Translation of
The Turobin Book;
In Memory of the Jewish community
(Turobin, Poland)

Translation of
Sefer Turobin; pinkas zikaron

Editor: M. S. Geshuri

Published in Tel Aviv 1967

Published by JewishGen

**An Affiliate of the Museum of Jewish Heritage—A Living Memorial to the Holocaust
New York**

Turobin Yizkor Book

The Turobin Book; In Memory of the Jewish Community (Turobin, Poland)
Translation of *Sefer Turobin; pinkas zikaron*

Copyright © 2019 by JewishGen, Inc.
All rights reserved.
First Printing: December 2019, Kislev 5780

Translation Project Coordinator: Dan Feder
Layout: Donni Magid
Cover Design: Rachel Kolokoff Hopper

Published by JewishGen, Inc.
An Affiliate of the Museum of Jewish Heritage
A Living Memorial to the Holocaust
36 Battery Place, New York, NY 10280

JewishGen, Inc. is not responsible for inaccuracies or omissions in the original work and makes no representations regarding the accuracy of this translation. Digital images of the original book's contents can be seen online at the New York Public Library website.

The mission of the JewishGen organization is to produce a translation of the original work, and we cannot verify the accuracy of statements or alter facts cited.

Printed in the United States of America by Lightning Source, Inc.

Library of Congress Control Number (LCCN): 2019954607
ISBN: 978-1-939561-76-3 (hard cover: 560 pages, alk. paper)

Cover credits: Cover Design Rachel Kolokoff Hopper
Front and back covers: Page 461 Modzitz Nigun (Melody) from the Turobin Tradition
Front Cover: Page 280 (Page 220)
The Hopen Family. Top row from the right: Mordechai, Golda, Yehoshua, Devorah, Itamar. Second row: Elazar, Y. Moshe, A. Rivka, Perl

JewishGen and the Yizkor Books in Print Project

This book has been published by the **Yizkor Books in Print Project**, as part of the **Yizkor Book Project** of JewishGen, Inc.

JewishGen, Inc. is a non-profit organization founded in 1987 as a resource for Jewish genealogy. Its website [www.jewishgen.org] serves as an international clearinghouse and resource center to assist individuals who are researching the history of their Jewish families and the places where they lived. JewishGen provides databases, facilitates discussion groups, and coordinates projects relating to Jewish genealogy and the history of the Jewish people. In 2003, JewishGen became an affiliate of the **Museum of Jewish Heritage—A Living Memorial to the Holocaust** in New York.

The **JewishGen Yizkor Book Project** was organized to make more widely known the existence of Yizkor (Memorial) Books written by survivors and former residents of various Jewish communities throughout the world. Later, volunteers connected to the different destroyed communities began cooperating to have these books translated from the original language—usually Hebrew or Yiddish—into English, thus enabling a wider audience to have access to the valuable information contained within them. As each chapter of these books was translated, it was posted on the JewishGen website and made available to the general public.

The **Yizkor Books in Print Project** began in 2011 as an initiative to print and publish Yizkor Books that had been fully translated, so that hard copies would be available for purchase by the descendants of these communities and also by scholars, universities, synagogues, libraries, and museums.

These Yizkor books have been produced almost entirely through the volunteer effort of researchers from around the world, assisted by donations from private individuals. The books are printed and sold at near cost, so as to make them as affordable as possible. Our goal is to make this important genre of Jewish literature and history available in English in book form, so that people can have the personal histories of their ancestral towns on their bookshelves for themselves and for their children and grandchildren.

A list of all published translated Yizkor Books in the project with prices and ordering information can be found at:
http://www.jewishgen.org/Yizkor/ybip.html

Binny Lewis, Yizkor Book Project Manager
Joel Alpert, Yizkor-Book-in-Print Project Coordinator

JewishGen
Yizkor Book Project

This book is presented by the
Yizkor Books in Print Project
Project Coordinator: Joel Alpert

Part of the
Yizkor Books Project of JewishGen, Inc.
Project Manager: Lance Ackerfeld

These books have been produced solely through volunteer effort
of individuals from around the world. The books are printed and
sold at near cost, so as to make them as affordable as possible.

Our goal is to make this history and important genre of Jewish
literature available in English in book form so that people can have
the near-personal histories of their ancestral towns on their bookshelves for themselves and for their children and grandchildren.

Any donations to the Yizkor Books Project are appreciated.

Please send donations to:
Yizkor Book Project
JewishGen
36 Battery Place
New York, NY 10280

JewishGen, Inc. is an affiliate of the
Museum of Jewish Heritage
A Living Memorial to the Holocaust

Notes to the Reader:

We apologize ahead of time for the poor quality of images in the book. Often these images had been scanned from the original Yizkor books which were of poor quality to begin with, being copies of old photographs. Each transfer results in loss of quality. We have done the best we could, given the original material and the resources and technology at hand. Even though images often appear of higher quality on computer screens, that does not transfer to high quality images in print. A reader can view the original scans on the web sites listed below.

Within the text the reader will note "{34}" standing ahead of a paragraph. This indicates that the material translated below was on page 34 of the original book. However, when a paragraph was split between two pages in the original book, the marker is placed in this book after the end of the paragraph for ease of reading.

Also please note that all references within the text of the book to page numbers, refer to the page numbers of the original Yizkor Book.

The original book can be seen online at the Yiddish Book Center web site: https://www.yiddishbookcenter.org/search?search_api_views_fulltext=turobin& Submit_search=&restrict=

In order to obtain a list of all Shoah victims from Turobin, the reader should access the Yad Vashem web site listed below; one can also search for specific family names using family name option. These lists are continually updated by Yad Vashem, so it is worthwhile to periodically search these lists.

There is much valuable information available on this web site, including the Pages of Testimony, etc.
http://yvng.yadvashem.org

A list of this book and all books available in the Yizkor-Book-In-Print Project along with prices is available at:
http://www.jewishgen.org/Yizkor/ybip.html

Geopolitical Information:

Alternate names for the town are: Turobin [Pol, Rus], Turbin [Yid], Torbin

50°50' N, 22°44' E

Period	Town	District	Province	Country
Before WWI (c. 1900):	Turobin	Krasnystaw	Lublin	Russian Empire
Between the wars (c. 1930):	Turobin	Krasnystaw	Lublin	Poland
After WWII (c. 1950):	Turobin			Poland
Today (c. 2000):	Turobin			Poland

Nearby Jewish Communities:

- Chłaniów 5 miles SSE
- Turobin 6 miles SW
- Wysokie 7 miles W
- Gorzków 9 miles ENE
- Chrzanów 12 miles SW
- Tarnogóra 13 miles E
- Łopiennik Górny 14 miles NE
- Zdziłowice 14 miles WSW
- Izbica 15 miles E
- Goraj 15 miles SSW
- Szczebrzeszyn 15 miles SSE
- Bychawa 15 miles WNW
- Piaski Luterskie 16 miles N
- Krasnystaw 16 miles ENE
- Frampol 17 miles SSW
- Biskupice 17 miles NNE
- Trawniki 18 miles NNE
- Zakrzówek 19 miles W
- Zwierzyniec 22 miles SSE

MAP

BALTIC SEA

LITHUANIA

RUSSIA

Vilnius ●

POLAND

BELARUS

GERMANY

● Poznan

Warsaw ●

● Lodz

Turobin ●

● Prague

● Krakow

UKRAINE

CZECH REPUBLIC

SLOVAKIA

250 miles

0

0 250 Km 500 Km

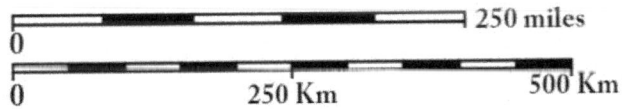

POLAND - **Current Borders**

Hebrew Title Page of Original Hebrew Book

ספר טורבין

פנקס - זכרון

הֶעוֹרֵד:

מאיר שמעון גשורי

בהוצאת ארגון יוצאי טורבין בישראל — תל-אביב. תשרי תשכ״ח

Translation of the Title Page of Original Yiddish Book

SEFER TUROBIN

Pinkas Zikaron

Editor:
Meir Shimon Geshuri

Published by

The Former Residents of Turobin in Israel

Tel-Aviv – October 1967

Table of Contents

Translated by Yocheved Klausner

1. The Portal

[Page 3]

The Turobin Yizkor Book Editorial Board

From right to left: **Yehoshua Ben Ari (Zilberklang,) Arye Goldfarb, The editor M.S. Geshuri, Itamar Hopen**

2

Irgun Yotzei Torubin Committee

Top row from right to left: **Moshe Efrat, Yehoshua Ben Ari (Zilberklang,) Arye Goldfarb, the editor M.S. Geshuri, Itamar Hopen**
Second row from the right: **Yosef Kopf, Moshe Gotbertz**
Third row: **Yaakov Friedler, Zalmen Frumer, Yaakov Mitzner**

[Page 7]

List of Photographs
Translated by Yocheved Klausner

Page numbers refer to the original Yizkor book pagination, not this translation.

4

6

Martyrs]

Heroes of the War of Independence

[Page 8]

<u>About the Book [English translation]</u>

[Pages 9-11 Hebrew] [Pages 12-13 Yiddish]

Editor's Preface
Translated by Meir Bulman

With awe and reverence, I hereby introduce this memorial book to the emigrants from Turobin in Israel and abroad. It was not a large Jewish community in Poland, but a smaller one. We have come to tell of the memories from that small community whose memory is dear to our hearts. It was a town much like the dozens of towns in the Lublin area, a lively cell in the body of Jewish communities in Poland. Its origin is in the distant past centuries ago and its end in the destruction of Polish Jewry within the mass grave of six million Jews, in the gas chambers among the souls of Jews who ascended to the heavens on poisonous fumes, its bones and ashes spread across the Polish lands of exile. This book is the fruit of the labor of a select few.

With the publication of this memorial book, in which the saga of Jewish Turobin is unfolded from its past to its bitter end, we light a candle in memory of the town members who lived, created and worked there for many generations. We Want to shed a light of love and compassion on the public, national, spiritual, religious, and economic lives of the Turobin Jewish community including the events and twists which occurred in the community across the generations. We are erecting a monument in memory of the Turobin community and the memory of its rabbis, activists and ordinary people, the passion of its youth and its pioneers who added a stone to the building of the nation and our land. We have come to tell of its light and shadows, the sun which shined upon the town and the clouds which darkened it, its rabbis and Hassidic greats which served in it since distant generations until before its destruction and the ordinary people who labored and suffered, who hoped and prepared for the future, in pure and total faith in mankind, who stuck to the vison of nations and the destiny and culture of humanity which will redeem any Jew wherever he may be. We have also come to tell of the warriors of free thought who recently emerged in the town, the generations of stirring up and rebellion, the foreseers of Zion, and its social and national activists who served as spokespeople for the tongue–tied masses. Jewish life in Poland before the destruction was rich and varied and Turobin was no different.

The emigrants from Turobin in Israel who arrived as pioneers even before the war of destruction would occasionally visit their hometown Turobin which had served as a warm nest for Jewish life and culture when the vast majority of the town was Jewish and Jewish life bustled everywhere. To this day, the past residents of Turobin in Israel and abroad long for that home in its glory and purity, in its simplicity and warmth, its quality and endearment, identify with it, are proud of its wholeness, steadiness, and its inner liveliness. They carry its memory like that of a mother, which has no equivalent nor can be replaced, and their longing and loving emotions are present among the pages if this book. The Holy Spirit floated along its alleyways and Jewish homes; to this day, its remnants, the remaining Jewish Turobin natives, have not come to terms with the horror of its destruction which is beyond human comprehension. It was as if misfortune thundered down from the sky and death crept up to them. In 5702, the Nazi executioner descended on the community, ended lives, and destroyed the graves of the dead. Thus the light of the community dimmed in such a cruel and tragic manner. Turobin of the physical world is no longer, and its survivors and remnants assimilated in Israel and continue to contribute to our future and culture, our struggles, and battles everywhere. Its Zionists, pioneers, and their sons are as an everlasting flame in memory of Jewish Turobin, a flame burning for past generations and those sacrificed in the massacre. The dozens of Turobin Jews living in Israel and abroad are orphaned and bereaved, one with the memory of their loved ones, cloaked in sadness.

Words cannot express our pain and grief over the deaths of the Turobin martyrs at the hands of murderous vile Nazis and their various collaborators. It is impossible for those of flesh and blood to write and summarize the events of the martyrologic 1939 – 1945. The heavens were sealed to the cries of our tortured brethren before their souls departed. The ears of the enlightened world were sealed when the occupying forces of the "nation of culture" Germany emerged armed with the best tools of destruction, to purge the world of the "global nation." The words of wrath by the national poet Hayim Nahman Bialik in his poem *The Nemirov Burden* come to mind.

In a conversation with an editor of a Yizkor Book for another town, he grieved the doubled destruction of the town; a general destruction like many other towns and cities, and the destruction of the intellectual workforce who could have written and described in various sections the lives and behaviors of the town Jews. Only when he approached editing the book were his eyes opened to the fact that he had much work to do due to a lack of people who could bear the burden of writing and resurrect the glorious past where they spent the years of their youth. And indeed, the second destruction is felt nearly in every Yizkor book, even the books of central towns who in the past served as Jewish cultural and literary centers. Turobin was not spared the loss of its intelligent gems, its forces of Torah and culture who made it famous across the region, and for that reason delayed publishing their own Yizkor book. Only after lengthy deliberation and difficulties, after the remnants of the town examined the situation considering reality and capability, came the bold decision to publish the Turobin Yizkor book. Of course, there is a great distance between intentions and deeds. All beginnings are difficult, in addition to its being a first and unique task for members of the town who were ill-prepared for that task in every aspect.

We did not have in our disposal archives and sources of the town itself, who were likely lost prior to the Holocaust for well- known reasons. But we utilized the few historical sources from which we could extract the material on Jewish life in past generations, with various discoveries. The material was gathered slowly and persistently, with sacrifice by the Turobin community. It was gathered [as if] out of thin air with limited resources and much difficulty. The book serves as a monument to the few happy occasions and many sad ones which the Turobin community members experienced, a vessel for blood and tears and a mark of good deeds.

The publication of a Yizkor book to Jewish communities in towns and cities that perished in the Holocaust is dependent on many variables; financial, administrative, and literary ability. We learned From experience that the first thing necessary for such a task is a person who is obsessed with one thing. Such a person could gather those able to contribute to the book, stimulate conversations with ordinary people and people of spirit, remember the forgotten, fundraise from those able to contribute to the best of their needs. He could also speak with community members in Israel and abroad and incentivize financial contribution by sending materials, memories from town life, sketches of characters and images of individuals, as well as enlist the help of those passionate about preserving memories who served as a source of income.

It should be noted that in that aspect the small and remote towns surpass many of the large Jewish towns. Lately, we have been witnessing a phenomenon where small towns publish a quality memorial book containing much material, while notable towns make do with Yizkor books making poor impressions, as if published to do the minimum, with sparse material which is not of significantly higher quality. The Turobin community was fortunate to find some activists who could assist in its time of need and invested their energy to complete the task.

The Turobin book is written in two languages, Hebrew and Yiddish which complement one another. The book contains only 400 pages, considered the minimum amount for Yizkor books. As the editor, I can say that more could have been added if not for lack of funds after requests for assistance by the Turobin community members in America and other countries were declined. The financial burden rested on the shoulders of the Israeli members alone. The extraordinary interest in the book by the members was awakened too late, after the book was sent to print and various sections could not be further postponed. Indeed, most town members did not believe in the task of completing the book, or at least completing it quickly, and regarded the matter with apathy, and also did not heed calls by the initiators for literary participation.

The wide-ranging historical overview of the Turobin community from the day it was established to the end of WWI was done by the editor who took the initiative and gathered, investigated, balanced, and edited material from centuries and made efforts to draw from the depths of memory many details concerning the town. He also wrote the overview of the chain of rabbis and righteous men across the generation In Turobin, in addition to other overviews of life in town and elsewhere. The editor filled a void which existed since the town elders perished without the opportunity to extract old memories from them, by authoring additional essays on town personalities.

We owe special gratitude to Yehoshua Ben Ari who contributed his valuable time, as well as Aharon Bumfeld who devoted himself entirely, and Moshe Gotbertz who worked tirelessly. We thank those who heeded the call and with all their hearts wrote about their experiences in town. We managed to publish here the list of martyrs who closed the last page of the history of Turobin. The list contains the names of most of the martyrs and was prepared carefully with the will to complete it. We must mention the efforts and contributions of an extraordinary man among extraordinary people, Itamar Hopen, whose initiative, energy, and tireless efforts through the years are a decisive contribution to the task of completing the book, as a participant in gathering the material, an author, and coordinator. We would like to sincerely thank the Holocaust survivors who described their experiences and testified of the final moments of the Turobin community. All are commended for their physical and intellectual assistance, to the point of personal sacrifice, for the sake of the book. Many thanks to all those who assisted and encouraged with advice, publication, preparation, and planning for the Yizkor book for the holy community of Turobin.

We know we have not obtained perfection, just as no Yizkor book published so far has achieved perfection. Of course, there will be additional sources and details, as well as people who were not fully and satisfactory described. Not all community members who were approached responded, and so, not all the values and discoveries regarding Jewish Turobin reached the full expression they are worthy of. Despite that, it seems that this book contains the image and soul of Jewish Turobin which was destroyed.

It is with great respect we present *Sefer Turobin* to the community members residing in Israel and abroad, knowing we have done our best to present the image of the holy community and memorialize it. We hope and pray that the pure image of the town martyrs sacrificed on the altar of destruction, their pure lives, and the sanctification of God and Israel, will forever rest in our memories and the memories of future generations and will serve as an eternal flame. We will follow in their steps and their memory shall never cease from our hearts. May this memorial book stand in the way of the Angel of Forgetfulness which might wreak havoc on the Jews of Turobin and those to follow. May this book rescue from the depths as much as possible the memory of the holy Turobin community in its ascension, peak, and destruction. May the words of this book remain in our hearts and the memory of the pure, holy, and beloved people will ascend and sanctify those cruelly uprooted from the land of the living. May their memory be blessed, and their soul bound in the everlasting bond of the nation.

May this book serve as bowing our heads and recitation of kaddish in memory of the martyrs.

———————

[Page 14]

Map of Turobin

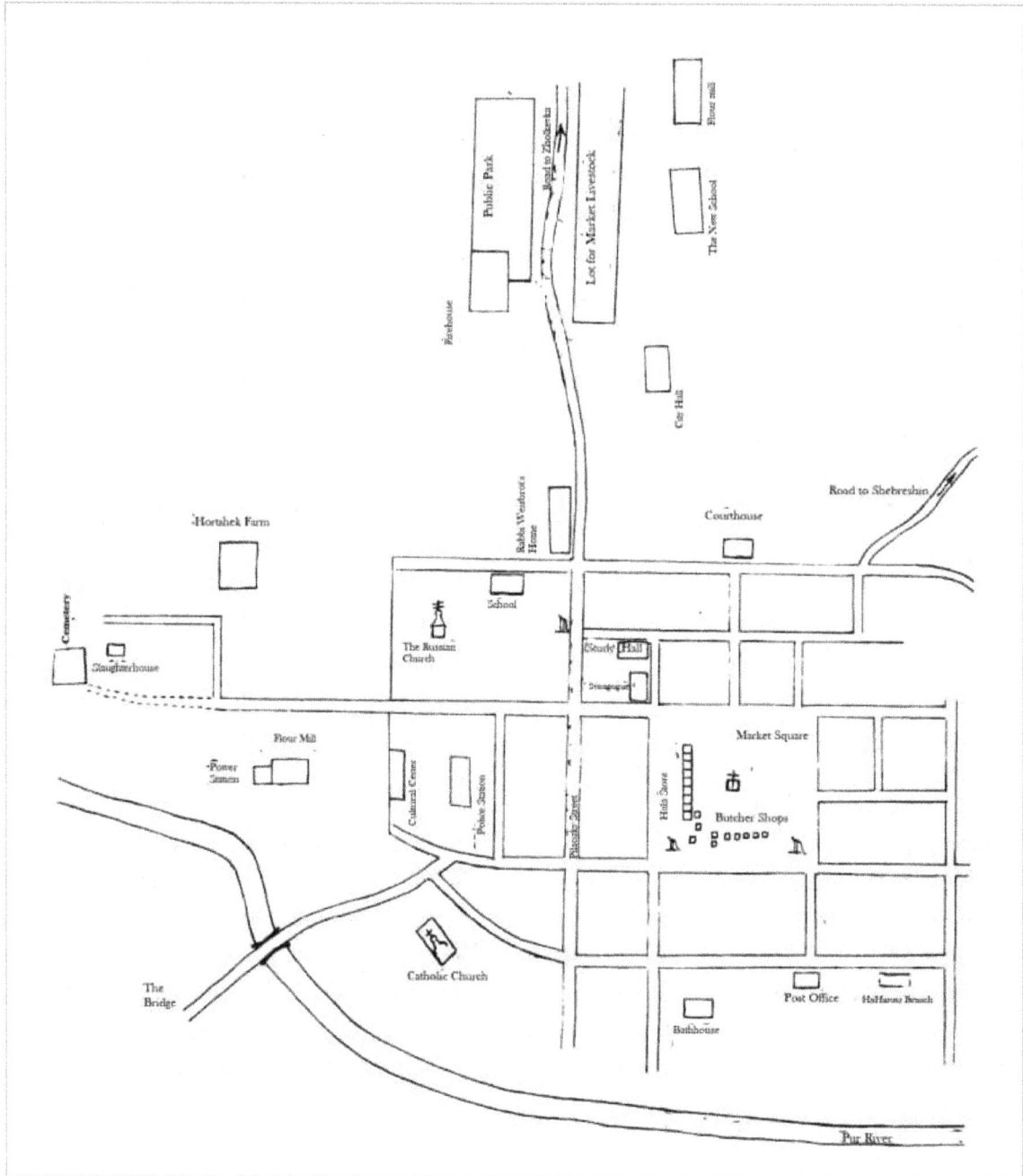

Public Park

Road to Zhólkiewka

Lot for Market Livestock

Flour mill

The New School

Firehouse

City Hall

Rabbi Wohlwein's Home

Courthouse

Road to Shebreshin

Hortshek Farm

Cemetery

Slaughterhouse

School

The Russian Church

Study Hall

Synagogue

Flour Mill

Power Station

Cultural Center

Police Station

Pilsudki Street

Hitls Store

Market Square

Butcher Shops

The Bridge

Catholic Church

Bathhouse

Post Office

Halfaraw Bench

Pur River

Map of 1939 Turobin drawn by Meir Af

[Page 15]

Demographic table of the Turobin Population
By Itamar Hopen
Translated by Meir Bulman

Year	Jews	Gentiles	
1936	1652	2016	The table is constructed based on a name list of those who perished updated to reflect: 40% of 400 families minimal birthrate over a 3.5 year period = 560 24% death rate compared to birthrate (8% of population) over 3.5 years = 1350 ~30 to 40 Jewish families residing in nearby villages, whose connection to the Turobin community was jurisdictional, traditional, and essential.
1939	425	686	
1939	200		
	135		
1942	2412	2702	**Total** Exiled to and perished at the Sobibor extermination camp and some at other extermination camps, other than refugees who came from Łódź and other towns numbering over 1000
	2277		

After the adding of the suburbs Olszanka, Zlobtsha, and Pshedmes'tse to the municipality in the 1930s the non-Jewish population comprised 55% of the population, excluding village Jews whose municipal designation was different.

14

In Israel and abroad

Israel	98
United States	15
Argentina	10
Canada	5
Uruguay	3
Australia	2
France	2
Total	**135**
USSR	4
Poland	3

[Page 16]

	Number of Jews				Emigration	
Place	**Before the War**	**1940**	**1941**	**1942**	**1941**	**10-12 1939 for the duration**
Turobin	1940	2220 [X]	3100 (1500+1600) [III] 3300 [IX]	3528 [4 III]		Over 1250 from Lodz, Kala, Konin, and others.

Settlement		"Evacuation" and Destruction		
1941	1400	1942	1942	1943
	From Lublin	10.5 – from surrounding towns	2750 – Sobibor, 10 – Izbica	

Note: It should be assumed an error was made when copying column 1 at the Institute for Jewish History in Poland instead of 2400 (1400).
This table was copied from pages of the Jewish History Quarterly of the Jewish Historical Institute of the Holy Martyrs of the Jews in Poland, January-June 1950.

[Page 18]

2. Chapters of History

[Page 19]

History of the Jewish settlement in Turobin

M.S. Geshuri

Translated by Meir Bulman

Preface

The regional Jewish literature, meaning the history of the various communities, has existed for some time now. Over a century ago, researchers, educated folks, and rabbis began to document their communities. Those were larger and older towns, who focused mainly on the distinguished genealogy, and above all on spiritual community leadership. Details on the lives of the general population were occasionally present through details on various institutions, although they were not the focus. A browse through those books indicates that sources from which authors drew their knowledge mostly tombstones, were those focusing on leadership. Of course, accounts pertained to historically significant and valuable tombstones. Such tombstones were better preserved than less significant ones. Sources used included preserved ledgers (mainly those by burial societies.) Endorsements by local rabbis were considered as sources as well.

Those respectable towns include (in alphabetical order:) Ostrów (*Memorial for Ostrów Greats*) Brisk (*Glorious City*) Grodno (*Town of Heroes*) Dubno (*Grater Dubno* and *Dubno and Its Wise Men*) Zholkeiv (*Sublime Town*) Lviv (*Notable Men* and *Holy Monuments*) Kraków (*City of Justice, Memorial Plaques, and Perfect Beauty*) Ruzhany (*Knowledge of Holy Men*) Lublin (*A History of Jewish Lublin* and others,) and Minsk (*Rabbis and Wise Men of Minsk.*) The books mentioned were published unrelated to uprisings, wars, and massacres but because of a feeling of respect for legacy communities, their rabbis, and wise

16

men. In addition, the purpose of those books was not to memorialize the lives of the communities, as those were still in existence, and it was unnecessary to establish a monument to a living community. Therefore, the authors chose not to utilize non–Jewish sources, be it due to the unreliability of such sources or out of lack of knowledge that there existed primary sources on Jews in public and municipal archives, as well as castles of nobles and ministers. Materials in such archives included licenses for local Jews, documents, and certificates from which one could learn of dates when synagogues and cemeteries were established.

We have mentioned above the source provided by ledgers that were composed for each community from the day it was established. We have all heard the ledger-recorded details about previous leaders, arrangements, and history. However, few have seen the ledger and were aware of its contents. Most communities were not aware of its value and did not store it for future generations when it was full and unnecessary to maintain as a consecutive source. But what was the fate of old ledgers? The few communities whose ledgers remain did not preserve them well and they were placed in dank spots until their pages withered, mold consumed it, or children played with it and ripped it to shreds. There were also cases of people who maliciously destroyed them as the ledgers recorded their names or their ancestors' names as transgressors subjected to fines, censures, or excommunications. After drastic changes occurred in the state or Jewish communities, many of the towns' notables and leaders declined in status while common men ascended and seized control of communities. Their first action was to shred or burn the ledger which recorded their sins and the sins of their fathers and praised the good deeds and status of those whose status declined. Thus, the number of ledgers that survived malicious intent was very small.

[Page 20]

The ledger was an all–encompassing detailing of the community which recorded town regulations and organization, appointment of leaders, rabbis, judges, activists, financiers, writers, cantors, synagogue administrators, estimates of community taxation, verdicts, punishments and fines imposed on those breaking communities rules or regulations, community revenue and fundraising efforts, especially expenditures – not even the smallest amount was spent without detailing its purpose, warnings and decrees, and censures. At times, the community's faithful servant, the ledger's author, was inspired and poured his heart out and described an important event, positive or negative, and described it in rhymes and simple heartfelt prose. In those days, it was impossible for a community to exist without such a ledger. Community members had to adhere to strict established guidelines, other than those that expired because of changes in the size or structure of the community. The ledger author had to constantly detail revenue and expenditures to refute negative feedback. He wrote what he was obligated to write, and so a detailed history emerged.

One who is even somewhat versed in our history books knows that without the few surviving ledgers it would be impossible to describe the state of our nation's culture, history, and past developments. Many matters of our events would be out of reach and completely sealed. Even those short and dry accounting lists spread across most of the pages are considered gems to the researchers. At times, details in the ledgers shed light on material in general history books. It should be noted that the ledgers have nearly identical formats in Lithuanian and Polish communities as if all community leaders convened and decided to enact rules concerning administration, the behavior of community members in public and at home, education, clothes, living quarters, modesty, family life, negotiations, and other similar matters.

Another important detail is that the language of the ledgers is evidence that our community leaders of the past felt that those ledgers were not written solely for the local needs of the time, but for future generations and Jews worldwide as well. All ledgers were written in Hebrew, though many community members did not understand Hebrew. At any rate, the few surviving ledgers serve as a primary source for researchers of communal histories, though rarely described in books where such details are evident.

[Page 21]

Another completely different source is Yizkor books published these days by members of various communities in memory of their hometowns destroyed by the barbaric Nazi Germans. In that aspect, those books are considered as monuments not only for individuals or select groups but to whole towns and cities. That task is therefore much larger, and for that reason significantly more difficult. The authors of the few books mentioned above encounterd a "living" cemetery as they could still browse the yellowing pages of various ledgers and could ask elders to describe stories they had heard from their ancestors. This as opposed to entire communities destroyed along with their

18

ledgers and other documents. Some no longer exist because of the war and the destruction it resulted in, and what remains is locked and sealed 'on the other side' and access is nearly impossible.

It is under such conditions that we approach writing the history of Turobin and its Jewish community. On the one hand, we find dates in the general Polish encyclopedias on Christian Turobin and from them, we know that as far back as 1389 Turobin (a town, village, or farm) was granted to Marshall Dimitri of Goraj by King Vladislav Yagello. From a similar date we know that in 1430, the Prophec Church was established in Turobin for local and nearby Christians. We also know of Polish influencers such statesmen and authors who resided in town. On the other hand, we have no sources detailing numbers and dates of the establishment of the Jewish community, the first Jews to reside there or their place of origin, what year the Jews established the synagogue mentioned in the general chronicle without listing the date of establishment, and we must cast about in the dark concerning matters regarding Jewish Turobin. And even if anything did remain as a testimony to those early days, that too was lost in the great storm of Nazi occupation. There might have been a ledger in the possession of the community council or the burial society. The Turobin natives residing in Israel cannot detail much from the town's ancient origins.

I have attempted to draw comparisons from published memorial books of nearby towns such as Frampol, Tomaszów, Bilgoraj, Zamosc, (Szczebrzeszyn has yet to tell its story aside from a few booklets.) Although Turobin is occasionally mentioned as a neighboring town it is difficult to find substantial details on its past. Even in books published about Lublin, the regional capital, no details are present about Turobin, as if the Lublin activists feared to lose any detail of Lublin proper. Three yizkor books were published about Lublin, aside from holocaust research published by former residents. Well, who would dare approach the great hidden void and unveil much or some of Jewish Turobin? who would dare accept such a great and difficult task to discover important or minor details of an ancient Jewish town whose natives residing in Israel and often reminisce about their hometown stand before an unbreachable steel wall? And yet, little me decided to do my part and discover at least a part of the history of the Turobin community, even though I have never visited it. The decision of the Turobin activists to publish a yizkor book in memory of their town encouraged me to stand by their side and add another component to the general history of Jewish Poland. All was done "so your descendants will know" that the Jews of Turobin were able to preserve themselves under various sets of conditions as a stable community and deserve to be documented in the great memorial book of Polish Jewry that will one day be written by expert historians who could assess how they greatly contributed to the world's nations and to the return to Zion.

[Page 22]

Chapter 1: Turobin's Origins

1389 first official date Turobin mentioned. Demintri from Goraj – master of town. Magdeburg Law in Turobin. Bazaar, market days, and Prophec Church. Destruction of town by Tatars in 1509. Soydov Reestablishes Town. Calvinism War in Turobin. Turobin moves to the Zamoyski Family Fee Tail. Since 1662, 4 market days in town. The Town during the 1648 Cossack Uprising. Census of the town in 1827.

The general history chronicle mentions the first event concerning Turobin in 1389, when the Polish king and prince of Lithuania Vladislav Yagello (1350–1434) gave Turobin along with many other villages to Dimitri from the nearby Goraj. He was the military chief of staff and later promoted to the role of the crown treasurer as a reward for his contributions to the military. Therefore, Turobin had an early link to the king of Poland who has contributed much to the country. Four years before the mentioned date for Turobin, 1385, Poland united with its large neighbor Lithuania, as a response to the threat they faced from the great German crusaders' kingdom to the north. That alliance resulted in a positive outcome for Poland and they beat the crusaders for the first time in 1410 at the decisive Battle of Grunwald. A more decisive victory came later, during the Thirteen Years' War (1454–1466), with the increasing importance of exporting wood and grains from Poland to Danzig in Pomerania. The victory was a decisive one and Pomerania joined Poland (as Royal Prussia) and Prussia itself (Eastern Prussia) surrendered to the Polish king, first dubbed Crusaders' land and from 1525 considered a part of the Prussian Kingdom.

Dimitri from Goraj who participated in many wars on behalf of Poland and Lithuania as a general fought devotedly and as a sign of gratitude King Yagello granted Turobin to him along with other regional villages. That detail is

20

mentioned in an essay by Krainski, who when addressing Polish treasurer Jan Dimitri from Goraj, wrote, "may the Crown's treasurer minster never decay. He observed Yagello's homeland from afar and in his heart remembered and loved the Lithuanian kingdom. He was rewarded for his service by his majesty king Ludwik of Poland and Hungary with a deed for the Szczebrzeszyn estate with the addition of Turobin and all villages in that region. Issued in writing in Kraków, 1389."

[Page 23]

Yagello was the second out of four Polish kings with the same name. As a great Lithuanian prince in a search for allies, in 1386 married Yadviga queen of Poland and was crowned king of Poland as Yagello II. That same year, he accepted Catholicism and worked to spread it among the Lithuanians. His victory over the Teutonic Order ended the Germans' eastward expansion and positioned Poland as a significant world power. He was a devout Catholic and heeded the advice of priests, including restrictions and various decrees unfavorable to Jews. The ancient academy founded by Casimir III the Great in Casimir, a suburb of Kraków, was renamed in his honor. To gain favor among the military leadership he granted them estates and villages and helped them to develop and turn them into towns by encouraging population growth. General Dimitri received Turobin, which had likely already reached a desired threshold of agricultural production and population. He also received a promise of royal assistance in developing his new estate in Turobin.[1]

Dimitri himself gained power after the big wars ended and he could enjoy the peace. He served as deputy treasury minister of the Polish kingdom and resided in the palace located in Goraj which he received as a gift from Ludwik I king of Hungary and Poland. The owner of Goraj, Alexander of Stroyantsha, managed to elevate it to the status of a town after he changed its name from Lada to Goraj. Goraj is located near Turobin and so likely added by King Vladislav as a gift to Dimitri so he can expand his territory and perhaps his income. Dimitri's actions to improve Turobin are ignored by the chronicle.

The date on which Turobin was chartered does not offer details on who founded it, when it was founded, or what its form – a village, estate, farm, or the like, or who its previous owners were. It is therefore likely that residential Turobin existed for many years but was not recorded in kingdom documents. The historical announcement granting its transference to Dmitri opened a new chapter and contributed to the economic and residential improvement.

The numerous Tatarian invasions of Poland are not to be ignored. The largest one occurred in 1241 and was thwarted in the battle near the city of Legnica in the Silesia province. The second Tatar invasion in 1259 and the third in 1287 affectedd Poland up to the Kraków area, which was destroyed as a result. After the country was destroyed during the Tatar invasions, from the second half of the 13th Century to the start of the 14th, a settlement movement grew stronger in Poland and was present across all Polish provinces. The settlers originated in Germany, who improved farming techniques with better equipment, and improved agricultural fertility with better seeding technique. The improved development resulted in villages' ability to trade produce. The expansion of the market contributed to the development of towns. At the same time, new towns were established. One of those towns was Turobin, which might have been previously established and destroyed by the Tatars. This time around, the king took notice and he and his advisors were determined to advance it and grant to trustworthy individuals. Since the first notice, there was a certain gap and it is unknown what occurred during that time.

The second chronicle entry about Turobin came 31 years later. It said that Yagello has agreed to grant Turobin regional rights according to German Magdeburg Law with a market day every Tuesday. An important step forward in the development of the new town is seen here; market days permitted all merchants to engage in free trade in the town. The development of the towns caused the formation of a new class in Poland, the civic class (Meishtshan.) Those rights afforded to Turobin attracted new residents to such an extent that in 1430, ten years after the charter was affirmed, the town owners established the first Prophec Church in town and perhaps the first in the region. The church was designated as a gathering place for the faithful and to attract wanderers to the churches closest to town.

[Page 24]

Since the founding of the church, no further events were recorded for eight years. Another item is presented recording an event which occurred in 1509. the Tatars, the veteran centuries–long enemies of Poland, periodically went on a ransacking operation due to a lack of borders between Turkey and Poland. On one of these operations, the Tatars burned Turobin and destroyed it. There are no further details on the destruction, and it was likely no different than that of other towns and villages in Poland whose residents abandoned the town, were killed, or captured by the Tatras who received a ransom in exchange. The following owner of the Turobin, Andrei Vincenti Soydov, showed interest in rebuilding the town and renewed rights for those who arrived to resettle it by granting constitutional freedoms. With the treaty signed between Turkey and Poland and due to their influence on the Romanian states, Turobin was spared further Tatar attacks and it could rebuild residentially and economically.[2]

The Polish chronicle recorded dates regarding churches and monitored clashes among the denominations. The strongest of the denominations was Calvinism, which was dominant in Turobin as well. Since the 16th Century, Reformation was popularized among the masses of *Shlakhta* [?] and Meishtshn[?] Polish classes in its various shades such as Calvinism, Lutheranism, Hussitism, and others. The Catholic Church wished to end Reformation by declaring war on the "heretics." A tumultuous time ensued in Turobin because of the spread of Reformation, until the Italian Optin Sochin spread the Arianic [?] religion. The Gorkin family who inherited Turobin converted the local church to a Calvinist one during the days of King Sigmund August, and established a Calvinist school near it, which was present until the end of the 16th Century. The Bishop of Chelm, Stanislav Gomolinski, was the deciding factor in that holy war and confiscated the church from its Calvinist owners, renovated it, erased all memory of its previous heretical owners, and eventually reopened it to Catholics. The chronicle says that the church was burned down towards the end of the 17th Century and was reestablished in 1713. That likely settled the conflict. The Calvinists likely made attempts to recapture the church.

There are no extensive details on the religious conflict among the residents of Turobin and the region. However, it is unlikely the conflict was non–violent, as other places witnessed incitement by churches which culminated in violent uprisings which further intensified. Jesuit students and wildly youths would burn houses of worship and raze protestant cemeteries, assault Calvinist ministers, attack funerals of heretics and drop the coffin, and more. There were casualties as well, and not even old hospitalized people were not spared. The Lutherans and Calvinists eventually adopted the Jewish technique of defense and payed "protection" fees to the unruly students, and would especially pay to protect their funerals. In Turobin things must have been [no] calmer and disturbed the peace in the otherwise quiet town. The Church contributed too much to the persecution of non–Catholics.

[Page 25]

Turobin changed ownership again. During its agricultural development, it was placed under the control of the Polish Great Chancellor Jan Zamoyski (1541–1605.) In 1600, he purchased Turobin and its estates and added them to the Zamoyski Family Fee Tail. He also returned it to Church authority. In 1618, 18 years after the purchase, Zamoyski examined the municipal documents and organized them. Some were approved, and others cancelled. Additional permits were approved in 1646. After the joining of the Fee Tail, things in Turobin improved. With religious peace returning to town, King Jan Casimir (whose time in office is regarded as "Days of the Flood") agreed to grant the right of 4 market days to Turobin. That was in 1622 and done to benefit the town fatigued from the continuous struggle and open a rehabilitation path. The Zamoyski Family Fee Tail and Jan Zamoyski saga will be written about later.

The next mention came after nothing was mentioned about the Cossack Uprising in 1648. Town residents suffered much during the Cossack conflict. Cossacks stormed town plundered and massacred residents. The awful riots began in Ukraine and spread to the Lublin region, and Turobin was affected as were all region villages. What is the purpose of the chronicle's silence on such an influential event, when everyone understands that the renewal of peaceful times was done to rehabilitate town and resettling it after residents had escaped? Turobin undoubtedly suffered plagues as well, especially in 1705, when cholera infected Poland and many died. The town also suffered considerably because of wars and feuds which took place in Poland in the 17th and 18th centuries, due to disparities in the states' foreign policy and nobility feuds. Of course, all those armed conflicts caused substantial suffering regarding security and economics.

No detail is mentioned about the town during the last thirty years of the old Polish kingdom from 1764–1795. Those were very tumultuous in both foreign and domestic politics. Three partitions occurred which put an end to the kingdom's independence. Turobin did not maintain its national affiliation, and during occupation of the Lublin region by the Austrian military, Turobin was occupied as well. But the chronicle is not to be questioned; at times it expands and at times is brief. The fact remains that no mention of Turobin during the 18th century is present, just as no details are recorded about its exchange of fee tails. Turobin is also not mentioned regarding The Kosciuszko

24

Uprising which erupted March of 1794 and ended in defeat. The ways of the Polish chronicle are mysterious; it ignored Turobin for a period of 165 years. Only in 1827, after the divisions and Napoleon's defeat in Russian and the annexation of Congressional Poland to Russia including Turobin, an item appears that there are 344 households in town and a population of 2026, who made their living mostly from fur processing, without mentioning if processing was done independently or initiated by the Jews who were already residing there.

[Page 26]

The chronicle had fewer entries during Russian rule, perhaps because the chronicling agency was intended to serve an independent Poland. After Poland lost its independence, there was a lesser need for entries that likely required permission from Russian authorities, which was more interested in maintaining Russian rule over Poland, whose people did not forego the possibility of restoring their independence. Turobin, which did not serve an important role in the history of Poland, was limited to statistical entries concerning the number of households and residents.

The Polish chronicle likely knew the rule which appears in the Talmud "to hide more than what is revealed." The Chronicle also supplied material to be read between the lines. There is not much that can be learned about the local Jews. The rare entries that did mention Jews were shrouded in mystery without dates. However, the events of Jews in Turobin are a story on its own which we will detail in the coming chapters.

There remains something to be said about the name "Turobin." The origin of the Geographic name of the town is unknown. Usually, towns were named for their owners, noblemen, princes, kings, or rivers and streams. Tomaszów, for instance, is named for Tomas Zamoyski. Janów was a common name in Poland since the name Jan was widespread among the various classes, and so a note was added so they can be told apart. Such is the case of Tomaszów Lubelski as opposed to Tomaszów Osbitsek, and Janów Lubelski near Pinsk or Janów Ostrov. Even Sosnowiec received two towns: near the Silesian border in the Zaglembie area, and near the town of Parczew, among many others. A second Turobin is a village in the Lomzhe district. Our Turobin is on the shores of the Por River without needing its help in identifying it. On the other hand, the name Turobin was inserted into Polish last names, such as

Turobinovitz, Turobinski, etc. as well as Jewish names such as Turobiner, now present outside of Poland after the destruction of Polish Jewry.

Chapter 2: First Jews in Turobin

A permit for Jewish residence. 1607 first date of Jews in Turobin – Soydov allows Jews in town. Jan Zamoyski estimates the Jews as a positive factor. [Another] permit for Jewish settlement. Jewish – Christian relations established. Businesses of Turobin's Jews. Jewish population growth.

[Page 27]

Like there is a basis to assume that despite the first mention of Turobin for the first time in 1389, the town itself existed for a while prior to that, we need to assume that the granting of Turobin by King Vladislav Yagelllo to marshal Dimitri from Goraj did not unlock the gates for Jewish settlement. First, since that king was a fundamentalist Catholic and a slave to priests who considered it a mission to restrict Jews as much as possible. Second, the ground was not yet laid to prepare for Jewish settlement in Turobin or the nearby towns, from an economic or safety perspective, especially because of the fundamental changes which were taking place in the social and political structure in Poland and the consolidation of the Polish noble class. On the other hand, recorded entries state that there were Jewish towns in Poland since the 11th Century. Poland's economy was doing poorly and had a great need for Jews. But the Tatar attacks starting in 1241 undoubtedly postponed for a long while the arrival and settlement of Jews in the region of Turobin. Third, a comparison can be made to other towns in the Lublin area, where Jewish settlement occurred later. Jewish settlement in those areas came later, initiated by owners of the towns who found the Jews to be a helpful element in developing trade and could contribute much to develop towns. So, the nobles published permits designed to protect Jews from attack.

The general chronicle ignores the existence of Jews in Turobin in the first centuries of its existence, even after it was promoted from village or farm to a town. Still, even if we have no direct entries, there are still reliable sources detailing the settlement of Jews in those places for centuries. We will mention two unique facts:

A. in 1607, the representative of Jews in Turobin, Shimon son of David Oyerbach participated for the first time in The Council of Four Lands (CFL) meeting. He signed various regulations heeded by all Polish Jews. This is the earliest mention of a Jewish presence in Turobin which should not be ignored.

B. Forty years later, the book *Yeven Mezulah* by Nathan (Nata) ben Moses Hannover mentions the many casualties of the Khmelnitsky Cossacks who massacred many Ukrainian and Polish Jews. When they reached the Lublin region, they massacred many Jews in Tomaszów, Szczebrzeszyn, Turobin, Bilgoraj, Goraj, Krasnik and others, and brought about the economic annihilation of the Jews. This is also a trustworthy source on Jewish residence which took place in Turobin.

However, we have no details on Jewish residence from 1389 to 1607, a period of over two hundred years and it is unknown whether Jews settled in Turobin only after it was made a town in 1389, or beforehand when it was a village. It is also unknown if from the first days of settlement the Turobin community was an apart of the autonomically Jewish communities of the Lublin region. That raises questions, if Jewish residence in Turobin was permitted by the nobility and authorities or if it began without a license but undisturbed by the authorities? What were the names of the first Jews to settle in Turobin? Where did they come from, larger Polish towns or various European countries they were expelled from? The general chronicle mentioned the establishing of a synagogue without detailing the date it was built, whether it was initiated by the town's noble or the king. There is no doubt that the cemetery was established by the Jews in Turobin with an agreement by the town's owner and payment for the plot or under conditions detailed in the permit. That document was probably archived in the Jewish community archive in Poland, and with a lack of preserving of the archive was lost with the other documents, who could have served as Urim and Thummim for all the unanswered questions.

[Page 28]

Although there is no direct proof of Jews residing in the Lublin area until the 14th–15th Century, their existence is a near certainty. It is inconceivable that at a time when Jews lived in the countries surrounding Poland from the east (Rysen) and to the west (Germany, Bohemia) and in Poland itself and traded in certain regions would avoid residing in the region. The new Jewish residents would first establish a temporary residence that would serve as halfway point as they travelled for business from east to west across Poland. In the 14th century, there were already Jewish communities in larger towns and later communities in smaller towns are recorded. In the 15th century, Poland was very backwards in its cultural and social development. The Polish noble class, the *Shlakhta*, required credit to raise the productivity of land and to provide revenue for the crown and the church. The activities of Jews in the realm of money–lending benefited the noble class. Therefore, there are grounds to assume that the development of town 1389 when Turobin was gifted to Dimitri of Goraj was slow. The enactment of Magdeburg rights and weekly market days awakened the town from its stagnation, to the point that the expanding population required the establishment of their own church in 1430, so they would no longer depend on a distant church. Since then, a certain advancement occurred in town, and it is possible that the first Jews arrived in Turobin at the time, be they passersby on a business trip, or to scout the town for residential purposes.[3]

At the start of the 16th century, the town was burned by the Tatars and its residents scattered, including the Jews. However, the owner of the town, Soydov, showed much interest in quickly rebuilding the town. His attitude towards Jews is unknown, but in his desire to rebuild the town, he chose a path like other nobles and invited Jews to settle in town as well. It is likely that Soydov opened the gates to Jews. Details on the first Jews are unknown: where they came from and what they did, whether they resided in numbers large enough to pray in a minyan, and began thinking of the first institutions required for every new community like a synagogue, mikveh, cemetery, etc. The establishment of the Council of Four Lands occurred when Turobin was already worthy of sending its own delegate, and 27 years after the establishment of the council, the first representative from Turobin worked on behalf of his community.

During development, an important transformation occurred in Turobin when Jan Zamoyski purchased it along with its estates. He knew to appreciate the Jews as a cultural and economic force, and his influence encouraged permission for Jews to settle in various towns. When Turobin joined the Zamoyski Family Fee Tail allowed it was able to further develop and expand. Turns out that Turobin was not the first town in the region where Jews had settled. Count Jan Zamoyski (1542–1605) inhered a majority of father's vast fortune in 1571. He studied abroad, a short time in Strasburg and five years in Italy, where he met the famed humanists and intellectuals who studied at the ancient university in Padova. There, he had the idea to establish a sort of Polish Padova, or in his words, an "Italian style" town, not only in its architecture but in its cultural and educational values as well. In a capricious effort by a wealthy man fighting the academic stagnation in Kraków, he established the town of Zamosc with the Zamoyski Academy at its center. Zamoyski showed a special interest in Sephardic Jews and granted them permission to settle in Zamosc. The Jewish community was at first composed of exclusively Sephardic Jews, an unprecedented action in the history of Poland. However, Ashkenazi Jews lived within Zamoyski's estates in other towns and cities. In Szczebrzeszyn, a town close to Zamosc, the main leaser was Yaakov ben Natan, and in nearly all of Zamoyski's large estates the Jews were the primary leasers and traders. Jewish Turobin also was in contact with the fee tail's administrator and could reside and work in town according to a permit granted to Jews.

[Page 29]

It should be assumed that the remit granted to the Jews of Tomaszów Lubelski was similar to permits for other towns. Due to the historical significance of that document we hereby detail a translation from Latin:

"In the name of the Almighty. For eternal memory. I, Zamoyski of Zamosc, governor of Kiov, Starost of Knyszyn, Goniadz, etc. hereby write to whom it may concern. When I decided a few years ago to establish a new town named Tomaszów, and I saw the daily expansion of the town. To successfully develop trade, I decided to allow the settlement of Jews similarly to other towns under my authority. As residents and citizens in that town, I have permitted them to build homes to house their families. Those Jews will have to fulfill their financial tasks, and pay the same taxes and fees levied on the town's Christian residents. I permit them to enjoy all rights and freedoms afforded to the residents in my jurisdiction, including conducting business, importation, and other honest professions needed to live. I also agree that they have equal rights in buying and selling products of all kinds, always, be it during the weekly market days or yearly fairs. In relation to this permit, current Jewish residents and future ones must pay me or my successor after 15 years a tax paid by all Jews, two florins per homeowner and 1 florin for neighbors, unrelated to other civil taxes equal to other Christian residents, to myself and my successor. In addition, Jews will be permitted to practice medicine equally to Christian doctors, and equal to Christian medics, Jewish medics will each pay me and my successor 15 florins annually.

If conflict or claims arise between Christians and Jews, they must attend arbitration by a Jewish rabbi. If the Christian feels wronged by the rabbi's verdict he has the right to approach my representative and if necessary, my court and me. Other than that, Jews may summon Christians to court concerning all matters, but only in civil municipal court.

[Page 30]

Moreover, I grant the aforementioned Jews the right to purchase lots at a certain distance from the church, for the purposes of establishing a synagogue, a residence for a rabbi, cantor, and teacher, and a shelter for the less fortunate. After those are built, they will be exempt from various taxes and fees placed on Jews when building their homes. However, I declare that Jews are forbidden to purchase from Christians or build more than 12 houses in the town market square. That figure includes existing homes of Jews. Anyone who violates that instruction and builds a house in that location will pay a fine to me. Jews are permitted to build as many homes as they wish on other streets. In addition, I release the Jews from the duty to repair the dams built near the town's suburbs to fortify the lakes, which Christian residents are obligated to do. Jewish homeowners must pay 3 pennies for town administration and recreation.

As validation, I have instructed this document be sealed in wax. Written in Zamosc 6 May 1621. Zamoyski."

It is evident the Jews were granted broader rights Compared to permits issued for other towns outside of the Zamoyski Family Fee Tail. They had equal rights to Christian residents and were also exempt from other obligations.[4]

The Turobin community was unlike its neighbors in the Zamoyski Family Fee Tail. Other towns were established at the same time the community was, so they did not to go through a period when there were few Jews who had to join other communities on Shabbat and holidays. It is likely the first Jews to settle in Turobin conducted business in wholesale and retail, and their businesses were not necessarily in Turobin proper but also outside of town. Later, handicrafts became a secondary occupation for the Jews of Turobin as well. The influx of Jews into manufacturing came only the 16th century and even more so in the 17th century. Their numbers increased across all Polish provinces, and they joined crafts which were nonexistent in the Middle Ages.

The steady increase of Jews in Poland through migration or natural growth, and the limited opportunities available in trading were important factors in the development of a class of handcrafters in Turobin. The largest of the crafts was fur manufacturing, which was imported from the Kraków area by professional craftsmen. Thanks to the development of trade and manufacturing, the Jewish population in Turobin expanded and obtained a recognized positioning in the general population. The right of Jews to work in crafts was awakened after Christians had already succeeded in obtaining all the most profitable occupations. In Turobin, on the other hand, there was no limitation in Jewish fields, as agriculture was the dominant profession. The Turobin area was also one of the few places in the country in which Jews worked successfully in agriculture. In Goraj, a town near Turobin, many Jews made a living in agriculture, as well as those in surrounding villages who were given the privilege to own fields and gardens like Christian residents.

[Page 31]

Chapter 3: Representatives of Turobin at the Council of Four Lands

The Turobin community established. Turobin on the CFL map. The names of rabbis and benefactors of Turobin at CFL – Rabbi Shimon Wolf Oyerbach was the first Representative. Rabbi Menachem Chaioot – Rabbinic Court chairman in Turobin. Representatives of Turobin make decisions concerning other Communities. CFL canceled by Polish authorities in 1764. An important community in Turobin.

Turobin went through various stages before reaching the status of an organized community like other Polish communities. Undoubtedly, the Turobin Jewish community joined another local community, though it is unknown if they were linked to a single community or alternated. It should be assumed there were links between the town Jews and the Jewish communities of Lublin, Zamosc, and others. It is unknown who initiated an independent community in Turobin, whether Turobin locals or another town, or if Jews initiated it or the Polish authorities. However, one thing is certain: Turobin was a part of a historic faction of Jewish autonomy achieved through its socio-cultural institutions and rabbis, synagogues, cantors, shochetim, cemeteries, ritual baths, Jewish day schools, and charities.

The Turobin community, whose structure was simple, was established because of pressure by external and internal realities. It was like a municipal unit which represented the Jews locally and to the Crown's representatives. Later, the Council of Four Lands (Greater Poland, Little Poland, Ruthenia and Volhynia) was formed and existed over 180 years from 1580 to 1764. It gathered the communities' leadership with the participation of representatives from the communities and their rabbis whose influence on the public was immense. The community was like a government within a government. The rabbis and other leaders wrote many rules designed to strengthen religion and secure their status against the hatred of the nations they resided within. Thanks to the Council of Four Lands, Turobin obtained a respected position and participated in meetings and actions. Through their participation, we can learn the names of a few representatives and the scope of their actions.

, CFL was established in 1580. It published a map of Jewish communities in Poland and its territories. The map includes Turobin and near it are Zamosc, Frampol, Modliborzyce, Krasnik, Krasnobród, Bychawa, Szczebrzeszyn, Bilgoraj, Grabowiec, and Vasilisovitz[5]. Turobin was probably a part of "Zamosc Orientation District."

Various representatives of Turobin at CFL are mentioned twenty times. 1607 was the first time a representative of Turobin is mentioned as participating in CFL. It is unknown if Turobin was represented in previous meetings because 27 years had passed since the establishment of CFL and the mention of Turobin. It is possible they participated without attracting attention in the form of actions or opinions. These are the names of the representatives of Turobin whose names are mentioned in various meetings:

Rabbi Shimon Wolf ben David Tebbil Oyerbach, whose name is mentioned six times.

[Page 32]

Rabbi David Tebbil ben Eliezer. He is mentioned four times. Possibly a father and son.
Meir ben Eliyahu from Turobin. Mentioned twice.
Meir ben Yosef, five times.
Menachem Munish ben Yitzchak Chaioot, three times.

Moshe ben Zvi Hirsh Segal from Turobin, once.
Pinchas ben Shimon Wolf Oyerbach, once.
Yitzchak ben Uri Shraga Feivel from Kraków, four times.
Yitzchak ben Uri Shraga Feivel (Kraków not mentioned) twice.
Zacharia Mendel ben Arye Leib, four times.
Yehuda Leib ben Nafatli Yitzchak of Przemysl, from Kraków in Turobin, five times.
Yosef Yoske Katz of Turobin, Once.
Meir ben Rabbi S. of Turobin, once.
Meir ben Rabbi Y. of Turobin (Meir ben Yosef mentioned above)
Meir ben Rabbi El(i) of Turobin, once.

Of course, we do not have a record of everyone. But as representatives of Turobin, it is assumed they were active smart leaders who possessed traits of fluency and knowledge.

The Council of Four Lands was preceded by national Jewish institutions in Poland which did not operate regularly. The Jews were differentiated from the rest of the population and were enclosed in their communities. They were given freedom by the king to arrange their own matters among themselves if there was a financial benefit to the state because of the talents and excellent work ethic they were blessed with. The Jews had established communal order earlier, and in accordance with broad administrative authorities granted to communities by the Crown were allowed o to establish and care for their vital institutions like synagogues, hospitals, cemeteries, day schools and yeshivas. The head tax levied on the Jews since 1549, which they disliked, forced a census of the Jewish population. After various stages, in 1579, a general tax sum was divided among the districts and their communities. Most Historians attribute Jewish autonomy in the Polish kingdom to the change in the taxation method.

Turobin was probably considered a "large community" and, therefore, had the right to send representatives to the council. In 1753, CFL had a total of 25 representatives. The protocols ("ledgers") kept by CFL who were preserved since the mid–17th century is an important source concerning Polish Jewry. It bares more importance to Turobin, especially after the destruction of the town and its documents in the Holocaust. It should be noted that Turobin was near Lublin which had a large notable community in which the council's meetings took place.

[Page 33]

Matters in the state were far from tranquil. The incited masses, the priesthood, financial competitors, foreign invading armies, hurt the Jewish community, wounded, and tortured it relentlessly. However, the time of the Council of Four Lands was a grand time in the history of Polish Jewry, great in economic, social, cultural, and spiritual development. It was a time which signified creativity, activity, and growth in all fields. During that busy time, Turobin was a significant contributor to Jewish life. However, Turobin never hosted the meetings of the central committee, the rabbis and representatives always had to travel to Lublin or Jarosław to participate in meetings. Additionally, only Zamosc was fortunate to host the members of the central committee, during a time when there was a falling out with the authorities and financial difficulties, so the demanded tax amount could not be collected. Jewish Lublin was fortunate more than all other Polish towns and hosted CFL over 100 years. Thanks to those conventions, Lublin became a center which shaped not only the lives of Jews in Poland, as important matters and problems concerning the whole of the Jewish world in the 17th and 18th centuries were discussed in Lublin during CFL. It is easy to imagine that every time the Council convened, Lublin bustled with the many people who arrived from all over Poland and at times from other countries, accompanied by rabbis, scholars, activists, speakers, merchants, and adventurers. As happens sometimes, rumors came from CFL which either caused happiness or sadness, or a fighting spirit which threatened Jewish communities in Poland and abroad by causing conflict between brothers who bonded through troubles they experienced together. Turobin was near Lublin, and undoubtedly the conventions in Lublin left a mark on Jewish Turobin as well.

CFL gathered once or twice annually: the days of the fair between Purim and Passover (Gromnitz Fair) or the Shwanski Fair in May, and the fall (month of Av or Elul) at the Jaroslaw Fair. The fairs continued for 16 days each. Sometimes, the Council convened near Lublin (Belzyce, Tyszowce, Opole) among the conventions' participants there were rabbis and benefactors (Benefactors' Council of Four Lands.) However, the wars which took place in Poland from 1648–1655 caused an economic downturn in Lublin, and staring in 1683, the council met in Jarosław and other towns such as Tyszowce, Rejowiec, Konstantynów, Pilica, and others.

The community rabbi filled an important role within the autonomous frame of Jewish life in Poland. The autonomous control effectively rested in the hands of the rabbis of the Council of Four Lands. Outwardly, they were the representatives of the Jewish body tasked with collecting and paying taxes. Internally, they were the men who dictated the spiritual and cultural aspects, and no corner of the lives of people was hidden from them nor exempt from their guidance and judgement. The material found in the protocols of the Council of Four Lands names the rabbis and benefactors of the Turobin community which helped us when determining the relative importance of Turobin and its rabbis and benefactors within the great structure of autonomous rule. After an extensive reading we reached the conclusion Turobin had a very important role, and together with great rabbis and activists from other towns would intervene in the spiritual and social lives of Polish Jews.

They oversaw appointments within the communities, book publishing, recommended or censured, praised someone and rebuked another. When gusts of wind blew, and Judaism was shaken by proponents of new ideas, the rabbis of Turobin and its leaders battled on the front lines.

[Page 34]

Twenty–seven years after the CFL was established, we first read of Rabbi Shimon Wolf Oyerbach in Turobin. He was a link in a family chain of rabbis. The question arises if he was Turobin's first rabbi or if unnamed community leaders preceded him. At CFL, we can find the rabbi's signature among the council members. In 1607, the council convened at the Gromnitz Fair in Lublin and enacted rules concerning Polish Jews regarding many matters, including interest bearing loans, etc. The rabbi of Turobin added his signature and added, "I too hereby sign. Small among my peers, Shimon son of my beloved father, teacher and rabbi, Rabbi David Oyerbach of Turobin."

In 1643, the Council discussed mistakes which existed as prayer books were published in different styles, which might have caused inconsistencies in the accepted format of payers. After deliberation, the council decided to grant exclusive rights to print prayer books to a rabbi from Przemyśl (Shabtai bar Yitzchak Sofer) to publish a prayer book in a single format, and a decree was issued not to publish or distribute other prayer books. At the same fair, there is a mention of Rabbi Menachem "Munish" Chaioot, son of the Great Rabbi Yitzchak Chaioot, rabbinic court chairman in Turobin, who apparently took part in the council's deliberation representing Turobin. Thus, we have the name of a second community leader who resided in Turobin. With the discovery of the rabbi it might make it easier to find details on his personality an influence which represented Turobin at the main council convention[6].

In 1669, the representatives of the Tykocin community approached the council and complained their community was being discriminated against because they had to pay their own taxes to the Poles while the council sponsored other communities. It was decided that the council would fund the Tykocin community as well (the Council collected taxes from various communities and would budget for such needs.) Among the signatories to that decision is Yitzchak of Kraków residing in Turobin. He was likely a community leader and not necessarily a rabbi. Thus, we first encounter the name of a community leader from Turobin who could address the council and decide on many joint issues. On the other hand, it is possible that due to a lack of qualified representatives in Turobin, the position was delegated to a Jew from Kraków named Yitzchak to represent it at the council.[7]

In 1672, the council convened in Jarosław. They decided later to never conduct the meeting there again as Jews were permitted to reside only in two buildings in that town. That convention was attended by "Yitzchak son of his righteous father Yehuda Leib son of the great rabbi and teacher Naftali Yitzchak of blessed memory from Przemysl, from Krakow, on behalf of the holy community of Turobin." Here too it is unknown if it was a resident of Turobin or someone who agreed to represent the community after being approached by the community, be it due to the absence of the regular representative or some other reason.

In 1673, the representative from Pińczów complained to the council that there were many people wishing to settle in their town despite it being unfavorable. There was much poverty and not enough sources of income. They requested the council grant them the authority to forbid such migration to their community for the benefit of the longtime residents. The request by Pinczow was granted. Among the signatures affirming the decision is "David Tebbil of Turobin (son of Eliezer?).

[Page 35]

In 1678, 18 community leaders of Lublin gathered and signed a promissory note for the noble Georg Miltren fun Miltenburg, treasurer of the royal town of

Breslau. The note promises to repay the loan over 12 years "starting at the Elizabet Fair 1679." Among the 18 signatories is "Meir Yosef (should say ben Yosef) of Turobin."

A similar transaction took place at a meeting in Pińczów on 20 Tamuz 5433 (1673) when a compromise was reached regarding the promissory note. Among the signatories there is a different name representing Turobin, "David Tebbil son of the great rabbi Eliezer of blessed and holy memory from Turobin,"

On 5 Iyar 1678, the Council in Lublin deliberated and affirmed the printing of the Bible translated for Ashkenazi Jews by a man named R' Yosef Atiash from Amsterdam. Among the signatories was "R' Meir son of my beloved father Rabbi Yosef Yoske Katz from Turobin." The signatory is repeated a few times with small changes to the name, be it because of a lack of caution, or error.

That same year, The Council reached an agreement with the Tykocin Community to grant them a representative at the convention in Lublin on 4 Sivan 5438. That community bothered the council often with various complaints and often gave the council leaders a headache. One of the signatories is "Meir ben Rabbi Yosef of Turobin"

A few years later, in 1680, the Council received another loan from the nobleman mentioned above, Milteburg of Breslau, with a promissory note for installed payments for nine years. A signatory is "Rabbi David Eliezer (should say ben Eliezer) from Turobin."

In 1687, the representatives of the Opatów (Apt) community presented a similar complaint to that of the Pińczów community, that people were settling in town without the permission of the community leadership and causing an economic burden. The council granted the request and forbade Jews from other towns to settle in it. Among those signatories (26 Elul 5447) is Meir ben rabbi Yosef Katz of Turobin. Note that the same Meir appears as a representative of Turobin in various meetings.

In 1688, the Council granted exclusive rights to Rabbi Yitzchak Aberlash of Kraków to publish a book of Torah lessons. The agreement was signed on 27 Elul 5448. Among the signatories was "Zacharia Mendel son of my rabbi and teacher the great light, grand rabbi Arye Leib of righteous memory, residing in Turobin." He will be further discussed in the coming chapters.

In 1689, the council was approached concerning the dispute of the Melnyk land among the Międzyrzec Podlaski and Tykocin communities. The council handed its verdict on 15 Tishrei 5449. Among the signatories is "Meir son of rabbi Eli (maybe Arye Leib) of Turobin. Apparently, the matter was not properly settled, as on 20 Tishrei 5449 The council in Jarosław was approached concerning the conflict. The Council had to regather and give a new verdict. Among the signatories was Meir son of Rabbi S. from Turobin (likely an error, rabbi A. instead of rabbi S.) We have previously noted there are errors in the signed names.

[Page 36]

In 1689, the council granted a copyright to the author of *Zofnat Pa'aneach* Rabbi Yosef son of rabbi Moshe, and forbade others to print and distribute it for three years. A signatory is "Zechariah Mendel son of the great light, grand rabbi Arye Leib of righteous memory residing in holy Turobin and temporarily in Belz".

In 1691, The conflict concerning the Melnyk land reignited and was brought once again to the council meeting on 8 Tishrei 5451. The Council compelled them to uphold the verdict previously given by the council. Zechariah Mendel residing in Turobin signed.

In 1673, the Council deliberated the request of rabbi Shmuel Zenvel of Pińczów son of R' Chanoch of Lublin to publish his Torah commentary book *Divrei Shmuel* (Amsterdam, 5438) and the council agreed to forbid others to print and distribute it by bestowing their blessing on the author. Signed by "Yitzchak son of beloved father Uri Shraga Feivel of blessed memory, resident of Turobin."

In 1726, the Council provided a detailing of annual revenue and expenditures. The council also determined the sources of revenue and contribution appropriate for each community. The council decided to grant a discount to various communities. It is interesting to note that Turobin was granted a 600 rubles discount, like the discount granted to the Lublin community. Discounts were granted after accounting for the community's financial abilities or considering some trouble which had occurred. The very fact Turobin was put on the same level of the large and veteran Lublin community, proves beyond doubt that the Turobin community achieved a status of significance at the time. Sometimes it is hard to believe it was the same Turobin which later is not mentioned in books and its Jews did not particularly excel in spiritual or cultural matters. Sometimes the impression is made that Turobin of the Four Lands Council was larger and more stable, and more developed in other aspects economically, relationships with other towns, and notable rabbis which resided in it.

In the 18th century, we witnessed the crumbling of the autonomous structure because of the uprising by small communities against the oppressive large communities. The Polish noble class warned many times against Jewish autonomy and governmental councils adopted many resolutions against the taxation system which granted Jews the ability to hide the true income of communities. The common Jewish people also rebelled against corruption within the communities whose patience expired after witnessing the arrogance and selfishness of community leaders who exploited them for personal gain. In 1764, the Council of Foul Lands was dismantled.

We have mentioned various issues discussed at CFL with the representatives of Turobin, without mentioning many other important matters which were also deliberated and whose resolution depended on the council. As an example, we will mention the study of Torah and concern for those studying it and yeshivas and professionals who studied. Various social issues (like helping conduct weddings for poor girls) were also discussed. These details cannot be even briefly detailed here. The representatives from Turobin could watch and witness events taking place in the Jewish community of Poland through a national lens and learn about events in the Jewish world in Poland and abroad.

[Page 37]

Polish Jews saw the Council as a symbol of social greatness and a governmental mandate. After the Khmelnitsky Massacre, Rabbi Nathan Nata Hanover saw in them "The column of justice in Poland, like what was before the destruction of the Temple in Jerusalem" and the "leaders of the Four Lands were like the Sanhedrin in the Hall of Hewn Stones and had the power to rule on all of Israel in the Polish kingdom and mend fences and write rules and punish any man as they saw fit." That is an idealization of reality, but it reflects the public sentiment. After the dismantlement of the Council by the Polish authorities, Jews felt deeply insulted "that the great men and community leaders were removed from what little power they had, and even that small honor was taken from Israel." The Turobin community participated in that important council whose advice was heeded by all Jewish communities. They knew how to apply experience, delve into important and difficult matters, and could rule wisely.

It is good that authors and researchers decided to rescue the varied material of the autonomous council from the claws of forgetfulness. They published it in the form of books and papers. Thanks to them the names of the Turobin representatives were preserved; names of greater and smaller rabbis, activists, and leaders who accepted responsibility at the council. The representatives labored with no consideration for their personal needs and had to travel afar for meetings and suffer what they may have when outside of their homes and families.

As we mentioned the issues handled by the rabbis and leaders of Turobin, we must note the gap which occurred because of the 1648 massacres, when dozens of communities were destroyed, and the council could not function properly, and we need to focus on that gap.

The Jewish community in Turobin was one of the communities which developed economically to the point that in 1648 it was considered a notable community. Its roots were deep and the status of Jews was good from a spiritual and financial perspective. They lived comfortably, as Rabbi Moshe Isserles expressed, "it is better to have a dry slice of bread and peace in Poland than a house full of pleasures in Germany."

Chapter 4: Turobin During the 1648 Massacre

1648 troubles in Poland. The destruction of Turobin in the book *Yeven Mezulah*. The Destruction in the books *Tzok Ha'Itim* and *A History Jewish Tragedies* by C.Y. Gorland, *Za'ar Bat Rabim* by Ashkenazi and *Nahalat Yaakov Melitzot*. Jewish Refugees in Turobin as time passed. Kalmankish Yaffe, a refugee from Turobin, owns a printing press in Lublin. The Turobin community on the martyr list of Tomaszów. The rehabilitation of the community with assistance from the authorities. Dramatic events near town. CFL meetings renewed. 1669, Reb Yitzchak Parnas of Turobin participates. Turobin in a cycle of war and events.

The previous chapter details the period of the Council of four Lands and much material on the participation of the Turobin Jewish community in its

40

various deliberations attended by community representatives, rabbis, and leaders.

[Page 38]

In contrast, we had to limit the detailing of 1648, although Turobin undoubtedly suffered the pain inflicted by Khmelnitsky no less so than other communities in the Lublin region.

The 1648 Massacre was inflicted by Cossacks on Jewish communities in Ukraine and certain communities in Poland and Lithuania. The methods of Khmelnitsky are known; he drowned the towns of Ukraine and Poland in rivers of blood. Turobin suffered as well and in 1648 the Cossacks occupied the region and murdered many Jews.

Before Shavuot, horrifying rumors reached the area. Nobody knew where they originated and how ruthful they were, but they spread quickly. People in Turobin met at the synagogue and at home and told of a terrible uprising of Cossacks in the southeast region of the country. The two–day holiday passed peacefully, but a few days later, convoys from the east arrived and merchants told of Cossacks who allied with Tatars, the defeat of the Polish army, and two captures generals. The news intensified and quickly everyone knew that the Cossacks were attacking mainly nobles and Jews. They massacred the Jews and destroyed entire Jewish communities wherever they arrived beyond the Dnieper river. A few days later, the first refugees began arriving at the Lublin region. They were mostly wealthy Jews from Podolia and Volhyn who feared to remain in the east and escaped with their families. The refugees told of the massacres in the communities of Tsirin, Niemirów, Tulchin, Polonia, Konstantynów, Ostrów, and others. They told of horrific things done to the Jews; how they were skinned, their bodies thrown to dogs, maimed, buried alive, and the like. Tales were told of gutted Jewish children, pregnant women whose stomachs were severed, a cat placed instead of the fetus, and the like. In their nightmarish imagination, the masses saw the Cossacks storming towns and cities where Jews resided. Mothers cried day and night and looked fearfully through the windows as the murderers approached from the east.

Here are the words of the only historian in those days who witnessed the massacres, Rabbi Natan Nata son of Rabbi Moshe Hanover. He wrote in his book *Yeven Metzulah* (Venice, 1653) about Turobin and the area:

"Khmelnitsky the terrible traveled with his army, many people like the sand of the shore. They sieged the Zamosc community, a strong town with a doubled wall and a water trench surrounding it. As soon as the enemies arrived, the residents burned down the houses near the wall, so the enemies cannot hide there. The enemy was prevented from approaching the city and 1.8 kilometers surrounding itb&and during that time, they infested all the surrounding communities and killed many in Tomaszów, Szczebrzeszyn, Turobin, Rybczewice, Tarnogród, Biłgoraj, Goraj, Krasnik killed thunders of Jews."

In addition to the mentioned primary source, there are additional sources on those terrible events.

[Page 39]

Rabbi Meir son of Shmuel of Szczebrzeszyn details the events on a long prosaic poem titled *Tzok Ha'Itim* (1ˢᵗ edition Kraków 1649) and although over three hundred ears passed since the book was published it is still very valuable and considered a rare document. We bring the entire portion (*Tzok Ha'Itim,* page 17):

"During that time, about two thousand hostile troops traveled to the communities of Szczebrzeszyn and Turobin. Thousands were killed in Szczebrzeszyn, indescribable notable Jewish people, martyred for God. They defiled women and girls who shouted for help but to no avail. Their deeds prove their unchanged intentions. After they tormented them and were no longer aroused by them, the tossed their naked bodies aside. The rebels reached the synagogue and saw a Jewish man who hid there. They hung him in the tallit and tefillin he was wearing. They searched for survivors who were hiding and murdered them torturously. The dogs licked the blood of the victims, the dead were tossed in winding mountains. Hundreds of infants drowned in cement. Scrolls and holy books were tossed in the streets, ripped to pieces, and dragged through the mud, turned into a resting place for swine. The windows were smashed to smithereens, the ovens shattered. They did so in Turobin. They reached Lublin and destroyed a quality region.

Rabbi Meir slightly expanded the framework, but the details are unclear. A *History of Jewish Tragedies*, (Otzar Ha'Sifrut, Kraków, 1888) Published by C.Y. Gorland, explains that "Szczebrzeszyn and Turobin are two small towns in the Lublin region." The author of *Tit Ha'Yeven*, Rabbi Shmuel Feivish,

42

detailed in his book the number of those massacred at every sight in all villages and towns, how many households there were and how many were murdered, how many were captures and sold into slavery, without mentioning the towns of Szczebrzeszyn, Turobin, Zamosc, Bocki, and Tomaszów.

Thanks to the diligence of the researcher C.Y. Gorland in his above-mentioned booklets[8] Turobin is mentioned in some other sources as well. In *Grief of the Many* by Rabbi Avraham son of Rabbi Shmuel Ashkenazi in the alphabetically ordered kina "Eulogy for Polonia" in the rhymes starting with the letter W$ it is written, "I cry for the surviving Hebrews, the dear children of Boćki, the honest children of Brehin, the righteous children of Szczebrzeszyn, the wholesome children of Yavoriv, the brave children of Turobin, the glorious children of Tomaszów. the enemies came and slaughtered more than thirty thousand people in the area, clever people illuminating like the light of the heavens."

The book *Nahlat Yaakov Melitzot* by Rabbi Naftali Sofer Medina of Gniezno (1652) includes various musar passages and ends with grief poems by Rabbi Chanoch of Gniezno (Poznan). In "God of Vengeance Kina" (alphabetically organized, stanzas form an acrostic of the author's name) written about the tragedy of the massacres in Ukraine, the Volhyn region, and the Chelm region it says, "For that I weep, A sword was not returned to its holster, God has prepared a sacrifice of summer newborns, the holy Szczebrzeszyn and Turobin communities were slaughtered by the enemy's sword for God. How long will You not rest and not let them be?"[9]

[Page 40]

So, Turobin is mentioned more than once in works mentioning the communities in which the evil massacre took place (if not in all the grief poems). Details on the number of casualties and descriptions of the murders are not detailed. However, the condensation of the descriptions says much. Turobin was not a fortress like Zamosc and its Jews could not redeem their lives for twenty thousand gold coins. It was also not like the capital Lublin, one of the four large communities whose residents prepared to defend the city, workers took positions in watchtowers, the walls of the city fortified, ramparts constructed, trenches cleared of trash, and canons updated. But luck shined upon Lublin that time, as the new king Jan Casimir demanded Khmelnitsky withdraw in exchange for negotiations. He directed his troops to return home and Lublin sighed in relief. In 1651, Lublin was already able to host the reconvened Council of Four Lands and discuss methods of assisting the thousands of the afflicted in Ukraine and Podolia. The communities were instructed to each assist a certain number of refugees.

The Jewish refugees who reached the region probably arrived to seek shelter in Turobin as well. For generations following the events, people shook in fear when discussing Khmelnitsky the horrible. Emigrants from Turobin now in Israel know to tell that when Khmelnitsky and his Cossacks invaded Poland and were able to reach Rava–Ruska, people from a few Jewish communities came to Turobin. The spoke Germanic Yiddish and sang a song "Bogdan, Bogdan you are a traitor" or something along those lines. The Khmelnitsky massacres left their mark not only on grief poems and *El Malei Rachmaim* in memory of the martyrs, but also in folk songs which angrily mentioned the name of the bitter enemy.

Apparently, impoverished individuals who could not afford to escape to safer, more distant places, were murdered. The wealthier people joined the camp of those leaving their homes and traveled to escape death and rescue their families. After the massacred ceased, the refugees of Turobin, or many of them, returned to Turobin and began to rehabilitate their lives and livelihoods and overcome the horrifying past, though they could not forget the tragedies which were written in rivers of blood on the hearts of Polish Jews.

The economic status of Polish Jews was destroyed mainly by the events of 1648 following the terrible destruction which was unprecedented in the history of Poland. Their political status had previously declined for various reasons, mainly due to feuds among the noble class.

Due to a lack of details, it is difficult to assess whether Turobin was resettled only by residents who survived by escaping ahead of time or whether additional refugees arrived who feared to return to their homes in Ukraine and Vohlyn, at the recommendation of CFL or invited by the Turobin residents who wanted to return the population to its previous size. The pain of the bitter past was not quickly forgotten. The rabbis who convened at CFL decided to announce a fast day on 20 Tamuz, the day of the massacre in Niemirów, and permitted agunot whose husbands perished during the massacre to remarry.

[Page 41]

One of the reasons for the small number of notices about the massacre in Turobin is that there was not a single Jew from Turobin who was spared killing and could testify to the tragedy that befell the local Jews among the refugees or those imprisoned by Tatars. Of course, those who escaped prior to the massacre could not know how the massacre was conducted there. However, there was a Jew from Turobin by the name of Kalmankish Yaffe who settled in Lublin and established a printing house in partnership with Shlomo Zalman son of rabbi Yakkov. That printing house also printed, probably to memorialize the author, the book *Broken Tablets*, a commentary on the Torah and Talmud by the holy rabbi Yechiel Michel ben rabbi Elazar, yeshivah and court chairman in Niemirów who was martyred there in 1648 and was memorialized in many folk tales and brief poems about the tragedy. The book was brought to press by the brother of the holy rabbi, the righteous rabbi Yitzchak Mochaich, chief rabbi of Terebovlya in Podolia, residing in the glorious Zhovkva community in 1679. The name of the publisher from Turobin is on the books cover page, "Kalmankish Yaffe of Turobin. Printed in Lublin under the rule of the great king his majesty Jan."[10]. A special El Malei Rachamim prayer in honor of his pure soul is present in all books dedicated to the 1648 massacres.

In the old ledger of the synagogue in Tomaszów Lubelski (which was burned in the first fire in 1918) kept meticulous records of all the places in which the Khmelnitsky occupiers massacred Jews. The name of the Turobin community is also included, and it was customary to dig near the graves on the three days leading up to Shavuot.[11]

Turobin was on the first line of defense on Polish soil on the western bank of the Bog River, near the towns from south and north like Goraj, Krasnik, Tomaszów, Rybczewice, Tarnogród, Bilgoraj and others. The region delayed the tide of the belligerents who wanted to storm and invade the heart of Poland. They were the first ones to receive he blows from the troops of the horrible Khmelnitsky on Polish soil settled by Poles and Jews, not Ukrainians.

It is unknown if that line of defense with fortified towns such as Zamosc and Lublin could have held on for long if not for the crowning of Jan Casimir, brother of the deceased king Vladislav. Khmelnitsky's fatigue meant the king's order to stop the war was a lifeline. He seized the opportunity and ordered his troops to retreat from all Polish and other occupied territories. Turobin was one of the towns liberated a short time after they were invaded. The residents, including Jews, were able to return and rebuild the town. We do not have details on their return and the rebuilding of community life.

Because of the recording shortage on the murders of Jews of the Turobin community, it is unknown what happened to the deceased; if they received a Jewish burial in the local cemetery or in a mass grave as was done in the other towns Khmelnitsky invaded. Other sources say that the Polish Sejm came to the aid of destroyed towns and reaffirmed the rights and privileges afforded by earlier monarchs to the towns and the Jews which resided in them. The permit was given in 1678 by the owner of Turobin, Count Zamoyski. He afforded such rights for the sake of town development in 1646, two years before the Cossack uprising. The new king, Jan Casimir, granted 4 market days for Turobin. It is unknown if he did so on his initiative as he did for other towns, or if he was influenced by Zamoyski.

[Page 42]

The Turobin community was able to rebuild quickly due to its proximity to Lublin, the main community, and the seat of the CFL, though it remined wounded like all of Polish Jewry. Not all communities were rebuilt. Many of the destroyed communities were erased from the communities' map. Above all, psyches were destroyed, and a fertile ground was created for mystical messianic delusions. The mysticism was joined with religion and the Jews invested in it their longing for Geulah and ascension from the depths of reality. The victory of the Zohar and Rabbi Yitzchak Luria's kabbalah was a decisive one. The longing for redemption and faith in it gave birth in a roundabout way to Shabtai Zvi and his pupil Yaakov Frank[12]. It also gave birth to the Hasidic movement which also found fertile ground in Turobin.[13]

Many dramatic events which happened during the 1648 massacre in Ukraine probably did not happen in Turobin, although they did in its vicinity. It is told that when Khmelnitsky's murderous troops were nearing Krasnobród, local Jews began pleading with the town's nobles Bonded and Yadmov to come to their aid in their time of need. They agreed to protect them for a hefty sum and kept their promise. The ataman's forces rested on Yadao's property, while some troops stayed in the Bonder woods and did not enter the town. When they found a bride and groom in the synagogue yard exiting their chuppah they killed them both. The "lovely and pleasant" were buried where they were killed. Near the western wall of the synagogue, there was a stone marking their burial spot and the cohanim would not pass near it and walk instead on the path between the synagogue and bathhouse.

The Council of Four Lands reconvened and representatives of Turobin participated in its deliberations. In 1669, there is a mention of "R' Yitzchak Parnas in the Turobin community" among the signatories regarding a decision made by the council regarding the Tykocin community. It is very possible the Turobin representative was there was a leader instead of a rabbi for the first time after the Khmelnitsky's tragedies, since they did not yet have one who could navigate the complex matters of the council. In contrast, we see in later years notable men among the Turobin representatives such as R' Meir ben R' Yoske Katz, son of R' Arye Leib, R' Yitzchak son of Uri Shraga Feivel of Kraków "currently residing in Turobin" and others. Among the representing rabbis were those who served many communities in their long lives and came to Turobin to serve as a rabbi, or continued to another town after serving in Turobin.

By the time to wounds caused by Khmelnitsky healed, new troubled had arrived. In the fall, a plague broke out in greater Poland and residents escaped from the towns and villages to the woods to save themselves. The plague spread quickly and brought devastation to many.

[Page 43]

The Jews have not yet rested from their troubles when a short time later, enemies invaded again, the Russians from the east, the Cossacks and Tatars from south–west, and the Swedish king Carl Gustav from the North. King Jan Casimir escaped to Silesia and Carl Gustav advanced within Poland without meeting an armed resistance. The Lublin region, including Turobin, was saved from the Swedes but met a worse fate; the Cossacks and Russians invaded and caused much suffering to the population. The cycle of events continued until 1660. Lublin and the region were passed from one invader to the next. Merchants and craftsmen turned poor, and in one of his publications, king Jan Casimir described the dark state of Polish Jews. Turobin was linked to the series of events occurring Lublin. We do not know details on the daily lives of the Jews of Turobin at the time, the most difficult in their live.

The fate of Turobin was as risk along with all Polish Jewry in the 18th century, which brought new shocks to the Jews. Kings August I and II ruled the country. They were wild kings of narrow hearts who abandoned the Jews to their enemies. Jewish spirit declined as a result. The wall of Jewish autonomy was breached. The dwindling financial resources of Jews and the immense debt of the Council of Four Lands following the massacres, wars, and other tragedies were added to the undermining on the inside and competition by those motivated by personal gain. So, the Council of Four lands finally collapsed, the same council which Jews of Turobin could take pride in as they had representatives almost during the entire time it existed.

That same year, Stanislav August Poniatovski became the last monarch of Poland. He enacted some reforms, but the economic status of the Jews had sharply declined. That generation lacked great leaders who could withstand the tide. Instead, people of a progressive and liberal mindset took leadership positions. The Jews of Turobin and other traditional communities were not pleased by them and matters worsened.

In contrast to the period of the Council of Four Lands and the events of 1648, for which we had historical sources, we have no sources on the state of Turobin on the period of the three partitions of Poland. Turobin also experienced changes, no less so than other communities. Turobin exchanged hands several times and for a certain time was occupied by Austrian troops.

Chapter 5: Development of the Turobin Community and Institutions

Turobin in CFL documents. "Holy vessels" in the Turobin community. The history of the synagogue of Turobin. The role of a rabbi in the community. Rabbi Shimon Wolf Oyerbach. Rabbi Zachariah Mendel author of *Ba'er Heitev*. The tombstone of Rabbi Reuven ben rabbi Yeshayah in Lublin. The rabbis Natan Nata and Eliezer. Rabbi Noach Shmuel Lifshitz – first Hasidic rabbi in Turobin. The cemetery and burial society. Origins of Hasidism in Turobin.

[Page 44]

Turobin was a relatively notable community. it was first mentioned in the documents of CFL in 1607, in a manner demonstrating it was a rich community, and the number of documents of CFL mentioning Turobin had since increased. They are a valuable resource when studying the community. It shows it was structurally important within Polish Jewish autonomy. We mention it here in the overview of milestones in the history of Jewish Turobin.[14]

As in other towns, The Jewish community in Turobin was autonomously ruled and held judicial and administrative roles concerning the population in town and the region. The community was the administrative point of contact between the Jewish population and the municipal and national authorities. The community regulated the economic, social, and cultural lives of its members. Community leaders were appointed who wrote the community's budget and handled fiscal matters. They represented the community to the nobles, municipal and royal authorities. They had a say over permitting someone to hold a certain profession. They appointed rabbis, administrators, clerks, and community officers. Additionally, the leaders would appoint a person from their ranks as representative to the regional and central councils. Collectors of dues oversaw synagogues, burial societies, homeless shelters, old–age homes, charities, bathhouses, weeding funds and other philanthropic institutions, the shochetim, those ritually purging meat, and butchers.

There was a synagogue wherever there was a traditionally observant Jewish population. Most synagogues in the Lublin province were built in the 16th and 17th centuries. The synagogue in Turobin was built in the 16th century. As an older town, the town had a synagogue before other communities in the Zamoyski Family Fee Tail. Count, Jan Zamoyski the Fee Tail's owner, was generous regarding the construction of synagogues and allowed unlimited amounts of wood to be taken from the forest, as well as cement and stones, free of charge. The synagogue in Turobin was built with red bricks. It was probably once the same color as traditional synagogues, but fires which were prevalent in many towns likely happened, and changes were made to the exterior and interior design while doing repairs. After the tragic events of 1648, when many synagogues were plundered and burned by Khmelnitsky's gangs, community ledgers detail immense artistic wealth Jewish artists contributed to those prayer houses. Presumably, the synagogue in Turobin also had an artistic treasure which did not survive.

[Page 45]

In contrast, to this day, the magnificent synagogues in the nearby towns of Zamosc and Szczebrzeszyn, are famed. The most famous and ancient among the many synagogues of Lublin, was the Shlomo Luria synagogue. It was built in 1567 by authority of King Zigmont August. Square–shaped and at the center of the prayer hall were four columns surrounding the stage, linked at the top in half–circular arcs. The synagogue in Szczebrzeszyn, the interior of which was like the Zamosc synagogue, was among the most decorated synagogues in the Lublin region. Its exterior was also excellent, in addition to the interior ornaments. The Renaissance synagogue in Zamosc served as the first example of interior ornamental architecture and was gently and tastefully designed. Unfortunately, we do not have a description of the original synagogue of Turobin. The Russians did not spare it in WWI, and it was only rebuilt and renovated ten years later. There were many windows in the synagogue, elaborately decorated, especially on the wall which faced the sight of the temple in Jerusalem which was by the parishioners, next to it stood the ark (which housed the Torah scrolls) which was a customarily decorated. Near the ark stood a podium which the prayer leader stood in front of. At the center of the synagogue, as usual, there was a stage where the Torah was recited. There was a women's section too.

The community had salaried positions, headed by the rabbi who in addition to his role answering religious queries had an official, respected say on community matters. He would affirm community rules and the leaders' important decisions. He signed the tax form written by the accountants, and led appointments of the community leaders.

The Great Synagogue - views from East and South
(Photographed October 1966)

50

[Page 46]

He was the court chairman, and the one to issue an excommunication decree. He oversaw teachers, gave permission to speakers to give lectures in town. He signed official letters and community notices, etc. As time passed, the rabbi's authority decreased in favor of the leaders; he could not excommunicate without their consent, and his dependence on the leaders extended to other matters. The rabbi's position guaranteed a large income; he had a fixed salary, payments from weddings, circumcisions, divorces, a commission of compensation ruled by the religious court, a fee for affirming documents, etc. In addition, the rabbi was exempt from all taxes unless he traded.

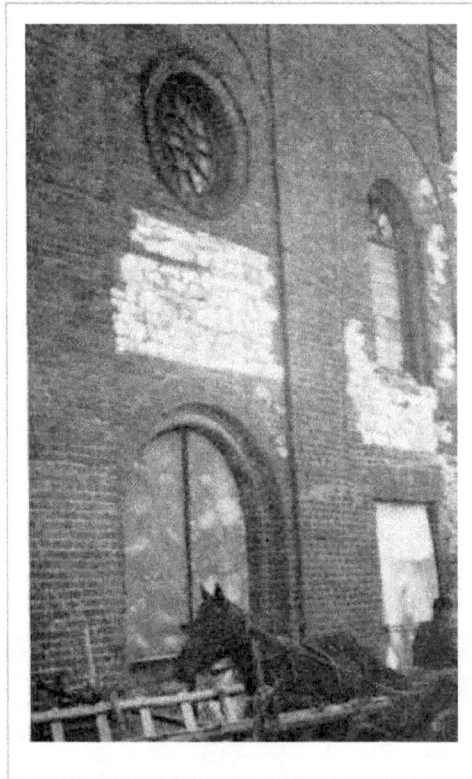

The synagogue became a barn

[Page 47]

Turobin had many notable, influential rabbis, and a few are mentioned with admiration in rabbinic literature and general Jewish literature. The great rabbi Shimon Wolf son of Rabbi David Tebbil Oyerbach was a rabbi in Turobin for some time and represented the community at the Council of Four Lands in 5387. However, rabbis in those days were travelers often relocated to a larger or more notable community. Rabbi Shimon Wolf relocated to Lyuboml, and a short while later, resigned as rabbi from Lyuboml as he was called to serve as a rabbi of Lublin. He served as rabbi in Lublin from 5339 to 5345. He then left Lublin, its masses, and noise, and was given the role of ABD in in Przemyśl where he ruled his community justly. During his tenure in Przemyśl, he was among those who approved the book *Yesh Nokhalim* (Prague, 5357.) He went on to serve in the Poznań community. He attracted admiration with his righteousness and there too he approved a book, *Siakh Yitzchak* (Basel 5387) on Shvat 19, 5387. He went on to serve as a yeshiva leader and ABD in the grand city of Vienna, capital of Austria.)5585) and towards the end of his life served as ABD of Prague where he passed on Cheshvan 7, 5392. His gravestone reads, "was ABD and head of the yeshiva in Turobin, Lyuboml, Lublin, etc. his Torah writings are printed in *Kav HaYashar* chapter 65.

The Symbol over the western entrance to the synagogue

52

[Page 48]

The synagogue viewed from a distance

He was the son–in–law of Mahrshal and father in law of Rabbi Eliezer Lipman Heilperin, father of the famed genius rabbi Ze'ev Wolf Halperin ABD of Olik. The details of the disagreement he had with Mahram in Prague, as well as he disagreement he had with Rabbi Yom Tov Lipman, author of Tosfet Yom–Tov, were written by the great rabbi Shlomo Yitzhcak Heilperin, rabbi of Brotchin, Ternopil. The great rabbi Shimon Wolf Oyerbach is quoted in the book Or Tzadikim by the great rabbi Meir Papas, Lev Arye (Devarim Parsha), Sha'ar Nefilat Apayim, Maharam's Responsa (Question 27), Korban

Shabbat (Ch. 3), and has approved the book Siakh Yitzchak on Hebrew grammar (19 Shvat 5377).

One of the most famous rabbis was Rabbi Zacharia Mendel, known for his book Ba'er Hetev on Shulchan Aruch, Yore De'a and Choshen Mishpat. He was Known in Kraków as Rabbi Mendel son of the wise Rabbi Arye Leib, also known by all as Rabbi Leib son of rabbi Fishel, after his father–in–law the great rabbi Fishel from Lviv. Rabbi Arye Leib was at first the chief rabbi and Yeshiva instructor in the Vienna metropolis and in Przemyśl and was later accepted chief rabbi in Kraków after the passing of the great rabbi Heshel of Lublin, who passed on 20 Tishrei 5424. The next year Rabbi Arye Leib already filled rabbi Heshel's throne. He published his book Tikunei Teshuvah in 5426 and others.

[Page 49]

Rabbi Zacharia Mendel, Rabbi Arye Leib's eldest son, had both Torah skills and greatness. He had a well–constructed large brick house in the Jewish street of Kraków. After the death of his father, Rabbi Zacharia was accepted as rabbi of the grand synagogue and Torah instructor in Kraków, and in 5434 he still had that position. Later, He was accepted as chief rabbi of Turobin. In 5448 he was at the Jarosław Council among the rabbis of CFL who approved the publication of the book Toldot Yitzchak, a commentary on the Torah by the great rabbi Yitzchak Darshan of Kraków. In 5449 he approved the new Tzofnat Pa'aneach. He went on from Turobin to serve as chief rabbi of Belz province. There, he approved the publication of Ktonet Pasim including Chaluka D'Rabanan on the Passover Haggadah by the author of Tzofnat Pa'aneach, signed as "the humble Zacharia Mendel son of the great light, teacher and rabbi Arye Leib of blessed memory, residing in Belz."[15]

At the old cemetery in Lublin there is a tombstone of Rabbi Reuven son of Rabbi Yeshayah, reading "Rabbi and scholar rabbi Yeshayah of blessed memory of Turobin, passed on 19 Av 5526 it is unknown if he served as a rabbi in Turobin or was a wise man versed in Torah without filling an official position.

Another notable rabbi is Rabbi Natan Netta, dubbed "The wise and righteous rabbi Natan Neta, rabbi of the Turobin community." He is quoted as a responder in the halachic inquiry book Beit Avraham but the wise rabbi Avraham rabbi of Tarla. He approved the book Asefat Yehuda in 5522 and signed "Natan Netta", residing in Turobin, son–in–law of the wiseman M. Baruch Kahana Rappoport." He was also descendent of a notable rabbinical lineage.

His daughter was married to the wise rabbi Yosef Te'omim who was the rabbi of Ostrovtza and in 5492 was hired as rabbi of Opatów.

Another righteous man well versed in Torah was the wise rabbi Elazar son of the wealthy Rabbi Yosef Halevi Segal Landau, halakhic scholar, and arbiter of the Kraków province. He was a chief rabbi in Turobin and is mentioned in the burial society ledger of Opatów in 5554. He rests with his ancestors in Opatów. His wife, Hadasa, was the daughter of the wise rabbi Yakkov Yitzchak, ABD of Zamosc.

His daughter Rivkah was married to the wise rabbi Yitzchak rabbi of Chelma and Zamosc who passed in 5685.

The first Hasidic rabbi in Turobin was the wise rabbi Noakh Shmuel Lifshitz (5540 – 5592)[16] who served as its rabbi from 5558 and like his father Rabbi Yehuda Leib Lifshitz who was a rabbi in Białaczów and Opoczno was of the followers and pupils of Rabbi Yaakov Yitzchak the Seer of Lublin. He was raised in the Hasidic tradition and also traveled to the rabbi Yisroel the maggid of Kozienice. Rabbi Noakh Shmuel raised and educated who would later become the "the righteous man of Gostynin" Rabbi Yechiel Meir Lifshitz, his nephew orphaned at a young age. He breathed the air of Turobin along with the moral air he absorbed in his uncle's house.

[Page 50]

Cover page of the book *Divrei Shmuel*
by rabbi S.N. Lifshitz of Turobin

[Page 51]

A cemetery was among the first concerns of every Jewish community and was the cornerstone when establishing a Jewish community. The cemetery was usually built outside of town, and as time passed was in the center of town. At the Turobin cemetery, there were ancient tombstones, half sunken in the ground. The Turobin cemetery was visited on certain days of the year; memorial days, 9 of Av, during the month of Elul, especially on the eve of Rosh Hashanah and the eve of Yom Kippur when many prayers were said, and charity was given to the poor in memory of the deceased. The date the cemetery was established is unknown.

The cemetery was under the care of the burial society, the company which cared for the needs of the deceased and was present in all Jewish communities. The members of the burial society and the fund collectors had various customs and rights. The privilege of caring for the cemetery was always considered one of the principles of religious freedom whose administration and care was legally established. Each burial society had a ledger which recorded various events and community guidelines. Regional authorities approved the decrees of the society. Of course, the Turobin ledger also recorded matters which concerned the general Jewish lifestyle and not unique to Turobin, as the social conditions expressed in community guidelines were not unique to the Jewish community in that town.

There was much responsibility placed in the hands of the chosen community council, and a special spot in the framework of Jewish autonomy in Poland was reserved for the rabbi. The autonomous rule was effectively placed in the hands of the rabbis of CFL. Outwardly, they were the representatives of the Jewish community, tasked with collecting taxes. Within the community, they were those shaping culture and spiritualty and were involved in every aspect of community life. There were additional religious officials in the community, shochetim, teachers, synagogue managers, and clerks. The rabbi's role was most influential, there was a reason he was called "head of the area."

With the demise of Poland came the demise of its flourishing Jewish autonomy. Indeed, before the demise of CFL of Hasidism rose in Poland. The rabbis of CFL could not negatively impact its fate in their final meetings, and quickly Lublin and Zamosc and the surrounding small towns were flooded with the bustling of the new movement, which entered Turobin silently and modestly. That reality was eventually recognized, and various sects of Hassidim established their own prayer houses. "Righteous men" visited and Hasidim would openly travel to their righteous men. Turobin also served as the home of some righteous man.

Chapter 6: Political troubles and the Joy of Hasidism in Turobin

Community reorganized. Jews settle in nearby towns. Census of Jews in 1764. Notable wise rabbis in Turobin. Turobin during the three partitions of Poland. The light of Hasidism in Turobin. The Rabbi of Turobin – student of the Seer. Natives of Turobin as rabbis in various communities. The Turobin area described by writers. Educated people and notable writers in the region.

[Page 52]

After the Cossack uprising of 1648, the Turobin community shared a similar fate to that of the rest of Polish Jewry. Most communities were destroyed. Refugees from Turobin were scattered near and far, waiting for a beam of light to arrive, without knowing from where. Polish Jewry was in decline. The fate of the Polish Commonwealth was visible and apparent to all. The conflict among classes and parties undermined the foundations of the state, which housed the Jewish community in Europe for centuries. Everything decayed. The king played with the nobles internally and the governments of Russia, Prussia, and Austria externally. The Jews of Turobin, who knew what was occurring in the country through their representatives in CFL walked as if on hot coals, between hope and despair. The nobles continued in their traditional feuds and self–preservation, and in the towns, a class war took place among the nobles and lower classes. Additionally, the Catholic Church intervened and preached hate towards other faiths and incited against the Jews with blood libel and other libel.

But after the Jews returned to Turobin following the Khmelnitsky massacre, their numbers increased in the town and satellite villages so that they were able to reestablish aa new organized community. Settlements took place not only in Turobin but also in the surrounding area in towns and villages for which Turobin served as the main community. Jewish residence in Turobin was not entirely forbidden (Non tolerandis Yudia)[11], as opposed to many other towns and cities of church strongholds. The growth in the Jewish population, as in the rest of the Polish kingdom, came about through natural growth, developed family traditions, religious lifestyle, especially the widespread tradition of marrying young, combined with the immigration of Jews from distant placed where access and reconstruction were unrealistic.

58

A shocking change to the Polish Jewish community was the dismantling of the Council of Four Lands by King Poniatovski in 1764. Until that time, the Council collected the head tax from the Jews. The representatives of Turobin in the Council took part in its decisions concerning many communities and had an idea of what was happening across the Jewish community in Poland. The dismantlement of the Council silenced an important chronicler of Jewish Turobin. The cancellation was caused by the suspicion that the communities were collecting fewer taxes from the lower classes. To maximize tax revenue, the Sejm decided to collect taxes from everyone. That removed the need for community leaders, rabbis, and regional leaders and diminished the value of the Council of Four lands, the great organization of Polish Jewry which radiated beauty and royal awe for centuries. The Sejm of 1788–1791 was concerned about the Jewish question and many solutions were proposed to solve it.

Most advocated forced assimilation, cancelling the communities' autonomy, replacing Yiddish with Polish, replacing trade with agricultural work. After many deliberations, the proposals were postponed to handling in special committees whose entire purpose was a perpetual delay of the Jewish question and avoiding a solution in the spirit of liberalism. The Jews attempted to influence the king Stanislav August Poniatovski through friendly ties wealthy Jews had with the king and his staff. Undoubtedly the representatives of Turobin were involved through various channels. Eventually, the Kingdom of Poland was partitioned a third time and independent Poland was lost.

[Page 53]

In 1764, the government conducted a census of Jews, which continued into the first months of 1765. The census was conducted in relation to the individual tax the Jews were demanded to pay, as opposed to a lump sum as before. Children less than a year old were exempt from the tax and so were not counted. In 1765, the Turobin community and the surrounding area had 985 Jews[18]. It was then a town in Chelm district.

However, the true number of Jews in many places was larger than what the census accounted for. Since the purpose of the census was raising taxes on Jews, they made an effort to report a number as low as possible, especially children which could be hidden more easily. It is unknown how many non-Jews resided in Turobin at the time as the non-Jewish population was not counted. The sources from the time, like the memoirs of Bar of Bolekhiv, confirm the underreporting of individuals to municipal and national authorities, especially the number of children.[19]

As we investigate those days in terms of cultural wellbeing on Polish Jews and ignore for a while the downgraded political and economic situation, we are shocked at the flourishing of the Torah and its study during those bad times. On one hand, a sword of persecutions was being waved by the Church and nobles. On the other hand, Torah was studied day and night in the Poland ghettos. Turobin was home to notable wise rabbis whom the Jews of Turobin took pride in. The rabbis of Turobin studied much Torah as they served as instructors in yeshivas for local and regional students. It seems that there was no bigger rise in the study of Talmud as in those days in the regions of Kraków, Lviv, and Lublin as in those days, in which the sound of Torah study was loud and it flourished and achieved unprecedented advance. The communities of Poland served as the cultural warehouse for the Western European communities. All the great rabbis in Germany, France, and Holland and others came from Poland. Elite yeshivot were established which produced thousands of Torah scholars while the well did not run dry and "gentle Poland of Torah and greatness" was not deprived of Rabbis. Rabbis of towns like Szydlowiec, Wodzislaw, and Opatów filled important roles in their communities. It is possible rabbis from Turobin served as rabbis in communities abroad without their names being mentioned like rabbis from other communities which were occasionally mentioned. Polish rabbis served In London and Amsterdam as well. In addition, Poland had many rabbis and wisemen. Beautiful responsa books on halakha and commentary were published often, in the Turobin area as well like *Mishnat Chachamim* by Rabbi Yosef Hochgilrenter of Zamosc. A rabbi who was a refugee expelled from Vienna expressed his conclusion, "I came to Poland where Torah and greatness are one of the same, and from which the light of Torah illuminates, as they spread Torah in Israel even in poverty and hard labor, especially the burden of head taxes, property taxesb& ten men wear a single tallit and study Torah." (Rabbi Nafatali Hertz Lenglezu in the introduction to his commentary *Naftali Ayala Shelukha* on *Midrash Raba* (Frankfurt)Oder) 5452)[20].

[Page 54]

The names of the rabbis of Turobin shine like gems of light to this very day in rabbinic literature and halakhic commentary. The name Turobin was well respected in Jewish councils, yeshivot and Torah students from Turobin were accepted in many places as important people. From that aspect, there was no place for residents of Turobin to be ashamed in comparison to other places. The wisemen who interpreted the name of the town as a combination of the words 'Torah' and *binah* [wisdom] were not overlooked.

Since the census of Jews, the last thirty years in the events of old Poland were tumultuous in foreign and domestic policy. Three Partitions occurred and ended Poland's independence. The three large neighboring kingdoms of Prussia, Russia, and Austria were the partitioning states. After Poland was divided a third time in 1795, Austria occupied a part of the Lublin province including Turobin. After the annexation of the province by Austria, changes occurred in community organization and the lives of Jews. The community was governed by Austrian inventions which limited Jewish trade, in addition to other restriction placed on Jews. By direction from Austria, authorities began an initiative to introduce the Jews, like in Galicia, to a civilization process to prepare them for receiving civil rights. That is how Jews were forced to add Polish last names to their Jewish ones. As opposed to Galicia, where names were chosen by clerks, the Jews chose the names themselves and names from that era like Turobiner and others like it remained.

The taxation burden was not smaller under the Austrian regime. The meat tax which was leased to Jewish contractors, and the candle tax, a tax levied on every candle lighted in Jewish homes on Shabbat and holidays, two candles at least for every married woman. Those taxes remained in effect even after the town was annexed to the Warszawa Principality. In 1809, the whole province was conquered by Prince Yozef Poniatovski, and the Lublin province including Turobin was returned to the Warszawa Principality. The wars of Napoleon and his conquers which shook the world and awoke it form its Middle Ages slumber brought a spirit of freedom and tolerance to all oppressed nations including the Jews. The Jewish nation, which was depressed by the persecutions of the Middle Ages, began a resurrection and the rumors about the founding of the Sanhedrin and equal rights for Jews in Europe filed their hearts in hopes of a new and brighter future. But the righteous rabbis of Poland, men of the holy spirt, predicted that if the laws of equal rights were enacted, they would cause the assimilation of Jews and they labored to cancel that so called "gift."

There is no doubt that during the events which shook the leaders of Hasidism relating to reforms was also present in Turobin. The town served as a halfway point between Lublin, Kozienice, and Galician Rymanów whose righteous men stood at the helm of the spiritual excitement. Messengers wandered many towns and stopped in Turobin as well, making it a party to the Political – Hasidic arguments about the future. Turobin was one of the first towns which were affected by the new light of the Hassidic movement and conquered many hearts and fresh spirits[?]. The religious star of Rabbi Noakh Shmuel ben Rabbi Yehuda Leib rose in Turobin, and he participated in spreading Hassidim across the country.

[Page 55]

At the end of the 18th century, a new fire ignited and spread across Eastern European Jewry –the Hasidic movement. It came bearing powerful psychological tools and overtook the souls of many. It first gave God to the ordinary Jew, from which he drew solace in dark days. It touched on many ecstatic emotions of mystical religion. It also possessed a surprising psychological phenomenon of ignoring the grey reality, creating an elevated world flowing with love and kindness. With the philosophy of mystical emotion, in which the righteous man served in a central role, every believer was directly connection to his Creator and could pour his heart out to him. The barriers present in thick volumes of Jewish law fell. God was no longer in the law but in song, prayer, and faith. The large wave which swept through the Jewish community reached Turobin in its early days, where it encountered no objections. Even the elaborate rabbinic tradition of the community could not withstand the force of the new movement and new winds began to blow. The foundation was than laid for Hasidic Turobin, the part of the Jewish community which stood out within the diverse picture. Here too there is more that remains a mystery, but the name "Rabbi Noakh Shmuel Lifshitz of Turobin" which was common among the many followers of Rabbi Yakkov Yitzchak "The Seer" of Lublin says much.

Just as Turobin was previously linked to Lublin as the main seat of the Council of Four Lands, so too Hasidic Turobin continued to be linked to Lublin, where the Seer resided. He was the founder of the Hasidic movement in Poland and inherited the Hasidism of the Baal Shem Tov. The Seer began his leadership between the first and second partitions of Poland. During those thirty years the Seer led, Poland was divided a second and third time, with changes in government and kings in many of its provinces. The French revolution arrived, and Napoleon and his conquers merged with the founding of the Warszawa Principality and the notion of equal rights for Jews. Those years also marked the development and spread of Hasidism in Poland which had arrived from the edges, from Vohlyn and Eastern Galicia.

The spiritual essence of the Seer who was born in Lublin and the time in which he operated marked the importance of Lublin and designed the unique image of the Hasidic leader, which was not only a community leader but a spiritual guide. His many followers and students were attracted by his method of worship, the way of total excitement and dedication. The Seer was a mystical expert, Kabbalah scholar, establisher of redeeming rituals, and writer of prayers. He was the student of the great Maggid of Międzyrzec Podlaski and Rabbi Elimelch of Lizhensk and had all the qualities which attracted followers. And so, a great community of Hassidism was established in Lublin and added to the many great students who were famed as leaders during his life and after his death.

The Hasidic community in Lublin brought the Seer to them in about 5554, after he resided in Cyców for about seven years. However, there were a few Hasidic people in Lublin (perhaps in Turobin as well), although the Hasidic movement was not yet pronounced in what was previously a scholarly center, the city of Mahrshal and Maharam. Indeed, the rabbi of Lublin in the previous generation, Rabbi Shaul Margaliot, was from a Hasidic home and even visited the Ba'al Shem Tov with his notable wise father and right hand man of the Ba'al Shem Tov, Rabbi Meir Margaliot, author of *Meir Netivm*. However, they were hidden and persecuted by community leaders.

Turobin was one among many followers of Hassidic Lublin, which was considered the first and main town and the one to spread Polish Hasidism. The first in nearly the entirety of Poland was Rabbi Yaakov Yitzchak "The Seer" who was admired by all Hasidic leaders and considered the father of Polish Hasidism. His battle to spread Hassidim in Poland was a rough one, but he overcame his opposition. After his victory, Lublin became a center of Hasidic leadership lineages and home to thousands of Hasidic people. Hundreds of followers came to him, including famed Torah scholars.

[Page 56]

If we want to examine the power of Hasidic influence during the period of the Seer in Lublin province we need to read the work of his students. Those include Rabbi Avraham, rabbi of Rejowiec who left many behind, Rabbi Eliezer Bar of Grabowiec brother– in –law of Rabbi Mordechai Yosef from Izbica, Rabbi Arye Leibush of Biłgoraj, Rabbi Ze'ev Wolf rabbi of Biyozipof, Rabbi Yosef Kesis of Chelm, Lubartów, and Janów. Rabbi Yitzchak Moshe Azriel Licht of Belzyce, Rabbi Lemmel of Wahin and Modliborzyce, Rabbi Moshe Chaim of Mboskovitz, Rabbi Moshe of Janów, Rabbi Noakh Shmuel Lifshitz of Turobin and Biezun[21], Rabbi Nehemya of Józefów, Rabbi Nata of Chelm, Rabbi Kalman Yitzchak of Belzyce, and more.

Turobin was located among towns and cities full of Judaism and Hassidism in all directions; Szczebrzeszyn, Janów Lubelski, Biłgoraj, Goraj, towards Lublin. Goraj is a small town from which the famed righteous man Mendli of Kotzk originated. Also worth mentioning is Motelle Gorajer who was considered by Jews in the region as a crypto–righteous man. Indeed, Szczebrzeszyn and Zamosc were known as progressive communities. Y.L. Peretz was born in Zamosc and studied Torah in Szczebrzeszyn as a student of the wise writer Yaakov Reifman who was reputable and well known in the region. Hasidism was the undeniable ruler of Jewish life in Turobin. Its liveliness and roots still fed on the first–generation Hasidism in Lublin of the and the Rabbi of Zaklików. Hasidic devoutness was dominant and did not allow any other breach of spirit in Jewish life. The Lublin rabbi Moshele Tverski and the rabbis of Turiysk visited towns annually and were hosted in Bilgoraj, Turobin, Janów, and Frampol. The writer Y. Bashevis describes in his book *Satan in Goraj* the troubles of the faithful on their journey to the rabbi in Bilgoraj and the coaches which sank in the swamps of Frampol. Biłgoraj produced the well–known writers Israel Joshua Singer and Yitzchak Bashevis-Singer who wrote many works in which they described various images from our area and its views. Janów Lubelski was well known for its scholars, God-fearing, righteous men of good deeds. In the Lublin area, Turobin was situated between the towns of Janów, Wysokiei, Tarnogród, and Biłgoraj, surrounded by forests and many unmarked villages. I.J singer wrote a beautiful story about Frampol and Turobin, a story read breathlessly. Bashevis too described the regional scenery in his book *Der Hoyf*.

64

There were times when a Jewish community was evaluated according to its spiritual leader, and the sense of gratitude and appreciation was estimated by how many great rabbis it had produced and by the number of great rabbis who resided in it. Turobin had a small population but was large in the quality it produced. The rabbis who served in it gave it renown. The wise rabbi of Frampol with the majestic appearance, Rabbi Eliezer Shalom Feder, originated in Turobin and was considered one of the great rabbis of Poland. He was a staunch opposer of Hasidism, as well as very impoverished, caring for children from his first and second marriages. He passed suddenly one Shavuot and the rabbi of Biłgoraj, Rabbi Metelle Rokeach (who made aliya after the war,) instructed the rabbi not be buried until Friday after the holiday[22].

[Page 57]

Jewish Turobin represented a large concentration of wise rabbis and Godfearing men and its scholars were well reputed in the region. Turobin was approached when there was a need for a halakhic scholar. Turobin could be proud of its Torah scholars, and many communities in Poland were blessed with yeshiva leaders and Torah instructors who originated in Turobin. Nearby Zolkiewka needed a rabbi so they invited Rabbi Simcha Plhandler, one of the Torah scholars of Turobin. Rabbi Bunem Ostreicher was invited to serve as an instructor at the Chakhmei Lublin Yeshiva. Rabbi Yeshaya Nata Tregger, son of Rabbi Ozer the Coachman from Turobin was invited to serve as rabbi in a Polish town.

In addition to the grand *Beit Hamidrash* in Turobin in which lives of scholarship and Torah were flourishing, Hasidic life flourished at the synagogues of the Gur, Alexander, Turiysk, and Kreshnik–Turobin sects. The rebbe Yaakov Leibelle whose every deed was honorable was Admired by the Hasidic community for his personality. He resided in Turobin for many years in a house with a garden surrounding it. He had many followers in Turobin and the region. Once, a Hasid from Turobin came to ask for a blessing from Rebbe of Belz who resided beyond the Austrian border near the Polish border. He likely did so thinking there was no equivalent residing in Turobin to bless him and provide support in his time of need. The rabbi of Belz refused to do as requested and said, "you have Rabbi Yaakov Leibelle, why did you travel so far?"

The Hasidic awakening and the influence of the residents of Lublin and its world–renowned righteous men ignited the Hasidic passion in Turobin and the region. As a result, there was no place for the members of the Jewish Enlightenment, even though an Enlightenment leader, Yaakov Reifman, resided in nearby Szczebrzeszyn. Later, the area learned of the Enlightenment enthusiasts who gathered in Zamosc as admirers of Y.L. Peretz. However, the Jewish Enlightenment movement was not accepted in Turobin which was sealed in Hassidism.

Chapter 7: Jewish Turobin Under the Russian Burden

Exchanging Polish rule for Russian rule. Three nations in Turobin. Jewish farmers near Turobin. Persecution by Russian authorities. Between the Polish rock and a Russian hard place. Apathy towards Polish rebels in Russia. Nearby Goraj, the birthplace of the Rebbe of Kotzk. Jewish residence in nearby villages. Draft dodgers, emigrants. 1905 rumors of a pogrom in town. The last census in town.

The Vienna Congress expanded the borders of European Russia and added to it the entire Warszawa Dukedom under the name of "Polish Commonwealth." Turobin exchanged hands many times and so, its residents did not foresee harm.

[Page 58]

Turobin was one of the towns in Congress Poland in which the Jewish population was almost completely separated from the Christians. Those were two separate worlds alongside one another. The two nations did not know one another and there were no social connections between them. Even the Russian clerks knew the Jews from the outside only and saw them simply as targets for persecution and exploitation. What could have served as an equal ground for Jews and Poles was prevented by both. It should be remembered that the Turobin area had several Russian Orthodox Christians. The authorities attempted to expand the minority of Russian Orthodox by building Russian Churches and adding believers. The Russian clerks controlled the state, and villages were annexed and given to members of the Orthodox Church. Russian bishops and priests made efforts to expand their influence on the region. The suspicion the Church showed the Jews was a barrier no less than opposition by Hasidic or ultra–religious Jews.

66

The ruling class hated Jews. It saw only the success of a few Jewish businessmen and not the horrible poverty and hunger of the Jewish masses. They only saw appearances and the often revolting sight of the expulsion of persecuted Jews. The Jewish population in Poland was expanding. The trade in Jewish communities was scarce and profits were slim. Many made a small living from unsecured positions. The number of craftsmen was grater than the demand, and so their work was scarce, and their earnings limited. Thousands heeded the call of Czar Alexander I to work the land. There were towns and villages In the Turobin area in which there have long been Jewish farmers whose diligence resulted in productivity. That would often awaken the envy of Polish farmers, envy which more than once alienated the Jewish farmers and caused them to relocate and look for other sources of income. The Russian authorities remained hostile to the Jewish population and refused to acknowledge its positive talents.

In the Turobin community, there were Cantonists who returned to their hometown after they completed their service in the Russian military. They were boys aged 12 or even 8 and 9 who were enlisted for the expressed purpose of uprooting them from their area for a period of 25 years and their enslavement to Christian influences. The Jewish parents saw their enlisted sons as lost. They had little chance of returning after 25 years, and if they finally did return they were strangers to their parents. The descriptions of those who returned were shocking; their prolonged religious struggle, the first meeting with their parents, their first return to the synagogue they attended as children. The returned Cantonists were surrounded at the synagogue by children and adolescents who wanted to hear what they went through in the depths of Russia. This is not the place to detail the horrors the Jews endured under Nikolai's rule, and an echo from that time of persecution was recorded in stories, memoirs, songs, and expressions[23]. The Jews of Turobin were party to all those events, but suffered less than others since they were distant from the centers of power.

The difficult life of Jews in the cities and towns of Poland, including Turobin, did not break them. The Russian barbarism was unable to enslave the Jews and take their liveliness away. In times of peril, they continued to guard by prayer, tears and fasting with a firm belief in God. They thanked God with the intention of not surrendering easily, but to stand bravely. Ideologies sprouted like mushrooms; Zionism, Messianic faith, socialism. The Jews fought for and against them and their spirits were firm to the point of personal sacrifice. While activism and clashes were scarce concerning matters of tradition and faith, secular activism did not enter Turobin early on.

[Page 59]

The Racial–Traditional barrier the Jews had constructed as an answer to the dangers posed by assimilating with the Polish Christians was more pronounced than in other towns, where there were assimilators and "Poles of the Jewish faith." The barrier saved many from joining the ranks of rebellion against the czarist regime. The majority of Turobin Jews were faithful to the tradition which advocated love of Zion and Jerusalem, and two national loves cannot coexist. Jews in Turobin longed for redemption from the harsh exile and emigrating to the distant Holy Land. It is possible the Jews of Turobin could not understand the motivation of the Polish rebels. The territory of Congress Poland had shrank from the previously vast territory which included Ukraine and Podolia to the Black Sea and the Baltic Ocean, but the Poles nevertheless remained in their homeland. Indeed, the government was a Russian one and the Poles, although invaded by Russia, remained in their national homeland but still could not come to terms with their situation and occasionally were motivated to rise against the Czar with an armed rebellion. The small–town Jews were between a rock and a hard place among the Poles who promised them freedom and equality in exchange for resisting the Russians, and the Russians who promised them leniency as long as they did not participate in a war they were not concerned with on "foreign" soil.

There are no events recorded about the attitude of the Turobin Jews towards the Kościuszko Uprising. He had extended a special call to Jews to aid him in his war against the Russian oppressors. The slogans of rebellion did not impact their target audience in Turobin during the later uprising in Russian ruled Congress Poland in 1830 – 1831. Community leaders and rabbis in various towns negotiated with military commanders and requested the Jews be exempt from the war, and instead pay a tax, claiming Judaism forbids bloodshed[24]. In many towns on the fight path the Jews did not want to participate even in a militia and proposed a doubled payment of tax ('recrotovi') in exchange for exemption from service in the gvardia or militia. In Lublin, near Turobin, Jews did much for the sake of the uprising despite the hostility shown by the non–Jewish population. There were those who supplied the rebels with equipment and grains, and there were some who spied on behalf of the Poles.

In the second Polish uprising in 1863, the approach of the Jews in the towns surrounding Lublin was apathetic or hostile. Only the Jewish intelligentsia was usually pro–Polish and assisted the rebels. In contrast, devout Orthodox Jews were staunchly opposed to those trends. But Lublin was a key position in the uprising and the participation of Jews in the rebellion was quite large there. Suffice it to say that the Russians retaliated against rebels they captured. Poland became part of the Russian state and Russian laws were imposed on its Jews. In the eyes of the Jews of Turobin, those Jews who assisted the rebels seemed like strange people, who instead of helping themselves during an economic crisis offered their help to outsiders. The Russians occasionally returned the favor to the Jews for not rebelling.

[Page 60]

Hassidic rabbinic tradition was enhanced in Russian Poland. In place of the two righteous men in the days of the Warszawa Commonwealth, Rabbi Yaakov Yitzchak "the Seer" of Lublin and Rabbi Yisroel the Maggid of Kozienice, new lineages of Hassidic rabbis emerged. Rabbi Mendel Morgenstern was born in Goraj[25], a town near Turobin. After he relocated to Tomaszów Lubelski, he established The House of Kotzk (1826 – 1859) where he did not build palaces or chase donations but appreciated the study of Talmud and delving into mysticism. Hasidic synagogues were established in Turobin, and Hasidic leaders occasionally appeared and attracted many followers to their tables. The Hasidic environment had much idealism and advocated pure, perfect morality. In a time of external pressures and the imposition of the military on Jewish youngsters, the power of Hasidism served as an antidote to the hostile dark powers of the outside. Hasidim and righteousness softened the external blows.

The development of Hasidism caused the establishment of "Houses of Righteousness" in almost every town. As new houses were established, existing houses were inherited by the descendants who continued the ways of their ancestors. In Turobin, such a house was established and managed by Rebbe Yaakov Leibelle. He was a righteous humble man, miracle worker, a scholar who knew how to attract a large audience and had may followers in the town and surrounding area. The rebbe purchased a nice spacious home which stood within a well–constructed garden. He passed away in Turobin and a shrine with a nice–looking tombstone was built for him in the local cemetery.[26]

The persecutions of Polish Jews by the Russian Crown varied in degree of existential threat. In other places, they caused anger and hate of Jews by the Polish population. In Turobin, by contrast, relations between Jews and Poles were not damaged, and business relationships continued on the standard path. Farmers from the surrounding villages like Tshrenitshe, Delkovitz, Otrocz, Tarnawa, Zhavno Zakladia, Lipina, Zalovtshe, Zagruvla, Tokarov, Bozeivitz, Chelanov, Olszanka, Maydan, Tregovisko, Wierzchowina and many others would come to Turobin to purchase goods or spend time with friends conversing, drinking, etc. Those villages were also settled by Jewish families who worked in agriculture, crafts, and trade. Many Jews from Turobin visited the villages on business and exchanged goods. That relationship continued until the final Nazi war, following the Polish anti–Semites.

[Page 61]

Adjustment to state persecution was difficult. The law forcing Jews to enlist in the Russian military caused much destruction among the Jews of Turobin. Some avoided enlistment by relocating from their hometown to a more comfortable place like America, Canada, or Argentina. The tendency to avoid military service emerged among Jews because as people who were denied civil rights, they did not feel the need to sacrifice themselves for the sake of a foreign land. The Jewish exodus from Russia, caused by the frequent prosecution by the state, expanded each year. Jewish Turobin also participated in that exodus and due to that, there are Turobin community members in various countries. The young men who could not part with their parents had to enlist and were sent to distant locations in Russia for several years. The parents considered enlistment to be a harsh punishment. Many in Turobin were drafted, and their parents were unable to resist. Instead, an awakening occurred among the youngsters who claimed one must not sit idly by and wait for miracles.

The Kishinev Pogrom which was initiated by the Russian authorities shook Russian Jewry to the core. A mix of anger and shame overtook the Jewish community; anger about those subjected to slaughter and shame of their brethren who did not resist the rioters, and did not attempt to defend against the human–shaped predatory beasts. Those riots were the start of a series of pogroms against Jews in various owns.

At the end of January 1904, The Russo–Japanese War began. The number of Jewish troops who served in that war was about thirty thousand. However, the reactionary Russian press which was angered by the initial defeats of the Russian army and Japanese victories spread rumors that the Jews were assisting the "racially related" Japanese to avenge the Kishinev massacre. Many youths from Turobin participated in the war in the Far East and many fell or returned maimed.

The bloodshed in St. Petersburg on January 9, 1905 began the open uprising against the monarchic regime in which social and political demands were joined. The liberation movement in Russia and Poland continued to expand. But in place of demands for change, came the Cossacks' whistling whips and the soldiers' gunfire, and a second round of the Kishinev Pogrom occurred in many towns against the Jews. The riots reached their peak in October 1905.

Turobin too was not silent and serene at that time. Suddenly, a rumor arrived the Russian Black Hundreds wanted to conduct a pogrom in Turobin. The town had no organized forces, aside from a police chief and a few Russian policemen tasked with keeping the peace. The Russian military was in place only in Krasnik and Janów Lubelski, and would rarely appear in Turobin while practicing for parades on quiet days. Of course, the rumor of the pogrom, which was intentionally spread to cause a panic, achieved its goal and the Jews locked their businesses and barricaded their homes as they waited for the storm to pass. The market square in Turobin was inhabited only by Jews, and aside from the Christian–owned pharmacy, Jews operated all businesses. The homes and businesses were locked for more than a day. In the end, all remained peaceful and nothing happened.

The last rabbi in the Russian period was Rabbi Eliyahu Halevi Landa, who was also recognized by the authorities. He passed a short time before WWI and was buried in the Jewish cemetery in Turobin. Following him was the instructor and halakhic judge, Rabbi Yaakov Yehoshua who escaped to Lublin at the start of the war, where he was accepted as an instructor.

[Page 62]

The Czarist regime was possessed by anti–Semitic incitement, whose echoes were felt in Turobin as well, because Jews were a common scapegoat. The trial of Mendel Beilis who was suspected of murdering a Christian boy caused bitterness across the civilized world, and the Jews of Turobin were also brethren who rejoiced in his acquittal. That trial left a stain on the Russian Empire.

Economic and political reasons likely contributed to the fact the Jewish population in Turobin did not expand as quickly as in other towns. We previously detailed the figures from the 1765 census in which Turobin and the area had a combined Jewish population of 985. In 1856, 951 Jews lived among a population of 1408 Christians. The general census of Poland in 1897 listed 2377 people in Turobin, including 1509 Jews.

The poor state of the Jews in Russia and Poland was clear to whoever met them. But in Turobin, that did not decrease the drive for traditional education and preserving tradition. That alertness helped them to overcome the political struggles. The plague of hatred, which the Czarist authorities attempted to expand by tarnishing the relationship between Jews and Poles failed in Turobin, which served as an example for other towns in a mutual relationship.

Chapter 8: Turobin at the Front of the Russia–Austria War

Draft announcement in Turobin. First retreat of the Russians. First Austrian horsemen in town. Cossacks in town. Cossack torment of Jews. Turobin exchanged hands. Canon fire destroys town. Turobin in Russian announcements. Military sparring in town. The Duma patrols the battlefield and his horrific description of results. Senator Neidhart's report. Civilian council for those impacted by war. Suffering of the Turobin residents. Descriptions of the Jewish writer Z. Mindlin. "Assistance Work in the Lublin Province." List of Jews of Turobin requiring assistance. Special Committee to assist Jews. Jewish Chairman H. Kafman in Lublin. Strategic change in battle territory. Liberation of Galicia and Poland from the Russians. Storming the Russian front and its abandonment. Turobin repeated in Russian war announcements. Turobin far from the Front under Austrian control. Rebuilding the Turobin community. National awakening of Jewish Youth. News of the Balfour Declaration in town. *Tarbut* Library in town.

After 102 years of Russia on Congress Poland since the decision of the Vienna Congress in 1812, Russia's time to exit Poland arrived. But the troubles of that exit were not easy at all. There was a wind of approaching chaos, although hopes of resolve were t abandoned. But hopes for peace were loose and very moment, the canons could start the world concert attend by countries large and small, with commanders desiring a swift victory conducting. Russia was not willing to exit Poland peacefully, and as a result, a lengthy bloody struggle ensued, whose impressions remain fresh to this very day in the world historical events.

[Page 63]

Leo Tolstoy once expressed envy of the Jews who do not have a country, a military and wars of their own, and mocked Jews who longed for a land of their own. Tolstoy would never see how ridiculous his envy was, since in all the armies of each nation, there were Jews who fought one another. Among them were Jews from Turobin, the quiet ancient town in which the train tracks did not pass and as a result was not shaken by rumors and echoes of rumors which shocked the world about what was to come. It had not yet grasped the meaning of war when the armies were at its gates and battled for the crown of victory. In the meantime, the Jews of town were sentenced to plundering, the fear of death, and other results of war.

Since its founding 600 years prior, Turobin was not subjected to wars and battles in Poland, aside from the Tatar invasions, the Khmelnitsky Massacres, and the Swedish invasion. Then came World War I and residents became eyewitnesses to the struggle between the two camps. The war's sad results mainly affected the Jewish residents of the town, who had peacefully resided there and all made their living whether scarcely or well. The merchants somehow found their livelihood from their labor. The market days which took place in the town and nearby towns positively impacted the town's craftsmen and had a significant impact on the town's economy. Although in later years the Polish boycott began to diminish Jewish trade, still the financial status of Jews in Turobin was healthy. The farmers, after they learned that the Jewish merchant had lower prices, returned to buy from the Jews, and so the Jews lived peacefully in town and life continued its normal path.

The world bell began to toll; on July 28, 1914 Austria declared war on Serbia. On August 30 a draft was announced in Russia. Germany declared war on Russia on August 1. August 5, England declared war on Germany, and August 6 Austria declared war on Russia. The tolls were heard in most European countries and caused much tension. A few days later, the Jews of

Turobin experiences firsthand the meaning of those tolls which did not give them much time.

The news of the draft announcement by the Russian authorities quickly spread across the towns. Turobin heard the weeping sounds of the women, children, the elderly, and the youth whom the news penetrated like an arrow.

On that night of horror, nobody slept. Everyone thought of the upcoming world events and the war about to erupt at any moment. Nobody in the town knew who the war would be fought against and in which country. They did not know Where the war would be located and did not care, as long as it was not near them. Nobody thought the war would be there too since they were certain that even if a war broke out between Austria and Germany, our "brave soldiers" would not let the enemy approach the city limits.[27]

[Page 64]

The first days after the declaration of enlistment passed in grief and consoling, in hopes that soon the horizon would be cleared of the dark clouds and the sun of peace would shine again. Indeed, a few days later, they forgot what happened and life returned to its course. All returned to their work, the tailor to his needle, the cobbler to his punch, and the merchant to his store. No significant changes were observed in town other than the pause in mail delivery. It was as if Turobin suddenly departed from the outside world and stopped taking in interest in it, and only few people showed an interest in keeping up with world events. Only a few days later, the first refugees arrived from Lublin and the town learned that there was much turmoil in the world and the war had already commenced.

The Russian military retreated in the first days after the declaration of war without the residents noticing. The few policemen who were in town suddenly disappeared. There were those who said that when the Russian officials and policemen departed, both the Poles and the Jews rejoiced and the exit of Russia from Poland happened to test their relationship and see if violence would ensue. Before the residents of Turobin could make up their mind, horsemen appeared in the market square. Where did they come from? what it a mistake? The horsemen asked everyone they passed, "where are the Russians? How do we reach to Lublin?" They were not answered as residents were afraid of the armed Austro–Hungarian horsemen. They passed through town quickly and continued eastward. The town rejoiced as if a heavy burden

74

was lifted. The Poles were the happiest. People walked the street, there was no more fear for life, no more fear of robbery. The town was increasingly filled with Austrian soldiers. Bands of Battle–ready soldiers stood on every streets. Austrian soldiers searched homes for Russian soldiers.

Shots were heard on the other side of town. The gunfire intensified, the streets were emptied, and gloom spread. Some began hiding in cellars. Children ran through the street, they did not want to sit at home, they wanted to watch the pleasant sights of shots and fires. Not far from Turobin, towards Lublin, the Austrians stopped and immediately cleared Turobin and the surrounding area. Moments later, Cossacks on horseback were seen chasing the retreating Austrian soldiers. The Jews of Turobin suddenly found themselves in a war zone, a territory which rapidly exchanged hands.

As the Cossacks appeared, terrible rumors arrived of mistreatment of Jews by the Russians. Jewish lives were meaningless to the savage, bloodthirsty Cossacks who did as they wished to the helpless Jews. Saddening news arrived from the Radom and Kielce areas that Cossacks had inflicted pain on the Jews in various places like Staszów, Chmielnik, Radom, Krasnik, and other towns. The Cossacks extracted praying Jews from the synagogue and hung them in the market on allegations of spying. Jewish property was plundered in many towns and other harm was inflicted.

[Page 65]

The Jews of Turobin immediately knew dark days were ahead and felt the sword waving above their heads as the murderous Cossacks arrived, some the descendants of Khmelnitsky. After the Cossacks arrived, one could not go outside as every Jew encountered by those beasts was not spared from assault. On the first night the Cossacks arrived, fires consumed Jewish homes. The Cossacks began robbing stores. The fired did not cease, and before one fire was extinguished another was started. Apparently, the method of burning and plundering as many homes as possible was a strategic directive received from Russian headquarters whose propaganda and anti–Semitic sentiment echoed throughout the world and attested to the danger Jews were facing in the battle zones. Half of the town was engulfed by flames, and most of those homes were of Jews, while those of non–Jews were not harmed. The Jews had no choice but to pack some their belongings and escape. Most ran to Lublin and some to other places to wait until they could return. Soon after, an official decree was issued by the military chief under the authority of the Czar that all Jews must leave towns and villages and make their way eastward. Turobin was included in that expulsion decree. After the Cossack terrorists were in town for a few days, they retreated eastward. Though they were there for a short time, the damage they caused to the Jewish population was immense, while they had not harmed the Poles and the Russian Orthodox at all.

Horsemen from both sides clashed and attempted to learn about the methods of their opposition. The Cossacks asked, "how many kilometers from here to Berlin?" while the Austrians inquired about the distance to Lublin, without asking about Moscow and Petrograd as they were well versed in the geography of Russia. Jews lived in fear for their lives and possessions for the few days in which the Cossacks were in Turobin. The delegates of the Russian military instilled fear and accused the Jews of spying and aiding the enemy. The price of goods ballooned, and scarcity and poverty increased. The young men were enlisted in the military, as were the reserve forces which were not yet called when the war was declared. After the Cossacks retreated, Jewish refugees began to return to town and rebuild their lives and businesses.

Turobin was passed around in the first and second years, as they were at the front of the war between the Russian and Austrian forces, considered a "no man's land" subject to canon fire, guns, and other tools of destruction. When one of the sides was invading, it was easy to accuse the Jews of abetting the other side. The Poles especially loved to speak ill of the Jews and the military courts did not usually conduct a lengthy investigation and instead produced a quick verdict. The Jews of Turobin acted correctly when they escaped town ahead of time and reduced the libel and lynching which neighboring towns were subjected to. It was only a temporary stop for the Cossacks, a perpetration for the upcoming main battle.

[Page 66]

It was not long before the Austrians returned to Turobin and a large battle between the belligerents ensued. The names of regional towns appeared in official announcements from both sides, and Turobin filled a large role. The Austrian commander Dankel announced that on August 23 and 24, 1914 his forces achieved a great victory in the battle on Krasnik, Polichna, and Goraj, while the battle for Zamosc and Tyszowce took place from August 25 to September 1. The Russians announced that on August 1 the forces of the Austrian enemy approached the Zbikhost–Zolkiewka–Janów–Tarnogród front and breached a small area of Russian territory. The Russians thwarted the assault on the 3rd. "In the region of Tomaszów, Cossack horsemen pushed back the forces of the enemy and breached the Galician border." A second Russian announcement reads, "The enemy is concentrating mainly on the roads to Lublin where intense battles are taking place." A third announcement reads, "our forces in the south of Lublin have gone from a defensive battle to an offensive one. Although some battalions are in the seventh day of battles, the battle rages on. Many bayonet fights have occurred near Tomaszów. An intense war is ongoing in the region." And again, "enemy forces have attempted to breach our position between Lublin and Chelm. Victory is ours. The remnants of the defeated army are quickly retreating southward." An announcement from headquarters reads, "Austria's primary forces have concentrated across the frontlines in Zawichost, Janów, Biłgoraj, Tomaszów, and Belz, so they can storm the Lublin–Chelm frontline. The Tenth Austrian Corp, which attempted to breach those places was pushed back. West of Krasnystaw, the 48th Austrian Battalion was surrounded and taken as prisoners." The announcement from a few days later states that "on August 23 and 24, the Russians stormed the Austrian base in Tomaszów Northwest of Zamosc. The Cossack horsemen wiggled through the enemies' coaches in Frampol towards Lublin. The convoy which moved along the road from Józefów to Annopol were dispersed by our artillery regimen from the left shore of the Wisla. A Cossack battalion returned from Frampol with many prisoners in addition to horses and livestock."

We quote the announcements of Russian military headquarters published in Russia, which were not particularly objective. The notices by the other side were also unrealistic for the sake of battlefield morale. The Austrians breached Poland in Kielce and Radom as well and encountered no opposition. The Russians quickly retreated, fearing they would be surrounded by the armies of Germany and Austria, which could enter Poland on both sides. The Lublin and Chelm areas were already in a defendable territory. Turobin was within that territory, the no man's land, trapped between the two sides.

A summary announcement by the Russians about "The great battles at the front of Lublin–Chelm–Tomaszów." Among other things reads, "On August 12, (12 days after the war declaration) the Austrians began an all–out assault. In those days, our forces were not yet organized across a territory of hundreds of versts and could position only a few of our troops in the north to face the Austrians. The first assault was aimed at Krasnik, but they immediately shifted focus and transferred it to the Tomaszów area, where the Austrian reinforcement Forces were brought. On August 21 while we were conquering Lviv, additional Austrian attacks occurred. The enemy's position stretched from Opole to Bychawa and was a canon shot away from the Trawniki Station and surrounded Krasnystaw, Zamosc, and Hrubieszów. Near Józefów, two bridges were placed on the Wisła. On August 24, we captured in a surprise attack the enemy's position in Opole–Turobin a 60 verst stretch[28]. The battle which began on the 11th on the southern part of the towns of Lublin and Chelm, which were previously the grounds of the great strategy slowly advanced, a prime example of military talent which ended in the total defeat of the generals Openburg and Dankel. On August 22, the victories of generals Rozski and Brosilov allowed us to counterattack. Near Sukhodol, the we defeated the Austrians, and with a strong attack towards Turobin and Zamosc, we managed to sever communications between the Austrian battalions in Krasnik and Tomaszów."

[Page 67]

These telegrams from the frontlines demonstrate the importance of Turobin as a central point between the two armies. Turobin was indeed very damaged by canon fire, and damage done to property was immense. Nakotchini was dispatched as the Polish envoy to the region of the Russian Duma. He patrolled the Lublin district where battles among Austria and Russia took place. In a conversation with a reporter, he said that the battlefield encompassed nearly three quarters of the Lublin district. It stretched from the Wisla River (from the E?ubki village near Wawolnica) until Oher [?] near Wojslawice and Tyszowce. That whole swath of land is now rubble covered in piles of trash, with occasional villages which were spared destruction. [29]

When entering the Lublin district, The Austrian armies did not initially torment civilians and burn villages. But if they were defeated, they engaged in violent acts of cruelty. First, the soldiers robbed civilians and forced them to give them grains and livestock they did not pay for.

The war zone can be divided into three parts according to the amount of destruction. The edge of the Lublin district from the previous border of Galicia to Kshinzhomirsh. Krasnik was the first to be invaded by the Austrians and the destruction in it was relatively small. A larger destruction occurred in the region near Turobin, from Zolkiewka and Wysokie to Zamosc. Especially large destruction occurred around Józefów, Opole, Orzendov, Wilkulash, Nedzvitza to Trabnik. Only scorched earth was left behind in those places, and few saved villages. Hundreds of villages were destroyed. Opole was completely burned and destroyed. Józefów burned completely. Chodell was deafened by canons. Tomaszów was destroyed and turned to rubble. Zamosc was plundered as were the regional towns of Weislovitz and Khomentsisk . The once fertile land in the Lublin district was abandoned. Trenches were placed across many versts wherever battles took place. The dirt dug up from the trenches, especially where deep canon positions were placed, was infertile and rocky. Over a million people labored for three weeks near the trenches, and many people are now needed to make the land fertile again. The damage done to the residents of the Lublin district is estimated in the hundreds of millions of rubles.

The many bodies left in the battlefields were buried where they died. There were some buried near residential areas. The fallen were buried in shallow graves and the air was poisoned by their fumes. There were areas where the stench radiating from the graves reached many miles. Today we find residential areas near the forests where dead bodies are scattered. Those are the corpses of Austrian soldiers who hid when injured.

[Page 68]

That report, although from an official source, hides more than it uncovers[30]. It does not attribute the destruction to the Russians, who are experts at destruction and not construction, and is written in neutral language. In addition, we quote a short report by Russian envoy Neydhart, after he returned from war–torn areas, printed in papers of Petrograd. It states in part, "I visited one of the areas invaded by the enemy on behalf of the esteemed council for assisting refugees. I estimated the quality of care to the population which endured the troubles of war. I visited in the regions which suffered most, in the Lublin and Chelm Districts. In Lublin, a civilian council was established. The regions of Lublin were stormed by the enemy who displaced the population. 200,000 remained homeless. All food was confiscated by the enemy or destroyed. Residents have no horses nor livestock. In the Chelm district, most suffering was endured by the residents of BilGoraj, Tomaszów, Horbishov, and Zamosc, where 1,593 farming estates were destroyed, 250 homes destroyed, and 228 civilians were killed by the enemy. The damage to civilians in the villages alone is over 700,000 rubles."

The envoy from the Central Civilian Council traveled to Petrograd to meet with authorities and advocate for aid to civilians impacted by the war. The representatives took with them a memorandum in which they explained the scale of destruction inflicted on Poland in the first four months of the war, including some details on the Lublin region. Among the places which suffered most were four counties in the Lublin district, and five in the Chelm district. In Lublin: Krasnystaw and Janów and in Chelm: Robishov and Tomaszów.

In the section of "In Towns Around the Country" a reporter detailed the situation of the Lublin area[31] partly stating that the towns of Józefów and Chodel suffered much during the war. Fires burned there for two days, and most residents escaped to Lublin, Warszawa, or Opole. In the final months, some returned and resided in tents and mud huts. The towns Krasnystaw, Izbica, Bikhawa, Turobin and Riki suffered To a Lesser extent, although many homes were burned in those as well.

Jewish activists and writers assessed the situation and thought of ways to rehabilitate Jewish refugees. A picture can be gained from the essays of Jewish writer Z. Mindlin who published an article in *Hazefira* titled, "Assistance efforts in the Lublin District." In his first article (Shvat 24, 5675) he wrote[32], "The Lublin district became a battlefield in August, after the Austrian invasion and their subsequent escape. Later, the towns of Józefów and Chodell were burned and destroyed, towns whose residents were mostly Jews. The towns Krasnystaw and Turobin, and the villages of Mendrowitz, Visoka, and Sweitshichov were partly burned and plundered.

[Page 69]

Other areas suffered as well but to a lesser extent. All district residents reaching the district capital, which the Austrians could not reach, lost most of their property. Livestock was lost or eaten. Granaries were destroyed, the stores emptied. Clothes, and underwear, were either burned or plundered. The need to aid the residents quickly arose. The first step was to establish a civilian council in Lublin without regard to nationality. Among the Jews was chosen H. Kafman, and it appeared that aid efforts would enjoy the cooperation of Polish and Jewish communities. However, differences arose in the first days, and shortly thereafter it became clear that each nationality will separately handle aid efforts. Kafman is still a member of the council but that is mostly nominal as he has no practical relation to activities of the council, which became an exclusively Polish one. The supervisory Jewish council began to operate alongside the civilian council as an organization which aided Jews who suffered from the war. The civilian council, which accumulated significant resources, mainly from officials in the Tsar's estate, began activities in Lublin and regional towns, where the council has established twenty branches assisting mostly the Polish residents.

However, the Jewish council in Lublin, who had fewer resources, had similar activities to the civilian council. It opened soup kitchens for Jews refugees, and in December alone 300 meals were distributed daily. A home for over 100 children was opened. Shelter was supplied to 150 refugee families. Two stores were opened where free bread is given to 170 refugee families. Over 1,500 families purchase food at those stores at retail price. The Jewish council's activities were limited to Lublin only until the first days of December. Jewish residents in the satellite towns remained helpless with much scarcity. The regional minister, after a visit to the Jewish council, proposed establishing a council of local representatives without nationality differences. However, aside from Krasnystaw, most towns did not accept the proposal, which caused much damage to correct distribution. The Jews suffered most from the chaos."

[continued in next issue, February 9, 1915:]

"In the towns of Turobin, Chodell and Izbica, gmina officials proposed the rabbis compose a list of needy Jews. In some places (like Turobin), the lists were recorded, but not fully. Matters progressed sluggishly, since nobody knows the purpose of the lists and the possibility of receiving emergency assistance. In Turobin, a list of 120 families was submitted. The gmina clerk reduced the list, placing only 100 families on it, who received over 400 pood of flour and 471 rubles in cash. The list of 120 families was incomplete so a completion list of 152 families was sent to the regional minister to read and act upon. , From what is known, flour was unavailable for distribution and I wish additional flour will be recived. The inconsistencies in aid distribution caused a disruption in Lublin as well. Only in Krasnystaw, where a general council was proposed by the gubernator, members of various nationalities joined the distribution of aid which operated with no complaints. When local Poles were asked why only they are given clothes, shoes, and food items, they responded that Jews had to ask H. Kafman, head of the Jewish council in Lublin. Meanwhile, scarcity has increased across the district and is increasing as the weather cools. An unfairness was felt in the lack of organization which could truly aid suffering Jewish residents."

[Page 70]

In his second article in the same paper, Z. Mindlin (Adar 3, 5675) continues to write about "the economic state of the Jews in the Lublin district," from which we bring the relevant excerpt:

"Although the economic ruin occurred last August, still no external help came until December. Also, aid was organized by local government in the places with a Jewish majority until that time. Public works in Poland, especially in the Lublin district, are scarcely developed. There are no charitable institutions. When the war started, and people demanded help for those starving, locals did not know how to organize aid and who to request it from." The author wrote of the large need for food items, shelter, clothes, shoes, religious items like tallit and tefillin, prayer books, whose absence was pronounced.

He then wrote of rebuilding the burnt homes. "Two months later, the construction season could begin in the Lublin region, and hundreds of people from Józefów, Chodell, Krasnystaw, Izbica, Turobin, and others need the ability to rebuild their homes. In the absence of reconstruction return to normal in those towns is difficult. Dozens of families resided in makeshift homes and cellars as they waited for construction season. They reside in nearby villages, which the central municipal committee for refugees of burnt homes has assisted with. Trade has begun to resurface in those palaces, orders are places with craftsmen and repairs. Remaining in those places for a lengthy period is unsustainable, and assistance is needed in constructing homes to rebuild those towns. In contrast, not rebuilding those towns for a prolonged period can forever deny them as a viable urban area and attract locals to other, undestroyed towns. That fact can deny hundreds of Jewish refugees the ability to return to their previous work and turn them poor for the rest of their lives. The will to return to hometowns is very strong, since only the previous known methods life can return to course."

The author concluded the article with an announcement that "A committee named for the great princess Tatiana Nicholayovna was formed, whose express purpose is to provide aid to those harmed by war. Civilian committees were established in Poland and received donations from all over Russia. There is also a central Jewish committee. The means to aid Jewish residents need to be given by the authorities as well as by all of those organizations."[33]

82

[Page 71]

Meanwhile, large changes were made in the strategy of the warring parties, in southern Poland as well. The Russians, who had retreated almost from the entirety of western Poland changed to offensive warfare, and not far from Lublin region attacked eastern Galicia, conquered Levuv, Ternopol, and Brody, and reached the Kraków area. Later, they occupied Peremyshl Fortress and reached the Hungarian border. Turobin remained in the hands of the Russians for a few months and served as a passage point for its troops who breached Galicia through the Wisła and occupied the Bokobina region and its capital of Tchernovich. The Russians in Turobin, like in all Russian occupied territories, treated the Jews like foreigners. They robbed and plundered as they pleased, accompanied by explicit incitement by Polish civilians, who knew how to flatter military leaders and sic them at the Jews. The Jews who remained in the surviving homes barricaded their homes at night and feared to go outside. Young women especially hid in cellars and other hiding spots. Occasionally, horrifying screams pierced through the town. Store doors were shattered, and Jewish property stolen.

At the beginning of May 1915, the opposing army stormed the Russian front on the Doenitz river in western Galicia and scattered their enemies like dust in the wind. They recaptured almost all of Galicia and Bokobina, all Polish provinces, and invaded the Volhyn area. In the summer of 1915, it was clear the Central Forces were victorious in the Lublin area ss well. Names of Jewish towns in the Lublin district once more began to appear the announcements of Russian headquarters in the style of victorious retreat. That tactic was perfected by Kuropatkin during the Russo–Japanese war in Manchuria, where retreats were blended with victories. Let us detail some parting words from Russian military headquarters concerning the Lublin district, namely:

Tamuz 19: "The offensive war between the Weipsh and Bug rivers on the Zamosc –Sokal front is ongoing." Tamuz 22: "Towards Lublin, the enemy remains in contact with us along the Rivers of Viznitza and Pur (the river which passes through Turobin.)" On Tamuz 23, a notice was published titled "The Galicia and Lublin Region" which stated, "in the area of Onoploe – Krasnik – Turobin, canons fired on June 17 and 18. The advance of the enemy's front forces were thwarted by our gunfire. In the Turobin region, an immense battle developed on 18 June at dusk. The enemy's series of attacks were beat back successfully. The battle continued all night[34]. On the night of June 19, some attacks by the enemy were thwarted in the Krasnik area. On June 23, the enemy advanced after persisting battles at the front between Krasnik and the Weipsh river. Near Lublin, our offensive war spread across the region, from the edge of the Podlipa lake to the lake at the south of Bikhawa. The enemy continue their retreat. Battles continue at the Józefów – Bikhawa front. On June 27, the enemy continued to hold Hill 13 and Kobrsk Village and mounted a fierce counter–attack between Bistritza and the village."

The Russian military retreated from Poland, the echoes of canon fire were increasingly distant, until Turobin remined far from the front, which reached the Volyn territory.

Finally, Turobin was no longer the center of battles between the Austrian–German and Russian armies who ruled it intermittently. During that time, it was emptied of its residents who were scattered in villages and towns near and far. The Central Powers were victorious in Turobin. It remained under Austrian rule while the Russians retread and abandoned position after position. This time, they also left Lublin as they retreated East and nearly left all of Poland behind as they went on to defend Volyn and Lithuania. They remained for a while near Baranovitz and at the edge of eastern Galicia and Bukovina. However, the Austrian and German forces did not allow them to rest and chased after them as much as possible. The destroyed and abandoned Turobin was able to begin rebuilding. The Austrian authorities declared the return of the residents and eased restrictions for the sake of rebuilding.[35]

[Page 72]

Turobin became a passage town for Austrians and Germans forces who were progressing through Russia, but the road to complete victory was still distant. Meanwhile, Turobin and the region was still reeling from the horrors of war. Long convoys of farmer wagons brought the injured from the battlefields. Their screams were blood–curdling. Terror ruled all and nobody knew what tomorrow would bring. The large battles continued beyond Turobin, far away in the territory beyond the Polish border. They continued for months and years. Turobin remained in Austrian hands to the end of the war. The military authorities cared for the residents' welfare. The direct and indirect employment by the military was substantial. Local craftsmen supplied the army offices, and trade flourished as well. Despite military rule, the

84

authorities did not burden the residents. The Jews and Poles were able to unite for purposes deemed harmless by the authorities. Zionist and social organizations began to operate in town, relieved after months of harsh battles, when life and death served as pawns by the canons machine guns, and the many destructive tools of both sides; Jewish Turobin began to breathe again after its refugees began to return. The youth, which witnessed their parents' tough life of wandering began thinking of "Purpose." However, political activism was forbidden in wartime, so Zionist activities were done under the guise of culture.

Some time passed, and after America joined the war and Wilson's Fourteen Points, a new wind began to blow in Europe. In Austrian occupied Poland, preparations began for the day of liberation. Encouraging news reached the Jews; their rights to the land of Israel will be assured. News came that a council was composed by the Jewish leaders from the United States, England, France, and Russia (under Kranski) to reach those goals. More shockingly, news arrived that a large Jewish volunteer force from America was at the front of Eretz Israel and fighting alongside General Allenby to take the land from the Turkish. An unusual wave of awakening passed through the Jewish streets, especially among the youth which began to develop a national consciousness. They organized Hebrew language classes, invited guest lecturers, and ordered educational materials. A few influential and talented members from the town and nearby towns directed and led activities. The Austrian authorities did not disturb them, and even the Poles who were part of a national awakening and expectation of liberation could empathize. When the shocking news of the Balfour Declaration reached Poland in the winter of 1917, enthusiasm and joy swept the Jewish community. People wept in joy, and a "Geulah fund" was founded to which funds and valuable objects began flowing. Indeed, it is no wonder that when a rumor spread that the enlistment began for aliya, youths and adults from town and the area swarmed to enroll and save money for the trip[36].

[Page 73]

The first act came to fruition as the *Tarbut* library was founded by the youth led by Yaakov Leib Yaffe, Shmuel Abba Gitwortz, and Yitzchak Feder. However, the founding of the library awoke a conflict between fathers and sons who did not understand one another. On the other hand, even that skirmish was in the spirit of advancement. The nationalist cause threatened the return of the pre–war days as it demanded drastic actions in changing the way of life in the Diaspora. Not much time passed before Jewish Turobin sent its first oleh to Israel. More followed him, and thanks to that were saved from the Holocaust and established a network in the land of our Forefathers. Thanks to that network, this Yizkor book is published as a living literary monument for the Jews who are no more, but their memory will remain forever.

On November 11, 1918, the bells were sounded declaring the ceasefire, and the nations breathers a sigh of relief. The mass–murder ended. Independent Poland was resurrected. But new persecutions and trials would come to the Jews.

Chapter 9: Towns and Villages in the Turobin Area

The Turobin community as a center for new settlements in nearby towns and villages. Krasnystaw was off limits for Jews. Its Jewish community served as an example. Krasnystaw birthplace of The Seer of Lublin. "Yoshe Calf" resident of town. Alias Reb Moshe Chaim Kaminer. Radzin Tekhelet dispute in town. BilGoraj – an old community. Many forests in the area. Zifn [?] and economic foundation in town. Jewish Goraj worked in agriculture and crafts. Birthplace of Rebbe Mendli of Kotzk. Janów Ordintzki regional capital. Jewish farmers in Janów. Wisoki Lubelski– an ancient town. Meeting place for Jews from nearby villages. Piaski (Lublin province). Rejowiec, Modliborzyce and Gorzków. Villages surrounding Turobin with a Jewish population: Tchirnitchin , Zhavno, Trgovisko, Dlikovitz, Tokary, Chlaniov, Hortcheck, Otrocz, Olszanka, Zagruvla.

In the 16th Century, royal policy towards the Jews was generally more liberal than later centuries. Still, some towns and larger cities recived privileged directives which forbade Jews from settling in them. Such privileges were dubbed "privileges of non–tolerance to Jews (Privelgium de non tolerandis Judais)." Such privileges were in place in the Lublin area as well, and in Krasnystaw. In Lublin, Jews were permitted to live only in the Pod Zamkiem (under the castle) suburb and not in the town proper. However, Jews found a partial solution thanks to roles in trade and crafts and through protection from the ruling noble class. In contrast, Jews were not denied entry to Turobin almost from the day it was founded[37], perhaps due to its status as a royal estate or since the Church did not see an interest in limiting Jewish residence.

[Page 74]

Turobin was founded before other towns which were famed and developed quickly like Tomaszów, Zamosc, etc. But as Jews settled in Turobin, Jewish residence took place in surrounding towns and villages. Let us briefly describe the towns and villages which served as residences for Jews. First, we will describe Krasnystaw which was not included in the regions Jews were permitted to live in, and only during the Russian occupation did its pages open as they did in dozens of other towns.

Krasnystaw was a smaller town relative to its sister towns of Chelm, Hrubeshiv, and others, but it was different. The ratio of Jews to non–Jews was smaller than the towns mentioned. Krasnystaw excelled in its beauty, cleanliness, and its quiet and honest people. The town had houses of 3 or 4 stories with nicely painted exteriors. In the center of the town there was a beautiful park with walking paths. In the center of the park there was a nice stage where a military orchestra played all summer long from 6 pm to 10 pm. The town was physically elevated with two rivers surrounding it. The large roads to Zamosc, Lublin, and Rejowiec added much beauty, movement, and life to the town. The Lublin road continued for miles out of town with trees on both sides, yards with various fruit trees which emitted a pleasant scent. Grazing fields and tall and beautiful hills which proudly surrounded the nearby rivers and forests. All those things left their mark on the way of life and mood of its population, especially its Jews. In contrast to the area towns like Rejowiec, Krashnitchin, and others, Krasnystaw was a clean and polished town; the roads were straight and nicely paved with wide sidewalks which added aa happy and pleasant view to the town.

The town was considered historic in Poland. Once, when Casimir the Great ruled, a noble's fortress proudly stood there, and elderly residents told somewhat of a legend that Casimir the great constructed an estate where he would spend time every year with his Jewish lover Esther. In older times, when Jews were forbidden to live in town, there was a Jewish ghetto. In later years, Jews resided alongside Christians, as they did in the town center and the "Groblia" [?] which was separated from town by the Weipsh River. The garden–surrounded town left a great impression on all who visited. Jews were one fifth of the general population of 25,000, but that figure included the suburbs Hkrakovi and Zakrinchia where few Jews resided. About 20%–30% of the Jewish population resided in the groblia. The lower Jewish class resided there: cobblers, tailors, bakers, windowmakers, jewelers, and village–traveling merchants. The Christian population never regarded the Jews with outstanding friendship. There was a restrained anti–Semitism, but active anti–Semitism never reached the town.

The elderly generation was not concerned with politics and did not belong to political organizations. However, they did conduct large and varied social activity. The town had unions of merchants and businesspeople, craftsmen, a gemach, a bank, and a burial society. There were Zionist organizations in town, Mizrachi, Aggudah, Revisionists, HaKhalutz, Poa'lei Zion (Z.S.), Poa'lei Zion Left, a professional union, and the Peretz Library. The Bund found no place in town.

[Page 75]

Religious life was concentrated in two synagogues: the one in the main town, which was renovated after WWI, and the second in the groblia. In addition, there were two Hasidic synagogues of the Trisk and Ger sects. Hasidim of all kinds were not an unusual sight in the towns of Poland, as its core was inclusive of the entire Jewish population, and so of course, there were Hasidim of all kinds in Krasnystaw as well. However, the Hasidim of Krasnystaw did not resemble Hasidim in other towns. They were not unkempt, irritable, nor sulking. Quite the opposite; there they were well–dressed and well–kempt. They walked together in the town gardens regardless of affiliation and discussed everything: Hasidism, pilpul, Kabbalah, inquiry, Hasidic tales, and general and local politics until dawn. All of that happened quietly and civilly without disputes and skirmishes but calmly and with mutual admiration and respect. The peaceful life among the Hasidic sects was contributed to by an event: the two synagogues were situated far from the pleasant Jewish center since old times. Then the synagogue burned down. The Trisk Hasidim, were a large share of the local Jewish community, especially the Hasidim. They were also the wealthiest. And so, they established a large synagogue at the center of town, known as the Trisk shtibel. It then became a general synagogue, leading to mutual respect by the various leaders and their customs and everyone became one big Hasidic family.

The expulsion of the Krasnystaw Jews began during Passover 1942 and most were sent to Belzec. Memorial day for the Jews of Krasnystaw is Iyar 22.[38]

88

Krasnobrod (Lublin area) – the Town elders were proud of the Seer of Lublin who originated in Krasnobord and pointed to a house where his wedding took place. On the same topic, they told a story in which he was arranged to marry a lessee's daughter from Ktchuke village and the wedding was set to take place in Krasnobrod. Before the bride was led to the canopy, the Seer demanded he be allowed to look at the bride's face since "it is forbidden to marry a woman sight unseen." After he saw her, he refused to marry her, claiming he saw in her an image of the cross. Later, the bride indeed strayed off the Path and converted to Christianity. The Seer married a different woman and the wedding took place in the same house.

A band of musicians of Belz Hasidim were the ones who met Yoshe Calf in the Belz rebbe's house.. Band members testified at the rabbinic trial. Yoshe Calf resided in Krasnobrod for some time. He was the subject of the play *Yoshke Calf* by I.J. Singer. The story is as follows:

In Krasnobrod, there was a strange man named Yosef, nicknamed Yoshe Calv. He was considered a fool because he did not speak properly and would answer each question with a "yes" or "no." Residents would exploit him for every task and give him pennies in exchange. He did not tire, not of the tasks nor the payment. He mostly stayed at the cemetery, where the manager employed him as a grave digger and allowed him to sleep in his home and a piece of brad and tea as a salary. Yoshe Calf eventually learned to scribe tefillin and mezuzot, but he did not stick to that job and continued to work temporary jobs and remained around the cemetery. After the cemetery–keeper expelled him from there, he slept in the synagogue. So, he lived alone and neglected, crowned with the title of village idiot. Once, a plague started in town. The residents began to repent and soul–search. They then thought of the orphaned Yoshe Calf, and to appease the Angel of Death married him to the cemetery–keeper's daughter who was orphaned of her mother. A canopy was raised in the cemetery and a proper wedding, was conducted. The town's rich gifted them with a dowry, and the town rejoiced. Meanwhile, the plague subsided. After some time, Yoshe disappeared. Some said he left with missionaries and others said he was killed by farmers while alone in a field. Few days passed before Yoshe Calf was forgotten.

[Page 76]

Then, a rumor reached town that the son–in–law of the Rebbe of Zshinev, Reb Moshe Chaim Kaminer, disappeared a short time after he married the rebbe's daughter. It was a topic of conversation for a short time and then quickly forgotten. A year or two later, when rabbi Moshe Chaim Kaminer returned home, the Rebbe of Zshinev greeted him with joy and held a large celebration to which he invited his friends and many followers. The feast was hosted by brother–in–law, the Belz Rebbe. At that time, there were Hasidim who were invited from Krasnobrod by the Rebbe of Belz; R' Moshele Sofer, R' Mendli Fuchs, Elchanan and Eliyahu Shuster, and Berrish Greenboym. As the crowd was giddy from wine, the groom was introduced to the crowd. The Krasnobrod residents saw he was no other than Yoshe Calf from their town. Eliyhau Shuster got up and slapped him hard, and turmoil and shame ensued. The men from Krasnobrod shouted that the groom was not Moshe Chaim Kaminer but Yoshe Calf from their town and is the husband of the Krasnobrod cemetery keeper's daughter. The people of Zshinev wanted to rip them to shreds. "Can it be? Such libel? About the Rebbe's son–in–law?" Yoshe Calf sat silently. Those in presence divided across lines and turmoil erupted.

Eventually, it was decided the matter be brought to a bet din. Reb Moshele Sofer and the Krasnobrod cemetery keeper and his stranded daughter stated their case that they know him as Yoshe Calf who was born and raised in Krasnobrod and married the cemetery keeper's daughter on x day. In contrast, the Zshinev Rebbe and his followers said that Reb Moshe Chaim Kaminer knew details private among a husband and wife, and explicitly told the Rebbe what Talmud page they studied the night before he vanished. The testimony affirmed both sides. The trial lasted many months until a verdict was reached. The court ruled that Yoshe Calf, AKA Moshe Chaim Kaminer, must divorce his two wives, and after that can marry whichever one he wanted. That concluded the event which at the time stirred emotions and found its place in literature and even reached the theater[39].

The elderly Hasidim of Krasnobrod maintained unity and harmony in the town until trouble emerged in the form of the "Tekhelet Dispute" by the Radzin Hasidim who would tie a blue tassel into their tzitzit. As is known, the dispute was present across Congress Poland, but the dispute was especially intensified in the Krasnobrod area and the rabbis named it "the KRC Dispute", initialism for Krasnobrod, Rejowiec, Chelm. The dispute in those places reached fighting and physical altercations and hatred, to the point that residents avoided marrying their daughters to the sons of their opponents and brought brides from other towns. But there was a silver lining, as the community expanded and developed through establishment of partisan synagogues. The religious

90

dispute ended on its own. However, the hatred continued for years to come and caused the firing of Rabbi Zvi Yechezkel Michelzon, known also as an author and biographer.

[Page 77]

BilGoraj existed even prior to the Tatar invasions of Poland, although it is unknown when the Jewish community was established. BilGoraj is mentioned in Yeven Metzula and participated in the meeting of the CFL. It was in Congress Poland near the old border of Austrian Galicia, near Zamosc. It had 12,000 residents, among them 65% were Jews. It was a town of Torah and greatness. Its last rabbi was Mordechai Rokeach, son of the Belzer Rebbe Yissachar Dov. The market square was surrounded by Jewish homes and their businesses. Until the first war, there was a Cossack division stationed in town from which the town Jews profited considerably.

Although BilGoraj had its own river, religious divorces could not be performed since Tsar Nikolai changed the river's name to Lada.

There was a forest near the town which became regionally famous. It had ample fruit trees, and stretched from Janów to Zamosc. BilGoraj had many synagogues, a yeshiva, religious schools, *Yavne School* for boys and *Bais Yaakov* for girls, some Jewish banks, charitable institutions, and many Jewish sects led by great rabbis across many generations. Rabbi Moredchai Rokeach of Belz served in BilGoraj from 5687 up to the destruction of Polish Jewry. He passed away in Israel in 5710 and was succeed by a widow and a son from his second marriage (who was recently crowned Belzer Rebbe). The synagogue was established in 5640, was expensive and considered a glorious part of the city famous throughout the region. The first cemetery of BilGoraj was near the synagogue walls and has two tombstones which are difficult to read. The second cemetery was enclosed in a wooden fence, and it too had tombstones aged over 200 years. The last cemetery was by the sands, far from town, enclosed in a brick fence. The groundskeeper of the cemetery was a Christian. Trains did not pass through town, and travelers rode on coaches harnessed to three or four horses to Rejowiec on dirt roads and then continued by train. Only in WWI, when BilGoraj was occupied by the Austrians, a narrow train was constructed to Viznitz and from there a wide train to Rejowiec.

There were immense territories of woods from Krishov to Janów, Kraśnik which were owned by Zamoyski, with many royal forests. Some forests were owned by farmers who recived them as gifts from Tsar Alexander II. There was a large trade of timber in BilGoraj which continued for many years and owned by Jews, headed by the Jewish firms Herman, Honigboym, Schefer, Arbisfield, and Hirshenhorn. Among the first wood sellers in BilGoraj was Shmuel Eliyahu Shwrdshaf, a great Torah scholar, who exported wood to Danzig. All wood was transported on water.

BilGoraj developed the trade of Zifn [?]. It was the only town with such a market, not only in all of Poland but all of Europe. It offered a great manufacturing contribution to town.

[Page 78]

There was a large printing house in BilGoraj owned by Nata Cronenberg who transferred it there from Pyotrkov and printed many religious and secular books. It employed about twenty workers[40].

Goraj was a privately owned town within the Zamoyski Family fee Tail. It was situated on the shores of the Lada River, roughly 2.5 miles from the district capital Janów. The town was previously known a Lada. It had an ancient palace in it, given along with the region to Dimitri, deputy treasury minister, by King Ludwick of Austria and Hungary. At the request of the owner, Alexander of Srivantze, the village was promoted to the status of town and renamed Goraj, after the famous Gorajski Family. Ownership was transferred from them to the Firley family, and King Zygmunt I respected the rights of Mikolai of Dombrovitza, Lublin voivode, and promoted the town from a Polish system to a Magdeburg one. But that family converted to Calvinism and established a church which was still in existence in the 17th Century. The town was transferred to Count Stanislav Gorka, who renewed all the old rights in 1561, and after the town was destroyed in a fire, added new rights, approved by King Zygmunt in 1569. The town was transferred by the Gorkas to Jan Zamoyski, who added the town to the Fee Tail. Since he wanted to improve the town, he afforded it additional rights, as did his successors. Later, Goraj had to invite craftsmen and industry folks to avoid bankruptcy.

In 1864, Goraj had a population of 1,712 including 1,248 and 464 Jews, who mostly worked in agriculture, with the remainder working in crafts and small–scale trade. It had one brick home, 244 wooden homes, a synagogue, city hall, and a public elementary school. There were factories in town which manufactured simple fabrics for peasant coats, wool socks, and coarse material for sacks. There were weekly market days and six fairs annually.

Goraj had an established Jewish community where there were many scholars and Hasidim. Rabbi Mendeli of Kotzk was born in Goraj to his father R' Yehuda Leibish Morgenstern who served as gabbai of the burial society. Many great rabbis served in it, who had an important role among the rabbis of Poland.[41]

Zolkiewka was a private town in the Lublin province and Krasnystaw district, 25 versts from the district capital. It served as a famous location in the events of the Zholkeveieski family. The dynasty's patriarch, the Russian voivode Stanislav, converted to Calvinism and gave the church building to members of his faith. His son Stanislav, the patriarch in the 18th century, returned the church to the Catholics. Zolkiewka was under the ownership of the Staromirski family which was the staroste of Krasnystaw. In 1869, it was purchased by Mitchislav Frishel. The first wooden church building was constructed at an unknown time after the Calvinists destroyed all its documents. After they no longer owned the church Tomash Staromirski established a new brick church in 1773[42].

In 1868, Zolkiewka had 1,183 residents, including 790 Jews. It had 4 Brick buildings, 84 wooden homes, a post office, city hall, and 6 annual fairs. In 1939, there were 500 Jewish families in the town among a population 3,500.

[Page 79]

Janów Ordintski was a private town part of the Zamoyski fee tail was on the shores of the Biala River. On its south was the small Tishivatz stream which flows a half mile from the town along forests and ponds. The mail road from Lublin to Zamosc, Turobin, Goraj, and Krushuvitz passed through Janów. The town originated in a village named Biala, which was chartered by Vladislav IV on 21 July 1640. It was elevated to status of city at the recommendation of its owners, Katarina of Ostrog and Tomash Zamoyski. The Polish monarch then granted it Magdeburg Law and allowed unions of tradesman and craftsmen, like other towns within the kingdom. Eight fairs were afforded annually, and weekly market days, etc. A few years later, Jan Zamoyski changed its name from Biala to Janów, after himself. After the town suffered from the passage of various armies, plagues, and was destroyed by fire and combat, King Jan Casimirish approved the name in a permit published on June 10, 1653, in hopes of developing the town. The town's owners from the Zamoyski Fee Tail afforded rights and liberties to Janów various times, like Jan Zamoyski in 1664, and Mrtzin of Brezlav who in 1687 added fairs and alleviated certain taxes. The town was well–constructed and well–settled. Various skills were developed in the town, and a special reputation was gained by thin fabrics manufactured by a factory which employed 364 workers. In 1831, after the Polish uprising, the factory was damaged and closed[43].

In 1863, Janów had a population of 3,395, including 1,795 Christians and 1,620 Jews who were employed in trade, crafts, and especially agriculture. It had 26 brick homes and 456 wooden homes. Most beautiful were the governmental buildings including the square shaped courthouse, a jail, butcher shops, warehouses of fire extinguishing equipment, a wooden synagogue, and a mikveh. In the market square, which housed brick building, there were the offices of the district governor, the courthouse, and treasury. Surrounded by those buildings there was a park, where a monument was placed in memory the national hero Tadeusz Kosciuszko. Jews continued to be employed by small fabric factories which employed dozens of workers. There were also groups of cobblers, butchers, tailors, etc. which operated by permit from the fee tail. The town was the seat of the regional minister's office, the court, police station, invalid [?] center, city hall, tax offices, post office, elementary school, and a pharmacy. The town held six fairs annually and market days on Sundays and before holidays.

Wysokie (Lublin Province) – previously a town, which returned to the status of village in the Krasnystaw district, five miles from Lublin, and one mile from Turobin. Situated among mountain ranges, it was established in 1360 by Lukach Gorka and was afforded Magdeburg Law. It was owned by Tomislav until 1382, and 1836 was acquired by Dovislav, the palace minster of Lublin.

[Page 80]

In 1414, it was acquired by Stefan Bidzinski, one of the kingdom's heroes. It was passed down as an inheritance until the 16th Century when it was inherited by Calvinists. Until 1645, it was owned by the Lubinskis, well-known Arians. after they had to exit the kingdom, it was purchased by the

Yavlonovski who held it until 1839, when the final owner inherited it, Keytan Larnizkii.

Until the 16th century, there was a Calvinist church in town which remained until the 17th century. The Catholic church was built of wood and constructed in 1414. In 1800, princess Yavlonovska built a brick church. According to tradition, there was a lavish castle built by the Lubinskis in Wyskoi, in which king Jan Casimirish lived. Indeed, there was a castle, or rather a castle's wing, at the center of a beautiful forest.[44].

Piaski (Lublin Province) was a private town in the Lublin province and district, three miles from Lublin, near the road to Krasnystaw, on the shores of the Belz (or Giltchvka) river. In the 15th Century, there was a village there named Pogozhlistav, and in 1429 an estate owner named Yaakov Deloto lived in it. Later, the towns name was changed to Piaski, probably for the sand dunes. In 1531, Paul Trushchke and Mikoly Starichevski, the estate owners, established the church. The town was then acquired by Pavel Bogoslav Ozhikhovski, scholar and treasurer of Chelm, and later by his son Stanislav, Lublin treasurer. Both were members of the new faith. In 1627, the town's owner was Andzhi Sokhodolski, a wealthy nobleman. Behind the stream at he back of town there was a large estate with a garden in which the Ozhikhovski family previously resided, followed by the Sochodloski family, the ruins of which remain today. For a long time, it was an Arian meeting center. There was also a cemetery there, located between the two churches with many marble tombstones. The last owner of Piaski was Yozef Bobruski. In 1865, the town had a population of 1,733, and had 112 houses, a post office, city hall, and held six annual fairs.[45]

Rejowiec, was a private town in Lublin province in the Krasnystaw district, two miles from it. Mikolay Rey of Tolola [?] established the town in 1547 on his property near the Kovila village in the Chelm area and named it after himself. Zygmunt I, who wanted to prove his good relationship with Rey as a reward for his wonderful service. So, for the sake of Rey's successors, it was elevated to the status of town and afforded it Magdeburg Law. It was granted weekly market days, fairs twice annually, and all residents were exempt from taxes for ten years. In 1729, the town was owned by the Zhibuski family. Its last owners were the Woronitski dynasty. In 1866, the town had a population of 1,333 and had 98 houses, a city hall and six annual fairs.[46]

Modliborzyce – a private town in the Lublin province in the Zamosc district. It sits in a valley surrounded by mountains, on the shore of the Sessna River. The road from Janów to Lublin passes through it, and it is 7 versts from Janów. The town was founded in 1642 by Stanislav Wytozki, the chef [/butcher?] of Belz, by decree of King Vladislav IV. The town was destroyed in fires in 1814 and 1841.

[Page 81]

Emil Dulinski last owned it. In 1864, it had a population of 998 agriculturalists. The town had 106 wooded hoes, two brick homes, a brick church, a flour mill, brewery, and city hall. Six fairs annually and weekly market days.[47]

Gorzków was a privately owned town in the Krasnystaw district, Lublin province on the shores of the Zolkiewka river, 13 miles from the district capital. Founded by decree of Jan III in 1689, according to records held by the local church. Vladislav Blishnski owned the town. In 1866, the town's population was 738, including 160 Christians and 218 Jews, who were employed in agriculture, crafts, and small trade. The towns had two walled homes and 36 wooden homes.

Villages Near Turobin

Turobin resembled an open palm. The large town market was its center and the streets were the fingers. There were more than five roads and their perimeter was not proportional to the hand. They were stretched in all directions like an open spread–out palm. Towns and villages surrounded it and served as shortcuts for many passersby. Many of the villages had large or smaller Jewish communities who were in contact with Turobin and made a decent living. There were also villages where Jews did not reside. They too had business ties with Jews in nearby villages. Let us examine some of these Jewish inhabited villages:

Szczuczyn – a village near Turobin on the shore of the Pur river. It was part of the Zamoysky Fee Tail. In 1827, it had 67 homes and 467 people. Szczuczyn Wola was also a part of Szczuczyn. Four Jewish families resided in the village. Often on Shabbat and holidays, Jews from several towns and villages gathered to pray in a minyan with a wonderful cantor who made services pleasant.

Tanawa – A village and farm on the Pur river, Krasnystaw District, Turobin gmina. It was located West–East of Turobin on the expanded mountain range which stretched across the west side of the river. The village spanned in a 5–verst line in the Pur valley. In 1827, it had 66 homes and 537 individuals. The Village was part of the Zamoyski Fee Tail. 2–3 Jewish families resided in the village.

Zhavno – a village and farm in gmina Turobin, a large territory within the Zamoyski Fee Tail. It had many grazing and crop fields. On the south side of the village was the "Kilfars witches meeting place" about which many legends were told, and written about by A. Viniarski. The Zhavno forest connected to the Wysokie woods across a large territory. In 1827, the village had 50 homes and 360 individuals. Three Jewish families resided there.

Tregovisko – Even during the 15th century, Tregovisko existed as a farm and village. 35 versts from Krasnystaw. It had a wooden church. In 1827, it had 5 houses and 70 individuals. It was a farm rich with the land, grazing fields, forests, and more. It had one walled house and 10 wooden houses.

[Page 82]

3–4 Jewish families resided in it and was a meeting location for Jews from nearby villages and towns.

Dlicovitz – *aka* Dilstovitz was a village and farm in the Janów district. It was 54 versts from Lublin, 16 from Janów, and 51 from the Wisla. That village was also rich with lands of various types; farming, grazing, gardens, forests, yards, and some infertile land. It had three wooden houses and 19 individuals. In 1879, it was separated from the Kshanov estate. The land was muddy and swampy, excellent for growing potatoes. Jews did not always reside in it, but they were always present on visits, business, etc.

Tokar – a peasants' village in the Krasnystaw district and the Turobin gmina. In 1827, it had 57 homes and 326 people. The village was added to the Zamoyski FFT. That village did not have a permanent Jewish residence, but Jews were always in contact with peasants and the farm's owners.

Khlanyov also Khlanyovka, a farm and village in Zolkiewka gmina and Krasnystaw district. It was located 49 versts from Lubin, 28 from Krasnystaw,

14 from Szczebrzeszyn, 7 from Zolkiewka, 18 from the road paved to Izbitza and 18 from the Weipsh river. There were two brick buildings and 13 wooden houses. The village had much land. In 1827, it had 58 houses and 349 people. There were 3–4 Jewish families, employed in agriculture, small trade, and crafts.

Hortshek – a town owned by a nobleman who controlled vast properties, and large herds of livestock and employed peasants who worked in large gardens of fruit and decorative trees. Jews lived there for generations. The Jewish cemetery of Turobin was on a small hill on the landowner's property and was accessible through his fields. It was not in Polish geography books, just as many other places were excluded.

Utrutsh – a large peasant village in the Janów district, gmina Kshanov, 14 versts from Janów. It was on elevated, weak land. In 1827, it had 85 houses and 542 people. Before 1756, the Zamoyski Fee Tail founded a wooden church in Roman–Greek architectural style. In 1881, a general school for beginners was founded. The Lada river started behind the village. The peasants worked in processing fuel and beekeeping. The village was part of the Zamoyski FFT. There were Jewish families in the village, employed in small trade, crafts, and sales of local products.

Olszanka – a peasant village in the Krasnystaw district and Turobin gmina, part of the Zamoyski FFT. The village had much land. Two Jewish families resided in it.

Zagruvla – a village in gmina Turobin and Krasnystaw district. Due to its proximity to the town, it could be considered a suburb of Turobin. No Jews resided in it, but Jews were seen coming and going and it was considered a village with a Jewish presence.

[Page 83]

I detailed here only the villages which were involved in the Jewish community of Turobin but not the more distant ones or ones less frequented by Jews. The Jewish communities in the surrounding villages were satellites of Turobin which was considered the center of dozens of villages who were very attached to the community.

The Turobin community members residing in Israel are still emotionally attached to their hometown. When they reminisce about it, as they frequently do, they include the surrounding villages populated by Jews, where they spent much of their youths and enjoyed the natural sights. It is a shame that their light was extinguished by the destruction of Turobin and the whole of Poland.

———

Notes and Citations

1. Turobin, as a royal estate, was not off limits for Jews, in contrast to church estates, and their residence there was free and unrestricted.

2. The town was not central in historic or political events. No rival armies battled in it, and only in 1914, a fierce battle was waged near it.

3. In the Zamosc book, (*Zamosc: Its Pride and Fall* edited by Moshe Tamari, Tel Aviv, 1953) it says that in the Zamoyski Fee Tail towns like Tomaszów, Turobin, and others there were Jews from the day they were founded. That assessment is incorrect. Jews did not settle in Turobin for some time after its founding.

4. The Jews of Turobin were very active and were exceptional in their dealings outside of town as well. Yet, they were humble when publicity was concerned. It is a wonder that its earlier history cannot be found in books.

5. The number of regions in CFL was not always the same. As the Jewish population expanded, so did the number of represented regions. At first, Turobin was in the Lublin district. It was added to the Zamosc Ordination Region as it and its neighbors expanded.

6. Five years after the final date mentioned, the 1648–1649 massacres occurred, disrupting the activity of CFL. The massacres continued into the next year. In the mentioned year, CFL convened at the Gromnitz Fair in Lublin, headed by wisemen, yeshiva leaders, and rabbis. They discussed the situation caused by the massacre and deliberated the question of agunot. No Turobin representatives participated, probably because of a lack of a qualified person or a lack of a Jewish community in place. It is possible there were other CFL conventions without the participation of Turobin representatives, but we found only one such meeting, in 5428. That year, Turobin was represented by "Yitzchak of Kraków residing in Turobin." It is possible the Jews of Turobin did not want to give up their participation and chose a Jew from Kraków who resided in Turobin for that purpose who discussed matters concerning CFL with the town leadership.

7. The matters of CFL were recently discussed in various studies in our literature. Superior to all those is the book authored by Yisrael Halperin, *The Council of Four Lands Ledger* (Jerusalem, 1944) which contains most of the subject matter concerning the CFL. We found the matters concerning Turobin in the discovered documents, and it is possible more details are yet to be discovered.

8. Jewish historian Chaim Yonah Gorland (1843–1890) was among the first to gather material on the 1648 persecutions which was scattered across printed and handwritten documents. He published it in a series of pamphlets, "A History of Jewish Persecution (Events of 1648)" which were added to the collection *Literary Treasure* by S.A. Gerber, and later published as standalone pamphlets. Thanks to his efforts, we are no longer "in the dark." The pamphlets were published in 4 parts 1887–1889.

9. In addition to the details we found on Turobin, we found poems, memoirs, etc. like *Weary Scroll* by Rabbi Shabbatai HaKohen of Vilne where horrific details about the massacre appear, (printed at the end of *Shevet M'Yehuda* by Shlomo ben Wirga, Warszawa, 1883). The responsa *Eitan Ha'Ezrachi*, section 22, details various details on the 1648 massacres. Dr. Yaakov Shatzki in his *Introduction to the 1648 Persecution in Vilne* also detailed various sources.

[Page 84]

Additional reading: Meir of Szczebrzeszyn, and Rabbi Natan Nata Hanover (*Tales of the Tach Vetat Persecutions*, Jerusalem, 1965, Jewish History Department at the Hebrew University.)

10. Forms of that sort are in the Heikhal Shlomo Library in Jerusalem and at the National Library at the Hebrew University. It is surprising the only Jew from Turobin to establish himself as a publisher did not see fit to even briefly describe his experience of the 1648 massacre in his hometown or on the road.

11. See Shmuel Elazar Bronner in *Tomaszówer Yizkor Book* where he describes at length the content of the old ledgers from the burnt synagogue who were restored from memory in the new ledgers.

12. There were those who saw 5408 as the year of Geulah and searched for clues in the Zohar. Rabbi Shabtai Hakohen rhymes in his book *Weary Scroll*, "the year 5408 when I thought that 'thus Aharon will come to the holy place' but my fiddle turned to weep and my joy to grieving."
Yaakov Frank and his followers, after the debate in Kamyanets Podilskyy in 1757, spent some time in the Turobin area as well. The bibliographer Shlomo Robinzon, a Tomaszów native currently residing in New York, detailed in his research (written for the Tomaszów book, and probably not published in it because it was all in Yiddish) that during the days of Selichot, Frank and his followers wandered the streets of Tomaszów, looking to provoke the locals and instigate a conflict, and from there traveled to Lublin through Krasnystaw.

13. Most refugees from Polish towns returned to rebuild the ruins and their lives. There were towns which appointed rabbis and founded yeshivot immediately following the massacre. Undoubtedly, the Turobin community was resurrected by adding Jews from neighboring villages, although we have no details on it.

14. At the beginning of Jewish settlement in regions, they resided in three: Lublin, Chelm, and Belz, and appointed a state rabbi to serve all three. That great rabbi was Yehuda Aharon, ABD of Chelm. In 1522, he was confirmed by king Zygmunt I as rabbi of all three regions. After Rabbi Aharon's passing, rabbi Shekhna (student of rabbi Yaakov Pollak) inherited the role. The number of

100

Jews increased in those regions, and after rabbi Shalom Shekhna passed, the Belz and Chelm communities appointed their own rabbi, the great rabbi Eliyahu ben rabbi Yehuda Aharon without being dependent on the Lublin community. After that, Jewish communities were founded in towns like Szczebrzeszyn, Tyszowce, Tarnogród, E aszczów, Tomaszów, and possibly Turobin. Communities included synagogues, *yeshivot*, cemeteries, rabbis, and shochetim.

15. In the bibliographic work about the wisemen and rabbis of Tomaszów by Shlomo Robinzon of New York, which for some unknown reason was not included in the Tomaszów memorial book, there are some mentions of rabbis from Turobin, and we thank the author for that blessing.
    Rabbi Mendel of Turobin signed an approval of the book *Chelek Shimon* by rabbi Shimon ben R' Ephraim Yehuda, a Vilne native and of those expelled from Eisenshtadt settled in the Zolkiewka community (Prague, 5447), also signed by Rabbi Chaim ABD of Tomaszów, Rabbi Hillel of Zolkiewka, (Author of *Beth Hillel*,) and Rabbi Yoel of Szczebrzeszyn.
    In the book *Toldot Avrahm Yosef Igra* about Passover by the righteous rabbi of Zolin (Biłgoraj, 5698), he brings a lesson from his father, ABD of Turobin, the holy rabbi Leibish of Tomaszów.
    Undoubtedly, if we were to search the hidden archives and books for names of the rabbis who served in Turobin, like those by the aforementioned bibliography writer, we would find much treasure. It is unfortunate we do not have the time for that.

16. While determining the birthyear of Rabbi Lifshitz, an error was made by Rabbi A.Y. Bromberg in his book *The Good Jew from Gostinin* (Page 10) as well as Rabbi Arye Albert in his essay about rabbi Lifshitz in *The Rebbe of Kotzk* and *60 Heroes Surrounding Him* (page 451.) His true birth year was 5540 and not 5560.

17. The justification for segregated living quarters for Jews by the sinod [?] of Braslau is quite typical. He claimed that "Poland is a new organ in the organism of the church," and therefore there was a danger that "The Christian people will be infected by the Jews' superstition and lowly customs." The Church thereby admits that one of the purposes of persecution is to guard Christians against the possible influence of Jews.

[Page 85]

18. See "Turobin" in the *Russian–Jewish Encyclopedia* edited by Dr. Y.L Katzenlson published by Brookhouse–Iparon, Petersburg, volume 15.

19. See *Bar Bolichover: Memories* published by Dr. M. Vishnitzer, Berlin, 1922 page 116.

20. On this same topic, see the introduction "Polish Jewry During Hasdidic Expansion" in *The Maggid of Kozienice: His Life and Teachings* by Zvi Meir Rabinovitz, Tel Aviv, 5707.

21. A more expansive list of the students of the Seer of Lublin by Yitzchak Alfasi was published in the annual publication "Sinai" on Torah and Jewish studies. Volume 59, Av–Elul 5726.

22. See *Sefer Frampol* published by *Yotzei Frampol* in Israel. Edited by David Shtokfih, March 1966, Tel Aviv.

23. Varied and interesting literature developed around the pamphlets, in which the Jesuit [?] cruelty of the Russian Tsars who tried to convert Jews with many methods is evident.

24. The two elders would fearfully mention the Polish Uprising in the region, when many estate owners and rich folks supported the rebels and drafted many of their workers into the uprising. However, Russian authorities took harsh vengeance against the estate owners by distributing many estates among practicing Russian Orthodox to strengthen their influence on the region.

25. See more about the Kotzk Rebbe and his birth town of Goray in the two volumes of *The Rebbe of Kotzk* and *60 Heroes Surrounding Him* Published by Netzach in Tel Aviv. There is also material presented on rabbi Shmuel Noakh of Turobin.

26. I have received memorized details from Zvi Kopf from Tel Aviv, the eldest of the Turobin emigrants in Israel, and he somewhat clarified the chronicles of the Hasidic rabbis in Turobin. According to him, there was a rebbe in Turobin before rabbi Yaakov Leib whom many Hasidim visited. Rabbi Yaakov Leib was related to Rabbi Bar. In general, since Hasidism arrived in Lublin, Turobin was home to Hasidim and righteous men.

27. About a similar fate that befell the neighboring town of Kraśnik see the essay of Yitzchak Rosenberg, "Life in One Town at the Start of the War: Events that Occurred and Deeds I Witnessed" serialized in the weekly publication "*HaMizrachi*" volumes 43–50, 1920, Warszawa.

28. Notices by Russian headquarters were published in all papers in Russia. Among the Hebrew language newspapers remain only *Hazefirah* published in Warszawa, in which updates from the battles appear. The paper was distributed only where Russians still controlled and could not reach the towns occupied by the Germans and Austrians. After the Germans occupied Warszawa, *Hazefirah* ceased publication and publishing resumed only six month later. I found the issues of *Hazefirah* from the WWI period at the National Library at the Hebrew University in Jerusalem.

29. The details of Nakotzini's survey of the battlefields in the Lublin area appeared in an article titled "The Cruelty of the Austrians" from 5 Tishrei, 5675.

30. The short report by Neidhart was published in *Hazefirah* from the Petrograd papers, issue 247, November 2, 1914.

31. See *Hazefirah* issue 20, 21 Shvat, 5675.

32. The article about the situation in the various provinces describes more details in the Lublin province in general and Turobin especially, see the issue of 24 Shvat, 5675.

33. The second article was published in *Hazefirah* issue 30, Adar 3, 5675. It contains important details on the Lublin area and proposed solutions on repairs of destroyed towns.

34. As the Russians retreated from Turobin, they no longer had anything left to destroy after the destruction and loss they had previously caused. Perhaps they ran out of time to destroy since they quickly retreated. Turobin was mentioned in announcements by Russian headquarters in *Hazefirah*, issue 141, 23 Tamuz, 5675. In addition, an announcement by the Lublin province minister Smerlinov (*Hazefirah*, issue 133, June 12) that as the Russians retreat from the region, civilians mentioned must join the retreating forces and not permitted to stay in enemy territory.

[Page 86]

35. Another interesting detail published due to the events of the time. The report states (*Hazefirah* issue 141, June 20, 1915):
"The Lublin province is part of few provinces where reconstruction efforts of Jews were organized. That was mostly because no war activities took place in the region during last August, and therefore there was no mass expulsion of Jews. Of course, the war increased the number of local needy people.
"By consent of the authorities there are activities by the Jewish communities to aid those impacted by the war, and its activities are spreading throughout the region. The total number of places aided by the council reached forty. Aid is given to approximately 15,000 people.
"As we passed through the number of known places in the province it must be emphasized that Lublin, as before, aid is almost exclusively in the form of economics; shelter and employment. Aid also includes bread distribution to refugees and local impoverished people. In the distribution of lunch by the soup kitchen (over 400 meals per day), a teahouse economy[?] was founded, as well as a home and soup kitchen for children. Finally, there is also food distribution at a discounted price. The council spends 800 rubles per month on leasing homes to refugees.
"With the help of the Petrograd council, employment assistance was established in Lublin. Founded already and in operation are factories for the manufacturing of shoes and baskets. There is also an office established for job placement. To maximize efficiency, the council has begun fundraising operations in Lublin and has approached the idea of self–taxation for those impacted by the war."

36. Cultural activities and nationalist organizations and political parties will be expanded on below.

37. This can be inferred from the general encyclopedia (in Polish) by the Orglebrand brothers, Warszawa, 1867, volume 15, page 751.

38. The Jews who emigrated from Krasnystaw have yet to publish a yizkor book, aside from a short book published in Yiddish published by Bafreyveng at the General Council in Munich, titled, "*Yizkor Tsum Andenk fun di Kduohey Krasnystaw Redagirt*" [Memorial and list of Krasnystaw martyrs] by Arye Shtunzeiger, 1948, 152 pages.

39. We have found it fitting to only mention here the most interesting details about Krasnobrod, as told by the Krasnobrod Yizkor Book edited by Mordechai Kroshnitz, published by Yotzei Krasnobrod in Israel, 5716.

40. See *The Destruction of Goray*. Material gathered by Avraham Cronberg, Tel Aviv, 5716. It is unfortunate that such an important city has not yet had a historical yizkor book about it.

41. A yizkor book has yet to be published on Goray, and its name has not been mentioned by traveling journalists. Some details were published in the essay about Hassidic Goray in this yizkor book.

42. Zolkiewka was a Jewish town, although the Jewish community in it was more recently founded. The town was not included in the list of places off limits to Jews. It is likely the town's owner initiated it to improve its economy. There are nearly no mentions of it in Jewish sources.

43. There were many towns and villages named Janów in the country. Hence the joiner Ordinitzki, not be mistaken with Janów–Lubshov near Pinsk, also a town with important rabbis. Janów Ordinitzki was home to its rabbi Moshe, among the students of the Seer of Lublin, who was known as "A righteous man, of the world's foundation, virtuous and divine." Rabbi Yosef Keziss also served in it as ABD and it was the birthplace of Rabbi Avraham Naphtali Hertz ben rabbi Mordechai Zvi Yenner. There is more to be said about the rabbis of Janów.

[Page 87]

44. The Jewish community in Wysokie is absent from rabbinate and literature. Its community was new and initiated by its owners for economic reasons.

45. The name "Piaski" is also prevalent in Poland as a name for towns, villages, rivers, and streams, likely because of the sandy ground ("piaski" is Polish for 'sand.') But our Piaski was unique in its lively Jewish community and the Jews called it "Piusk". It was common for Jews to change names of geographic terms according to their manners. The town did not produce notable individuals in literature or rabbinate, although it is described in fictional works in Yiddish.

46. Rejowiec was a Jewish community, although it did not leave a significant impression in the lives of Polish Jewry. It produced no great rabbis, although Hasidism was developed there no less than other places.

47. It was a weird and unconventional name and was renamed Mezel–bozhitsh. That community was also an ordinary and newly founded. The community could not self–fund its religious objects and coordinated with neighboring

communities. A rabbi served as a joint rabbi of Lemil Wahin [?]. He was a student of the Seer of Lublin and rebbe Simcha Bunem of Pieczyska, who later travelled to Kotzk. He passed in 5628.

―――――

2. Sources for the History of Turobin

Undoubtedly, authentic materials could have been retrieved from primary sources like the archives of the municipality, district, or province. But obtaining such material from Poland, especially through the mail, involved various difficulties which need not be detailed here. Therefore, we had to make do with other sources, old encyclopedias which shed light on the early history of the town and its events.

From the **Geographic Lexicon of the Polish Kingdom** (1892) volume 17, p. 646–7, Warszawa:

A municipal settlement, previously a town, Krasnystaw District, Turobin gmina. Near the main road from Lublin to Janów and Zamosc, 49 versts from Lublin, 35 from Krasnystaw, 40 from Zamosc, and 12 from Zolkiewka (post office.) In it are a brick Catholic church, a brick Greek–Russian Orthodox church founded in 1882, two synagogues, a shelter for the handicapped, an elementary school, seven Jewish day schools, gmina offices and accompanying loan bank [?], a pharmacy, 366 houses (15 brick houses) 3949 residents (in 1883) including 1548 Jews.

In 1827, the town had 344 houses, 2026 residents, and the population was employed in fur processing.

In 1377, large properties in the Goray and Krasnik areas were granted to Dimitri, King Ludwick's treasurer and his brother Ivan. In 1389, King Yagello added Turobin and the neighboring villages. It must have formerly been the village of Targobisko.

Turobin was granted local municipal rights by king Vladislav Yagello in 1420 at the request of the nobleman Dovrogosta of Szamotuly, whose wife Elezhbita, granddaughter of Demitri of Goray, granted Turobin as a dowry.

[Page 88]

The first local church was likely founded by the town's owner in 1430. The current brick church building was built in the 16th century.

At the start of the 16th century, Turobin was owned by the Shweider family, and its sons Vincenti and Andzhei renewed local rights in 1510, as the previous permit was burned during the Tatar invasion in 1509.

While king Zygmunt August was in power, Turobin was owned by the Gorks, who converted the local church building to the Calvinist faith in 1570 and founded a school for members of the faith near it. That school existed until the end of the 16th century, meaning until the time when Turobin was purchased by general and chancellor Jan Zamoyski. He added it to his fee tail, and the church and school buildings were confiscated from the Calvinists. In 1595, Stanislav Gomolinski, Chelm bishop, overtook the church and after thorough renovation was reopened by bishop Swirski. The church burned at the end of the 17th century and reopened in 1713.

Turobin is the birthplace of the theologian Paul Razitcizki, who donated his self-portrait to the local church. It is also the birthplace of the educated attorney Jan Turobinski, a professor at the Academy in Kraków. Turobin was the only place where notable statesman and economist Stanislav Stashitz served as a priest, who was an anti-Semite but also acknowledged their positive attributes.

Known poet Shimonovitz, who wrote his poems in Latin, resided Near Tchernicin.

The immediate Turobin region housed 5312 people. Gmina Turobin was part of the district court in Wysokie and the post office was in Zolkiewka. The Turobin gmina spanned 18,893 morg [?] with 9481 permanent residents (including 280 Russian Orthodox, 1803 Jews.)

From the **General Orglebrand Encyclopedia** volume 25, 1867 Waraw, p. 751:

Turobin, a private town in the Lublin province Krasnystaw district, on the Pun [?] River. 12 km from the Zolkiewka post office. In older times, it was part of a royal estate but was granted as a gift in 1389 to marshal Dimitri from Goraya, deputy royal treasurer, along with many other villages. Dimitri's granddaughter, Elizabet, who married Dovrogusta Shmotolski, kshtaln (city minister) of Posna and military affairs minister of greater Poland, owned the town after the Goras.

By request of Dovrogusta Shmotolski, king Vladislav Yagello granted rights to the town following the Magdeburg model as an administrative framework including weekly market days on Tuesdays.

After the Tatar attack, the permitted towns were burned, after which point Andzei Vicenti Soydov, inheritor of Turobin, renewed local rights in 1510 and granted its residents a constitution and freedom. After that, Turobin was transferred to the Gork family, who turned the beautiful local church into a Calvinist church while king Zygmunt August was in power. They founded a school near it for members of their faith.

[Page 89]

However, by the end of the 16th century, the great chancellor Jan Zamoyski purchased the Turobin estate and returned it to Church rule. The Church than received the building and the neighboring school. That was thanks to efforts by Stanislav, the bishop of Chelm who began his term in 1623.

After joining Turobin with his other properties, Jan Zamoyski examined the town's relevant documents and granted it rights on July 19, 1600. Tomasz Zamoyski approved or canceled other rights in 1618, and some other rights were approved by Jan Zamoyski in 1646. Finally, King Jan Casimiris granted 4 market days for Turobin in 1662.

Two hundred years later, Turobin was populated by 2482 people who lived in 330 houses and had 6 fairs annually.

From **The Towns of Poland in its 1000 Years if Existence**. Volume 1, published by Oslinski, Wroclaw–Warszawa–Kraków, 1965:

Formerly a city, now a village in the Krasnystaw district, near the Pur River, a stream which leads to the Wieprz, 35 km south–west of the district capital, somewhat distant from the rail tracks. There is a paved road to Lublin and Krasnystaw.

At the end of the 14th century, Turobin was joined with the Goray estate which spanned from Kraśnik to Szczebrzeszyn. The town is quite ancient, and in the Middle Ages was on the road leading from Kyov Vladimir–Wlinsk to Kraków. In the 15th century, it was purchased by the Shamotolski family and thanks to its efforts it was granted the status of a town in 1420. The town experienced A period of growth in the 16th century. At the time, it was owned by the Gorks, and then owned by the Zamoyskis. The Gorks converted the town to a Calvinist center and founded their own church and school and built a local palace.

108

In 1564, Turobin included 245 houses and 1225 residents. It is the birthplace of a notable lawyer, a professor at the academy on Kraków, Jan Turobinski, whose last name was inspired by his hometown. After 1772, the town served as a passage point to Zamoyski's tribunal.

In 1810, Turobin was home to 1963 residents. The population expanded to 3942 in 1887. The professions which dominated the town were agriculture, minor trade, and among the various crafts, fur processing received special attention. In the second half of the 19th century, the town lost its rights. Later, the situation in town did not improve and its population decreased and reached 1592 in 1921. However, in the twenty years between the world wars, the population doubled, but WWII brought about the destruction of the population; in 1943, 1297 residents lived in it.

After the town was liberated from the Nazi occupier the town was uplifted. Electrical lighting was instated, and first work began on canals, a brick mill opened, and some small factories began operating, basic institutions for the public good were established, yet agriculture was the town's main source of employment at 64% of the population. In 1959, 1050 individuals resided in Turobin. There is an old church in the town in the style of the Renaissance.

[Page 90]

Editor's Note

We have quoted the material which has just come off the presses in Poland as is (translated into Hebrew). It is more efficient in its knowledge than the previous sources. However, it also raises unique interest as it ignored the Jews which lived there in 5 centuries of the millennia it existed and have contributed much to the town: economically, professionally, and politically. Even if the hand of the Nazi murderers impacted the Jews of Poland to such an extent that nearly none remain there, still certain artifacts remain; the centuries old cemetery, and synagogues which due to a lack of Jews have fallen as a "legacy" to the local Poles which must serve as housing or cultural warehouses. Does the good that the Jews contributed to Turobin necessitate ignoring and forgetting? And especially in the Bolshevik period which officially supports the war on anti–Semitism and advocates equality for all nations? Is that the payback to the Jews who held on to it for many generations despite persecution and bloodshed by various infamous criminals, and returned to it in masse to reconstruct its ruins and renew their residence? Does their constructive input warrant overlooking and erasing their memory which due to lack of Jews was demoted from town to the status of a pathetic village?

However, Turobin is not alone in the forgetting of Jews. There is not a single book published in liberated Poland abut towns and cities which this outlook of ignorance does not rule. We see no distinction between explicit and implicit anti–Semitism regarding the Jews who settled in Turobin and carried the burden of all municipal institutions and taxation no less than other residents.

Even more regrettable is that there has yet to be any response from any group on this implicit anti–Semitism in the new Poland. The intentional ignorance is itself being ignored by the Polish envoy to Israel as if we do not see what is happening in the world of Polish literature. They have the impression we are deaf and blind to this malicious harm by a nation which was a target of Nazi fire and their wild murders. This is the thanks the Jews get. It is good we are responding here to this injustice by the authors of liberated Poland who are continuing this anti–Semitic trend like olden days, as if a global revolution, especially in Europe, a social and idealistic revolution for the humane and moral rights among all nations. As if the leaders of Polish national democracy were not punished for their crimes and constant torment of Jews until the last war.

From **The Jewish Encyclopedia** (in Russian) by the Brookhouse – Iparon Company for Jewish Science Books, Petersburg, Volume 15:

In the period of the Polish Republic, Turobin was a town in the Chelm district. During the Khmelnitsky uprising, the Jews of Turobin were destroyed. In 1765, the regional community included 985 Jews. Now Turobin is part of the Lublin Province, Krasnystaw district. Its Jews were not always pressured. [?]

In 1856, there were 1408 Christians and 951 Jews. According to the 1897 census, it had 2377 people including 1509 Jews.

In May 1942, the the Jews of Siedlce, Rabka, Turobin, and other towns were expelled (The Zholkov expulsion) and transferred to Krasnystaw where the Jews of Wysokie, Turobin and other regional towns were transferred. Only the Jews who had work permits remained.

[Page 91]

According to testimony by Shmuel Lerer and Esther Perner.

Those expelled from Turobin were led for two days to the Krasnystaw train station where they were loaded on a train and transferred to Sobibor (testimony of Berish Friedenmerg.)

Jewish communities near Turobin:

While we use the Jewish Encyclopedia (in Russian) we will quote entries from the same source about neighboring towns:

Goray

Jews resided there without bother since Polish rule. In 1856, it had 483 Jews and 1,352 Christians in 1897, the population was 1,738 including 473 Jews.

Gorshkov

Under Polish rule, the town's gates were not wide opened to Jews: in 1856, 176 Christians resided in it and 227 Jews. In 1897, the population size was 641, including 303 Jews.

Wysokie

Under Polish rule, the town was part of the Masovian Voivodeship. In 1765, 62 Jews resided in it who were subject to the Chikhanov community.

Zolkiewka

No roadblocks to Jewish settlement were in place under Polish rule. In 1856, it had 336 Christians and 568 Jews. In 1897, The population numbered 2,110 including 1476 Jews.

Modliborzyce

Under Polish rule, the town was part of the Lublin Voivodship. In 1765, 350 Jews resided in it. After the Russian invasion of Poland, it was added to the Janów district. Since it is 21 versts from the border, in the years 1823–62 was off limits to non–local Jews. In 1856, it had 364 Christians residents and

576 Jews. According to the 1897 census, the town's population numbered 1792, including 859 Jews.

Piaski

Under Russian rule, it was added to Lublin Voivodship. In 1765, there were 602 payers of the Jewish tax. In 1765, it was home to 104 Jews. Its name was later changed to Greater Piaski. In 1856, 520 Christians and 1883 Jews inhabited it. The 1897 census did not include population figures.

Rejowiec

Was one of the places in which in old times Jewish settlement was unrestricted.

[Page 92]

In 1856, 311 Christians resided in it and 824 Jews. In 1897, the population numbered 2175, including 1605 Jews.

Janów

Under Polish rule, it was part of the Lublin Voivodship. B. Tanner notes that in 1678, local Jews owned homes and real estate. In 1765, 461 Jews resided in Janów. Under the Russians, it became a district capital and Jewish residence was unrestricted. In 1896, it was home to 1049 Christians and 875 Jews. In 1857, the district's population numbered 117,000 including 11,600 Jews, 8,000 in Janów including 2770 Jews.

———

3. Chronology of Turobin

General municipal:

1389 King Vladislav Yagello gifts Turobin and may other villages to marshal Dimitri of Goray.

1420 Vladislav Yagello grants Magdeburg rights to Turobin, including market days on Tuesdays.

1430 The town's owners founded the first church in town, which was intact up to the Tatar invasion.

1509 The Tatar on their journey to occupy Poland burned and destroyed Turobin.

1510 Andzei Vincenti Soydov renewed the town's local rights and granted a constitution and freedom to those rebuilding it.

1511 Jan Turobinski (1511 – 1575) is born, a great scholar and lawyer, author of books (in Latin) and poems.

1564 245 Houses in Turobin and 1225 residents.

1570 The Gorks, inheritors of Turobin, converted the local church to a Calvinist one during the period of king Zygmunt August and built near it a school for members of their faith, which existed to the end of the 16th century.

1595 Stanislav Gomolinski, Chelm Bishop, seized the local church building from the Calvinists and in 1630, reopened it after renovations.

1600 Turobin and its estates were purchased by the great chancellor Jan Zamoyski who returned it to Church authority.

1604 Residence of the greatest Polish poet, Shimonovitz, at the Szczebrzeszyn estate near Turobin.

1618 Jan Zamoyski, after adding Turobin to the fee tail, examined the town's documents, approved some and canceled others. Other rights were subsequently approved in 1646.

1662 King Jan Casimir approved four market days for Turobin.

1772 Turobin served as passage point to Zamoyski's tribunal.

[Page 93]

1780 Stanislav Stashitz (1755 – 1815) a priest in Turobin, later promoted to royal statesmen and economist.

1810 1963 residents in Turobin.

1827 344 Houses and 2026 residents. Population employed mostly in fur processing.

1856 A population of 1,408 Christians and 951 Jews.

1867 The town has 330 houses and a population of 2,482

1882 Orthodox Church founded.

1883 366 houses, 3949 residents including 1548 Jews. The gmina, a territory of 18,893 morg [?] is home to 9,481 residents (including 280 Russian Orthodox and 1803 Jews.)

1897 The census records 2377 town residents, including 1509 Jews.

1921 Town's population is 1592.

1943 Population: 1297

1959 Population: 1050

Jewish Community:

1580 – 1764 The Council of Four Lands is in existence for the Jews of Poland, whose authority included the Jewish community in Turobin and the names of its leaders mentioned in the Council protocols.

1607 Shimon ben David Oyerbach of Turobin is among the 10 council members who signed various rules for Polish Jewry.

1632 Rabbi Shimon Wolf Oyerbach, formerly rabbi in Turobin, passes in Prague.

1643 Rabbi Menachem ben Yitzchak Chayoot, ABD of Turobin, participated in the Council's deliberations on the inconsistent wording of prayer books at the fair in Lublin.

1669 R' Yitzchak Parnas of the Turobin community, is a signatory on the CFL decision on the Tykocin community's complaint.

1672 R' Yitzchak, son of the righteous rabbi Uri Shraga Feivish represents Turobin at the CFL meeting in Jarosław, in which it was decided the council will not return to that cursed city.

1673 David Tebbil of Turobin participated in the Council's decision to empower the Pińczów leadership to restrict relocation to their town due to a poor economy.

1678 Meir Yosef of Turobin signed with 18 Jewish community leaders on a promissory note for the nobleman Georg Miltren fun Miltenberg, treasurer of Breslau.

R' Meir ben rabbi Yosef "Yoske" Katz of Turobin joins CFL approval of publication of the bible in Yiddish by R' Yosef Atiash of Amsterdam.

1861 R' David ben Eliezer of Turobin joins the members of CFL on another

114

promissory note by the aforementioned noble to be paid in installments in the next 9 years.

1687 Meir ben Yosef Katz of Turobin was a signatory to forbidding more Jews to settle in Pińczów due to economic straits.

1688 Zechariah Mendel ben Arye Leib of Turobin signed a CFL document granting exclusive publication and distribution to a book's author.

[Page 94]

1688 R' Meir ben Arye Leib of Turobin signs a ruling on the dispute between the Tykocin and Międzyrzec Podlaski communities.

1689 R' Zachariah Mendel of Turobin signs a copyright decree to the author of *Zofnat Pa'aneach* and forbidding others to print and distribute for three years.

1691 Zacharia Mendel of Turobin signs a verdict upholding a previous ruling on the matter of Miedzyrzec Podlaski vs. Tykocin.

1726 600 rubles granted to the Turobin community by CFL in the wake of a strained economy or other troubles.

1648 – 1649 A slaughter by Khmelnitsky's gangs in Tomaszów, Szczebrzeszyn, Turobin, Bilgoraj, Krasnik, and economic annihilation of their Jews

1850 A map of Jewish communities in Poland published by CFL mentions the communities in Lublin province: Zamosc, Frampol, Modliborzyce, Krasnik, Turobin, Szczebrzeszyn, Bilgoraj, Krasnobrod, Bychawa, Grabowiec, and Vasilisovitz.

1765 985 Jews in the Turobin area

1766 Av 19, passing of the rabbi and scholar Reuven ben Yeshaya of Turobin in Lublin, where he was buried.

1856 951 Jews living among 1408 Christians

1897 1509 Jews and 2377 Christians

1910 Rabbi Eliyahu Halevi Landa, 40–year ABD of Turobin

1926 *Divrei Shmuel* by Turobin rabbi Noakh Shmuel Lifshitz, a student of the Seer of Lublin, is published.

1942 20 Tishrei – 20 Cheshvan, Jews are expelled by the Nazis to Izbitza.

[Page 96]

3. Life in Town

History of the Town

Yehoshua Ben–Ari (Heshel Silberklang)

Translated by Meir Bulman

A.

When was Turobin founded? Who were its founders? How did it develop
and root itself in the distant and recent past? When did Jews settle in it and
how?

Those questions and many others remain unanswered for a simple reason:
there is nobody to ask. Every possible source was denied to us across
generations either accidently or maliciously, archived in the dirt or burned in
the flames of the hell our brothers and sisters were cast into. The few
survivors who luck smiled upon are mostly young and the wisdom of the
elders has yet to be absorbed in their wounded and fractured consciousness.
Few of us know the history of the town in which we were born and raised. Our
parents could not pass it along and we grew and entered local life as if it was
born and created with us.

Those questions resurface and bother whenever we return in our thoughts
to the place in which our ancestors were born and lived, and where we too
drew our first breaths. It was our hometown and we knew no other birthplace
in our lives. Eretz Israel was in our consciousness like in a mental archive,
vague in the magic of the ancient legend, along with the creation of the Earth,
the times of the national Forefathers and the wonders of Genesis. It seemed to
us like on a distant star in a different universe.

The reality we lived was Turobin and thousands of other towns. The pain of
the Holocaust which eats us is therefore multi–emotional and pours into the
depth and with of our pain and suffering. The deep and fracturing pain in our
soul for the destruction of the lively, culturally varied Diaspora which spanned
across many generations, bothers, and feeds on it. The more we try to ignore

116

and suppress it, the more it resurfaces. As if it has a mind of its own it stands before us and raised many questions. Our minds' eyes wander and we wonder as they examine the view, the natural background against which we were raised. It was there that we grew, learned, played, and lived our lives, a normal life as we perceived it, lively and deeply rooted lives in a world of institutions and cultural values which were not created overnight. Where did it all come from? When did it begin? That nostalgic curiously, a powerless dig in a past which was uprooted, or that we were uprooted from, is an act of historic cruelty.

A legacy spanning many generations was eradicated from the world in one fell swoop and is no more. Those were generations which despite the troubles which impacted our nation occasionally, did not cease, until the final generation. Still, they settled in the ground, grew fruits, and expanded their trunks, and in rivers of blood they were fruitful and multiplied. Their fate was sealed in ancient times when they were commanded, "when thou wash in thy blood, Live!" They lived in rivers of blood, lives full of creation, thought, and deed, as if life was fertilized and fed on the blood and suffering.

Could we uproot it all from our hearts in one day and forget it all?

Now that I am so distant from them, the ancient tombstones in the Turobin cemetery speak to me, consumed with age, as if they want to tell me much about the history of the town, its people and its history. The Synagogue that was destroyed, and its twin – the *beth midrash* both try to explain events from the depths of history, and tell me divine secrets from a world that is no more. That library full of ancient holy books in the *beth midrash* could have told many stories.

[Page 97]

When we began gathering material for this book, it was obvious to us that we had to find some description of the history of the town. We contacted some historians who promised to obtain the required material but to no avail. Our town was small, sperate from the large Jewish arena of the large towns. Its roads did not find their way to the hearts of the large Jewish community, despite its geographic proximity to Lublin (50 – 60 km), a large town bustling with culture. We can barely find our town on the map. The historians who deal with that region of Poland see in their mind's eye the entire region and their focus is primarily on the large towns, the centers of activity and culture. We almost gave up on the possibility of penetrating the history of our town, when one of the members found Mr. Yisreal Halperin's book on the Council of Four Lands (Bialik Institute of the Jewish Agency) where we discovered twenty mentions of Turobin. However, an irritating disappointment occurred since we found nothing about the town itself.

The name of the town is mentioned in relation to events which occurred in other places and the name of a representatives of the town appeared in relation. Absent any other choice, we made due with that scarcity for the time being. At least we know that our town existed 400 years ago, that great men served as rabbis in the town, and that the community representatives participated in the activities of that important council, which led Polish Jewry for about 240 years, since the start of the 16th century.

Not all towns were fortunate to be represented in that council, whose authority and position in Judaism of that time could compare only to the Sanhedrin of old. For example, it is told that Tykocin gained representation at the council only in 1678. Matters concerning that town were often discussed by the Council, and it is likely it was an important town with communal significance. It demanded representation at the Council, the request was deliberated and granted. Among the signatories, we found Meir ben Yosef of Turobin, who must have been a longtime member of the council.

This is not the place to delve into that important council. We will just say, that it convened mainly in Lublin. The bulk of the activity was twice a year, mainly at the Gromnitz Fair, and continued for several weeks. Jews from all corners of Greater Poland gathered in Lublin at the fair, which usually gathered between Purim and Passover. They would state their issues or deliberated in front of the Council. The Council would hear their complaints, disputes, or questions on matters of Torah, and would clarify, decide, and render a verdict. Its verdicts were adhered to like a governmental decision. The verdicts and decisions were recorded in a ledger, which, much to our dismay, has vanished and is no more, aside from the few surviving documents. From the end of the 16th century, Poland granted the Council de jure authority as representing Polish Jewry. Its title, "The Council of Four Lands" relies on the fact that its authority spanned across Russia, Lithuania, and the two halves of Poland.

118

[Page 98]

The Council of Four Lands heard the voices of the notable communities and its positions were filled by important notable people of Jewry of the time, in the Torah world, of course. As previously stated, Turobin was represented at the Council, and rendered opinions on matters concerning all of Polish Jewry.

In the absence of details or stories which could shed light on the long chronology of town events, I found some solace that some issues ruled on by the Council of Four Lands were signed by Turobin's representatives. That confirmed reality about our town can make us proud that our town was not at all a weak one within the Polish Jewish community.

These are the details:

1. In 1607, at the Gromnitz Fair in Lublin, the Council enacted regulations obligating all Polish Jews including issues of interest on loans, etc. among the signatures is also:
"I too hereby sign, small among my peers, Shimon ben my teacher and father David Oyerbach of Turobin"
Turns out that Mr. Shimon Oyerbach was ABD of Turobin at the time and was an in–law of the great Talmud commentator Mahrshal.

2. In 1643, the Council discussed misprints in prayer books published in multiple versions. The Council decided to grant exclusive rights to the rabbi of Pshmishel, Shabtai ben Yitzchak Sofer, to publish a single version of the prayer book and decreed that no other prayer book be published and distributed.
At the same fair in Lublin, where the Council came to the aforementioned conclusion, there was a man named R' Menachem "Manesh" ben Yitzchak Chayoot, ABD in Turobin. He probably represented Turobin at the council's deliberations.

3. In 1669, the representatives of the Tykocin community complained the council was discriminatory in its practice of collecting taxes from residents to the Polish Sjem, while the Council covered the same cost for other communities. Among the signatures is that of Yitzchak of Kraka, residing in Turobin. He was likely a community leader and not necessarily a rabbi.

4. In 5432, the Council convened in Jarosław, and decided to no longer convene in that cursed town (Jews were permitted to live only in two houses in that town.) In that convention participated also "Yitzchak ben harav Uri Shraga Feivish" representing Turobin.

[Page 99]

5. In 5433, the representative of Pińczów complained to the council that many people relocated to their town while it was detrimental to its residents. Poverty was widespread in town and few sources of income existed. They requested authority to forbid such immigration, for the sake of its longtime residents.
   The request of Pińczów was affirmed and signed also by David Tebbil of Turobin.

6. In 5438, 18 Jewish community leaders gathered and signed a promissory note for the nobleman Georg Miltren fun Miltenburg, treasurer of the royal city of Breslau. The promissory note stated the loan was to be paid back over 12 years, "starting at the Elizabet Fair 1679." Among the signatories was the aforementioned Meir Yosef of Turobin.

7. That same year, the council approved the publication of the bible with a Yiddish translation by R' Yosef Atiash of Amsterdam. Among the signatories was "R' Meir ben rabbi Yosef Yoske Katz of Turobin," (probably the aforementioned Meir Yosef, or ben Yosef, although the signature is sometimes shorter.)

8. A few years later, the Council received another loan from the same nobleman of Breslau and signed a promissory note obligating payment over 9 years. Among the signatories was R' David ben Eliezer of Turobin.

9. In 5447, the representatives of Opatów posed a complaint similar to the one previously made by Pińczów (that people were settling in it despite economic straits, and that only one street allowed Jewish residence) and a decree was issued that no more Jews will settle there. Among the signatories was Meir ben Yosef (Katz) of Turobin.

10. In 5448, the Council granted an exclusive right to a rabbi to publish and distribute a book. Among the signatories was Zacharia Mendel ben

120

rabbi Arye Leib of Turobin (it is told that he was a wealthy man and the author of the book *Ba'er Hetev* on *Shulchan Aruch, Yore De'a,* and *Choshen Mishpat.*)

11. In a dispute between the Tykocin and Mezritsh communities about a plot of land brought to and settled by the Council was signed by Meir ben Arye Leib of Turobin.

12. In 5449, the Council granted a three–year copyright to the author of *Zofnat Pa'aneach.* Among the signatories was the aforementioned Zacharia Mendel of Turobin (it is likely that Zechariah Mendel and Meir were brothers who both served Turobin.)

13. In 5451, the Mezritsh dispute was renewed and the Council forced them to adhere to the previous verdict. Among the signatories was Zacharia Mendel of Turobin.

14. In 1726, the Council detailed its annual revenues and expenditures. The costs included a tax to the treasury for the sum of 220,000 "yargelt" to the master [?], 12,000 to the royal treasurer, and more. The Council also detailed the sources of revenue and levied taxes on each community. Some communities were grated a discount. It is interesting that the Council granted the same 600 silver [?] ruble discount to Lublin as they did to Turobin. Discounts were based on the community's finical state or some other troubles. The entire budget numbered 288,300 gold.

[Page 100]

The very fact Turobin and Lublin were placed on the same plane proves that Turobin reached a status of importance at that time.

In a later book, published in 5672, titled *Mekor Chaim* [life source] dedicated to the *rebbe* of Tzanz, Chaim Helberstam, and his lineage, (p109) the following story appears:

"I was told by zh"b [?] R' H.M [?] Shekhna of Turobin traveled to the Mr. Khrabbi [?] A. near there, with vexlen [exchange/ IOU?] worth several thousand rubles to collect his debt. He (the khrabbi) took the vexlen from him to pay and immediately tore them up. Bitter, he travelled to Tzanz. On Friday, he arrived at the synagogue, where some dispute was taking place: what is preferable, being a rabbi or a merchant. The Holy Rav came and said being a rabbi was preferable, and added, 'ask Shekhna, he will tell you.' After he did not proclaim [?] and told him everything, he said to him, 'travel to Lublin,' and so he did. While there, he saw a gentleman he was acquainted with, who saw he was sad and inquired about it. He told him. That gentleman then saw the debtor and made a large effort until the debt was repaid."

That was about 100 years ago. Among the rabbis who travelled to the Tsanz *rebbe* was ABD of Turobin, Rabbi Yuda Leibush and Zolishtchik (page 117.)

B. Changes in Turobin

The town was about 50 km south of Lublin.

I was 13 when I left it and would return home only on holidays. In 1935, after a few years of pioneer training, I made aliya. So, I cannot recall details on the town's history, its people, and institutions, except in a vague and general sense.

If the book *The House of Israel in Poland* edited by Yisrael Halperin is to be trusted, the town was founded at the end of the 16th century. Although the name of the town is not mentioned in the book, Krasnystaw, Zamosc and other neighboring towns in the Lublin province are mentioned in relation to [expulsion] privileges and allowances the gentile residents of those towns received in 1555. Privileges were not implemented until king Zygmunt August approved them, and Jews from those towns were expelled. At that time, the noblemen requested the king to extract the Jews from his royal towns and resettle them in towns and villages owned by nobles. Their intention was to enjoy their taxes, trade, etc. Thus, many Jewish towns and villages were founded in the 17th century.

"Ask your father and he will tell you, your elders and they will say to you," goes the verse, but when father and grandfather are absent there is nobody to ask. That is the additional tragedy to the destruction of Polish Jewry, which also destroyed an important chapter in the history of the Polish Jews who were experienced in suffering and bloodshed.

[Page 101]

The surviving population is comprised mainly of youths who were mostly children when the tragedy took place, and the only remaining option is piecing chronologies from crumbs and speculation.

Indeed, we can estimate the town's origin is somewhere in the 16th century with some Jews who came to settle under the jurisdiction of the nobleman. The Jews of the time needed a minyan, and a minyan required a community, a community necessitated institutions, and so on until a gathering established with patterns typical to that time: a community council, rabbi, shochet, circumciser, synagogues, cemetery, bathhouse, charity institutions, etc.

Truthfully, the town was no different than others. It was muddy, almost detached from the outside world, its genesis rife with struggles for existence and livelihood, and enjoyed autonomy with minimal governmental intervention. The parents worked hard to earn a living, and the youths, other than those apprenticing in their parents' profession at a young age, either studied Torah or completely inactive. The adults in their free time took up as "hobbies" matters such as a dispute, Hasidism wars, appointing or dismantling the community council, praising or else smearing the rabbi, etc.

There was one difference between the town and the neighboring towns like Zolkiewka, Goray, Wysokie and others, in that it had many Torah scholars and religiously observant and its reputation preceded it. The name Turobin was explained in the joining of the words 'Torah' and 'binah' [wisdom.] Its true Polish name was Turobin. The study of Torah in town was constant. Those who themselves did not or could not study would listen to instructors and leaders between prayers, on shabbat, and holidays. For a boy, the study of Torah began at age 3 when he was "tossed" in a festive ceremony to the *dardeki* [toddler teacher.] At age five, approximately, he left the *dardeki* and graduated to a higher-level teacher taught Torah with Rashi commentary, and some Mishnah. From that teacher, he passed on to a greater one, until the age of 10, approximately, he knew a chapter in Talmud. Above such an age a teacher no longer necessary, and he began attending the *beth midrash*, where boys studied on their own in the company of older boys who were better versed, or with the aid of the elderly scholars who only slept and ate at home and the *beth midrash* was their home in which they also rested. I remember that the study of Talmud was done in public at the *beth midrash*, while the adults, the breadwinners, were busy praying, teaching, or labored on religious literature along the two sides of the tables placed along the walls of the *beth midrash*. The back and forth of melodic Talmud study mixed with the notes of prayer. The atmosphere inside the *beth midrash* bustled like a beehive from the early morning hours to the late hours after midnight. The debate was fierce, the will of the youths to outdo one another was natural and ambitious.

There were boys aged 15–16 who already swam freely in the sea of *poskim*. The *Shulchan Aruch* and Maimonides were the source of much knowledge and pride, and the envy of scholars increased wisdom. On that note, I recall one episode among many:

[Page 102]

There was a family which particularly excelled in that field, the Estreicher family. The patriarch, a large Jew with the looks of a wiseman, owned a fabric store and was a follower of the Alexander *rebbe*. He had three sons: Bunim, Yechiel, and Yerachmiel. They were the only Alexander Hasidim in town, as most Hasidim in town were Ger Hasidim. In addition to being unusual, they were also very studious. So, Ger Hasidim were prideful and dismissed Alexander Hasidim like dirt. Thus, the family became socially isolated. In response, the father enacted a strict Torah study regime on himself and his sons to rebuke the Ger Hasidism. The father, as he labored in his store, did not cease studying Torah as well and that family fulfilled the instruction "you shall study it day and night." They rose early and departed late. They studied even at home in the late hours of the night, the sound of Torah was heard echoing. Thus, they reached a status which very few could attain.

Moreover, town boys were not sent to the only secular school in town which was run by Christians. Each tried to attain elementary knowledge in literacy and mathematics and made due with that. The knowledge of Torah overshadowed the need for secular education which was barely felt. In contrast, the girls attended the elementary 7–class school. The boys later attained their secular education from the girls as if it was a game.

The *beth midrash* served not only as a center for prayer and Torah study, but also a social and cultural center for the residents of the town. Deals were made between the afternoon and evening prayers, and were marriages were arranged. Disputes took place there, passionately debated, be it about *aliya la'torah* or a spot by the eastern wall. All wedding canopies took place and funeral processions began in the yard. Lecturers came to the synagogue and recited their lectures from the stage at the center. Fundraising took place there for support of yeshivot, orphans, impoverished brides, etc. It was also a gathering place for passers–through and peddlers who wandered the area. They gathered near the entrance, and as they exited, the crowd would contribute their pennies or invite them for lodging and meals.

124

Despite the disputes and fights among the various classes and Hasidic sects, all residents were still one community, united in joy or mourning, good or bad. When a wedding took place, all its members, including the elders, women, and children partook in it. If there was a funeral all residents came as a final act of charity. If trouble overtook the town, chaos included all. I remember the drowning of three sisters and the awful panic which encompassed all. If gentile youths rioted in town, all the youth untied against them.

Alongside the *beth midrash*, some of the youth went towards progress. The pioneering and Zionist movement was imported to town by youths who were exposed and influenced, secretly read external books, visited the big city, befriended a stranger who settled in town, and matters began to organize. Thus, chapters of *HaKhalutz*, General Zionists, *Mizrachi*, and *Ha'poel Hamizrachi* were founded. They found large grounds to operate among the many youths who were free from the worry of labor and wasted time. The burden of providing a living extended to older sons and daughters. The daughter awaited a groom and the son a good arrangement from the outside. [?] The *beth midrash* no longer attracted them, aside maybe for prayer. Envoys from the movements oversaw their establishment. Reading and thought–provoking material was common. The secret liberation from the bind of tradition induced happiness, and party activity had much content. Fundraising, lectures, endless ideological debates. There were also socialist youth, members of the Bund. They were mainly the craftsmen who were the third step after the attendees of the *beth midrash* and the various Zionists. They did not have much time to run wild; they worked hard to make a living and dreamed of the socialist revolution to rescue them. And if the messiah came before that – how wonderful, and therefore they continued to pray at the synagogue.

[Page 103]

Thus, the town was divided into three layers, which added volume to the liveliness. In addition, among the Hasidic sects and among the chief rabbi and the halachic instructor, the disputes were added among the many Zionist movements and among them and the Bund members, with almost complete overlooking of the poor state of life in town and the almost total disconnect from events occurring in the big outside world.

An outside observer would probably shake his head at the sight of the naivete of the town's residents, the excitement in such debates and the seriousness of debating trivial matters. But those things were an important prat of the community atmosphere and reflected the character of that small community, its alert thinking, its activity, and energy from a social–communal aspect. It was all done without taking away the wholeness of the community, the devotion, and care for one another in times of need, and the saying of "All Israel are responsible for one another" as they occasionally competed in charity. Anyone who requested help received is it, and many acts of charity were made anonymously.

What I clearly still remember is the beautiful views and the natural blessings of the place and region. They were so captivating and fascinating, so it is natural that the Jewish residents knew how to be happy and joyous with all their being, despite the difficulties and various troubles which occurred, which at times had enough strength to depress the will to live. The fields with wildflowers in all colors of the rainbow, the trees, the silent flow of the river, the intoxicating scents in the fall and spring seasons, the song of the birds and all the rest served as a calming and sweeting drug for the Jew in his troubles.

The town was on an agriculturally rich and fertile soil. It was decorated by many mountains, forests, and villages. Along its south side flowed a narrow and long river stream which went on for many kilometers beyond it. That river served the youth as the only sports arena where they swam, dived, immersed, jumped, and gathered for entrainment. Everyone in town knew how to swim, thanks to the river. A hut hidden among thick brush in one part of the river served a meeting spot for romantic couples or a cold mikveh for choosy Hasidim. Entrance to the hut was not free and entitled a small payment to a gentile farm owner through which one had to pass. The passage was on narrow wooden boards which bridged water along the path. Special agility was required to walk down that path without getting wet. There were some which an athletic challenge in the long swim from the edge of the river by the main road and surprised the lone bathers in the hut, much to the joy of all.

[Page 104]

In the winter, the water froze, and the icy arena served for skating as the winter sport. All skated, sometimes on nailed heals, at times ripped ones. Chunks of ice were divided into squares, loaded on coaches, and led to town, where they were stored in cellars or piles of sawdust and used as refrigeration during the summer. As spring arrived and the snows melted, the river rose and flooded a significant portion of the fields and farms mainly at the eastern part of town, called "*przedmieście*" (suburb), an area which resembled a miniature Venice. passage to the homes was done on temporarily placed wooden planks or bricks which never failed. I remember how much I enjoyed that charming site when I happened to pass through the place with my father who went to visit a gentile he was acquainted with. I was very jealous of the young gentiles who accompanied by their dogs steered small boats or rafts along the river among swimming ducks and chicks.

At another part of town, at the North–West edge, was the estate of the aristocrat of the town Hortshek, whose ancestors must have seen to it that Jews settle in the area. That nobleman controlled large plots which produced many goods. His private residence was surrounded by gardens and fields full of fruit and decorative trees, and large dogs swarmed the property. I was always attracted to the enchanted spot spurred by my imagination as mysterious, with a fearful curiously. Accompanying my father, I managed to see much of it; the stables and cowsheds, granaries, the big herds of cows, horses, swine, chickens, and the people laboring like slaves from sunrise to sunset, all for the nobleman, the supreme leader who rarely was at his residence.

The nobleman's fields led to the permeant resting place, the cemetery, which was on a small hill to the west within the landowner's tree field, hidden among tall trees and marked the unique status and its holy aura. Today I confess my sins; there was barely a funeral which I did not participate in (almost all did), but all because of my attraction to that wonderful place more so than a feeling of obligation to the deceased. Those green fields, the fruit gardens, the scent, all induced in me a lively spirit and joy. As a rambunctious boy I dared to pick fruits on the side of the road, apples red and fresh from the landowner's gardens, although they were fenced and guarded. I returned home more than once with tattered trousers and scratch marks on my palms as my heart beat in fear of the barking dogs.

On my way back from there, I would sneak a peek at the large wood chipper and the motorized flour mill which was in operation nearly 24 hours a day, illuminated by blinding electrical lighting. I liked to listen to the sound of the motors and watch he movement of the peasants who stood in line with wagons filled with wheat and barley for milling for self–consumption. The scent of the chipped pine trees was pleasant and intoxicated my senses.

Not far from the farm, on the left side, was the town firehouse. The firemen were local Christians volunteers. Their uniforms were colorful, and they wore shiny copper hats.

[Page 105]

They extinguished fires which were common to the area, and in their free time practiced playing wind and percussion instruments. There was not a festivity or ceremony they did not participate in. The Jewish youth could only watch them and listen to them, but not be one of them. I liked listening to their rehearsals and in my heart, I envied them and cursed them.

On the road, more inwardly and widely spread, were the public institutions like the elementary school, the local council building, and the courts. It was interesting is that those institutions operated at the edge of town and not at its center, as Jews mostly populated the town proper. The non–Jewish residents resided mostly at the edges of town but not in its center. What symbolized the Cristian control of the town was the church and its uniquely elevated dome, also at the edge of town a large cross atop it. It was a nuisance of the market center which was surrounded by a large square of Jewish homes and businesses. Later, gentile–owned operated there as well. Those businesses were mostly restaurants and pubs which spread a scent of alcohol and fried pork at night, much to the dismay of Jews. After those businesses closed for the night, Jews governed the whole town. When boys reached the age of compulsory enlistment in the Polish military, it was customary to impose on oneself a weight–loss regime, in the hopes it would harm their health to evade enlistment by failing medical examinations. Boys of that age did not only fast, but also let loose for whole nights in the town's streets, shouting, singing, and occasionally fighting.

One of the mischiefs perpetrated by youths during those nights was rearranging the business signs. The next morning, one could find a sign in Polish declaring the sale of pork placed atop the lavatory in the square, and a sign for a Jewish business hanging atop a gentile's pub.

The town square was the center of the town's economic life. On market days and holidays, the square was filled with people and livestock who arrived in large crowds from the neighboring villages. Chaos was prevalent during

128

those days. Drunks rolled around in every corner. Violent disputes were abundant. If fate dictated that one was to be stabbed by his foe's knife, he likely died public in that square. The chaos increased in such circumstances. I remember one market day when some village leader was knifed to death by a local Christian mercenary. The chaos, escape, and fear which ensued did not deter us, the youth, from approaching and looking at the victim's severed stomach whose guts spilled out.

The unemployed Jewish youth gathered in the square and wasted time. You could find them near a kiosk or some other business, calculating the end of days and waiting for *Ge'ulah*, or debating important issues.

The streets and buildings in the town were not unique in any sense nor architecturally impressive. Dirt roads led in all directions from the market square. Those were the streets and alleys of the town, occupied by wooden houses surrounded by fenced yards. They were home to the Jews Including their large families, grandparents, goats, and chickens, and in certain homes also cows and horses. When it rained, the streets were muddied and with puddles, and during the cold winter they were covered in head–high snow.

[Page 106]

Before I made aliya, the first road was paved, on the main road which led north to Lublin. Then, a bus line which traveled daily to Lublin and back was founded. That bus was a novelty and a big attraction to the locals. It opened a larger window to the outside world through which civilization began entering. At roughly the same time, electrical lighting supplied by the flour mill was installed in the homes, gardens were planted, some brick houses were built, and there was a feeling of change. I do not know what caused that. Was it an enlightened council chairman? I cannot recall one single public effort which benefitted the Jews until then. What I do remember was tax collection and business permit enforcement, which were done with much force and no public service in exchange. There was no sewer, no roads, no sidewalks or anything of the like, and the change was sudden.

The Jews did not expect nor wait for services. Suffice it to say they never dared to request anything substantial. Their demands were minimal. If there was no light, one walked in the dark or carried a flashlight. The rain and storms cleaned the unfenced areas. The trash was somehow absorbed in the ground. If one became ill, divine help was prayed for. Meanwhile, the ill person was cared for with warm chicken soup or used cures based on grandmother's advice, or summoned the local doctor, the fletcher (medic.) The medic also had to work as a hairdresser[?] and when he could not make do with that, his wife contributed as a midwife. As most mothers received assistance from the experienced elderly women, the fletcher turned to liquor to drown his sorrows. After that, nobody used his services.

He was a character, the healer, "Leiser *der Fletcher*" he was called, a tall handsome man. I do not know how that man came to be in that town. He was a living symbol of the disregard showed by the locals towards modern medicine. Even when someone was very ill they did not want to summon a doctor. First, a minyan was gathered which recited Psalms and prayed for the life of the ill. Or a few people stood by the ark, opened it, and wept bitterly and loudly. Those sights always depressed me, but miraculously, most of the sick healed without the aid of a doctor or medic. Nature immunized people and selected them at a young age and people were strong and healthy. There was also another practitioner with the title of doctor, but only the wealthy used his services, and they were scarce. The common folk trusted their God or ran to the *rebbe* and handed him a note (a *kvittel*), received the blessings. Sometimes they also got a talisman which worked occasionally and elevated the rabbi's prestige to new heights.

Thus, the public had no need special services from the local authorities. They thanked God for not intervening with excessive taxes, repossessions, disrupting business, nor with the autonomous administration of the community.

The municipality was represented in town by a Jewish resident who was somewhat of a tribe leader who was the point of contact between the authorities and the residents. A sign, "village leader" (in Polish) was placed by his house. All government inquiries were done through him. He also supplied his services to the authorities but remained loyal to his tribe. When he learned about a plot forming against someone, he warned him ahead of time. His name was Isaac Obroweys and had a son who was the apple of his eye. The son was among the first members of the Zionist pioneering movement in the town. He has been in Israel for the past 30 years and is a member of Kibbutz Alonim (Yisrael Amir.)

130

[Page 107]

C. Economics in town

Town residents depended on regional peasants for income. Some also made a living from one another. Most income was drawn from the market days or Christian holidays. Every Thursday, a regular market day took place, and a few times a year there were also large fairs. On fair days, merchants from more distant places also arrived. During that time, many peasants and merchants gathered in town. The farmers brought their produce and traded it for essential items needed at home or in the field. Between each deal, they gathered in the pubs and drank.

The Jewish merchants and some Christian ones supplied everything and purchased everything. There was much preparation for market days. All prayed for a successful market day, because weekly income of most residents depended on it. If it was a pleasant day and the roads were dry, many arrived at the market and much was traded. However, if it was a rainy day and the roads were poor, income was scarce and sadness common. All depended on the heavens, which were not always charitable. Trading took place in stores or temporary booths.

The livestock market was separate and located at the northern entrance of town. That market drew my attention. The mixture of man and animal was a living picture of the atmosphere of the entire region. They depend on each other; the animal was the main tool, the dominant mode of transportation, and sometimes food. Man and animal worked alongside one another to provide a humble income for the peasant.

The land was very fertile. It had rich soil, evergreen forests, many fruit trees, whose fruits fell on the side of the road with little attention paid to them. Much grew and expanded in that agricultural area. Wondrously, the peasant was impoverished and had little money, but a few noblemen and landowners controlled most of the land and wealth. Most of the population leased land as a reward for the backbreaking labor. I began understanding that only once I matured, and only then did I understand why that country experienced very little independence in its history. Its neighbors always resented it, and it was subject to invasions, wars, and bloodshed, much of it due to its agricultural wealth and potential. As the people were divided and resentful, it could not be sustained for long. In that hateful and violent environment, Jewish communities existed in segregated clusters and always scapegoated.

Interpersonal contact and business ties between the Jews and the mass of peasants was operational if the city folk or the wealthy village intelligentsia did not sic them on the Jews. In times of peace, trade and business proceeded in a manner that benefited both sides. One bought, another sold and they shook hands giddily and playfully. The peasant loved his animal and had a difficult time parting with it. When the transaction has completed, a bottle of vodka was shared and they patted each other on the back as they said goodbye, the peasant with tears in his eyes and the Jew was happy. Those sights captured my heart, although I could not explain it to myself at the time.

[Page 108]

Agricultural products purchased from the peasants were a small portion of local consumption. Most of it was exported goods to Lublin or Warsaw. On the road, it passed through various middlemen, during market days and fairs in other towns and cities. Thus, the command of King David, "go and sustain one another" was fulfilled. The trading of such products was mostly done by Jews and included grains, chickens, eggs, etc. The Jewish merchant also supplied the peasant with work tools, cooking utensils, oils, spices, premade clothes, footwear, furniture, writing utensils, home improvement tools, and professional services. In most cases, the merchant was also the manufacturer.

The main professions among the Jews were tailors, seamstresses, cobblers, porters, locksmiths, and hatters. They manufactured their own products and sold them on market days. The only professions in which few Jews were employed were construction and blacksmith. I do not remember a Jewish blacksmith in my area who cast horseshoes, nor a construction worker building homes. I remember a great and admired Jew from a neighboring town who was specially invited to repair and reconstruct the crumbling synagogue roof which was a carefully detail. Baking was also the dominated by Jews, aside from one gentile named Polski who competed in quality of product and had a developed business sense. He conducted his business at his home near the church in order and style which was the envy of Jewish merchants. He was a wealthy gentile and conducted decent business also with part of the Jewish population. If I recall correctly, he was not involved in local politics.

132

After bicycle riding became popular, the two Yaffe brothers repaired and sold bikes. A third brother owned writing utensils kiosk near the church and was also the only one to deal in musical instruments. They were enthusiastic Zionists, and the progressive Zionist youth gathered around them. One could always find they had some "forbidden" book to read. To the youth, they symbolized progress.

There were 10 families who operated the Lublin line. Coaches departed twice weekly since the 50 km journey to Lublin was lengthy. It was a journey full of obstacles and adventure with stops at roadside inns. The road was entirely dirt. When it rained, you would drown in the mud, and the winter absorbed by snow. The passengers served mainly to help the horses pull the wagon or pushing it through puddles and mud. When the morning finally arrived, and the destination was reached, it was difficult to recognize the human form of passengers. The coachmen of the town were strong Jewish men who worked hard to provide for large families and their animals. They persisted in their work despite the difficulties. They provided well for their families and raised good children. One of them survived; a good Zionist, a veteran pioneer who currently teaches at a school in Nahariya. (Yaakov Avituv.)

[Page 109]

Additionally, there were community servants whose income depended on it, from the synagogue custodian to the town rabbi. There was a small group of wealthy businessmen who represented town, as their business extended far beyond the town. They maintained business ties with the wealthy noblemen of the region. Among them were forest merchants, land leasers, and some in finance, foreign currency, and loans.

Work and business life was very well developed relative to the size of the town and its population, thanks to the rich land and the talented and diligent human resources of local Jews. Although income cannot be said to have been plentiful, it was always available, and only a few required community–financed welfare. A significant portion was wealthy and lived a life of abundance. Those families searched for arranged marriages for their sons and daughters with established high–class families from other towns.

Quite often, a lack in cash was felt, as all trade was done on credit. The merchant and craftsman required working capital but it was not difficult to obtain funds, whether as a low interest rate or a *gemach* loan. Two banks operated; one for crafts and the other a general *gemach*, and financial matters were generally stable. It was only difficult when a zero–return expenditure was needed, like a dowry for a daughter or an unexpected expense, but there too things worked out. People worked hard, so they knew to value pennies and saved them when possible. The humble lifestyle and the low demand for luxuries enabled saving for a rainy day.

D. Lifestyle

Every adult resident worked to provide for himself or his family. When trading, he was almost always helped by his wife and older children. The family unit was whole in all aspects. On many occasions, families continued living together after a son or daughter married. The prime authority was in the hands of the patriarch.

The hardest working and most admired figure was the matriarch. She was the first to rise and the last to go to bed. She was usually the wonderful figure described in "Woman of Valor:" "The heart of her husband doth safely trust in her...She seeketh wool, and flax, and worketh willingly with her hands. She is like the merchants' ships; she bringeth her food from afar. She riseth also while it is yet night, and giveth meat to her household," etc. etc. It is the same song that the husband sang to his wife when he returned home on *Shabbat* night after he greeted Queen Sabbath. The Jewish mother in the town was like that. She rose literally while it was still night, kindled stoves and ovens, and prepared food and clothes. After that, the husband went to the morning prayers at the synagogue, or when not possible prayed at home wrapped in a tallit and wearing tefillin. Each at his own pace and words; one thanked his God for his blessing from the day before and asked for his blessings for the starting day. The boys and girls also woke early and prayed and helped the mother. Young girls went to the municipal school. Young boys ran to their various Torah teachers or to the *beth midrash* to study. Working youths started their day. Activity was everywhere and there was much work to be done.

[Page 110]

The household was based upon purchasing only base materials: wheat was bought and ground, or firewood chopped. There were also lumberjacks and water deliverymen who did so for a living. In the basement there were flour sacks for baking, and fruit and potatoes collected during the season. There were various pickled vegetables and baked goods prepared by the housewife. Strings of dried fruit hung in the attic. Under piles of straw, you could find softening pears. Straw was gathered during the season to feed the household livestock. Whoever had a cow supplied milk for himself, and you could find clay jugs full of milk for cream, cheese, and butter in almost every home. There were several chickens which laid eggs in the yard and fully or partially supplied the household's consumption of eggs. During the spring or summer, the children gathered eatable plants while the cattle grazed in natural grazing lands or while on a walk. In the nearby woods, wild mushrooms and strawberries were gathered. I can still taste those strawberries in cream. When the cabbage ripened in the fields, household members crushed and pickled it. When the barrel was full, it was covered with a heavy rock and left to freeze over winter. It was very sour cabbage served as a side with meat. When radishes were ripened they too were pickled and put aside for cooking on holidays or other days.

The matriarch ruled over all those activities. She planned, knew the seasons for each item, worked and supervised, and bore children without too many calculations or pampering. She raised them, educated them, cared for them, and put them on the right path. If the patriarch was the protector and provider, the mother was the supreme authority. Decisions were based on her will. If she became ill, God forbid, chaos ensued in household operation and the pattern of life was disrupted. But she was immune and rarely sick.

After morning prayers and breakfast, the businesses opened. The workshops were open all day and closed in the evening in time for prayers. The mother and her daughters worked at home doing laundry, cleaning, repairing clothes, cooking, and baking. The store owner was glued to his store, the craftsman to his workshop. The merchant left at dawn for the area villages to trade with the peasants or landowners.

After the workday was over, the men gathered once more at the synagogue to pray and study a page of Talmud or at the very least to listen to those teaching or studying. At that same time, the mother prepared dinner at home, which was the main meal of the day. After the meal ended, in the calm atmosphere of the neat home, everyone continued personal interests and personal hobbies. The progressive youth gathered in the various youth movements. The studying youth returned to the *beth midrash*.

The girls who did not take part in the youth movements, meaning most girls, met their friends at homes and spent time in discussion, reading a book or doing homework, etc. After a full day of hard work, the matriarch was busy with her hobbies which were the small chores like knitting, repairing socks, ironing, making raisin wine for shabbat and the like. At about 9–10 everyone went to bed for the night. Neighbors met in the summers at the front of the houses and in yards, and during winters by the fireplace. Things continued that way until the market day, when the noise increased, and life became a bit more energetic and active. Everyone worked for success that day. As stated, that day determined the joy levels for shabbat. When that day was over, the weekdays were essentially over too.

The preparations for shabbat began on Thursday evenings. "the vigilant are early in the performance of mitzvot," and it was also necessary to hurry, as everything was self–prepared and there was much work. At sundown, mother prepared the dough to rise and be ready to bake at night. That same evening, chickens were slaughtered, or meat purchased and prepared, Intestines were cleaned. Almost in every Jewish home a stew (cholent) was placed in the heated oven overnight. The atmosphere was active and uplifting. All women in the family participated in kneading the dough and baking cakes, challah, and cookies of all sorts. The scent of baking spread warmly and sweetly. Whole wheat or barley bread was baked to be used throughout the week. When the baking was completed, the meat–filled pots and cholent were placed in the oven which was sealed until *Shabbat*.

Friday was devoted mainly to completing and summing up the work of the entire week, purchasing missing goods, a thorough cleaning of the house and the yard, debt repayment, haircuts, etc. As noon approached, businesses began to close, and men made their way to the bathhouse and in the summer also to the river. A rushing movement could be felt on the streets. Fathers returned from the bathhouse with their sons, thoroughly clean, red–cheeked, and wet–haired with an aura of calmness and satisfaction. Everything was cleaned and polished that day; human, animal, home, and farm. One waited for shabbat like a groom waiting for his bride, and *Shabbat* is referred to as a queen for a reason. You felt that the preparation was being made for a large and very important matter, the most important in the lives of each community member. *Shabbat* was a day of release and rest for all. That day, the Jew departed from earthly matters and ascended to holy purity.

136

As I look back on those days, I understand the meaning of the "extra soul" which was added to a person on that holy day, an unfortunately meaningless term in our modern world today.

One cannot understand it ever if he did not witness shabbat. Family members walked together on late Friday afternoon to the synagogue, wearing their best clothes. They shined with a light of happiness, prayed, and sang. They returned home joyously and greeted shabbat in their illuminated home with the whole family and often a guest at the set table.

[Page 112]

Hymns echoed from every home in sweet voices. He who did not feel the elevation of the spirit and the calmness of the soul will never comprehend it.

I am a non–practicing Jew today. However, I believe that shabbat and holidays observed happily and willfully by most diaspora Jews motivated them in foreign lands. It encouraged them to be, and to develop an independent life within the dark exile rife with blind hatred for a period of roughly 2000 years. It lasted until the cruelest destroyer in human history rose and erased it all within a few years in an ocean of blood and indescribable suffering.

E. The Jewish Institutions

Community matters were governed by an elected or appointed council in which all classes were represented. The tone was always determined by the wealthy and respectable. The council collected taxes and covered the expenses of the community servants and supplied the remaining needs of the community. It also represented the community when dealing with the municipality, maintained a *gemach* fund, and was involved in local politics.

I recall conflicts between various sects and the town rabbi who was always a factor in those disputes. The "middle class" belonged mostly to the sect of the rabbi's father. For some reason, the other Hassidim and the studious, the town's "elite," did not value the rabbi and his son and bothered them often. They did not need their assistance, not in questions nor advice. Most were very learned and were proud of it. At one point, as I recall, they brought a second competing rabbi. The partisanship made the town livelier. All residents participated in that fight, and passionately debated and argued between services.

The central institution was the *beth midrash*. It served not only for prayer and Torah study, but also the main cultural and social gathering place of the community on most days of the year. One met friends there, listened to lectures, and studied Torah and wisdom. Community matters or other important matters were debated. There, one found the enlightening atmosphere, where one was together and felt a sense of belonging to the community and their experiences, found solace from the troubles at home, spirits were elevated, and one felt secure within the community. All joys and sorrows were concentrated in that holy abode.

Near the *beth midrash* was the other synagogue which was partially destroyed in WWI. It was a large, tall brick building with tall columns supporting a giant dome. In my mind's eye I pictured the destruction of that building to the destruction of the Temple. The building was abandoned and broken. When we were young, we feared ghosts and demons, so we did not enter. I do not know why the community leaders left that magnificent building in its abandonment all those years. It is likely the community fund could not budget for reconstruction.

I remember that before I left home, a Jewish craftsman and his son from a neighboring town constructed a very large wooden dome in the synagogue yard. They were considered excellent wood artist and were in high demand for tasks of that nature. I forgot their names, but I do recall the lean and noble face and the pointy beard and sidelocks of the artist. He was very religious, and I perceived him as a remnant of the Levite tribe. He worked on measuring and assembling arks since dawn, and in the evening, the parts of the dome seemed like one piece.

[Page 113]

Around those two buildings was a gated yard where the youth spent all day. In that same yard, wedding ceremonies took place, and from there the funeral processions began. It was also where the faithful danced on Simchat Torah and where they mourned the destruction of the Temple on Av 9.

The second center was the *rebbe's* estate. It was crowded only on shabbat and holidays or when the *rebbe* visited town. There was the spacious residence of the town rabbi, a synagogue, a large yard, and the *rebbe's* followers visited it often.

In addition, there were also the small Hasidic synagogues the "*shtiblech*" of the Ger sect, the Trisk sect, and more.

The progressive youth had the various youth movements; *HaKhalutz*, *HaShomer HaTzair*, *Betar*, General Zionists, *Hapoel Hamizrachi*, and the Bund.

Time was abundant. The day was devoted to work and trade and the night to social gatherings or Torah study. The residents of town did not travel often, and if someone left town it was a short trip to arrange a marriage or on business. Wondrously, boredom was not felt and even in such a limited lifestyle one found an interest in what existed and in one another.

F. Cultural Life

People thirsted for knowledge. The majority studied Torah as a reward of its own. Study also included much Hasidic literature, Zohar and kabbalah. There was a large and often used library of Torah literature and at the *beth midrash*. Mishna, Talmud, and *poskim*, were the most widely used. Maimonides' philosophy was also studied and many traveled with his *Guide for the Perplexed* as if it was their own. One could find young devoted scholars discussing the creation of the universe and its purpose. The bible was scarcely studied, and many did not have proficient knowledge of it. The knowledge they had of the bible was from the study of Talmud or the recitation on shabbat and holiday. Folks studied a daily page of Talmud or a chapter of Mishnah.

The progressive youth secretly read "banned books" and expanded their knowledge of Zionist or socialist literature. Marx's *Capital* was covertly passed from person to person and people studied it and were well versed. The primary newspapers arrived in town almost daily and were read cover to cover. The Zionists read *Haynt*, the progressive merchants read Moment etc. each with his own paper. The *Nasz Przegląd* was also delivered and people were aware of world evets. Of course, the town did not have a theater, movie theater, radio, and the like. All knowledge was drawn from newspapers, books, lecturers, or a guest from out–of-town who stopped for the night. The youth movement had amateur theater companies, and during festive events produced various plays for their members from Jewish or biblical folklore. During Purim, some youth movements or individuals would wear a well–designed costume and portray biblical heroes accompanied by music, song, and dance. For instance, The Sale of Joseph, which brought much joy to all. In general, holidays were celebrated with much festivity, with special decorations, unique dress, and special foods, all fitted for the holiday and one's traditions. During those days, it was hard to tell the rich from the poor. Everyone had a happy royal face. Every festive event like a circumcision, bar mitzvah, or wedding brought joy to the whole town. Everyone was like one family. The weddings especially were celebrated joyfully, and every wedding had a jester and a local Jewish band who played and joked until they ran out of steam.

[Page 114]

G. Figures

Every resident without exception was a unique figure. There were many characters, and a talented artist could find much material to draw, sculpt, or write. They were rare and dear figures. But where is the memory and talent that could illustrate it? Not one figure was absent from the town. It even had its own *meshumad*, named Eliezer. He was a convert for spite. He drew special satisfaction from standing in the synagogue yard and biting into a *treif* sausage in front of everybody. He was disparaged and isolated. It was told he returned like that from the military after WWI ended. But he was an anomaly. The favorite figures were among the scholars, community activists, craftsmen, the coachmen, the public servants, in short from all types and classes. The figures still exchanged in my mind are the two Shochetim of the town, a lovely pair. Two short-statured elderly men, with an appearance evoking honor who were respected by all. They were also the circumcisers, and never departed from Torah study. One of them, R' Isaac of blessed memory, was a courteous man of the Hillel worldview, with a musical sense, and an addition to his official roles also led services on shabbat and holidays. He had a pleasant and awakening voice. He knew many hymns and songs, some of which he composed. At his side, was a mixed choir of old and young and when they led services prayer was divine and enjoyable. All his grandchildren were in his choir, although they were progressive and dabbled in Zionism. One of them is our friend Moshe Gutvirtz who is here with us,

The second, R' Yitzchak, was of a stark expression of the Shamai worldview. I do not recall his children. He always leaned over large Talmud volumes and studied day and night. He was our neighbor and when I had to pass by his house I was careful to not make any noise, fearing rebuke. In my mind, he and his wife were a pair of doves who were always with each other; he studied and she served him readily and devotedly. The two *shochtim* were community servants and Torah scholars. Nobody knows where they came from and how they were rooted in town. They were cherished figures who were like two pearls in a Torah crown.

The chief town rabbi was Rabbi Mordechai Veisbrot, son of the Turobin *Rebbe*. That is what the *Rebbe* was called even though he resided in Kraśnik. He was a man of the people and his disciples were the common folks in town and neighboring towns. He had a majestic appearance and the pronounced figure of a *rebbe*, as I remember. He often visited town and stayed with his son. There, he led his table in the traditional Hasidic manner. As a boy, I was very impressed by him. I anxiously observed the Hasidim who gathered en masse.

[Page 115]

Way of Life

Yaakov Avituv

Translated by Meir Bulman

Our town looked like hundreds of other towns in Poland. I did not know them all, but those I visited resembled our own. The large square was surrounded by hundreds of homes pressed together with their entrances facing the market square and mostly used as stores. To the question "how can there be so many stores? Who were the customers?" the answer would be the area peasants who came to buy their products in town. That was the way by us and in the nearby towns Goraj, Frampol, Janów, Modliborzyce and all the towns I visited in my youth,

Market Day

One day a week, regional peasants from villages near and far gathered to sell their produce and buy from the Jews. Most trading was of products manufactured by the Jews like shoes, clothes, ropes, saddles, sewing items and products brought by coachmen from Lublin such as kerosene, salt, herring, sugar, etc. There were Jews who owned pubs and on market days peasants gathered in their houses to drink alcohol between purchase and sale. That was the world of Christians and Jews who peacefully coexisted and respected one another, for instance, on shabbat, no peasant came to try to buy something. Similarly, Jews did not travel to the villages to buy anything on Sunday. Many years passed like that, since the day the first Jew settled in the town.

by his door with notes in their hands written by an assistant and how they left his room glowing with hope and happiness. His son, the town rabbi, had a majestic appearance, but he was likely not the most studious. Because of that deficiency, the scholarly Hasidic "nobility" in the town plotted against him at every turn. That was expressed by their appointment of competing rabbinate, and a persistent dispute with him and his followers. I was always revolted by that atmosphere. However, truth is it was an inseparable part of community life which activated and sparked spirit and absent that, boredom would likely wreak havoc.

Every figure could be described but the obstacle ridden memory and time left their marks. Etched I my memory are those from the Hasidic sects and the *beth midrash* attendees of which I was one. There were cherished Jews and picturesque figures, the bedrocks of the community. Mainly the common working folks among the coachmen, bakers, tailors, cobblers etc. and the various merchants. Their images appear before me in their glory, but unfortunately, I cannot describe them on paper.

All I have left to say is: We mourn those who were lost but not forgotten.

[Page 116]

The elders said that the town existed from the time of Casimir the Great. The chronicles of the town were never recorded. And if someone handwrote it, I have not read it. Our town was different from others in that at the center of town there was a large cross which was visible almost from every Jewish home, to remind and remember the nation of the land and who really controlled it. A few times a year, the Christians had processions near that cross, and during that procession from the church to the cross it was dangerous for a Jewish child to be seen in the street or near the cross.

At the southwest corner of the square there was the wall of the Great Synagogue destroyed during WWI. I heard many conversations by respectable people about the reconstructing of the synagogue who said, "If we will be fortunate to rebuild the synagogue, the messiah will arrive." Of course, we children awaited the moment the synagogue will be built. One evening, between the afternoon and evening prayers, R' Yisroel Mordechai ascended the stage at the *beth midrash* and said, "My Jewish brethren, it has been many years that our synagogue, the gem of our community, is standing in ruins as we sit at home and enjoy life. Why are we not ashamed? May each contribute according to his ability so we can begin construction." R' Yisroel Mordechai's words were well–received by the community, many contributions were made, and a date was set to begin construction. We children were very happy. It was no small matter; A) we will be rid of the ghosts and demons who float around the synagogue at night in the synagogue area and B) They will most likely remove the stretcher used to carry the dead to the cemetery from the synagogue yard, and the taharah board will be gone from the destroyed synagogue's gate. And most of all, the messiah will arrive once construction was completed. Five years later, the construction was completed but we were not fortunate to see the messiah, nor were the burial society's utensils removed from the synagogue yard.

And we, who until then feared to pass by the synagogue, still feared when its repair was completed. Not only were we not redeemed, but the state of the Jews worsened. Hate crimes against Jews increased. The National Polish Party declared an economic boycott. Their slogan was "Do not buy from the Jew!" The very fact that a public institution publicly declared a boycott on Jews was enough to awaken hatred within the Polish people and consequences followed.

There were occasional acts of murder. Once, R' Fischel Kopf from a neighboring village was attacked and murdered. I still remember it as if it was today. It was between the afternoon and evening prayers. R' Fischel's sons began bitterly weeping, and the rumor of Fischel's murder quickly spread in the synagogue, which was packed. Fischel's sons recited kaddish as they choked back tears, among them his little son who stood on a chair and recited kaddish. I cried too, as did many in the audience. Many years passed, and those bad omens were forgotten, and life returned to its normal course. Jews were also involved in social and economic life of the area to come to the correct conclusions.

Yet, occasionally, Jews began about emigrating to the Holy Land. However, most talk was not translated into deeds, aside from a few who left town and made aliya and are currently with us in Israel. That awakening and the emigration of a few were also forgotten by most. Only the youth remembered, and the prayers we recited each day did not remain as words alone, as we began to comprehend the meaning of *galut*, although the non–Jewish locals tolerated the Jews aside from the occasional uprising.

[Page 117]

The Youth and the Aging

The awakening which began a few years following the Balfour Declaration took root in the hearts of the youth which began to organize around the *Tarbut* Library. The leaders of the youth were Yitzchak Feder, Yaakov Leib Yaffe, and Shmuel Abba Gitwortz.

Those who got involved in public Zionist work had a tough decision-making process. The aging, who were usually very devout, were not neutral and almost decreed that nobody rent a room to the criminals who were forcing the End of Days and unifying in Zionist groups. I do not know who initiated that, but even the rabbi, Mordechai Veisbrod of blesses memory, who was a pious Jew and tended to be more compromising, joined the detractors. Wealthy homeowners probably initiated the leasing boycott against *Tarbut* Union. After exhausting negotiations, Azriel the carpenter agreed to lease his workshop to us which became a meeting place for the youth at night. The winter was rough, income decreased, and many began blaming the *Tarbut* youth of incurring the wrath of God, and 'who knows what else the Zionist criminals will bring to town.' There were Jews who decided to eliminate the library using many tactics. One of those tactics was forbidding their sons and daughters to attend meetings.

Many tragedies affected almost every family, and the parents fully believed the library was leading to apostasy, God forbid. The first winter with the *Tarbut* library passed and spring arrived. As opposed to the rest of the world, in which spring symbolized the renewal of nature and man, in our town, early spring was when large swamps began to form. They were frozen all winter and as the snow melted the dirt began to thaw as well and the stench rose. Due to the swamps, the days before Passover saw the peasants absent from the town and the shop owners idled in front of their shops, yawning in boredom.

R' Yerachmiel Bronshpigel passed his hands through his beard and said, "Gentlemen! we see clearly that all the troubles have come upon us because of the criminals and the library. It disseminates those books among our sons and daughters, who day and night read what is forbidden and improper. Why

144

are we still silent? We need to begin a holy war. Otherwise, this anarchy will rule us and who knows what will be of our sons and daughters?" R' Yerachmiel words made a strong impression on the audience. Some attendees, mainly the Ger Hasidim, gathered in corners to contemplate. The craftsmen gathered at the tables by the southern wall of the synagogue, not far from the door and listened to R' Yerachmiel. R' Shalom Fleischer then addressed the Jews and said, "Tell me, people, why does R' Yerachmiel care that the youth is reading books? Where in the Torah does it say that it is forbidden to read books that our wisemen wrote in our time and ancient times?" R' Barak the tailor, who was a good man whom I think never once in his life forgot to pray and recite psalms, said, "let us ask someone who knows Torah, and learn." They both approached R' Mordechai the teacher who was known as a great scholar. R' Mordechai contemplated and said, "it is written, 'You shall not do as they do' and it is also written, 'you shall meditate therein day and night.' If one must mediate on Torah day and night then there is no time left to study other books." By the facial expressions of R' Shalom and R' Barak I understood the answer they received was not to their liking. They returned to their table.

[Page 118]

That took place between afternoon and evening prayers on the week of Purim. The members of *Tarbut*, led by Yitzchak Feder, prepared to present the play "Joseph in Egypt." The synagogue swarmed like a beehive. Everybody talked about the event scheduled for Passover. The members of *Tarbut* were also at the synagogue, but the Ger Hasidim were not bold enough to approach and start a debate, as they knew they would be defeated. They therefore limited their activity to talking and shouting about the fire burning in town which may burn it all down. The leader of the incited speakers was, as stated, R' Yerachmiel of blessed memory. He was followed by other notables like R' Shmelki Drumler of blessed memory. He was a well-natured Jew, studious and a skilled businessman whose entire presence, even his appearance, demanded respect. His wide face constantly bore a smile, his long silvering beard was long, and he wore a tall Jewish hat and an Atals velvet kapota. He never fought anybody. After he heard R' Yerachmiel, he stood for a second and contemplated, as if to say, "calm down, Yerachmiel, anger is idolatry. What needs to be done must be done sensibly and mercifully. 'Even when Jews sin, they are still Jews.'" R' Shmelki spoke as he saw spirits were heating around the "Treater" [theater?]

The youths gathered to the west of the synagogue stage not far from the craftsmen who cast doubt that Yerachmiel's war on the youth was indeed a holy one or whether a hidden political motive was at play. Hidden political agendas were frowned upon based on precedent; in our town there we the *shtiblech*, small synagogues of the Ger, Trisk, and Kraśnik hasidim. A Jewish man appeared in town and convened for a long time with the Ger Hasidim. The public then learned that the man was an envoy from *Agudath Yisrael*, and all the *shtiblech* became branches of *Aguddah*, almost against the will of most of parishioners. Thus, the common Jews were suspicious and hated politics and served as the neutral backbone of *Tarbut* members in town. Those common men smiled covertly as they saw others fuming over the Passover play. R' Melech the carpenter expressed approval of the youth and said, "they are great men. My wife and I will be the first to go to the treater." Of course, many common folks awaited the play which they have heard of since it was also produced in large Polish cities.

[Page 119]

The sun warmed the muddy dirt. Gradually, dry paths that could be skipped were seen. Occasionally, peasants were seen coming to town to buy goods and Jews began baking matzah. There was a group of Jews by the well drawing water for *shmurah matzah*. R' Shmelki Drumler of blessed memory stood among the Jews, drew water and played with the edges of his girdle, deep in thought. R' Shmelki always thought and had what to think about. His household was not whole, as his youngest daughter, Chantche, was an active member in *Tarbut*, and not just that, she was a friend of the committee member, Yitzchak Feder, an energetic man of action. The rumor in town was that he swore an oath that during his lifetime his daughter will not marry Yitzchak, who was considered in town to be a heretic and the disseminator of Zionism and its culture. R' Shmelki's contemplation stopped as Jews debated who should bake the matzah; R' Leibish ben Baruch or someone else. By the way, the debate interested me as well, as R' Leibish ben Baruch Cooper was my uncle and sometimes I helped in placing the matzah in the oven before Passover, not the *shmurah matzah* but the plain kind. The large business of *shmurah* was reserved to the Hasidim.

As sated, shortly before Passover, the mud began to dry but in some alleys the mud lasted long after Passover. If it was a cold year, even two weeks after Passover. The muddiest was the butchers' street on the route to the flour mill.

There, it was good if one party to the conversation lived opposite the other and could be heard clearly from a distance. If the conversation partner lived farther away, for instance from R' Shalom Fleischer to R' Henik Fleischer, 200 meters, the voices of those conversing could be heard from a great distance. Conversations were mostly about livelihood, taxes and the like, and at times abut arranging marriages. There were many marriages to arrange as they had many descendants, who were strong as bulls. Most married according to their class and profession. If there was no suitable partner within town, a groom was brought from a neighboring town. There were occasions in which Jews wanted to marry people of a different profession, in which case the father promised a substantial dowry and fund the couple for a few years until the young man was able to have his own business and make a living on his own.

In summer, the *beth midrash* men studied Talmud, be it independently or with a study partner. If someone studied and could not grasp the concepts or had a difficult time, he would ask R' Chaim Yosef or R' Alter Scherf. R' Chaim Yosef, who sat on the eastern side of the synagogue near the ark, was asked complex difficult questions, and R' alter was asked simpler questions. We honored R' Alter very much as it was rumored he was a Tzadik Nistar. And where did we get that from? It was told in the *beth midrash* that when he was young, he served several years in the Russian army and in all those years kept kosher. Even after being so cautious, he was still not certain that he adhered to kashrut, so he avoided many foods and lived on salted bread and water. Lest you think other food was unavailable to him, his wife Zippah was a woman of valor and a great baker. Almost all the folks studying at the *beth midrash* bought her products, and R' Alter's home was close to the *beth midrash*. We were also amazed that we never saw R' Alter in casual conversation. Instead he would sit and study or pray in his corner. The Kraśnik *Rebbe* took him under his wing, and during the third meal of *Shabbat* honored him with the hymn of *El Mistater*.

[Page 120]

R' Alter had a wonderful voice, his thin beard would shake as he sang, his eyes shut. The crowd was long silent and R' Alter continued as if he was floating in the heaves. Who knows, maybe he was. One day, a rumor spread that he had passed. Everyone wondered, "How? He was not even sick."

There were many Jewish houses on the street near the synagogue. As the children matured and needed housing, the lots had not expanded and the town remined as was. Instead, another apartment was built in the yard, until the overcrowding was even greater and no passages remained, only narrow paths between each father's house. Such a home was that of R' Hirsh Leib Golberg of blessed memory whose property was separated from R' Pini Gewirtz on one side and R' Berish Gewertz's house on the other only by a narrow path. All three homes had balconies and shops facing the market square. The residents of those houses were, of course, the homeowner's household members.

R' Berish Gewertz had large family. I think he had three daughters and five sons. He was a God–fearing man, a wonderful singer, and a scholar. The town residents respected him very much due to his great traits. When he was bankrupted and had no income, community members sent their children to him to learn Torah and the Way of the World and compensated him well. That income was still not enough to support his family. God had bestowed upon him a woman of valor and she took responsibility for a large portion of the income. Thus, they made a living and married their daughters to good men of quality lineage and savvy businessmen. In that manner, for instance, the firstborn daughter married Leibel Gewirtz, R' Pini Gewirtz's granddaughter. They were probably related, since they had the same last name. R' Pini was a fabric salesman, a silent type, and he earned a reputation through town as a stingy man [although] he invited impoverished people to meals every shabbat, and those who entered his house hungry came out satisfied. The Goldberg house, as stated, was owned by R' Hirsh Leib. He was a serious man, tall, with a long grey beard. I have never seen him laugh, and even when my father of blessed memory would tell jokes, R' Hirsh hid a smile under his beard, as if to say, "we are in Exile and happiness is lost here." His son Moshe "Toto" followed his exact path.

He was the son–in–law of R' Yitzchak the baker. His father–in–law was also tall and thin. R' Yitzchak always looked like he was just immersed in a mikveh, a sort of holy aura expressed on his face. He was also silent by nature. From the cellar of his bakery there was a constant chirping of crickcts. It always seemed like R' Yitzchak maintained some big secret. Once, on *Tisha'a B'av* as we walked to the cemetery, we saw him waling quickly ahead of us, so that we had to run. And why did we follow him? To discover his secret, as it was said that R' Yitzchak disclosed his secret by the large tombstone of the mysterious man who was said to have renewed the Turobin community. Indeed, R' Yitzchak walked directly to the tombstone above the

148

holy grave and talked as if to himself. He asked the deceased to be a messenger to God, to send a worthy spouse from his youngest daughter. We thought, "is this the secret he keeps? Is this the reason he never smiles, and is it worth it?" Yes, it was worth it, as his two sons–in–law Moshe ben Hirsh Leib and Shlomo Greenberg, were good, God–fearing men. R' Shlomo was a great scholar, and adhered to customs of Ger Hasidim but was uninvolved in politics. When the Zionist pioneers came to his son–in–law to ask for work, he proposed he let us chop wood for the bakery.

[Page 121]

His recommendation did not always help the pioneers, who heeded the teachings of A. D. Gordon to value and love labor. They were unemployed for long periods of time and the chapter fund was empty. When someone wanted to make aliya, it was postponed because of the 200 zloty "*Hakhalutz*" headquarters required. It is possible that many of those who perished in the Holocaust would make aliya had the rich men of the time contributed support the *olim*. Instead, young men and women trained for several years but were unsuccessful in their aliya efforts. That in turn diminished the will of others to enter training. Some also left training as pessimism overtook most of the members *hakhshara* communities. The entrance to the Land was sealed, and illegal immigration efforts were yet to start, but we will discuss that at a different opportunity. We will return to describe our beloved brothers and sisters who perished in the awful Holocaust.

Shabbat and Holidays

If during the week the reality of the town was simple and concerned with income, it was unrecognizable on shabbat. The narrow streets were cleaned almost in front of every house. The aroma of cooking fish filled the air. From the early afternoon hours, the spirit of *Shabbat* was felt in the town. The town residents begin to prepare to greet *Shabbat*.

Jews and their sons hurried to the bathhouse at the east of town and returned with their faces blushing and beards and sidelocks still dripping with water. The bathhouse of Turobin is worth describing, as it was the only one in town and attended mostly by Jews. There were many reasons for that; the gentiles likely did not wat to mix with Jews, and Moshe "Bdr" was very adamant that everyone payed the entrance fee. Moshe instructed those entering to take a broom [?] and a wooden bucket, as without those utensils there was not much to do inside. My father would say the warm vapor and the broom were an effective method against illness and the higher the bench the better, and if one followed those rules his health was almost guaranteed. The Hasidim would come on *Shabbat* morning to immerse in cold water in the morning before prayers. Generations continued their ancestors' tradition in that manner.

As stated, during the weekdays, preoccupation was with livelihood matters which were surrendered to, but on shabbat all carried their Judaism proudly. Families marched to the synagogues with their heads held high. Almost all Jews passed through the square which was surrounded by the village homes, passing through to the previously ruined, now renovated grand synagogue. For instance, one could see rabbi Yeshayahu Shternfeld calmly walking on his long legs.

[Page 122]

R' Yeshayahu was a tall, Jewish man with a majestic appearance. It was rumored that when he painted his house he did not even climb on a chair to reach the ceiling. His wife, Pearly, would walk by his side, as did R' Moshe Shternfeld and R' Moshe Eisenberg from Yanov, grandson of the R' Isaac, a shochet and cantor who married R' Yeshayahu's daughter. From the northern corner of the alley, near the house of R' Reuvli the ropemaker, appeared his uncle R' Chanan Gutvilik, who was also called R' Chanan Jordan, since he was a very tall man and could cross the Jordan in one step. He and his son Yaakov and Chaim Hersh would walk slowly and calmly, as the tassels of their *tallitot* peaked under the long kapotas, fearing the eruv was torn in an unknown spot, making carrying the tallit on shabbat forbidden. R' Chanan was not the only one who did not carry his shawl, and most who were devout did so. And who in town was not devout? The closer to the synagogue, the more men were seen walking wearing velvet or silk kapotas. Some wore plain shabbat hats and others a velvet "*samet*" hat made by R' Leib the hatter. Leib did not have children and donated most of his fortune to writing a new Torah scroll, completed it, and majestically led it to the synagogue. The Jews who owned a velvet hat wore their hats atop the yarmulke which was also made of velvet and formed a double decker hat!

The Ger *shtibel* was hosted by my uncle R' Ozer Kleiner. He too was tall, wide–shouldered, and handsome. To this day, when I read the passage "from his shoulders and upward he was higher than any of the people," I remember

R' Ozer Kleiner. He was a kind man who was never angry, just pinched cheeks if he caught any of the children. The Ger *hassidim* prayed enthusiastically. They had full faith in their *rebbe* and traveled hundreds of kilometers to be in his presence for a few days. The prayers were led by R' Yisrael Mordechai's sons. God gifted all six sons and their father with wonderful voices. The Ger Hassidim's devotion to God and their pure and strong faith shined upon their families and their surroundings. Even those among them who were impoverished were happy. On Saturday night, the Hassidim held the *Melaveh Malka* meal. The food served was simple; onion seasoned herring and potatoes with radishes, and some liquor for *l'chaim* and happiness to accompany Queen *Shabbat* on her departure. During the meal, one of Ozer's sons gave a short Torah speech. Everyone was intoxicated by the sweet atmosphere and the memories of the *Shabbat* that had just departed. Eventually, someone began singing and everyone danced an enthusiastic Hasidic dance. Their extra souls still beat within them, as they were all dressed in their shabbat clothes and the weekday was yet to overtake them. Those Jews had a tough time parting with their extra soul, and they conformed to reality only because they had no choice.

[Page 123]

No less than them were the Trisk Hassidim whose *shtibel* was hosted by R' Yehoshua Yennis Rosenfeld of blessed memory, an honest Jewish man who was faithful to his rabbi, Nachumtche of Trisk. R' Yehoshua's house also served as R' Nachumtche's lodging when he visited town. When he visited his disciples in Turobin, he met with his flock at R' Yehoshua's house, which was a large home with many rooms. Although his daughters Leah'tche and Sheindle were very friendly and were members of our youth group for a while, I still was not able to visit every room in that house. Not the whole house was R' Yehoshua Yennis' residence. As said, one room was he *shtibel* for Trisk Hasidim. It was a long room, on its eastern side was the ark, and in the middle of the room was a sloped table where the Torah was recited on Monday, Thursday, and *Shabbat*.

[Page 125]

The *Beth Midrash* in Turobin

Yaakov Avituv

Translated by Meir Bulman

It was wintertime, and it was snowing. The windows of the *beth midrash* were covered in a thick layer of frost. People were arriving for afternoon and evening prayers. The synagogue slowly filled with Jewish men, wearing heavy, long kapotas and fur hats which blended with their *payot* and beards. Among those Jews were various men: craftsmen, merchants, and unemployed men, who nobody took any interest in knowing what they lived from and how they fed their families. Yet, they somehow lived, and raised generations, and if not for the axe of the murderer raised upon them they would be alive today, they and their descendants.

Morning and evening, every Jew came to the synagogue to pray, and if one did not appear, everyone thought he was ill or absent from home, traveling to some fair. There were Jews whose scarce income relied on the synagogue. They sold cigarettes, frozen apples, and seeds. There was usually a break between afternoon and evening prayers, which was used to converse on various matters like arranging marriages, sometimes a lecture. Sometimes discussions centered on the quality of the shochet, the rabbi, the Ger Hasidim or Kraśnik–Turobin, Turiysk, etc.

We the children would crowd by the fireplace and discuss our own matters. There were children among us who were nearly starving, and they always steered the conversation to food. One evening, we were on a break from R' Mordechai the melamed. He usually occupied one of the long tables at the south–west corner of the synagogue. We usually sat there from the morning until 8 pm or 9 pm, but on Hanukkah or Nittel, meaning Christmas, we had a vacation. That evening, I passed through the synagogue and listened to peoples' conversations or to conversations of boys who were not in R' Mordechai's class. I heard a conversation which grabbed my attention, which I remembered just this morning. It left an impression and it probably resonated with me, as I still remember it.

The topic was a young man named Yechiel ben Eliyahu Akerman, who traveled through villages with his merchandise and made a difficult and deficient living. Yechiel was a diligent and smart boy. His family was poor and did not have a home. So, his large family lived in rented apartments, sometimes damp, like that of Dan Goldstein. Then, Yechiel became ill and was hospitalized in another town for a long time. When he returned, he had a limp in one foot and was supported by a cane. Yechiel asked his friend, "Tanchum, have you eaten dinner yet?" "not yet," replied Tanchum ben Yoske Frumer. "And what's for dinner?" asked Yechiel. "I think we're having buckwheat and meat," answered Tanchum. "Wow, how much I would want to eat that beloved dish, but what can I do? my father is elderly and ill and cannot travel to villages and earn a bit." "We also have nothing to eat at home," said Peretz, the Fogel widow's son.

———

[Page 126]

In our Bet Midrash

By Mordechai Yoskovitz (Hopen)

Translated by Meir Bulman

Synagogues in Polish Exile served as spotlights and marked havens in the dessert where a fortified wall was built to guard against assimilation and intermarriage. Our *beth midrash* also contributed much, and many of us drew our saving light from it. I will divulge just a bit, and will devote this holy hour to draw from memory and add a brick to this important structure, the book we are publishing. This is a big day for us. Today, we build a monument and light an everlasting candle to memorialize our town which is no more.

[Page 160]

In the book of Ezekiel (11) the prophet says, "will I be to them as a little sanctuary in the countries where they shall come." "Said Rabbi Yitzchak, those are the synagogues in Babylon (*Megilah* 29a). From this we learn that a *beth midrash* in *Galut* is considered a temple, and with the destruction of those in Poland it is like the destruction of the Third Temple. I will attempt to describe the general attributes which signified the atmosphere in our *beth midrash*, since the memory is at risk of being lost.

The *beth midrash* had many faces. Let us picture the synagogue on weekdays and 1st of the Hebrew Month, shabbat, holidays, Rosh Hashanah and Yom Kippur, *Simchat Torah*, Chanukah, and Purim. The added spirit of Shabbat and its holiness, the awakening repentance on Rosh Hashanah and Yom Kippur, the happiness on *Simchat Torah*. The courage of the Maccabi beat in our hearts on Hanukkah when the candles were lit by R' Mottel the *shamash*. On Purim, we exchanged *Mishloach Manot*, the recitation of the book of Esther by members of each household, a special inspiration in those days of the (damned) Polish exile. Let us dwell for a moment and consider our feelings during prayers on the Days of Awe, when R' Isaac the shochet served as cantor with the choir headed by R Yechezkel and his booming baritone. R' Isaac the music lover sang the tunes of the Apta *Rebbe* in his pleasant voice and added his own flavor. When we heard him recite "I... of poor...deeds," the prayer of *U'netaneh Tokef*, and the Kaddish of Musaf we were shaken and gripped by awe. The inspiration we have gotten then remains in our hearts (even when distracted.)

Let us turn to Shabbat. On early Shabbat morning, the *beth midrash* was full of craftsmen and working men. Among them were lovers of Psalms who recited them joyfully. They were awakened by R' Alter's call echoing through the streets of town. R' Alter was well-known to fulfill that mitzvah, which he did to the end of his days. Some from the class of the Psalm reciters. concluded with verses commemorating the sacrifices in the Temple.

[Page 127]

By the tables, one could see some standalone Torah scholars immersed in Torah or *poskim*. As I said, I will describe the Torah–center aspect of the synagogue. I see the scholars before me, traveling like on a conveyor belt.

I see R' Shmelki, a town leader. He was an honest, pleasant man, who led the study of the daily Talmud page. His voice filled the house as he learned and taught. Also, R' Yisrael Mordechai led his clearly explained Mishna class, a role which he was very pleased by and maintained for many years.

At the center, were young men supported by their fathers–in–law, filling the space with Talmud, *poskim*, *Shulchan Aruch*. Sometimes, they raised a glass to celebrate the completed study of the entire Talmud. The completion of writing a Torah scroll was also celebrated with a procession to one of the synagogues.

The *beth midrash* left the strongest impression on me. I recall winter nights at the synagogue. It was the peak of the intensity of studiousness [?] in the hearts of many in attendance. After evening services, seats were taken on

154

first–come–first–serve basis. Book in hand, all began studying, each with his own tone and tune. Together they raised the souls of the ancient sages. They raised a longing for Zion in their voices, as the vision of resurrection and the hope for Redemption was in many of their hearts and filled their soul and spirit. All in quietly, within the *beth midrash.*

The golden age of Torah in Turobin began in the second half of the 19ᵗʰ century. Two wealthy men, R' Yechiel and R' Shechna, were ordained as rabbis. They were accepted as leaders by residents and led social life in the town. If a dispute arose, both parties came before them and they ruled, and everyone accepted the verdict, whether in one's favor or not. R' Yechiel was nicknamed "House of Shamai" since he was strict, and R' Shechna was dubbed "House of Hillel" since he was lenient. They both faithfully served in their roles, expecting no reward. R' Yechiel published a book, *Leket Marhryt* (*Collected Works of Rabbi Yechiel Tuvia*) a collection of in depth exploration of Talmudic interpretations. He was well–known as a man of Torah, and had a gifted son, Rabbi Leibish, who was appointed as rabbi of Lodz. R' Shechna was also very knowledgeable on Torah, and his son Yaakov Yehoshua was gentle, wise, and appointed a rabbi in the Lublin rabbinate. Rabbi Simcha of Zolkiewka and the Rabbi of Turobin were among the attendees [of the bet midrash]. Many other ordained rabbis also have originated in our synagogue.

Our *beth midrash* was also home to figures worshipping in Torah and prayer, fasting, and self–imposed austerity. I will name three. The first was R' Shaul (Mendel Shiae's), a Ger Hassid whose faith was his guiding force which he expressed through fasting and austerity. Of the same age, was R' Alter (Moshe Chaim Shmuel's), a Hassid from Uman (Russia). His wife was a professional baker. One fateful day, R' Alter parted with secular life and decided to spend all of his time at the bet midrash. He also imposed on himself never to enjoy his wife's products, although she urged him to eat and drink. R' Alter made a living by fixing kitchen utensils. He worked one day a week and lived off that for the rest of the week. He spent his time praying, studying, and austerity. In his final years, he fasted daily from dawn to the emergence of three stars. He did so until his body was weakened, and he was bound to his death bed. He paid for medicine brought to him. His humble and devoted wife could not persuade him to use her money. She quickly summoned his friends, led by R' Shmelke, and they attempted to persuade him but to no avail (I was present at the time.) He vehemently rejected the idea of a loan or other form of aid and said only, "I will not benefit from anything but my own work." His pure and holy soul departed a few days later. I was fortunate to aid him during his illness, to wash his hands, and wrap him in his shawl and tefillin while he was weak. May His Soul Be Bound in the Bond of Everlasting Life.

Lastly, R' Shechna Zuntag also followed the ways of R' Shaul and R' Alter. He studied much Torah and prayed much and worshipped through fasting and austerity. MHSBBEL. There were many other beloved figures which should be memorialized in this book, but my memory betrayed me, for which I apologize.

We have summarized and detailed the spiritual asset that was our noble synagogue. And now, the holy house is abandoned and lonely, pathetic with a mark of shame. And a weeping is sounded, reaches the heavens, and asks, "is this how Torah is rewarded?"

[Page 128]

Rabbis who Served in Turobin
Translated by Meir Bulman

A. Rabbi Zechariah Mendel

Rabbi Zechariah Mendel is well known for his *Ba'er Hetev* commentary on *Shulchan Aruch*. He was known locally as "R' Mendel Ben Ha'Gaon [Son of the Wiseman]" and possessed both Torah and greatness. He had a well-constructed brick house on the Jewish street in Krakow. After the death of his father, the Great Rabbi Aryeh Leib ABD of Krakow, R' Mendel was accepted as rabbi and rabbinic judge in the High Synagogue of Krakow. In 5704, he still served in that position. Later, he was appointed as ABD and Yeshiva master in Turobin, and at the end of 5448 was at the Jarosław Convention of the Council of Four Lands where they approved the book *Toldot Yitzchak*, a commentary on the Torah by the Great Rabbi Yitzchak Darshan of Krakow. At the end of 5449, he endorsed the reprinting of *Zofnat Pa'aneach*. From Turobin, he went on to serve as rabbi of Bełżyce and the region, where he endorsed the book *Ktonet Pasim* also named *Chaluka M'rabnan* by the author of *Zofnat Pa'aneach*. He signed, "word of the small one, Zechariah Mendel son of the Big Light Rabbi Aryee Leib, residing in Bełżyce." (*Klilat Yofi* by R' Chaim Natan Dembitzer, Krakow, 5648. vol. 1, P. 89)

B. Rabbi Natan Netta

The righteous, wise Rabbi and teacher Natan Netta, ABD of Turobin. He is quoted in the responsa *Beth Avraham*, edited by the Great and wise ABD of Tarla. He also endorsed the book *Aseifat Yehuda* in 5522, signed, "Natan Netta, residing in Turobin, son–in– law of the wise M. Baruch Kahana Rappoprt."

His daughter was married to the wise Rabbi Yosef Te'omim, who was first an ABD in Ostrovtza and accepted as ABD of Opatów in 5492.

[Page 129]

C. Rabbi Eliezer Landau

The Wise Rabbi Eliezer son of the wealthy R' Yosef Levi Segal Landau, judge and teacher in the Krakow region, was an ABD in Turobin. He is mentioned in the 5554 burial society ledger of Opatów, where he is buried. His wife, Mrs. Hadassah, was the daughter of Rabbi Yaakov Yitzchak, ABD of Zamosc. His daughter Rivka married the great wises Rabbi Yitzchak, ABD of Chelm and Zamosc who passed in 5585.

D. Rabbi Reuven ben Rabbi Yeshaya

In the old cemetery in Lublin, there is a tombstone which includes the rabbinic description, " Our learned teacher, Yeshaya OBM of Turobin, passed away 19 Av, 5526." (*History of the Jews in Lublin.*)

E. The Wise Rabbi Shimon Wolf of Turobin.

The famed wiseman Rabbi Shimon Wolf ben Rabbi David Tebbil Oyerbach was an ABD in Turobin for a period, and from there continued to Lumbla. Shortly thereafter, he resigned from his position in Lumbla after he was invited from Lublin to serve as their community leader. He later left Lublin with its masses and noise and traveled to Przemyśl. There, he sat on his throne and differentiated and justly ruled upon of his community according to law. While he served as an ABD there, he was among those who signed an endorsement of *Yesh Nochalnin* (Prague, 5357). From there, he was accepted as ABD of Posna, as his humble righteousness attracted the attention of many. There, he also endorsed the book *Siach Yitzchak* (Basel, 5387) on 19 *Shvat*, 5387. From there, he continued to the role of ABD and Yeshiva leader in the capital, Vienna (Glory of the elders extends to the descendants, 5585[?]), and towards the end of his life was accepted as ABD of Prague, where he passed on 7 *Cheshvan*, 5392. He was quoted in *Kav Ha'yashar*, chapter 65.

———

[Page 129]

Great Scholars and Debaters in Torah and Hassidism
by M.S. Geshuri
Translated by Meir Bulman

A. The origins of Hassidism in Turobin and the Area

As Hassidism grew in popularity among the Jewish masses in Poland, it also met resistance by rabbis and scholars. We cannot know if it met similar resistance in Turobin, because the ledgers and town documents of the community and *shtibels* in Turobin were lost. After the first period of Hassidic origins, resistance was slowed and no longer resulted in boycotts and censure. Hassidism left its mark; it conquered hearts, expanded its reach, and spread the wings of its control of social and spiritual issues on large districts which housed many Jewish communities. If there were debates, forceful or less so, they concerned methods within Hassidism, between *rebbes* and their communities, like two shades among many colors.

[Page 130]

In the Lublin district (voivodstva), Hassidism left a deep mark. Right when it appeared in a storm and deeply captured everything. Homes of righteous men were found in Lublin, Przedbórz, Kozienice, Warka, Goraj–Kock, Gur, and

158

more. Not long passed before resistance ceased. Jewish Poland became inhabited mostly by *Hassidim*, and even the giants of Torah and yeshivah attendees were *Hassidim*. Rabbi Yaakov Yitzchak Horovitz, the Seer of Lublin (1745–1815) was born in the Lublin area to his father, Rabbi Avraham Eliezer Horovitz, rabbi of Józefów, not far from Turobin. Lublin became a Hassidic metropolis, and almost all the following *rebbes* of Poland and Galicia were disciples of the Seer or were influenced by him. It is possible that some Turobin residents were among his disciples and followers without us knowing their names.

In the various shades of Hassidism in Poland, Kock took a leading role. *Rebbe* Mendeli of Kock, the founder of a method which achieved fame and became a phenomenon, was born in Goraj, which is near Turobin. R' Mendeli was born in 1787 to his father, Rabbi Aryeh Leibush, and his mother Esther (Atia) in Goraj, Lublin district. His father, Rabbi Leibush ben R' Menachem Mendel of Kirov was among the most notable and respected in his community. Aryeh was a great scholar, the finance officer for the burial society, of a significant lineage. He is the grandson of Rabbi David Halperin, son of Yisroel Halperin, Rabbi of Ostroh and Izyaslav, known as Rabbi Yisrael Charif. The lineage of the Halperin family was very well known. On one side, Rabbi Mendeli was descended from the family of Krakow rabbi Shlomo, author of *Maginei Shlomo*, and Rabbi Heshil of Lublin.

R' Mendeli's family was spread throughout many towns in Poland, mainly in Lublin district, mainly Goraj and neighboring Turobin. Rabbi Leibush of Goraj established a large family and had seven boys and two girls. The eldest, the sharp, righteous man Rabbi Yisroel Morgenstern resided in Turobin and was the in-law of *Rebbe* Henich of Alexander. He passed in Turobin on 7 *Cheshvan*, 5602. The fifth son, Rabbi Yekusiel Isaac, resided in Turobin and married his niece, Rabbi Yisroel's daughter.

R' Mendeli, second son to his father, spent his childhood and youth days in Goraj. Even as a child, *Rebbe* Mendli was different than his environment. A Hassidic legend tells that when he was three years old, he would jump enthusiastically and strongly chant the verse "My heart and flesh sing to a living God." (Psalms 84) Sometimes, since he was deeply devoted, he fell into mud without noticing and continued enthusiastically chanting. He received his education at the cheider in Goraj. He quickly surpassed his peers in his skills and knowledge and no longer found his place there. Even as a child he was modest and shy, a persistent scholar, and studied Torah day and night. He was a rare talent, of a sharp mind who dissected and critiqued the heart of each matter. He obtained remarkable knowledge of Talmud, memorized Talmud and *poskim*. He paid no mind to his impressive lineages. He recognized that each person had to grow and obtain perfection on his own merit, and would often say, "I do not have time to be fenced by lineage." "You have grown fat and grown thick" was the clever remark he would direct at the detractors and the various "grandsons," meaning, "although you have grown fat i.e. of a lineage of great quality, you can still be coarse and thick." While walking with his friends, he would suddenly leave them and vanish. After they searched, they found him resting on a tall mountain, hands and legs spread out, chanting "My heart and flesh sing to a living God."

[Page 131]

In his youth, he was an outspoken critic of Hassidism. His Misnaged parents ensured that he be filled with Torah and fear of God and not be distracted by other matters. His raising in a family of Misnagedim had its influence. But his heart was torn, and many envoys from the houses of the righteous in Lublin, Kozienice and others, told of many miracles and signs from there. The boy listened to the tunes which captured his inner soul.

Rebbe Mendeli was quoted as saying, "my family was a family of Misnagedim who opposed *Hassidim* and Tsaddikim, their customs and way of life." When he was 15, he travelled to The Seer of Lublin without requesting his parents' permission. He stayed there until word reached home that Mendeli was captured by a 'cult'. His father hurried to the Seer's house to return his son to the right path. The father angrily asked his son, "why did you stray from the customs of your ancestors to follow Hassidic customs?" The son calmly replied, "in The Song of the Sea it first says, 'He is my God, and I will praise him,' followed by 'my father's God, and I will exalt him.'"

He was asked where he turned to *Hassidim*, to which he replied, "in my hometown Goraj there was an elderly man who sat in the *beth midrash* and would tell tales of *Hassidim* and tsaddikim. That elderly man told what he knew, and I heard what I had to hear and became a Hassid." A spirit came over him and he travelled to Lublin. He then became a disciple of The Holy Jew. Later, to expand on the teachings of The Holy Jew, he became a disciple of *Rebbe* Simcha Bunim of Peshischa. He improved and deepened the methods

of his *Rebbe* and recruited more disciples. The leader among the disciples was Mendeli, the future *Rebbe* of Kock.

The young man from Goraj was ignited with fiery passion, like he could not or would not mix dishonesty with his studies. Even as a child, he was well known for his sharp replies. He never tolerated hypocrisy. *Rebbe* Mendeli did not marry as young as the Jewish custom at the time and chose instead to continue his studies. Only in 1807 at the age of 20, he married Ms. Glikkel, daughter of Rabbi Isaac Noy, an important man from Tomaszów. The agile, sharp-minded, warm-hearted prodigy of Goraj with the concentrated walk and joined eyebrows then left the yeshivah. He relocated to live with his father-in-law who supported him in Tomaszów Lubelski near Lublin.

It is told that *Rebbe* Mendeli once returned to his hometown of Goraj. He went to visit his first teacher, the one who taught him the aleph bet. There was a second teacher who taught him Torah, Mishnah, and Talmud. The second was insulted and asked rabbi Mendel, "why did the *rebbe* not come to greet me? I taught him more than the first." *Rebbe* Mendel replied, "you taught many things the truth of which I am uncertain. One explains, and another comes and contradicts him. But the first teacher, who taught me the aleph bet, his Torah is true, since everyone admits that aleph is aleph and bet is bet."

The Influence of *Rebbe* Mendel of Tomaszów and Kock was very present in Turobin. There were as many of his followers in Turobin as there were wonderful educational legends about him. *Rebbe* Mendel visited his two brothers who resided in Turobin often, since Kock and Tomaszów were not far from Turobin. The Jews of Turobin knew to greet him with the respect and admiration proper for such a wonderful Tzadik and dwelled within in his teachings and presence.

[Page 132]

Rebbe Mendel passed at the age of 72 on *Shvat* 22, 5619.

Rabbi Yisroel Morgenstern, the brother of *Rebbe* Mendeli of Kock, resided in Turobin. His father R' Leibush of Goraj named him after his great-grandfather, Rabbi Yisroel Halperin. Halperin, known as Rabbi Yisroel Charif, was the rabbi of Ostroh and a famed miracle-worker. It is told that he once cursed an informer which was fulfilled when the informant drowned in the river. Rabbi Yisroel Halperin was the son of the great wiseman Rabbi Eliezer

Lipman Halperin, rabbi of Tarnogród, son of the wise and righteous Rabbi Yitzchak Isaac Halpern, rabbi of Tiktin. After Rabbi Yisroel passed on the eve of the first day of *Shvat*, 5491, his son, the great wise rabbi Dovid, was appointed to fill his spot of the rabbinate. He was a devoted disciple of the Ba'al Shem Tov and it is told that when the BST visited Zelów (where Rabbi Dovid relocated from Ostroh to serve as rabbi and passed on 15 *Tamuz*, 5528) he stayed at the home of rabbi Dovid Halperin.

Rabbi Yisroel of Turobin was a Torah scholar and a disciple of the *Rebbe* of Alexander Rabbi Chanoch Henich HaKohen. He is the root of a large family tree. The daughter of the Alexander *Rebbe*, Mrs. Bracha Shifra Miriam, married R' Mendel son of R' Yisroel of Turobin. R' Mendel Morgenstern resided in Lodz, a righteous scholar, and a working man. His sons were Gur *Hassidim*, the famed R' Pinchas Leibush and R' Yisroel Mordechai Morgenstern of Lodz. R' Yisroel passed in Turobin on *Cheshvan* 7, 5602.

In the hometown of *Rebbe* Mendeli of Kock Goraj were the graves of his ancestors (mother father, grandfather, and great grandfather.) With the destruction caused by the Holocaust, the cemetery on Goraj was likely destroyed along with the ancient tombstones. Therefore, it is of historical value to record the tombstones and quote them here. According to the president of the Goraj community, Moshe Hoyt in his 5698 letter to researchers, the tombstone of the father of the Kock Tzadik was broken into four pieces and had to be pieced together so that they were legible. The father's tombstone is as follows:

And God said Yehuda shall go up

Passed Iyar 2 5573

Ascended to the City of Warriors An honest man

of many deeds Walked

on the true path

Hero of Torah the lion

in the bunch among the holy masses

You sat on the seat of wisdom

The wonderous rabbi (missing)

pure, walker on the straight path, cycler [?]

Grew in talent and did much of note

and glory the honor of his name is great

in Israel Known in Juda Son of

the famous Sharp Rabbi

of great lineage (two words missing, likely descendent of)

holy men Our rabbi and teacher Menachem Mendel

His memory will live in the World to Come MHSBBEL.

[Page 133]

Tombstone of the mother of Rebbe Mendel of Kock:

Passed Av 13, 5570

Here Lies

An educated woman, humble

In deed and fear of God

And she shall walk (missing)

A lioness among lions

Seven cubs she reared

Sons of distinction and Torah

The name of the great woman is

ESTHER daughter of Issachar Bear

Gravestone of the Tzaddik *Rebbe* Mendeli of Kock:

Gravesite of our great holy rabbi may his soul be at peace

The town of Goraj birthed. Tomaszów raised its beloved. Woe is Kock for its beauty was lost.

Here lies the man of God, Our master, teacher, and rabbi, God's anointed, our very life breath, master of Torah, source of wisdom and depth of knowledge, leader of the wisemen and the holiest of the holy, foundation and wonder of the world, the cavalry leader of those in Ariel Exile, light of Israel and rabbi of all wise and righteous men of his generation, like an angel of God is he, his name holy and awe– striking, our rabbi and teacher Menachem Mendel His soul treasured in the Heavens, ben Rabbi Yehuda of blessed memory. The generation sinned and he was gathered to the Holiest and returned to God in his Seventy Second year on Thursday of the portion of "and to Moses he said Rise to God" on *Shvat* 20 of the Year "Woe to us The Ark of God was taken" (5619). His memory will defend each generation and at every time may he defend all of Israel's brethren.

R' Yisroel of Turobin established a large family which was spread through many places. His brother and son–in–law Rabbi Yekusiel Isaac resided in Turobin his whole life. In contrast, his brother Mendel (son in law of *Rebbe* Chanoch of Alexander) resided in Lutomiersk and Alexander. Rabbi Dovrish in Zamosc, Rabbi Itzak in Soloveitsh, Rabbi Zalman various places, and the two sisters married residents of other towns.

Tomaszów and Kock were an integral part of the new Tzadik movement. Kock was the deepest and most complex subject of Hassidic chronology in Poland. Even geniuses and holy men did not fully comprehend nor easily grasp its nature and content. Thus, Kock was a new link in the golden chain woven from the days of the BST. Turobin and Goraj were the first origins in the life of the Tzadik and his family.

[Page 134]

B. Rabbi Noakh Shmuel Lifshitz, ABD of Turobin

Rabbi Noakh Shmuel continued his spiritual legacy not only in his written works but also during his life. His soul's song was not in words alone but also in the holy worship and the message of Hassidism. He and his father were party to the foundation–laying of Hassidism in Lublin and the rest of Poland. They were disciples of The Seer of Lublin who faithfully and lovingly contributed to the spread of Hassidic teachings. He was the first Hassidic rabbi of Turobin and laid the groundwork in the town for the new movement. Hassidism livened the masses whose souls yearned for big personalities to show them humility and love of Israel not just in study but also in concrete reality.

Rabbi Noakh Shmuel Lifshitz (5540–5592) was the firstborn son of Rabbi Yehuda Leib Lifshitz, rabbi of Blashaka and later Opoczno. *Rebbe* Yehuda Leib was a disciple of the Seer of Lublin and visited the Maggid *Rebbe* Yisroel of Kozienice. The Maggid very much valued his righteousness and would forward to him Jews who needed salvation. Rabbi Ze'ev HaCohen ABD of Lask (known as R' Velvel Charif) anointed him with the title of "Righteous, wise, famed, miracle of the generation." He was the brother of the famed wiseman *Rebbe* Yechiel Michel Lifshitz. *Rebbe* Yehuda Leib passed in 5563.

R' Noakh Shmuel achieved fame in his youth as a Torah prodigy. When he was 12, he memorized Maimonides' *Mishneh Torah*. At 13, one of the wealthy men of Kazimierz, R' Ze'ev HaLevi Wolman, arranged for him to marry his daughter Ms. Chaya Sarah. In remained in his father–in–law's house several years. There he studied Torah, worship, and Hassidism, and ascended to a height of the holy Torah. When he turned 18 in 1798, he was invited by the Turobin community to serve as chief rabbi. That was his first rabbinic role. After a short time, he was famed as a genius of Torah, and there were many rabbis and scholars who wanted his company and were in correspondence with him.

His devotion to Torah study was immense. Every year, he would complete all volumes of Talmud on 15 *Shvat* and hosted a mitzvah feast. Every day, he would study 18 chapters of Mishnah, and intermittently slept, no longer than three hours; two hours at night from 10 to midnight and during the day – one hour. Most of the day, he was adorned by tefillin. On shabbat, he spoke only Hebrew. Along with his genius in Torah he was also a Hassid, a disciple of the Seer of Lublin and the Maggid *Rebbe* Yisroel of Kozienice, and would quote their commentaries in his books. He quotes the Seer of Lublin: "I heard from my master and teacher, The holy light of Lublin, who interpreted 'she works with willing hands' in the sense of path: When a person does a Mitzvah [he is repaid] for example, by giving to charity his hands heal or by walking to the synagogue his legs heal. That is what is meant by 'she works with willing hands.' I also heard he interpreted 'God is righteous in all of his ways etc.' to mean that a tzaddik worships God in 'all of his ways' and not 'all of his deeds,' but is virtuous in all of his deeds."

[Page 135]

He also quoted interpretations by *Rebbe* Meir of Stopnica–Apt, R' Zisheh of Annopol and others.

He traveled often to Lublin to witness the Seer and was considered one of his most important disciples. During his stay in Lublin, he lodged with his relative, the famed wiseman Rabbi Azriel Halevi Horowitz ABD of Lublin, known by all as "The Steel Mind." and although Rabbi Azriel was among the fiercest critics of The Seer, he viewed Rabbi Noakh Shmuel in a positive light. The often–debated Hassidism and Torah; Rabbi Azriel proposed many questions, Rabbi Shmuel Noakh found an answer for everything, and Rabbi Azriel always admitted he was aiming for those answers. Additionally, Rabbi

Azriel helped him with financial matters by writing letters he wrote on his behalf to the wise author of *Baruch Ta'am* and to Rabbi Mintz. The hostility to Hasidism was deeply entrenched in Rabbi Azriel's heart but did not adversely impact his treatment of Rabbi Noakh Shmuel.

The rabbinate in those days did not provide a large income. Rabbi Ze'ev HaCohen ABD of Lask mentions in a letter that in Poland it is very difficult to find a rabbinic role that would provide for the family as the country became scarcer, "and may God have mercy on our brethren and bring good times soon." The residents of Turobin very much respected and were proud of their wise rabbi, who was well–liked by The Seer of Lublin who once even sent messengers to summon him. The Maggid of Kozienice directed people who needed redemption to him since he was considered a man of the Holy Spirit and a miracle–worker. Although he did not wear the crown of a righteous Tzaddik, he was a visionary. In addition, he attracted talented Torah scholars to his lectures since he was strongly and thoroughly knowledgeable. The salary he received in Turobin was not enough to provide for him and his household. His low salary is mentioned by Rabbi Yaakov Orenstein, ABD of Lvov (Author of *Yeshuot Yaakov*) in one of his letters (*Shvat* 21, 5570.) Rabbi Orenstein wrote R' Feivel [?] that Rabbi Shmuel Noakh was "well known in his good deeds which flourish like grain, yet his livelihood is not dependent on improper methods such as charging a fee for arbitration. He earns only what is budgeted by the communal fund, and the remainder he covers on his own." His father–in–law from Kazimierz provided for him and always covered the necessary difference. His father–in–law proposed that he resign his position in Turobin and return to Kazimierz where he would be supported as he studied and worshiped. Rabbi Lifshitz initially refused since he hoped to receive a more important role in a larger town. He labored to obtain such a position.

The Maggid of Kozienice addressed a recommendation letter (*Tevet* 3, 5570) to the Opoczno community. He requested that they accept Rabbi Noakh Shmuel as their rabbi in place of his deceased father. In response to the approach of members of that community, he highlights the need for livelihood in the rabbi's ability to teach and learn. The Opoczno plan was Likely not executed despite the recommendation of the Maggid, who had a strong influence throughout Poland. In 5572 he was invited to serve as chief rabbi and Rosh Yeshiva in the Dessau, Germany community as evident from a letter by his relative, the Wise Rabbi Gedalya Lifshitz, ABD of Khasdeish. However, the role in Prussia was not to his liking so he did not accept and continued

166

searching in other communities. In all the letters recommending his services as a rabbi, his title is "ABD and rabbi of The Holy Community of Turobin."

[Page 136]

It was an honor for the town, although his income there was scarce. He eventually agreed to the pleading of his father–in–law to return to Kazimierz, where he rested and studied Torah and was well–supported by his in–law. After his father in law passed, he had to renew his search for a rabbinic position. For that purpose, he wandered from town to town and country to country looking for a position. He also sought endorsements of the books he authored in his youth and maybe during his role in Turobin.

His books were A) *Divrei Shmuel*, a pleasant collection of works on Shbbat Tracte including laws, legends, and wonderful interpretations sweeter than nectar and honey on the topic of 'if a candle becomes extinguished.' Also included were collected works on words of Our Sages and new interpretations of the *Magen Avraham* and the *Turey Zahav*. B) *Minchat Yehudah*, a commentary on *HaMachriah* by the wise rabbi Yeshaya di Trani author of *Tosfot RID*. Additionally, according to his grandchildren, there are many manuscripts of other works: an essay on *Tracte Brachot*(Wonderful Essay Wondrously Wondered), a responsa on the four volumes of *Shulchan Aruch*, answering questions by many distinguished and famous rabbis, including responses to the Holy Rabbi Famed Among Israel, Our Teacher Shimon, ABD of Żelechów known by all as Rabbi Shimon Deitsch. Also included was a response to the famous wiseman R' Yitzchak Moshe [?] ABD of Bełżyceitz. He also left behind an essay on rules and composition on the Torah and most volumes of Talmud. All those manuscripts were likely lost and never published.

His sister Sarah married R' Yaakov Zvi, who was a God–fearing Torah scholar who passed at a young age while his son Yechiel Meir was still a small child. The orphan was taken in by the Rabbi of Turobin who raised and educated him and served as his uncle, father, and rabbi. He learned Torah from him until he became independent. He often mentions his uncle in his speeches, and is the same Yechiel Meir who later became the famous *Rebbe* of Gostynin. Years passed, and Yechiel Meir continued to grow. Circumstances in his uncle's house changed as well; his uncle the rabbi of Turobin had to leave home often and wander great distances in search of a rabbinic position to provide him with larger income. He then brought his orphaned nephew to the city of Kutno where he studied in the Yeshiva led by the Great Wiseman Rabbi Moshe Yehuda Leib author of *Zayit Ra'anan* (who made Aliyah towards the end of his life in 5615 and passed in 5625 in Jerusalem.) In the Yeshiva, he made great progress and achieved fame as a prodigy. Thanks to Rabbi Noakh Shmuel, Turobin was fortunate to be the first residence of a youth who later became the famous Tzadik of Gostynin. Rabbi Noakh Shmuel was accepted to be ABD of Bedzin, were he passed away in 5592.

C. A Turobin Native – Wise Rabbi in Jerusalem

Jewish Turobin contributed much to the personality of rabbi Yisroel Ze'ev (R' Velvel) Mintzberg who adorned Jerusalem with enchanting beauty in a coat fitting "the Joy of the whole earth." R' Velvel Mintzberg, a Turobin native, was one of the most wonderful figures of the beautiful Jerusalem backdrop. He loved Jerusalem with every fiber of his being and illuminated its paths with his rulings and directives for over half a century. Through him, Jewish Turobin made its contribution to the *olim* and the builders of the holy land, in a time which long preceded the period of pioneering and *aliyah* and love of Zion. By being there for over half a century, he became a part of it and was like a foundational stone whose public and spiritual being is based on. He kept his birth town of Turobin on his mind throughout his life.

[Page 137]

R' Velvel was not only a great Torah scholar but also descended from a great lineage. He was born in Turobin near Lublin, which was dubbed "Jerusalem of Poland." His father, the Great Wise Rabbi Moshe Zvi Mintzberg was the grandson of *Rebbe* Moshe'le (Biderman) of Lviv and The Holy Jew of Peshischa. R' Moshe Zvi was the son of the wise rabbi Avaraham'che, Rabbi of the Tshmilov and Józefów communities, who was known as a miracle worker. R' Avraham'che married the daughter of the great Rabbi Yitzchak Dovid Biderman. It is told that in the wedding contract there was an explicit clause that mandated the young couple settle in *Eretz Israel*. They were financially supported by their grandfather, The *Rebbe* of Lviv who lived in Przedbórz and was preparing to make *aliyah*. He wanted to sound his shofar at the Western Wall to hasten the end of days. His will was not realized, since he became ill after he arrived in Jerusalem and was too weak to walk to the Western Wall. He instructed his sons to carry his bed there, but he Arabs rained stones on him and they had to turn back. Two weeks and two days later, the *rebbe* passed away.

The clause of the wedding engagement was not fulfilled, because R' Avrahamche's parents prevented the young couple from doing so. He was their only son and therefore, had difficulties parting with him. The *rebbe* of Lviv wished upon them they he not remain their only son, a blessing which was fulfilled when a son was born to them, but the young couple still remained in the foreign land. Rabbi Avrahm'che then ascended to the rabbinate throne. His family grew, and many sons and grandsons were born. One of them was R' Velvel, whose life chronicles were detailed by author Aaron Sorski. The chronicle was detailed by the Turobiner Rabbi in his humble abode in the Arab effendi neighborhood Katamon in southern Jerusalem, where he settled after the surrender of the ancient Yishuv in Jerusalem and its abandonment. [?]

My father, R' Moshe Zvi, left home while I was a toddler and wandered to Austria, because he had to escape Poland due to persecution by the army. At six years old, I immigrated to Israel on my own on a ship which sailed from Galatz, a Romanian shore town. I was to exchange Jerusalem of Poland with the actual Jerusalem of *Eretz Israel*. My grandfather R' Avraham'che also traveled to Israel, separately. A terrible fire consumed most the town of Józefów, and Grandfather saw in that a sign from God that he had to fulfill the clause in his engagement contract and immediately begin travelling to the Holy Land. That was in 5639.

R' Velvel was taught Torah by his grandfather R' Avaraham'che and was raised by him after being orphaned of his mother at a very young age. He went to live with his grandfather and they were inseparable. He was quickly discovered as a prodigy of rare talent, a scholar who studied day and night and blurred the lines between a night devoted to study and a night devoted to sleep. When he was 13, his uncle, the Wise Rabbi Yerachmiel Yeshaya Mintzberg of Łukowa, among the wisest scholars in Poland, said that 'he will grow into a great tree'. His persistent study of Torah bore fruit. The wisemen of Jerusalem began whispering of R' Avrahamche's grandson "he is skilled in study." He corresponded with great Torah scholars including Rabbi Shneior Zalman of Lublin author of *Torat Chesed* and Rabbi Yehoshua Leib Diskin the Rabbi of Brisk. He gained a reputation among yeshiva students, even the Misnagedim, who at first were skeptical of the reality of a Hassid who is a greatly proficient and sharp Torah scholar. His reputation was mainly gained through his rulings on halakha. He achieved a uniquely high status and his responses reached all corners of the world. The name "R' Velvel Mintzberg" became a household name as a Halakha scholar among the rabbis of the Diaspora.

[Page 138]

R' Velvel published various scholarly pamphlets, especially about the Halakha of *Eretz Israel* and *Agunot halakha*. He published a pamphlet about Shimtah (5675). He also authored "This is the Law of Torah" (5680), about the forbidden appointment of women to the national council. Additional works included "*Shelichut B'Truma*," (5688) the pamphlet "Yishuv *Eretz Israel* (5690), and a booklet "*Heter Agunah*" (5704). He prepared *She'erit Israel* for publication in his lifetime without witnessing the fruition of that task,

It was published by his son Rabbi Chaim Yudell (5723) and includes 325 pages of through responses and deep interpretations of *Halakha*.

R' Velvel was a beloved figure within the walls and would befriend even children. He was loved even more than admired. He was a posek and ABD of the Hassidic community. Still, he was not patronizing but a man of the people. He was short–statured, introspective, humble, and modest, with a soft yet deep voice. It was difficult to be accepted by all factions In Jerusalem, yet he managed to do so without using excessive flattery. All factions recognized his status; *Hassidim* and Misnagedim, Lithuanians, Ashkenazim, and Sephardim.

In his 84 years of residence in the Holy Land, he only departed once. In 5665, he visited the center of Judaism in Poland and Galicia. He was among the last defenders of the Old City of Jerusalem until it fell to the forces of King Abdullah of Jordan in 1948. He accepted (along with the Rosh yeshiva of Porat Yosef Rabbi Ben Zion Hazan) the dangerous task of walking toward the enemy lines with a white flag to announce the readiness of the last remaining defenders of the Old City to surrender. That move, which R' Velvel took upon himself the very last moment, saved the lives of 2000 residents and protectors of the besieged Old City. He saw that heroic rescue as the achievement of his life.

After he exited the walls, he took up residence in the Katamon neighborhood. He continued his attentive study Torah and Hassidism as before. He was on his death bed for several years. His freshness and clarity of mind remained until the age of 90. On Friday, Adar 17, 5722, R' Velvel Mintzberg reached the end of his wonderful life saga, that of one of the most wonderful figures of Jerusalem.

170

[Page 139]

D. Rabbi Eliyahu Halevi Landau, ABD of Turobin

A little over fifty years have passed since the death of Rabbi Landau in 5670. Yet, it is still difficult to obtain details on his personality. Some of his sons, daughters, grandchildren ,and great–grandchildren survived the Holocaust and some reside in Israel. Still, it is difficult to obtain details about their ancestor's life; how he arrived in Turobin, where he was born, what yeshiva he studied in and received ordination, where and whom he married, and details of his rabbinic service, whether he served in other towns before Turobin. It is known that his service in Turobin spanned 40 years until his last day in 1910 and is buried in the Turobin cemetery. His grandchildren in Israel have not visited his gravesite and do not know what is written on his tombstone, what titles, and if a shrine was erected there. It is unlikely that such a shrine was established, as that is a Hassidic custom, and he was a rabbi and not a *rebbe*.

R' Zvi Kopp is the only Turobin survivor who told us of the famed Rabbi Eliyahu, without providing additional details. Only few among us survived. Rabbi Eliyahu's great grandson Rabbi Yehuda Halevi Rozhani resides in Lower Motza near Jerusalem. We found in possession two volumes of Mishnah with Eitz Hachaim commentary from the library of Rabbi Eliyahu of Turobin, marked with a round stamp common in the first half of the 19th century, "Eliyhau Halevi Landau, ABD of Turobin" and the name of his wife *Rebbe*tzin Haddasah. Rabbi Eliyahu published his Torah commentary and authored a book, *Kol Eliyahu*. It was not published despite Rabbi Eliyahu's proximity to Lublin, well–known in the Jewish world to have quality printing houses. many libraries and manuscripts were destroyed during the Holocaust and that manuscript was also lost.

There are grounds to assume that he originated from the house of a former ABD of Turobin, the Wise Rabbi Elazar ben R' Yosef Segal Landau. Rabbi Elazar is mentioned in the 5554 burial society ledger of Opatów where he is buried. Rabbi Eliyahu's wife Hadassah was the daughter of Our Wise Teacher Yaakov Yitzchak ABD of Zamosc. It is also known that Rabbi Eliyahu was a direct descendant of Rabbi Yechezkel ben Harav Yehuda Halevi Landau, author of *Noda Be'Yehudah*. The *Noda Biyehudah* was one of the greatest rabbis of his generation, the generation of Hasidism founder, the BST. The *Noda Biyehuda* was born in Opatów on *Cheshvan* 18, 5474 (1713). His father R' Yehuda ben R' Zvi Hirsh was a town leader and a member of the Council of Four Lands. In his youth, he studied Torah under the guidance of Rabbi Yitzchak Isaac Halevi of Ludmir. At the age of 14, he studied at a *Kloyz* in Brody in the company of talented youngsters who were known as "lions and tigers of Torah and of pure Godly faith." He was eventually appointed as one of the *Kloyz* Wisemen. After he served as *dayan* in Brody and as rabbi of Yampol, Podolia, he was invited in 5515 to serve as rabbi of Prague, capital of Czechoslovakia, replacing R' Dovid Openheim. There he operated a great yeshiva and held a daily lecture on Talmud. Among is students were great and famed rabbis. He stood before angels [?] and knew to judge wisely. His efforts on behalf of his people were not in vain. R' Yechezkel was of the lineage of Rashi and wrote, "since I am of the clan of Rashi, I have labored to reconcile the words of Rashi." R' Yechezekel passed in Prague on 17 Adar 5553 (1793), and many legends illustrating his wisdom and sharp mind were inspired by his illuminating figure. 10 books of his written works were published.

[Page 140]

It is unknown if Rabbi Eliyahu signed endearments of books. We have found only one such endorsement on the book *Birkat Yosef*, a commentary on the Five Books of Moses. which was published by his son Rabbi Yosef Zvi Halevi, a Turobin native who was rabbi of Ostrovtza. It was published in Warsaw in 5655 recently printed in second edition 5725 in Jerusalem (Hathiya Inc. Publishing.) We hereby quote the title of the endorser: "endorsement of A.A. [my father and master?] my teacher and rabbi, the wise, famous, sharp, well–versed, great etc. his honored holy name Rabbi Eliyahu Halevi Landau may he live long amen, ABD of Turobin, descendant of the Noda Be'Yehuda and the successor to Rabbi Yechezkel Segal Landau:"

Today I have seen the holy and beloved writings of my son, the sharp, well versed, great, etc. on the Torah. It was a pleasure to see his deeds and the beauty of his wisdom with such deep and nuanced knowledge. It is full of the width of the Talmud, Kabballah, and the writings of the Arizal. Wherever I looked I have found flavor and deep thought built upon golden columns. It will bring joy to the educated reader whose heart and eyes are open to grasp the bright light. It is a worthy source and I hope that as such it will prove its beauty to all who witness the joyful illumination, and pleasing God and man. May Hashem strengthen his spirit and his well shall never dry and quench the thirst of all who year the Word of Hashem. Signed, the author's father in Turobin. Tuesday, *Lech–Lecha* portion, 5649. The small one, Eliyhau Halevi Landau.

Rabbi Eliayhu had three sons who lived in Turobin. The eldest one was Rabbi Yosef Zvi, ABD of Ostrovtza who went on to serve as rabbi and leader of the Grochów near Warsaw. His second was rabbi Yechzekel, and the third Rabbi Noakh. Rabbi Eliyahu was not a Hassid and did not travel to any Hasidic leader, nor was he a staunch opposer of Hassidism, and lived at peace with all. We have already mentioned that in Turobin there was no dispute between Hassidism and Misnagedim. *Hassidim* conquered the town early on, in the days of The Seer of Lublin and some of its chief rabbis were Hassidic. According to a description by a relative, he was tall statured with a patriarchal appearance. He often traveled in the Lublin district to watch that there were no cracks in the wall of religion. He observed the district alongside other highly influential rabbis from several towns. Rabbi Eliyahu was considered one of the greatest halakhic scholars of his time, one that combined the mystical Torah and common Torah. His home in Turobin was a center for wisemen, and occasionally regional rabbis would gather to discuss contemporary issues. His was influential in the Lublin and Chelm Districts and admired by the masses.

Even if Rabbi Eliyhahu was not himself a Hassid, his sons were close to that movement. The eldest founded his own dynasty in Grochów and attracted a community of disciples. Rabbi Yosef Zvi was a great scholar and wrote about 40 works mostly on Kabbalah named alphabetically; *Aimrei Yosef, Birkat Yosef*, etc. The last one was called *T'eomei Yosef*. only the first two were published while the rest remained as manuscripts. He founded the Grochów Dynasty in a town of the same name 10km from Warsaw. Rabbi Yosef Zvi was a disciple of Rabbi Meir of Opatów and Rabbi Mendeli of Kock. After his death, his disciples added to him the title of Tzaddik. The dynasty was a new one in Polish Hassidism, and only two generations of it followed before the final destruction of Polish Jewry. He lived 70 years, and passed on *Simchat Torah*5673, three years after the passing of his father the ABD of Turobin.

[Page 141]

On an interesting note, Rabbi Eliyahu of Turobin was persecuted by Polish authorities along with all offspring of the Noda Be'Yehuda, for the sole reason that the Noda had ties to the Czech and Austrian royal dynasties. Rabbi

Eliyahu's sons changed their last name to Rozhani and all three sons were known by that new name. the three were rabbis of various towns. Rabbi Yosef Zvi would visit his father's gravesite on his yahrzeit, but only managed to visit three times since he died in the fourth year. The two other sons also served as rabbis in towns near Turobin. many of their descendants perished in the Holocaust, but some survived and reside in Israel and abroad. Hashem did a kindness for Turobin which was fortunate to find some of its sons who were willing to publish this memorial book for their community and establish an everlasting legacy of the destroyed town, its rabbis, and rich cultural.

Rabbi Eliyahu was succeeded by the *dayan* and rabbi Yaakov Yehoshua who served as Turobin rabbi until the start of WWI. Starting in the first months of the war, Turobin was situated at the front of the battles between Russia and Austria. The Jews were the main victims and were subjected to plundering. The rabbi and his family fled the town with the other community members. He was then accepted as *dayan* in Lublin. After the war was over and the Jews of Turobin began to return to their town aided by various charitable institutions. It was then that chief rabbi Yaakov Weissbrod was appointed rabbi, following his previous role as ABD of Fokshivintza near Tsoizmer. The Kraśnik community then invited him to serve as their rabbi, and Rabbi Mordechai Weissbrod replaced him as ABD. He served until WWII, when he perished in the destruction with most of the Jewish community Z"L.

[Page 142]

E. The *rebbe* of Turobin Rabbi Yaakov Weissbrod

Shimon Halamish

Translated by Meir Bulman

The influence of Hassidic *rebbes* on Poland was immense and they attracted many disciples and admirers. The *rebbes* headed different dynasties, and although there was seemingly no difference among them there was still fundamental differences among the *rebbes*. Differences were seen in administration and relationships between the *rebbe's* estate and his disciples.

Some *rebbes* travelled cross country to meet their disciples. They conducted a *tisch* wherever they arrived, Torah lectures. They received *kvittles* (notes requesting health, income, children, etc.) and pidyon (the tax to the *rebbe* resembling a [Temple] sacrifice and was devoted to the administration of the estate.) There were also *rebbes* who did not leave their homes and conducted their kingdom within the estate. They also, of course, received *kvittels* and pidyon which was generously contributed.

Some *rebbes* did not know the shape of a coin and had no financial dealings. Such matters were left to estate *gabbaim*. *Gabbaim* wandered Jewish communities, met Hassidic activists, and publicized the deeds of the *rebbe,* his greatness in Torah and worship, and the miracles he performed. Those assistants contributed much to *rebbe's* estates and gathered crowds which contributed enthusiastically.

Many Hassidim, especially Torah scholars, traveled to their *rebbe's* estate on holidays and remained to absorb spiritual inspiration from the *rebbe* on which they relied for the rest of the year. Before the High Holy Days, Shabbat Chanukah, or Simchat Torah, large crowds attended the estates. Many traveled to receive the *rebbe's* aid in attaining divine help, because as is well known, 'what the righteous man decrees, God fulfills'. Some also arrived on an ordinary shabbat, especially Shabbat Rosh Chodesh, and would stay as long as the *rebbe* bestowed his will. If a Hasid was uneasy he needed advice and guidance from the *rebbe*. He would consult about his business, household matters especially matchmaking, the boys' military service etc. He would run to the *rebbe,* receive a blessing or advice, and all was well and there was no need to worry.

In every *rebbe's* estate there were disciples who were unique and stood out from the crowd. There were great Torah scholars, sharp minded individuals, and some wealthy who generously contributed as the *rebbe* advised. There were also talented men with a beautiful voice or artful dancers who performed on holidays and brought the audience to holy ecstasy.

In our town there were those who followed "the working man's *rebbe*," Rabbi Yankele Weissbrod ZT"L, the *rebbe* of Turobin. In his final years he also succeeded the *rebbe* of Krasnik. During WWI, Rabbi Yisroel HY"D was martyred when the Tsar's forces, executed by hanging along with three other

Jews after a libelous accusation. Such libel accusing Jews of spying was common in that time.

There were Hassidic craftsmen who followed dynasties of other *rebbes* such as the *rebbe* of Rozwadów and the *rebbe* of Bykhaw, Rabbi Yitzchak Rabinowitz (A descendant of The Holy Jew) who was also an avid Zionist and a member of Hamizrachi. Here I want to tell of the visit of the Turobin *rebbe* to our town which unfortunately is no longer. As I mentioned, the craftsmen did not have distinguished positions in the *rebbes*' estates, although their wives often visited the *rebbes* for *kvittles*. The craftsmen were not seen in the *shtibelch* at all and instead formed their own synagogues.

[Page 143]

In our town of Baranów Sandomierski the craftsmen gathered in the Turobiner *Shtibel*. They prayed there on shabbat, and the leader of the Torah recitation was a young man whom they invited from the *beth midrash*. During the High Holy Days they prayed in the general synagogue and parted to their own minyan for Torah recitation.

It is therefore easy to imagine the joy and enthusiasm when the Turobin *rebbe* visited our town. All residents of town were swept up in the joy of the Hassidim. The *rebbe's* fixed lodging was in the home of the Avraham Velevels the butcher who had a large apartment which was renovated and improved. The walls were freshly painted and everything was sparkling clean. The girls were sent to their uncle Chaim Berlin and everything was ready for the *rebbe's* annual visit.

When the day arrived, all work stopped in town. The tailor abandoned his pin and the cobbler his leather punch. Everyone adorned their festive shabbat clothes and went out to greet the *Rebbe*. Coaches were cushioned with fresh hay, and the procession was led by the town nobleman's coach which was designated for the *Rebbe*. The greeting procession made its way to Godziszów.

At the greeting ceremony, glasses were raised *l'chaim* as was tradition. The *rebbe's* convoy was immediately led to the special coach and the procession retuned to the town in song and dance. The *Rebbe*, his two sons, and his assistants were led to Avraham Velvel's house where they comfortably settled and prepared to greet their followers.

176

From then on out, the *rebbe's* house swarmed like a beehive. Tailors, cobblers, carpenters, carriers, and other common folks made their way to the *rebbe* with a joyous expression in their eyes. Everyone was excited, and a festive aura was sensed; "we also have a *Rebbe!* The scholars are not so special!"

Immediately following the evening prayers, the wives of the Hassidim also arrive with their small children. They approached the *rebbe* with reverence and awe so he could confer upon them his blessings and holiness. Of course, the *rebbe's* aid, R' Benim'le, assists in preparing the *kvittel* properly. In the *kvittel* they confide in the *Rebbe*. They plead that he plead to God on their behalf that their sons be God–fearing and scholarly. Others request healing for their husband, parents, or other relatives. There are those who ask to make a good living so that the Melamed could be handsomely rewarded and raise the boys to be upstanding scholars of Torah. There were also some unusual requests, such as how to deform the eldest sons to escape the burden of the gentile military. One requested a heling of a gallbladder infection, another asked that God will make her fertile. The assistant R' Benim'le listens attentively to all requests, properly records everything on the note. He then utters words of encouragement, and humbly extends his hand to accept the contribution which the woman happily hands him, as her eyes tear in a mix of sadness, joy, and faith.

The next step was the second assistant, Yellow Elazar, who also dos not oppose any form of currency and collects the entrance fee to the *rebbe's* room. They pass through the doorway, their heart beating, deeply excited and somewhat afraid. Sometimes, the husband, wife, and children stand together and in a shaken voice the woman addresses the *rebbe* with her request note and the fee. The *rebbe* strokes the coins with his blessed hand, as if playing with them. He grants his blessing in the order presented in the note, gives advice and proposes a charm, and holds the boys' hands as he blesses them. The family then leaves the *rebbe's* presence, light–hearted and faithful, like all their wishes have already been granted and the road ahead is smooth. The assistant's wish of good night accompanies them on the way out and adds to their feeling of security. Blessed is the man who has a *rebbe* who will always support him in his time of need.

[Page 144]

The presence of the *rebbe* in town exempts the residents from work during the week, including the nights. People gather in groups, tell stories which pass from person to person with some help from the Gabbai and Yellow Elazar. A favorite of the working Hassidim is the visiting of some notable scholars, disciples of other *rebbes* who visit the *rebbe* and engage in conversations on Torah. They especially enjoy watching them discuss important issues with the *rebbe's* two sons. God has provided to these poor craftsmen a slice of joy and peace in their world. The mind expands, the eyes shine and sometimes secrete tears of joy from the awakening soul. "Happy is that people for whom such is the case."

On Friday, the whole town is in upheaval. The inspiration of the approaching Day of Holy Rest overtakes all and much preparation is underway. Everyone anticipates the *tisch* ceremony. Even the scholar who usually mocks the Hassidim and their rabbis comfortably makes his way to the *rebbe's* house. Let's see this great scholar who is always exuding cleaver puns and words of Torah and secrets show his powers to the *Rebbe*. Let that smug arrogant man demonstrate his abilities to the *Rebbe*! What is also wonderous, is that he and the other "Torah scholars" grab the *shirayim* before the humble Hassidim manage to get their hands on any of it.

The residents have gathered at the town's bathhouse to bathe and purify in honor of the coming day. The craftsmen, the heroes of the day, prevail. They skip to the front of the queue to bathe in the mikveh and dip seven times while they disregard the geniuses waiting in line behind them. It is their day and they shall know it is their day!

On Friday night, the *rebbes'* rooms are densely packed. Young and old appear. The faces of the men illuminate in joy as they arrive from every direction. All dressed in festive clothes, the children in new outfits in honor of the occasion. Everyone listened with holy awe to the song of *Lechu Neranena* sounded by R' Mordechai Yossel the deaf man [artisan?], and when they reach *Lecha Dodi* everyone joins the singing. The singing echoed through the whole town. And he, the *rebbe* blinks his eyes and sometimes opens them wide, and a sigh of pleading sadness, "Oy Tateh Zisser, how I love You! Come to the aid of your people Israel and bless them with kindness! Oy, oy rescue and aid us!

178

[Page 145]

The silent portion of services is reached. People whisper their prayers, only their bodies swaying back and forth. Occasionally a sigh pierces the silence. Folks glance back to see if [the person behind has finished praying so] they can step back. Services end, and all crowd in front of the *rebbe* to exchange with him a Gut Shabbos. The *rebbe* replies to all, young and old, with a beaconing face, and illuminates as the Shabbat Queen hovers above. Some people who are new in town meet the *rebbe* for the first time. "Shalom Aleichem," they approach him in humble awe, and he replies in his pleasant voice, "Aleichem Shalom! Aleichem Shalom!"

Now folks run home to make kiddush and quickly eat the Shabbat meal, so they can get a good seat near the *rebbe's* table later. The table fills with those diligent early arrivals. Those who have prolonged their meal are sorry to see that all seats are taken. People squeeze into one another and the crowding is immense. Women and children stand outside looking in through the windows. The eyes scan to see of the husband has obtained to get close to the *Rebbe*. They are happy that the husband (may he live long) indeed found a spot near the notables.

The door opens. The *rebbe* and his entourage enter. All rise in holy awe, the Shalom Aleichem rises from all uniformly. The *rebbe* blesses the wine with deep intent. After that comes the rinsing of the hands and the blessing accompanied by "raise your hands in holiness." The *rebbe* slices the bread, and dabs some in salt and eats to fulfill the mitzvah. Then the saga of *shirayim* begins. All grab their portion from the gabbai's hands. Then the Shabbat dishes are served; fish, noodle soup, meat, etc. The *rebbe* only samples the food to fulfill the joy of Shabbat. The Hassidim busy their hands, struggling forcefully for every portion of *shirayim* which reaches them despite the overcrowding. Sometimes the portion falls from the spoon and the recipient makes do with licking his finger.

The enthusiastic crowd begins to hum hymns. The humming intensifies until loud singing pierces the dark town. They sing such songs as *Kol Mekadesh,* and *Menucha Ve'simcha.* The joy is high, and the material world fades away. The spiritual light and the holy sparks overtake one's being. The world is immersed in a sea of holiness. Suddenly, like by a magic wand, the crowd falls silent. Mouths agape and the eyes shine as they are fixed on the *rebbe.* They watch him like it was the giving of the Torah at Sinai.

The *rebbe* speaks calmly and pleasantly. His words are not audible to all in presence although people try to listen. The *rebbe* continues, comments on acrostics, reveals deep secrets, and then his voice intensifies. His enthusiasm grows and excites the Hassidim. He divulges the secrets of the Torah which foretold the sorrows of the current exile. He sighs in pain as he speaks of the exiled holy spirit. He speaks of this world and the World and Torah to Come. The *rebbe's* words are highlighted by a choir of sighs and um–hums which periodically rise from the crowds in waves. The sighs of Shmuel Tanchum's and Leizer the tailor rise like soloists within the choir.

[Page 146]

Suddenly, the crowd erupts in song, claps, and stomps their feet. Their core is forgotten in the flames of passion. When the food is no longer being served, the post–meal blessing is recited. Then, there is no table, house, nor space. All converges with the circle of dancers. The circle thickens and widens, everything become one, the crowd dances in grand celebration. The *rebbe* is at the center, as if floating midair, his eyes raised to the heavens. He claps his hands, raises them, and mumbles prayers and thanks sprinkled with short pleas, "*Tateh zisser, ah! helf shoyn dyne kinder!* See how they value Torah and mitzvot! Ah, Have mercy on us, oh Merciful Father, *un zal shoyn zeyn di Geulah!*"

Slowly, tiredness overtakes the dancers, its source is not hard work and shortness of breath, but a tiredness of enjoyment, an overflow of pleased spiritual ecstasy which overtakes those present and brings them to a release of their worldly being. It is total purification and a link to the holiness above. The fire of joy which moves the body and operates its organs slowly slips away. The energy released in the sparks of holiness fades away, and leaves behind a pleasant tired feeling cushioned with eternal joy and a feeling of soul ascension.

The Hassidim disperse to their homes. Their excited wives who followed them all evening once more follow. Their hearts treasure love and it shakes their core as they yearn for what is to come.

*

On Shabbat morning the Hassidim gather at the *rebbe's* house again. They Pray enthusiastically and recite the weekly Torah portion from a small scroll which the *rebbe* always carries with him. The Leader of recitation is of course the man who reads weekly at the *shtibel*. The number of aliyot is increased to please as many people as possible. Everyone makes a *Mi She'berach* for the *Rebbe*, bless and are blessed. After prayers, they once more run to the table to grab some *shirayim*. Now the kugel is distributed. There is ample kugel since every wife who is well versed in preparing kugel sent an offering with beer or mead bottles to the *rebbe's* house. The *rebbe* of course samples each kugel to infuse it with his blessing, and the gabbai ensures that each man receives his fitting portion. Then, on to the hymns; "Blessed is He Every Day," "Freedom Shall be Proclaimed," "Shabbat Today for Hashem."

The *rebbe* offers words of Torah. He begins with what is known and moves on to the hidden and tells of secrets, as he connects them to contemporary issues. Concepts are linked to the journey of the Messiah. He praises men of action who combine Torah and the Way of the World and fulfill the words of 'your brother shall live among you.' The *rebbe's* praise is no small matter. The *rebbe* finishes with "And You shall purify our hearts to worship You truly, may we witness the full *Geulah*." After the speech a wave of music erupts and reaches the heaves. The devotion links all and forms one soul burning with passion.

After the post–meal grace, everyone dances. Dancing lasts all day until the afternoon prayers, and resumes during the Third Shabbat Meal. The *rebbe* recites words of Torah as is tradition, hymns are sung until dark, and then on to the evening prayers. After the evening prayers, the high spirits begin to somewhat subside. There is a feeling like the additional soul is hastening its leave. The weekdays approach along with their worries and labor. Once more it will be necessary to labor and create, to provide food for the children. On Sunday morning, the Hasidim still make an effort and accompany the *Rebbe* on his journey out of town. They part ways teary-eyed and sorry. The *Rebbe* calms, encourages them, smiles, and blesses them. The *Rebbe's* smile and blessing which he luminated stood before the eyes of his followers. The laboring and poor men recalled them throughout the year and shined their paths as a pillar of fire and conferred upon them much faith in their destiny and future. They trusted him for his blessings will always be by their side and through it they will be redeemed in this world and the next.

[Page 147]

*

I devote this wholly holy essay to the Tzadik of Turobin who was a devout shepherd of his flock for over a generation. He led them spiritually and materially so they can confidently tread their rough path of lowered social conditions and sense of inferiority when compared to the upper classes of the wealthier and scholars. Their income was always low and was not enough to comfortably support their families. When school tuition payment was necessary they did not always have the funds. As a result, their education suffered, and they left cheder early on to help support their family, usually training in their father's craft. When attempting to study Talmud and *poskim* they were not always in luck and remained commoners like their fathers. For those working poor the *Rebbe* was like a guardian angel and he instilled in them faith, happiness, and hope. He brought them into the fold of the Jewish people and ensured each person's afterlife and his status within the nation.

The murderous Nazis made it their goal to destroy the nation of Israel and did so indiscriminately. They made no distinction between righteous men, men of action, rabbis and *ADMURim*, businessmen and craftsmen, *shochetim*, coachmen, judges, cobblers, merchants, matchmakers, teachers, revered leaders, and simple idle men. All were led into kennels, humiliated, tortured, stripped of their image of God, and led to the crematorium to fertilize fields with their ashes. Entire holy communities were uprooted and their children, homes, temples, and tombstones are no more.

May these words be a living monument for the sake of all those who miraculously survived and grasped at the rescue boat of Zionism and the State of Israel.

[Page 147]

When Shabbat Arrives in the Town

By Itamar Hopen

Translated by Meir Bulman

Every Jew no matter his profession, was shaken by mitzvah feeling if sunset was looming and he had not yet completed his weekly work. He hurries to end the work and report to the greeting of Shabbat Queen. The coachman who returned to town late whips his horses, the merchant hurries his last customers to hasten their shopping for Shabbat is coming and claimed that he was selling only candles for Shabbat. The craftsman stopped his work early and made his way to the bathhouses as others returned, each hurrying along with his chores.

[Page 148]

At sunset, the Shamash would pass with his hammer–shaped stick and knock on the shades of homes and announce: "Shabbat has arrived!"

The Jews hurried to the synagogue illuminated in the light of Shabbat. All candles in the chandelier were lighted as were the candles on the service leader's podium. The early arrivals read the Song of Songs and the latecomers began the afternoon prayers. The cantor R' Yerachmiel (*Shechna'lit*[?]) Zuntag approaches the podium and begins *Lechu Neranana* in his booming voice. The walls tremble and the crowd follows his recitation. Some of his assistants accompany his singing followed by *Mizmor Shir*. When they reached the verse "And Israel shall observe the Shabbat" there was an awakening and everyone recited loudly, for 'In the right of Shabbat observance Israel will be redeemed.' The service ended and the audience rushed home. The poor wait by the entrance, awaiting an invitation to a Shabbat meal. Our brethren are compassionate and not a single poor man remained without a Shabbat meal. The hurry in walking home had several reasons; the burning time of the candles was limited and it is better to greet Shabbat in the light so the children will not fall asleep and will be party to the joy of Shabbat, and the food will not get cold, for igniting a fire on Shabbat is forbidden.

After the Jew returns home he begins by singing Shalom Aleichem and invited Queen Shabbat into his home. The kiddush was recited and the meal was served. Ample meat, fish, and many delicacies were prepared since it is a mitzvah to eat on Shabbat. The shabbat *zemirot* echo from each home. More than once, a gentile stops by a Jewish home and looks in, wondering, 'what are these customs and lifestyle?' "The Jews are so strange," he comments and walks away. Try and explain the flavor of Shabbat fish to a gentile.

The streets also changed form since Shabbat had an inadvertent influence on Christian life. There was barley any traffic and only scarcely did a coach appear. Trade was suspended, and the shops were shuttered. The Christians did not trade with one another since they preferred trading with the Jews. The Christians went about their business at home which was very easy to distinguish from a Jewish one by the lit Shabbat candles. The singing from the Jewish homes could be heard from the streets and the festiveness of Shabbat was sensed in the air. The extra soul dwelled in each Jew. The young men and women of the town made their way to their youth movement activities and were the only ones outside. The older generation went to sleep, certain in their faith as the younger generation stood guard[?]. The youth walked through the streets in a cloud of new ideas and worldview, surrounded by an unforeseeable future.

———

[Page 149]

The Deposit
Zibn gute yor[1]
(From *Folktales* by I.L. Peretz)

Translated by Meir Bulman

In the holy community of Turobin there was a porter whose name was Tuvia. Tuvia suffered in poverty. the edges of his shirt were tucked into the rope around his waist. He was willing and able to carry a load to provide for Shabbat. Tuvia looked around. The shops were empty and the owners sat by corners tables, yawned or aimlessly wandered the store entrances. The sun rose above him. it was midday and still his satchel was empty. Tuvia raised his eyes the heavens and said a brief prayer, "Master of the Universe, help my Serril and the children. Do not turn my shabbat into a weekday and may I not be beholden to other beings."

184

As he spoke, a hand grabbed his coat form his back. Tuvia turned and before him stood a German hunter wearing a green uniform with a shiny feather in his cap.

"How can I help you, Mr. Hunter?"

The hunter spoke to him pleasantly in fluent German:

"You should know, Tuvia, that you are destined for seven good years. Seven years of blessings and success. You will be able to buy the whole town with this market place and stores. You have one choice, which is when they will start. You can choose for the riches to arrive today. Before the sun sets, your luck will shine like gold. However, at the end of the seven good years you will return to the status of a poor porter. Or else you may choose that they come at the end and you will pass away as a rich man with the honor befitting such wealth."

I do not need to tell you that the man was Elijah the Prophet Peace Be upon Him, but Tuvia did not detect that and thought he was a clown mocking his poverty, or a wizard. He wanted to be rid of him, so he calmly replied,

"Leave me alone, kind German, and begone. I am penniless and cannot repay your favors."

But after the hunter pled and repeated the question twice and thrice, the words entered Tuvia's heart. He thought, 'maybe,' 'perhaps,' and, 'even if it will not help it will not harm.'

"You should know, my dear German, that I always ask my Serril for advice. I will go ask her and she will designate the time."

"A fine custom," replied the hunter, "I will wait here for you."

Tuvia untucked his coat from his rope and left the market square. He walked to his mud hut outside of town to ask his wife.

Serril stood at the doorway waiting for him. When she saw him, she ran towards him with her arms wide open for she thought that God had provided and he was bringing groceries for Shabbat. But Tuvia said that he has yet to earn anything, and he came to seek her advice since a hunter came to him and told him such and such.

[Page 150]

He told her all the hunter had said and Serril believed immediately. She did not inquire nor require much. She said, "Go tell him that the seven good years should come immediately."

"And in our old age, Serril?"

"God will provide! Every day God is great." She replied confidently, "and we have not the time to wait. Can you hear the children? They are out in the yard playing in the sand because they were sent home from the cheder. We have not paid tuition."

Tuvia was convinced and no longer deliberated. He ran to the Messenger and said, "My Serril said, 'immediately!'"

"And later, when your strength depletes and you can no longer bear your burden?"

"She said, 'every day God is Grea' She has faith. The main concern is paying tuition for the boys."

"And so it shall be," said the messenger. "Go home, there you will find the treasure."

The Messenger vanished. Tuvia returned home and went to the backyard where the children were playing in the sand. He saw the sand was not sand but Gold powder.

The Seven good years began.

*

Time flew by. As the seven good years approached the end, the Messenger came and told Tuvia that on that day the sun of his success will set. All his riches he has at home or deposited with others will vanish like a dream. He found him standing in the marketplace, his coat edges tucked in his rope belt, prepared to earn his keep by the sweat of his brow as before through bearing a burden.

And Tuvia said, "Dear German, you have come to tell me that the good years have passed. I will go and tell my Serril of the riches and honors which she possessed."

They both walked out to the field where Tuvia's house was. It was made of mud like it was before, and Serril the housewife was wearing rags like before. When the Messenger told her of the passage of time she was not shocked at all and said, "No mater sir. For us, the seven good years never began. We have considered the treasure to be a deposit from God. The house remained as was. Our clothes and the food and drink are provided by Tuvia's labor as before. We have only taken from the golden treasure in the sand to pay for tuition for the boys. The Torah is His and the gold is His, and with His gold we have paid for His Torah, and no more. If His Blessed Name has found people more equipped to handle the deposit, He can give it to them."

After she concluded, the Messenger rose and brought the matter to the Heavenly Court. A verdict was rendered that there was no person more fitting for the deposit than Tuvia and his wife Serril, and the deposit remained in their hands.

Translator's footnote:

1. Seven Good Years

[Page 151]

Sayings, Conversations and Typical Stories
by Berrel Zuntag

Translated by Meir Bulman

Turobin – a Grand Town

How did Turobin Become a Town? R' Isaac the *shochet* explained how it came to pass. As is well known, there were no roads in Polish towns and our small town was among those who needed a road. Before Passover, as the snow and frozen waters melted, swamps and mud were formed everywhere to the point that it was difficult to leave the town. R' Isaac said, "now I understand how Turobin became a big town. Some Jews arrived in town for Passover and could not leave. With no other options, they wrote their families and asked if they would be so kind as to come to Turobin. And so it was. The wives and children came to Turobin for Passover. In the summer, they did not wish to return to the big cities they had come from at the name time all the city folk were travelling to the countryside on vacation. And thus, Turobin became a town."

The Messiah Approaches

Once, Hershely Rothblatt saw Pini Gewirtz filling his mouth with laugher at the *beth midrash*. Hershely, knowing that Pini never laughs, said, "brothers. Know that we are in the time leading to messiah's arrival, for it says 'when God will restore Zion, Then our mouths will fill with laughter.' If not for the messiah approaching, it is inconceivable that Pini will laugh."

Hirsh Fershtendig Learns Hebrew

After the *Tarbut* School opened in Turobin, Hirsh signed up for Hebrew language classes. He began to diligently study Hebrew. After he would return home from Hebrew classes he slowly began to speak more Hebrew. His father Binyamin Fershtendig was not pleased since he was a Hassid. But his Mother, Chane'le would say, "no matter, children need to study everything, even at *Tarbut*, as long as they are studying." Once, while sitting at the table, his mother asked him to pour her a cup of tea. At the same occasion, Hershel asked his father in Hebrew, "*Abba, ata shoteh?*" ["father, will you drink?"] when his father heard his question he slapped him and cried angrily "you have just started going to *Tarbut* and already you are calling me a *shoteh* [fool]?" Hershel began to scream and yell that in his question he meant to ask was if he also wanted to drink and the phrasing he used was correct. His father replied, "I do not want your honey nor your sting. I do not want to fool your tea in your Hebrew."

188

[Page 152]

R' Binyamin Fershtendig

R' Binymain actually opposed being
photographed. A group of Zionists purposely
captured his image. They are smiling
because of the successful mission.

[Page 153]

To Not Grow Wide

When Shlomo'le Greenberg came to Turobin as Yitzchak Bekker's son-in-law, he regarded himself as one of the wisest Torah scholars of Turobin. Everyone remembers R' Yeshayahu the Torah instructor. He was a respected man and liked to be treated as such, but Shlomole disregarded his wishes. Rabbi Yeshayahu usually walked to the synagogue with a large bag of Talit and tefillin under his arm, and everyone he encountered would clear his path out of respect. Shlomo Greenberg was a revolutionary in that sense and would comfortably walk the width of the synagogue. Once, R' Yeshayahu summoned Shlomo and said, "young man, please, since are new in town you have to act differently." How?" asked Shlomo. "I'll illustrate this to you. I do not care if you regard yourself as a great scholar. You can add to your height all you want. But you cannot block my path. You must not add to your width."

Evil Eye Spell

Evil Eye is a Jewish folk term which denoted observing an object or person in envy and bad intent. Evil Eye or *"Enna Bisha"* in Aramaic came about as a belief that such a bad observation can result in tragedy to the observed party. In a Talmudic legend there is a spell against the Evil Eye, and since the Middle Ages there were many spells against it. Also used as a dispel is saying "without the evil eye," which is added when speaking positively abut a person or animal. In every town there were those who knew to whisper spells against the Evil Eye and decrease its influence.

Of course, R' Isaac Shochet was among those few in Turobin who knew the Evil Eye counter-spells. Whenever an accident or illness occurred one would run to Isaac. "Oh Isaac, save my girl," yelled the mother, "she just finished eating and is not feeling well. She's suffering with strong head and stomach pain and is screaming in pain. She cannot yawn [?] and overcome her pains." After carefully listening to the mother, he asked her name and her daughter's and began to whisper. After he finished whispering the spell against the evil eye, he told the mother, "You can leave now. Your daughter will make a full recovery." Right after the woman left, R' Isaac said, "she must have stuffed herself with potatoes and dough until she felt stomach pain. But what can I do? The woman thinks I'm a Hassidic *rebbe* and fully believes it. I have no other choice but to fulfill her wishes."

190

Secrets

Chaim Friedler's the butcher paid to slaughter an animal and the *shochet* said the slaughter was improper. The butchers who were around hoped the animal would not be *kosher*. It was very fat and expensive. The other butchers were very pleased by the animal not being *kosher* since they knew that if not for that Chaim would be selling the best meat in town. Many of the butchers were secretly joyful about the animal being dismissed and said, "a man like Chaim'el need not slaughter such expensive animals." There were also those who sympathized with Chaim for his loss. But since Israel is a nation of laws, the rabbis and *shochet*im gathered for a meeting and began deliberating. Chaim Friedler was a poor man and father of small children. He paid for the animal with borrowed money thus he will not be able to feed his children. The verdict was rendered that the animal was actually *kosher* and he would not lose so much. After the verdict rendered by the rabbis and known in public, Chaim went outside and began yelling, "who knows what else it says in the Torah that these thieves are hiding?"

[Page 154]

Two Lessons from *Shechita*

Once, R' Yitzchak *Shochet*, who had reached his eighties, was asked what he learned in his decades of serving as a *shochet* in Turobin. He replied that he learned two things, one, the length of a cake for a circumcision ceremony, and a second, the weight of a rabbi in town so he can be called Our Teacher and Our master.

First, it is known that R' Yitzchak was also a circumciser. Once, he went to perform a circumcision at a village. All the Jewish residents gathered for the mitzvah. Before the meal the villagers asked one another if they have prepared everything properly so as not be ashamed and laughable to the *shochet*. The main concern was if the cake was lawfully prepared. One of the attendees said that in regard to the cake, it is lawful if one is permitted to recite the bread blessing on it. He places the cake on the table and measured it against his arm. When the cake reached his elbow, he said, "yes, this is a cake long enough to be *kosher* for a bris."

Second, when the butchers of Turobin came to R' Yitzchak to slaughter their animals, they recounted the events of the livestock market. They discussed matters such as who found a bargain, who was on the verge of making an important purchase but a the last moment the deal was spoiled, who made a bad purchase. Etc. The *Shochet* was subjected to all the stories told by those who provided his income. Once, a butcher entered mid conversion and said, "guys, I also have something to tell about today." "What happened?" asked the other butchers. "Today I have purchased a *moreh morenu* ['masterful teacher.'] "Is that so?" asked the other listeners, "How much does it weigh?" "it weighs six pud." He replied. "Six pud? Than it is truly a masterful teacher." Ever since, R' Yitzchak *Shochet* knew what he was told the town's butchers: a master rabbi is only worthy of such a title if he weighs six pud.

———

[Page 154]

Nicknames of Towns in the Lublin District

by Shimon Halamish (Shlepferman)

Translated by Meir Bulman

1. **Turobin**. The members of the town gained a reputation of ignoramuses and so they were called "Turobiner Barteks" a Polish name and a name for a Jew not well versed in Torah.[1]

2. **Goraj**. For some reason they were called "The Goraj Dead." the town was quite small, and the clowns said that when coach enters the town, its front wheels are already outside of the town. Religious divorces were written there.

[Page 155]

3. **Zolkiewka**. The residents were called Zolkiewka Moysrim (snitches) since it was a small town and most of its residents sold moonshine or other contraband items which the authorities imminently informed of.

4. **Rejowiec** was a small, calm, silent, and stagnant town. Local authorities did not bother the Jews during the 1648 massacres and other times of turmoil. And so, there was an expression "quiet like Rejowiec." It was told that its residents had no money issues and lived peacefully and comfortably.

5. **Janów Lubelski** was a Count Zamoyski territory near the Biali River. For some reason, religious divorce documents were not written there. The

residents were named Yanover Codekkes after the Cordecs, sandals made by tough leather soles bound to the foot with rags and laces traditionally worn by peasants.

6. **Modliborzyce** – in Yiddish the name became Mazl–bozhits. The residents were nicknamed "*Modliboshitzer yoykh*" (broth) after the year–round mud resembling broth in a bowl on the streets of town.

7. **Piaski Luterskie** residents achieved a reputation of famous thieves. They did not recite "How precious is Your gift," the Psalm which is usually recited when momentarily cover the head while cloaking in the tallit. There once was a man excitingly recited it while wrapping his tallit and at that very moment his tefillin were stolen.

8. **Rachów** (**Annopol–Rachów**) A town on the shores of the Wisłă . Its goats rest on the rooftops and eat the straw which replaces the tiles, or the weeds growing in the walls of every home. The Goats of Rachów oppose culture and progress and when announcement are posted in the streets they quickly chew the paper and lick up the glue.

9. **Biłgoraj** was a great Jewish town. According to *Tzok Haitim* the whole community was destroyed in the 1648 massacres. Its residents were nicknamed "*Biłgoraj er Zifers*" (sieve makers) after the swine whiskers which are used when manufacturing sieves.

10. **Szczebrzeszyn** was a town of great wisdom and Torah. Some enlightened folks interpreted its name as "shav rishon" [the first returned] or "Shever shen" [broken tooth] after events that occurred. Its residents were nicknamed Shebrishiner plakhatess (sheets) after the regionally famous quality sheets made of simple cotton which they manufactured.

11. **Zamosc** – birthplace of I. L. Peretz, acquired a reputation as a town of gluttonous eaters, "*Zamoshtsher Fressers.*" Being a stronghold of Haskalah, the fundamentalists hated it and in the eyes of Hassidim it was a town of rebels. They interpreted the name of the town as a culprit; Zamosz is he numerological equivalent of heretic.

12. **Kazimierz** was a well–known town to Jews and the nation, built by Kasimir the Great in the 14th Century and named after him. The old synagogue housed silver candlesticks and a gold woven curtain of the ark for many years. Still, the residents were nicknamed "*Cosamirer*

Meshumadim" after a *meshumad* named Khatzkele Hogge who was there and stank up the town.

–*Yeda Am: A Center for Jewish Folklore*, edited by Dr. Yom–Tov Lewinsky, Tel Aviv, Vol. 1&2.

———

Editor's note:

1. The opposite is true. It was accepted in the town for generations that Turobin produced many great Torah scholars. it is probably an unsuccessful joke.

———

[Page 156]

Soul

by Itamar Hopen

Dedicated in memory of my mother–in–law
Aliza Serkis of Johannesburg
Passed away 22/7/67

Translated by Meir Bulman

A town does not only have a name, but also a soul. A person has name and also a soul, a river has name and a soul. Everything has both a name and a soul.

A person is born with a soul and his name is given eight days later. A river is born with a soul and a name is given to it later. But a town is first given a name, but its soul is continually formed in the generations to come.

After a person who passes away, his name is forgotten but his soul remains. The soul struggles and wanders, becomes mystical and gains form until it achieves peace. A river that dries, its name is forgotten, and its soul is no more, not a trace remains of the river, other than memories. (witnesses say that after the destruction of the Turobin community the river Pur cried until it dried.)

When a town and its community are destroyed, its name is gone, but its soul still exists. Only then does a town know how crucial its existence was. It does not die even after its tombstone is placed – it only serves to prove that spirit lives on. The Jewish people live on, despite the Spanish Inquisition. 470 years have since passed the nation will continue to survive as long as Yom Kippur survives.[?]

Name and soul are known terms. But what are they? Can one obtain them? can they be sensed? Can they be felt? Can they be seen? Yes! Of course! Distinctly and as a group.

The human soul is well known although it is not a human. "He is a dear man with a golden soul." "He is a sweet person with a gentle soul." "The soul and its presence can be seen in one's eye." "After death, the souls will roll in tunnels and reach Eretz Israel." "Dear Soul, a good soul." "in Your hands I commit my spirit," "Nishmat."

If you please, you may listen. A river also has a soul: the river flowed, the river shrank! The river demands its yearly victims! The river is gushing! The river is silent and shines. The river has fish, crevices, etc. The river has hiding spots. It has a heart too, the river has a head – the source of its waters, feet.

The river accepts everything, even sins during *tashlikh*. When a town mourns, the river mourns with it. It can be clearly observed when the river is kind, large, raging, sensitive, or grand.

A town and its soul: R' Baruch the *shamash* awakening the residents, with a mallet–shaped stick. When he knocks three times it is ordinary. If, God forbid, he knocks twice it means someone in town has died.

R' Hershel called everyone to the bathhouse and also whipped the town's important people on the tallest bench. If it was not hot enough everyone would yell, "*a shaifele*!" meaning a water bucket needed to be poured over the heated stones which emanated the hot vapor.

[Page 157]

R' Alter Shneiderberg summoned people to recite Psalms on Shabbat morning. R' Alter awoke people with a pleasant singing voice. R' alter had another role; he walked the streets on Friday and called out "bread for the poor!" R' Hershshle gathered the bread in a sack and distributed to the needy anonymously.

Everyone walked quickly to the synagogue, but returned slowly. Between the afternoon and evening prayers there was noise at the synagogue, important business was conducted then.

If a woman was having a difficult childbirth, the cheder students customarily tied a thread from the holy ark to the bed of the mother as a good luck charm.

The *beth midrash* did not have a lock, because there were always people in it studying. The passersby heard the pleasant voices of those studying well.

The yard of the two synagogues also had use. All *chuppah* ceremonies took place in it, shine, or frost. The groom stood under the canopy, his eyes covered, waiting for his bride. If the bride lived on the other side of town, that trip lasted an hour and a half or more. That was an unpleasant experience for the groom. At that aimless and sometimes dangerous time, haters friends and even of the groom were jealous he got such a good bride. They would honor him by throwing snowballs at every available surface and he could not dodge since his eyes were covered. If the groom would have known of that wild judgement ahead of time he would have probably delayed the wedding. A Jewish soul cannot be estimated.

On Friday night after prayers, the Holy Spirit rested upon the town. Everyone wore their festive Shabbat cloths, and the streets were silent and pleasant. The light of the shabbat candles emanated from every Jewish home, and the pleasant hymns were clearly audible in the streets.

On Shabbat day, everything was in motion; the various praying folks, the scholars at the *Beth midrash*, the Zionists in their prayers, lectures and gatherings. Everyone knew it was shabbat and acted accordingly.

On Yom Kippur evening after *Kol Nidrei* all was silent, a silence bordering fear as the world stood before the heavenly court. The fear gripped all, even the fish in the waters trembled. The fast ended and the prayers were completed with the verse, "Next year in Jerusalem!"

On Simchat Torah, the weekly portions recited were completed and Jews danced joyfully. When the Hassidim danced, so did the whole town. Of course, one drinks *l'chaim* and eats quiche before dancing. R' Shmelke, a large and fat man, a follower of the Gur *Rebbe*, is intoxicated and the ground cannot hold him. He climbs the two–meter high awning owned by Mrs. Tishah and intends

196

to jump from it. When his Hassidic friends saw him, they begged him to have mercy on Mrs. Tishah's room. Do you know what power drew R' Shmelke from the roof? A delicious quiche was brought and R' Shmelke was told he must taste it.

R' Shmelke was a Hassid of the Ger sect. A story about him is told. One market day, another Hassid of the same *rebbe* entered his store, crowded as usual on market days. R' Shmelke greets him with a"Shalom Aleichem, R' Yaakov," and tells him that if wishes to discuss business he will have to wait shortly, but if he wants to discuss Hassidism he is ready immediately. Such is the power of a Hassidic soul.

[Page 158]

When A Jew could not afford Shabbat, other Jews fundraised for Shabbat. When a Jew could not afford to marry off his daughter, there were Jews who fundraised for him. When A Jew became ill, Jews aided him. Who else would he go to, the gentiles? The Jews approached the gentiles when there was a dispute in town, and not for help but to inform and snitch, by authority of the Torah, of course. Can you imagine a Jewish soul?

R' Shaul Mendel Shia's vanished from the town for a few months. The women gathered and whispered, speculating he was in a dispute with his wife. How can it be? A Jewish man leaves behind a young woman and four little children and a flourishing leather business and vanishes? But the Hassidim knew he missed his *rebbe* so he travelled to him for a few months. Imagine a Jewish soul.

Mordechai Greenberg's wife worked while R' Mordechai taught a group of students at the *Beth midrash*. It was said that R' Mordechai was a philosopher, a great scholar. If it happed that one of his students did not understand the material, he bit his own fingers until he bled. Or he would roll his pointed beard into his mouth and bite, bite and spit and the beard got smaller. Imagine a Jewish soul.

R' Alter Chips fasted his whole life, like Rabbi Zadok, but R' Alter did not eat dates. Instead, he ate breakfast, lunch, and dinner together at three in the afternoon. He was a spirited man, a dear soul. Jews of his kind can no longer be found.

The coachmen traveled the road and between each station studied a page of Talmud. The craftsman studied and worshipped. The water deliverymen also enthusiastically studied and prayed. Even Elazar the apostate stood longingly by the synagogue on Yom Kippur. Can we imagine the quality of a Jewish soul?

Let us gather and speak of that a town and its beloved people. There were pure and kind souls, servants of holiness, philosophers, honest people, its own bathhouse, rabbi and holy utensils, and a river. The question is raised, did that town have a soul? Of course, it had a soul, a beloved soul indeed.

[Page 161]

4. On the Way to Zion

Cultural Activities in Turobin

Aryeh Goldfarb

Translated by Meir Bulman

After WWI, anew spirit began to spread throughout the world. Many nations whose national freedom was previously denied and who were mentally and physically enslaved by dictators achieved national recognition and state autonomy. The walls surrounding Jewish life also began to crumble. New ideas penetrated through the cracks and the bells of freedom tolled everywhere. The Jewish masses had lived among the nations for millennia and had traveled a long and winding path rife with physical and economic persecution, their lives often hanging on by a thread. They constantly struggled for social and material survival. Their hopes were imbedded in messianic destiny and they began to open their eyes and observe their surroundings. They, too, awoke alongside the nations in which they dwelled and demanded their right to exist. They resisted their national enslavement and resisted, with intensifying force, against economic persecution and social

198

restrictions. This change was greater in Poland which was liberated from the burden of foreigners and achieved national freedom. In that state, the Jewish life force was strengthened and advanced.

The role of the Balfour Declaration in the Awakening of the Diaspora

The Balfour declaration publicly declared to the world that the Jews are a nation like all others and have the right to self–determination like other nations. It galvanized the Jewish masses and instilled strength and bravery in their youth. November 2, 1917 was etched in the diaspora Jews as a distinguished date. It predicted redemption and advanced the wonderous event which until then was just a vision for the "End of Days."

The Zionist movement, small in its founding days, began to rapidly expand and added masses of people who were previously indifferent to the Zionist ideal. The World Zionist Organization began spreading culture and education among the masses. Hebrew schools were founded, as was a vast network of cultural and educational institutions among the diaspora communities under the framework of the cultural organization *Tarbut*. At the *Tarbut* school, Hebrew was the language of instruction. As a result, it spread among youth as a living and spoken language, making its way towards its final purpose as the natural and living language of the Jewish nation in an independent state. There were also night schools founded to teach adults the Hebrew language and its culture, and to bestow upon them the joys of renewal.

Turobin's Part in the National Awakening

In our Turobin, most residents were craftsmen, merchants, and middlemen between the village and the city. It was detached from a large Jewish center. Turobin also began a Zionist awakening which gained popularity. Until then, socio–cultural life was concentrated within the confines of the synagogues. As the bells of liberty began to toll across the country, they reached the town as well. Youth were thrust into turmoil and waves began to crash upon the calm surface. The days were no longer silent.

[Page 162]

At the initiative of Yitzchak Yaffeh, Sarah Yanover, Yitzchak Feder, Silka Drimler, Shmuel–Abba Gutwertz, and Yechiel Cooper, a *Tarbut* chapter was founded locally. That institution eventually became an important factor in the cultural and social life of Turobin. The chapter maintained a stable correspondence with headquarters in Warsaw. It purchased a dwelling and its first move was founding a library with many books in Hebrew and Yiddish which were loaned to local youths. *Tarbut* became the central point of youthful life and energy. Local youth, which until then had aimlessly squandered their time, enthusiastically tackled the books. Reading opened them to new worlds and they set goals which they had not considered before. Their aims changed as they uncovered new issues in Jewish culture and lifestyle.

Librarian Chava Rothblatt invested much of her energy and courage. Every evening, with great devotion she engaged in curating and distributing the books. She also customized reading materials fitting the interests of those not versed in catalogues. She did so as a volunteer and expected no reward.

Many discussions took place at the library about Zionism, socialism, Marxism, and Social Zionism. The debates echoed into the late hours of the night.

Night classes for Hebrew language instruction were also established. There were lectures about current events in Eretz Israel and worldwide. Periodically, guest lecturers were invited from Warsaw, Lublin, and other central locations; they enlightened locals on matters of interest. The audience expanded each time. Occasional discussions on literature took place.

The Theater Company of Turobin

Participants in the drama company founded in Turobin were: Leiser Streicher (the town medic), Yitzchak Feder, Leib Yaffeh, Hadas Lerrer, Sara Yanover, Yossel Gutwertz, Uri Gutwertz, Neihoz, Moshe Goldshmidt, and Temmeh Feder. Shmuel–Abba Gutwertz and Moshe Shneiderberg were the directors.

The company successfully produced several plays. Revenue was dedicated to the library and the *Tarbut* general fund, which was usually underfunded due to the many expenses for instructors, lecturers, etc. The Jewish community council was under the influence of Agudath Israel members who were a majority on the council. Not only did they not support those institutions but, from the beginning, they also battled them with all of their power because they considered Zionism "an evil culture" and an obstacle to traditional Judaism. They thought that the library disseminated to their

200

children heretical and idolatrous material in those forbidden books and they saw in it a danger to the future of their children. They feared that youth would be "carried away by the murky tide," "taste the tree of knowledge" and stray off the path they had walked on until that day.

[Page 163]

Struggle Between Old and New

At the head of those battling the new movement were Yerachmiel Bronspiegel and Shmelke Drimler. They did everything in their power to strangle the activities of *Tarbut* and went so far as breaking bread with the Strosta[1] in Krasnostav and pressured him to shutter *Tarbut*. The authorities did not relent as the official policy regarded Zionism positively at that time. They did not do that out of love for the Jews but saw in Zionism a means to drive Jewish emigration out of the state, which was beneficial to them on all counts. When the men of Agudah failed in undermining *Tarbut* through the authorities, they began to handle matters on their own. They invested a lot to prevent offspring's defection. They literally made them stay in their houses and forbade them to leave. However, the youth did as much as possible to evade house arrest and secretly left home for the gathering place to taste of the forbidden fruit. Among them were the children of activists mentioned above. When their parents sensed that (the children were escaping), they set up an ambush outside (they dared not enter as they would not set foot in an "impure" place) and waited for them to exit. Then stirring scenes occurred. Slaps and blows came from every direction, accompanied by name–calling and swearing directed towards the *Tarbut* activists. The assaulted and humiliated victims, among them also older girls, did not continue coming, and were fearful, ashamed, and pained. But when they could no longer "overcome their urges," they returned, blushing in shame and fear. The encouragement they received from the club members instilled in them a spirit from above. They were strengthened and encouraged to stand up to their guards and detractors. The struggle manifested in various forms until the stubborn parents realized they were defeated. They would not be able to stop their offspring and then the "belt was loosened."

The library also suffered a lot because of the struggle and lost many books which were ripped or burned by the parents who, after diligent searches, had discovered the "impure goods" in their children's possession.

In addition to the attention to cultural activity, attention was also paid to physical education. A gymnasium was founded next to the *Tarbut* club. Early on Shabbat morning, members travelled a few kilometers from Turobin to Zelshvika where they exercised. Football also drew many enthusiasts. Hours were spent exercising in nature and they returned to the town refreshed.

A council to benefit Keren Kayemet was also founded by the club and included several devoted members. Thanks to them, in cooperation with Keren Kayemet representatives from Warsaw, Keren Kayemet achieved much fame among the locals.

Locally, Keren gained fame among all classes. Even the most sworn and extreme detractors among the Gur Hasidim and the leftists came and filled the synagogue to listen to the lectures. The lecture topic was 'Keren Kayemet L'Yisrael (KKL) and Eretz Israel.' Among the lecturers was Shimon Shleferman who excited his audience.

The Zionist organizations of the right and left took part in that activity and volunteered their time. Even ordinary expenses were paid with their own money. That work was many shades. The collection boxes were distributed at movie days which took place on certain occasions such as Lag B'omer, Hanukah, the 20th of Tamuz, Purim etc. Sometimes movie days were conducted on market days and then the local peasants were also graced by (given) KKL armbands to decorate their clothes.

Among the activities were various fundraisers on festive occasions like weddings, family gatherings, and tree planting in the KKL forest. During Torah readings, pledges were made to KKL, especially at the Zionist shtiebel[2]. The balls hosted on the 20th of Tamuz in memory of the Founder of Zionism also raised funds for KKL.

Another form of income was the distribution of fruit bags from Eretz Israel on Tu Beshvat. Bags included dates, figs, carob, etc.

Youths enthusiastically gathered the funds from KKL collection boxes; on a monthly basis, they went door to door. There was not a single instance of a box being empty, not even in the poorest households. The women saw it as their sacred duty to drop a coin in the box before candle lighting on Friday because is there a bigger mitzvah than redeeming the land from the hands of foreigners?

The First Group of Halutzim to Immigrate to Eretz Israel

Top row from the right: **Mordechai Hopen, Itamar Hopen, Bluma Greenberg (Zilberklang), Moshe Gutwertz, Yaakov Friedler**

Seated: **Yehoshua (Heshel) Ben–Ari (Zilberklang), Aryeh Goldfarb, Yerachmiel Frieberg, Aharon Bumfeld**

Hahalutz and Hakhshara [training]

Alongside the *Tarbut* club, other clubs formed including Hakhalutz, Hakhalutz Hatzair, the Friehyt, and Beitar[3]. For some time, there was also Hashomer Ha'leumi, a Jewish branch of the scouts headed by a motivated and proactive leader, but after he left that movement dismantled.

Zionist inspiration penetrated the bet midrash[4] and the men who studied it as well. Yehoshua Zilberklang (today Ben–Ari, a legal consultant for the Israel Police), Zvi Rothblatt, Baruch Katz, and Berrel Zuntag founded the Hapoel Hamizrachi[5] chapter in Turobin. It was founded at the initiative of Zilberklang who founded a number of training grounds in the Lublin district on behalf of Hamizrachi. Two Kibbutzim were founded in Kean Village, 17 km from Lublin, and in another village whose name I forgot.

Therefore, Turobin was a town blessed with activity. It had active, lively youth organizations and councils with much blessed action. The Jewish community was alert and thirsted for the redemption and the restoration of the nation, until the destroyer rose and severed it from this world.

May their memory be blessed and forever in our hearts.

Editor's Footnotes:

1. Strosta – may have referred to the mayor or the head of the government area

2. Shtiebel – a place used for communal Jewish prayer. In contrast to a formal synagogue, a shtiebel is far smaller and approached more casually.

3. Hakhalutz, Hakhalutz Hatzair, the Friehyt, and Beitar – Jewish youth movements

4. Bet midrash – a Jewish study hall located in a synagogue, yeshiva, kollel or other building

5. Hapoel Hamizrachi – a political party and settlement movement in Israel;s one of the predecessors of the National Religious Party, which later became the modern–day Jewish Home Party

---

Traditional Life and Zionism in Town

(Memories)

By Shimon Halamish (Shleferman)

Translated by Meir Bulman

In memory of my uncle Moshe Shleferman and his family who

perished in the Holocaust

As I come to write in the Yizkor book for the martyrs of Turobin, the town populated by Jews in the Lublin district and has been mentioned even before the events of 1648, my hand shakes as my heart sinks. Is this town really no more? The same town which was home to beloved Jews, who built it devotedly and loyally, now remains without any Jews, and all perished, including its women and children, due to the murderous Nazi Germans aided by the Polish, among six million of our people, the glory of the nation? And it should be noted that the Jews of Turobin observed tradition and Torah. Each of them labored to enliven their soul in crafts and trade (the devout, in order to observe mitzvot and go to heaven). The women usually worked to provide while the men studied at the bet midrash. Everyone strived to raise and educate their children to establish the next generation as their fathers before them. Sadly, the days of the Holocaust arrived and the German and Polish murderers erased the Jewish town from the face of the Earth. We do not know where the bones of the martyrs are buried.

[Page 166]

I find it a divine obligation to draw from my memory beloved Jews who lived in Turobin. They built it across several generations, established community values and produced Rabbis and rebbes, men of Haskalah[1], and the pioneering builders of our nation.

I had known of Turobin before I visited it. During WWI, heavy artillery was directed from the Austrians and Germans and the town burned to the ground. Its residents left and became refugees. One of these came to our town of Yanov and succeeded in settling there. In our home we hosted the Ashnberg family (daughter of R' Isaac, the town shochet.)

Every year, the Turobin Rebbe also visited our town during the winter week of the Vayechi Torah portion. During his stay, the town became a holiday for his disciples and admirers. They were usually men of action, meaning craftsmen – tailors, cobblers, butchers, etc. who saw him as their spiritual leader. He would draw them in; they confided their troubles and handed him notes and his fee. Every night after work they came to R' Avraham Velevel's; he had a large house.) Avraham hosted the Rebbe so he could pray near him during afternoon and evening services and converse with the gabbai[2] between services. (The assistant (gabbai) was seen as assisting holiness and therefore holy himself.) The Hassidim were delighted when their day arrived and they were respected like scholars. After the evening prayers, each Hassid entered the Rebbe's room according to the appointment set by the Shamash[3] (of course, according to the amount of contribution he received.) The entrance to the Rebbe was done with awe and an accelerated heartbeat. The Hassid cautiously placed the note (written by the assistant) and the fee. The Rebbe rose and shook hands with the Hassid. After reading the note, he responded with kind blessings. The couple then left the Rebbe's room with a glow on their faces, happy as if a burden has been lifted. Therefore, the town was near and dear to my heart. I was also the Ba'al Koreh[4] at the shtibel of the Hassidim of that Rebbe.

As luck would have it, my step–uncle Moshe Shleferman became a resident of the town when he married the daughter of R' Alter Snheiderberg (Barik). R' Alter taught young children and, while also making a living, ensured his spot in heaven. Every Shabbat before dawn he would awaken the town residents from their slumber as he announced, "Awake, rise to worship the Creator, for that is your purpose, (Yiddedn, shtyt oyf L'avoydas Haboyreh.") Every devout Jew would rise and wash his hands (into the bedpan) so he could walk more than 4 steps. He would then dress and say, "Hashem created the mitzvot to enlighten our eyes." Then men would go to the synagogue. Some prayed and some recited psalms, the weekly portion, or a chapter of Mishnah. On weekdays, too, many Jews rose early for prayer and grace. After the morning prayers, many remained to study Talmud. The businessmen went about their business as the cheder[5]students went to their studies. The youth, adapted to that lifestyle which spanned generations, was now seeing influences of new ideas spreading through the country and Turobin.

206

[Page 167]

After the Austrian occupation during WWI ended and Poland gained independence, the Jewish youth began to open their eyes. Footsteps of redemption were heard. Zionist movements were founded, as were libraries, *Tarbut* schools, and various pioneering youth movements. In that newly created environment, wars were waged among fathers and sons. The youth strived for Aliyah and rebuilding the land so they invested much energy and devotion in activism on behalf of the national funds: Keren Kayemet, Keren Hayesod[6], and the Eretz Israel Fund. Despite fierce opposition by the religiously devout, which were the town's majority, the youth left the bet midrash. They began reading other books and newspapers. Hebrew courses were founded, and at the Zionist Movement's club, gatherings took place. The youth movements hosted discussions on topics concerning Israel. A group of Maskilim[7] was founded which marched alongside the national renewal moment in Turobin. It is interesting to note that the founders of the national movement had been excellent Torah scholars at the bet midrash and among the children of the community's holy men. They included the granddaughter of R' Isaac the shochet and his daughter Yetta Blima whose home became a center for Zionist activism. They worked alongside Yitzchak Feder, the Yaffeh brothers, Aryeh Goldfarb (who is here with us), and Sara Yanover who is also with us. They organized the local Zionist movement and the various institutions which derived from it.

As the movement's activity gained ground, a change of events took place in town. The religiously devout objected to all of Zionism and the rescue movement. They were subservient to important rabbis who opposed hastening the "end of days," especially to all actions by Hakhalutz and the advances made in Eretz Israel by the Zionist movement. They dubbed them 'criminals' who were not waiting for the messiah's arrival. As a result, a conflict arose among them and the Zionists, including the religious Hamizrachi and others. It began when Keren Kayemet collection boxes were distributed to homes, and when collection plates were placed in synagogues on Erev Yom Kippur and Purim. Aggudah men saw fit to wage war concerning the plates and the like, especially on the Days of Awe.

I had the honor of visiting Turobin several times and spent time with youth in the evenings. Friendly conversations and public performances took place. I saw the youth movements in action, especially Hakhalutz, an organization to which members relentlessly devoted their efforts. They left behind everything dear to their hearts, including their parents and their friends and, of course, those who did not agree with their chosen path. They traveled to training camps on the eve of their aliyah and thanks only to that physical and mental sacrifice are most of the surviving families – roughly 100 households – in Israel.

[Page 168]

While visiting the town, I visited a gathering of craftsmen (Handworker Fareyn) who were a subsidiary of the Folkists[8] founded by Prilutski. I managed to convince them to join our movement. They stood by the local Zionist movement and generously contributed to the Zionist funds.

I should note that the town residents were fortunate to have comrade Goldfarb the dentist who the residents went to for dental care. He also accepted the role of educator and guide to local youth. With his help, the activity of the Tarbut chapter was renewed; he was also a patron of Hakhalutz and participated in youth gatherings. He battled the Orthodox who often attempted to disrupt youth activities. He also helped found the drama club which produced living pictures of Jewish life. His late wife Tamar (Tameh) of Blessed Memory supported his efforts.

A Group of Zionist Activists

Standing from the right: **Shmuel–Abba
Gutwertz, Shlomo Diamant, Gutcheh
Hochman, Chana Drimler, Michael Yaffeh,
Zvi Fershtendik**
Seated: **Feigeh Mandel**

[Page 169]

I would like to examine another facet in the life of Turobin youth. Turobin
borders towns like Goray, an ancient small town whose residents were
devoutly religious. Anyone who spoke in favor of enlightenment was boycotted

and met a bitter end. In the face of the awakening in all the surrounding towns, Goray refused to join the awakening nationalist movement. However, it did have several young men and women who strived to join the movement, establish Zionist chapters and contribute to the national funds. However, due to their closeness to their parents, they were prevented from doing so. Rebellion was forbidden and they did not have the strength. A meeting between a young man and woman was strictly forbidden, but there were still those who dared to meet. Such meetings took place in secret in the grove outside of town or near the fountain. If such a couple was caught, meaning someone saw them conversing, they were declared caught, *gechefte*, and they met a poor fate.

I visited and organized many branches of Hakhalutz, mainly Keren Kayemet L'Yisrael branches and local Zionist movements. In Goray, I managed to organize a branch of the World Zionist Organization which included all departments of the movement. I knew that after the club was founded in Goray, youth from the entire area would join. The goal was that young women would attend the opening celebration and meet local young men, since the girls of Goray were not permitted to participate, fearing their parents who used whatever means available[?]. The risk that the girls of Goray would encounter meeting local boys was that, in the future, they would be shunned. That would lead them, G–d forbid, to stay single until their hair grew white (zy velen farzitzn.) As a result, the young women would be allowed to continue to participate after the opening in the remainder of the activities. The event was organized; for opening day, representatives from all local towns participated – Yanov, Bilgoray, Framopl – and the largest group was young men and women from Turobin.

As the procession of wagons reached Goray, they were greeted by a band with wind instruments that led the attendees to the location of the festivities. When the fathers of the town saw the hundreds of gatherers of both sexes, they allowed their daughters to also participate. The celebration was very successful. Of course, I was active in orchestrating the festivities. I gave an impressive speech, followed by speeches by the representatives of the convoys. The oversight of the Goray branch's administration was handed over to the people from Turobin and Frampol. That celebration, during which many extraordinary events took place, will never be forgotten. It is a pity that those fully devoted activists who gave their life for the Homeland were not fortunate

210

to reach Israel and were murdered by the Nazis and their Polish and Ukrainian collaborators, may their names be blotted out!

They should be remembered with the six million of our sacred Jewish brethren who perished in the awful Holocaust. Earth, do not cover their blood!

Editor's Footnotes:

1. Haskalah – a term referring to Jewish Enlightenment which was an intellectual movement among the Jews of Central and Eastern Europe

2. Gabbai – a person who assists in the running of synagogue services in some way

3. Shamash – often a salaried official in a synagogue whose duties generally include secretarial work and assistance to the cantor

4. Ba'al Koreh – a member of a Jewish congregation who reads from the Sefer Torah during the service

5. Cheder – a traditional elementary school teaching the basics of Judaism and the Hebrew language

6. Keren Hayesod – United Jewish Appeal

7. Maskilim – an 18th–19th–century movement among central and E European Jews, intended to modernize Jews and Judaism by encouraging adoption of secular European culture

8. Folkists – a political movement founded by historian Simon Dubnow in the aftermath of the 1905 pogroms in Russia

---

[Page 170]

The *Tarbut* Library in Turobin

Translated by Meir Bulman

Members of the *Tarbut* Library

The term Tarbut [culture] means the sum of the behaviors, methods of operation, and values according to which the individual and society implement spiritual and material life according to their understanding. The youth of Turobin who approached progress did not use "Tarbut" as a term, but as the name of an organization which centered on nourishing Hebrew culture and education between the World Wars. The youth of Turobin were very late in founding cultural institutions. In 1919, the Culture and Education Office was founded by the Zionist Organization in Warsaw to create and develop various forms of national life: cultural institutions, primary and secondary schools, and seminars with various lectures. The Turobin youth were not among the early ones, although the first signs of enlightenment appeared following the Austrian occupation during WWI. But compared to the deep political unrest among Polish Jewry during Poland's first days of independence, Turobin was silent and still. In 1921–22, there still was no trace of political life in Turobin. The town slumbered as if no change had taken place in Poland and its Jews. Only in 1929 was the Tarbut Library founded; it began to form the right environment to attract activists and lecturers from which the youth learned Zionist ideals. Youth also began to study the Hebrew language and read Hebrew books. The library was founded despite the opposition of pious parents who saw in every secular book a step toward apostasy and would tear such a book if it fell into their hands. The library was considered the fortress for town youths; they guarded it lovingly and developed it by occasionally adding new books.

[Page 171]

A group of young women active in the *Tarbut* Library
Standing: **Sima Greenberg, Gittel Feder, Mihal Zuntag, Yoptchi Tregger, Chaya Zilberklang** Seated: **Sheindel Zuckerman**

The *Tarbut* library had a reading hall with a varied collection of reding and text books. It operated in the 10 years preceding the Holocaust. Volunteer members did all operations. Dues were inexpensive and the funds were used to purchased newly published books. The *Tarbut* library included youth from all Zionist–pioneering sects.

[Page 172]

In the initial years, *Tarbut* also provided Hebrew language instruction and, due to a lack of funds,there was a gap in teaching. But starting in 1923, the teaching of Hebrew continued without interruption, not necessarily at *Tarbut*. Because of a scarcity of space, classes took place in the halls of Hakhalutz or *Tarbut*, depending upon conditions.

A group of *Tarbut* members at a reading in the forest outside of town

Standing from the right: **Yaakov Gutwilling, Aryeh Feder, Moshe Gewertz, Itamar Hopen, Shlomo Kupenbaum, Yehousha Hopen** Seated: **Yaakov Friedler, Yosef Gutbertz, Yosef Rieder, Yisrael Oberweiss, Yaakov Braverman, Yehoshua Zuckerman**

The First Pioneer's Aliyah

By Itamar Hopen

Translated by Meir Bulman

Shlomo Kopf, son of R' Fishel and born in 1896, studied at a cheder and received a traditional education. He was healthy in body and mind. He regarded people honestly. Shlomo was not talkative by nature but he knew how to quietly present his thoughts in an organized manner. He respected others and was respected by all. After he grew up, he helped his father's business. His father leased fruit tree gardens from villagers and area landowners. Shlomo spent much of his time in regional villages and was well acquainted with the area farmers. Under those circumstances, he experienced working the land and was also familiar with the hate expressed by the peasants towards the Jews.

As Shlomo lived through the period after WWI and the liberation of Poland and the deeply felt persecution of Jewish communities, his approach changed.

[Page 173]

In the 20s, like many young Jewish men at that time, Shlomo sought his path and future. As was tradition, his parents found the solution and arranged his marriage. Shlomo married a young woman from the neighboring town of Shebreshin. But the marriage was unsuccessful and Shlomo was unhappy. There were many reasons for that. Some said his wife did not agree to join him on his journey to Eretz Israel and others cited a different reason. Either way, Shlomo decided to immigrate to Eretz Israel. Since his wife did not agree to join him, overseas journeys were unpredictable, and he did not want to leave her as an *agunah*[1], they divorced.

Shlomo obtained a "Herzl Card." The card was either blue or blue and white; either way, that is what the ticket was called. Shlomo made Aliyah in 1924. As is known, a crisis occurred in Erez Israel then. But in his letters to his parents, he did not mention the crisis at all. He wrote about the hot sun, the bright skies, the pioneers. He also mentioned he was working on draining the swamps of Hedera and was feeling well. Malaria took hold in Hedera and Shlomo also contracted it. He was treated with quinine and recovered.

215

At the end of 1928, Palestine Potash Limited was founded, led by Moshe Novomeysky. Shlomo traveled with a group of pioneers who were specially selected for preparing the ground at the north side of the Dead Sea. The desert terrain which had been unsettled for generations took the lives of many of the first workers. Some contracted malaria or some other disease which was yet to be understood. Shlomo contracted sleeping sickness. After a lengthy hospital treatment in 1929, Shlomo was sent to his parents' home by the World Zionist Organization and the Palestine Potash company. That was the year of the massacres in Eretz Israel. At that time, many youth in the town were enthusiastic about immigrating to Eretz Israel and then fighting. Under such circumstances, Shlomo's return left a depressing impression on the Jewish youth in the town.

Shlomo, the first halutz[2], once strong as an ox, now walked the streets of town like a shadow. He did not recover from the disease, in spite of doctors' prediction that he would recover by switching climates. He would walk and doze slowly. He would slowly spit as he spoke and drool dripped from his mouth.

Anyone who saw him felt empathy. The pioneering youth in the town were not negatively impacted by Shlomo's return. The opposite was true. They attempted to befriend him and wanted him to tell them about Eretz Israel. Shlomo did not speak much since it was difficult to do so but everything he did say about Israel was about the good and beautiful. What happened to him was his personal, private tragedy.

The pioneering youth observed Shlomo with mixed feelings. Shlomo would mumble, "Come, descendants of Jacob, let us walk, for you have nothing to do here."

To make a change in his life, the doctors recommended he marry and in 1931, Shlomo married a woman from neighboring Yanov but his health did not improve. In 1937 after he had suffered much hardship and pain, Shlomo passed on to the next world.

Bless his memory.

Editor's Footnotes:

1. Agunah – Jewish legal term for a Jewish woman who is "chained" to her marriage. Often refers to a woman whose husband refuses, or is unable, to grant her a divorce document in Jewish religious law.

2. Halutz – a person who immigrates to Israel

[Page 174]

Herrish Bitterman Goes to Eretz Israel

By Israel Amir

Translated by Meir Bulman

Herrish built his home behind the synagogue. The house was constructed from bits of wood he had gathered for years. The home was his residence and wood workshop. The structure of the house was never completed and was also missing a floor. The family was large and poverty was even greater but Herrish was always content.

He was one of the best carpenters in town. Many learned the trade from him, for he who studied with Shlomo knew the job well. Herrish was never formally a member of any party, but Poale Zion[1] was close to his heart. His eight boys joined the Bund[2] and were devout members. There were those who said that the mother sided with the boys' party.

I recall a day in 1923 when Herrish came to me and told me his secret that he and two other men were planning to make aliyah on foot. One of the others was a Hassid from the Trisk shtibel[3], Yaakov Goistgaut, and another was Leibush Forer, a more progressive Jew from the neighboring town, Zholkeivka. Leibush's daughters were members of Gordonia[4] and he was likely influenced by them.

Three worlds had converged in this goal of aliyah on foot. I asked Herrish how he planned to make sure his family would be supported during his absence. He replied that his sons would work and they are trustworthy.

In the meantime, I went to kibbutz training. When I returned to town a few years later, my parents told me that the three indeed went on their dream journey. However, only one of them was successful in crossing the Austrian border. Herrish and the other person were stopped at the border and, after much trouble and torment, returned to Poland.

The failure had cost Herrish in health. As if that was not enough, the Hassidim and the Bund members widely mocked him. That did not deter him and he was determined to fulfil his dream of aliyah.

After I immigrated to Eretz Israel in 1939, I decided to find the one of the three who had succeeded, Leibush Forer. I searched intensely and found him and his family, whom he had succeeded in bringing to Haifa. Leibush, who had become an expert climber, was content with his lot.

That same year, the war erupted and with it came the Holocaust which destroyed, among others, all those beloved modest Jews who were the majority of Polish Jewry.

One bright day in 1948 I received a letter from the town's survivors in Germany. I found that Herrish was among them. He wrote me that two of his older sons survived as well and were with him in Germany. The boys were trying to convince him to immigrate to the United States but he was adamant to fulfill his dream and come to Israel. He wrote that he had obtained a small woodworking machine which he intended to bring with him to Israel.

[Page 175]

A year later, I received another letter from him. I found out that he had finally achieved his dream. He had arrived in Israel through Cypress and was now living in Beit Lid.

I visited him later and he retold the story to me with tears in his eyes. After he disregarded his sons' pleas to come with them to the United States and they arrived in the US, they proposed sending him to an old–age home. He had determined that he would not accept such an offer.

Although he was over the age of 50, he could still earn his living. I tried to convince him to come to our moshav[5], Alonim. I thought that such a good carpenter would be satisfied by living in Alonim. He almost agreed but in his next letter he wrote that he had met a woman in Beit Lid and they were relocating to Acre.

A year later I met him at the memorial ceremony for members of our town. I deduced from his words that he was well. Despite his age, he had a good

218

reputation among carpenters and had work. I asked what his boys were writing. He replied, "They do not write because they are upset with me. But I do not regret it, I fulfilled my dream and am happy with that."

Time left its mark. Herrish had been through many troubles. He never lived comfortably, even in his best years. Add to that the Holocaust and its consequences. He was able to enjoy only a small period of his life in his homeland for which he yearned. He passed away suddenly four years go.

Herrish the carpenter was a dear humble man. Through persistence, he somehow managed to fulfil his lifelong dream. May his memory be forever in the hearts of his town members in this generation and those to come.

––––––––

Editor's Footnotes:

1. Poale Zion – a movement of Marxist–Zionist Jewish workers founded in various cities of Poland, Europe and the Russian Empire around the turn of the 20th century after the Bund rejected Zionism in 1901.

2. Bund – a secular Jewish socialist movement

3. Shtibel – a place used for communal Jewish prayer

4. Gordonia – a Zionist youth movement.

5. Moshav – a type of Israeli town or settlement, in particular a type of cooperative agricultural community of individual farms pioneered by the Labour Zionists

––––––––

Hahalutz[1] in Turobin
By Itamar Hopen
Translated by Meir Bulman

The first Hahalutz chapter of Turobin was founded in 1925/1926. During those years, a training division was founded by the pioneers of Lublin in the agricultural grounds of Novo–Dvor, between Turobin and Wysoki. The estate owner was a liberal man, unlike the rest of the regional estate owners who were members of the Endecja, a fascist anti–Semitic organization. The estate owner agreed to accept young Jewish men to work on his land. The halutzim from the training unit often came to town to purchase groceries and pick up packages. Those men were among the best Lublin youths and made a good impression on the residents of Turobin.

About a year later, the unit dispersed. Some of the members made aliyah and some traveled to other places. The Hahalutz chapter in Turobin increasingly weakened and there were many reasons for it. 1929 was the year of riots in Eretz Israel and the massacres in the Hebron Yeshiva. The massacres angered Jewish youth of Poland. Most youth were willing to enlist and help their attacked brethren. If it were realistic, thousands of young people would have traveled to Eretz Israel with a deep desire to build and fight. Following those events, the Hahalutz chapter of Turobin was reassembled and a branch of Hahalutz Hatzair was also founded.

[Page 176]

There were 70 members of Hakhalutz and the same number in Hakhalutz Hatzair. There was some rotation of members as some went to training or aliyah. There was a time that Hakhalutz Hatzair numbered close to 100 members. The two organizations were practically one camp with a joint working plan, one building, etc. Much activity developed in those branches in both the organizational and educational fields.

Hakhalutz Hatzair members were divided into groups based on age and had a counselor for each group. There were courses in Hebrew language and geography of Israel. There were lectures on life in Eretz Israel, geography, workers' organizations in Israel, and the social structure of settling in Israel. In 1930, 5 members were set for training for the Shahrya group and others. In 1931, 13 members went for training in various places such as the Borokhov Kibbutz, Grokhov, Levendn (?) and more. Two members went for seasonal agricultural training at Kibbutz Magshimim on Count Potocki's estate near Wysokis–Litovsk.

At this opportunity I would like to note an interesting event I was part of. Yisrael Oberweiss and I were among those who went for agricultural training. The dates on the mission letters we had received were close, but Yisrael's departure date was sooner than mine. Yisrael was an only child and opposition to his departure from home was expected. Therefore, everything was planned and kept secret. In the wee hours of the night, we rented a coach and accompanied Israel to Zolkiewka and from there he continued by train.

220

Upon returning to Turobin with Yaakov Mitzner, the other member who accompanied Yisrael, we met Israel's father R' Isaac who meanwhile learned of the tragedy that befell him. When R' Isaac met me, he pointed his heavy cane at me and asked, "Where did you send my son? You have murdered me!" I saw that he was beside himself and instead of trying to explain, I instinctively escaped. Until I departed for training, I dared not pass on the street near his home. That was one of many similar events that took place during the pioneering activities in town.

Hahalutz Organization of Turobin 19 5/([?])33

[Page 177]

As previously noted in this book, most of the town's population was religious–Hassidic. For that reason, many members kept their affiliation with the pioneer and Zionist movement a secret. That made it complicated to recruit members and maintain financial institutions such as the Aliyah fund, the Hakhshara[2] fund, etc. There were also difficulties in raising money for the national funds which Hakhalutz members were most involved with.

Despite all the obstacles to Hakhalutz, it improved, conquered the hearts of most of the town's youth and became a force within the Jewish community of the town. Most of the activities – Zionist congress evenings, invited lecturers, messengers, and other gatherings – contributed to an appreciation of the pioneering spirit. There were other contributing factors to the path chosen by Hakhautz; these included the anti–Semitism which was present in all aspect of Jewish life and the explicit discrimination of Poles against Jews. Those led the Jewish youth to consider where to turn and what to do. Such objective conditions brought the Jewish youth to the clear understanding that we were a people lacking a territory. Education to turn oneself into a productive person and creating power in the Jewish homeland followed that spirit and path.

Such matters were the central focus of the members. Athletics were among the other activities. Under the guidance of Areyeh Goldfarb, who was very active in the branch of Hahalutz, they organized sports outings to the forests outside of town. Every Shabbat, members rose early and organized units to walk to the forest. After hours of exercise and playing football, the members conversed about politics and organizational matters. In the hours before noon, the pioneering camp returned to town. According to guidelines, members organized in units and marched through the streets of town. They sang in Hebrew and Yiddish as the residents exited their homes and watched them marching.

The Hahalutz branch of Turobin was considered one of the biggest and most organized in the area. In 1932 there were already 20 members in training units and several members waited in line for Aliyah. Comrade Yerachmiel Frieberg made aliyah that year as did comrade Boymfeld. All that contributed to the pioneering spirit in town.

That same year, a regional conference was held in Turobin. The event at the gathering was very valuable and widely attended. There were some inconsistencies among the headquarters and the chapters and the date for the conference was twice postponed. At the height of the conference, a negative factor darkened the spirits of those attending. It was a year when Aliyah stopped, a year after the issuing of the Passfield[3] White Paper. Many in attendance at the conference were waiting in line for aliyah and, without explanation by headquarters, the conference was postponed twice. Finally, Hakalutz headquarters found someone to represent them, comrade Feivel Ben–Dori, envoy of the Workers Organization.

222

[Page 178]

The conference was supposed to take place in Lublin but for some unknown reason, Hakhalutz leadership approached our chapter and asked if we were willing to host the conference in our town. 250 members participated; they represented 32 chapters. The conference took place in the new firehouse theater over two days. After Ben–Dori's speech, debates took place and decisions were made. "To open wide the gates to the Land," and "train the youth for labor," were the two most important decisions drafted by the presiding committee.

After that conference, comrade Goldfarb decided on aliyah. Hahalutz headquarters granted our chapter's request for a certificate. The conference brought about a change of attitude of the observant, many of whom wanted to know what was decided. Not long passed before religious Jews began purchasing certificates as shochetim[4] and rabbis. Some of them immigrated to Eretz Israel with their families, including R' Yosef Corndrexler and R' Zvi Kopf.

If anything deserves credit for the existence of the Turobin community in Israel, it is the activities of Hahalutz. Through Hahalutz, 25 members made aliyah legally or illegally. Among them were those who arrived by other means and were members of Hahalutz. The number of members reached 45. Among them are 7 in various kibbutzim and two in agricultural settlements.

A Group of Pioneers before Aliyah

From the right: **Yaakov Friedler, Yechiel Friedler, Israel Oberweiss, Zeev Geier**
Second row: **Moshe Gutwertz, Yehoshua Hopen**

Editor's Footnotes:

1. Hakhalutz –Jewish youth movement that trained young people for agricultural settlement in the Land of Israel

2. Hakhshara – a Hebrew word meaning "preparation"

3. Passfield White Paper – Issued by the colonel secretary Lord Passfield, it was a formal statement of British policy in Palestine made in the aftermath of the 1929 riots

4. Shochetim – people who have been specially trained and licensed to slaughter animals and birds in accordance with Jewish laws

[Page 179]

Hahalutz of Turobin

By Israel Amir

Translated by Meir Bulman

The Hahalutz movement was founded as a life force for the local youth. Otherwise, the youth would have progressively deteriorated. All forms of existing organization no longer fit the times, as new winds began to blow in the Jewish community including our town.

We could no longer make do with working for the Zionist funds, the Zionist Congress Shekel or ballroom dancing. Our mission was completely different: organize and train, through social and cultural work, youth who were healthy in body and mind, study the Hebrew language, and organize workshops to familiarize people with Socialist Zionism and the workers movement in Eretz Israel and worldwide. The goal was to maintain a strong and healthy chapter in which each member would be knowledgeable and would first work on self-development.

It cannot be said that we succeeded 100%. Still, we did succeed in our work despite the various obstacles. Turobin was not a progressive town like others in Poland such as Vohlyn, Polsia, Bilistok, and Vilna which had Hebrew schools and progressive communities. Turobin was under the firm control of Agudath Israel[1] and the sects of Gur, Trisk, and Alexander[2]. They objected to not only activities of the Hahalutz but even ordinary works in support of funds, which could therefore not be properly maintained. Everything related to Eretz Israel was dismissed and forbidden.

On the other side, the Bund and even Beitar[3] posed some obstacles. We still did not relent and worked diligently and faithfully because we knew what we were moving towards. The road ahead was rough but true and just. So we progressed until we formed a strong chapter. We attracted youths from all classes: children of craftsmen and merchants, Bund sympathizers, youths studying at the bet midrash[4], etc. We worked persistently until the Hassidic and Agudist town members learned to recognize us as people who knew where to lead the local youth. Our aim was to change everything. We succeeded.

Our members' mentality, way of dressing, and behavior were different than that of other youth in town. Our members knew how to wisely respond to our detractors from all sides. That was our biggest accomplishment and the reward for our work. Parents and other folks began to understand their sons and daughters and realized they were doing right and good things.

Our members began going to training and some made aliyah. There were also failures. There were some who could not succeed in training. But we overcame the difficulties and obstacles.

The Hahalutz branch in Turobin continued on the path forward and changed the town. Hahalutz of Turobin caused a true revolution and became the strongest and liveliest branch in the region.

The headquarters in Warsaw allowed us to visit regional branches and organize them for a big conference in the Lublin district. The conference was well-organized. The days of the conference became celebratory, not just for Hahalutz members but for the whole Jewish population of Turobin. Everyone remembers the conference days and the happiness expressed by youth and the joyful town. On Friday, all day and before evening, convoys of pioneering youth from the entire region, hundreds of pioneers, arrived on foot, wagons, and bikes.

[Page 180]

Even the gentiles knew the "Palestinists" were convening. It was probably unusual to see a large crowd planning emigration to Eretz Israel. They were not exactly sure what this whole fair in Turobin was about. The joy increased even more when it was announced that Feivish Bendori, a special envoy from Eretz Israel, had arrived especially for the conference. The impression of his presence was very strong and granted much respect to our branch. Even the flaw of Bendori arriving in town on Shabbat was not enough to spoil the spirits in town. It was apparent that Hahalutz was a very serious and desirable for local youth. The conference and the Zionist deliberations were dedicated to discussing the future of the Jewish youth, especially Hahalutz.

Hahalutz in Turobin

[Page 181]

After the conference, regard for us changed considerably. Even town leaders asked us, "What did the envoy tell you about Eretz Israel? Can non-members also go on aliyah?" We reached a point that even parents we had not considered it came with their young children and asked to enroll them in Hahalutz. The victory was tremendous. The branch expanded and developed. We rented a larger hall and hired a Hebrew teacher. We organized additional classes in Hebrew and Israeli history.

Hahalutz became a point of light in the darkness and a warm home to hundreds of youths. There was a rotation as some members made Aliyah and new and younger members joined. Younger members were active.

I was among the last who made Aliyah. In 1939, I met the remaining members who envied me. Of course, I spoke to them and attempted to encourage them but there was negativity in the air which we all sensed.

Some went to summer training camps and none considered they would not return to continue their blessed activities for and among the youth. No person among us knew what awaited us or anticipated such a quick and soon tragedy. The Holocaust descended on our nation. The Nazi German monster brought destruction to the Jewish people. We will remember the young men and women who were not fortunate to be with us in our homeland and taste the joy of becoming a free Hebrew man in his land.

Editor's Footnotes:

1. Agudath Israel – founded in 1922 to serve as Orthodox Jewry's umbrella organization

2. Gur, Trisk, and Alexander – Hassidic dynasties

3. Beitar – a Revisionist Zionist youth movement founded in 1923 in Riga, Latvia, by Vladimir Jabotinsky

4. Bet midrash – Jewish study hall located in a synagogue, yeshiva, kollel or other building.

Hamizrachi Movement
and Hapoel *Hamizrachi*[1] in Turobin
By Yehoshua Ben–Ari

Translated by Meir Bulman

It can be said that *Hamizrachi* was the first local Zionist organization. I was the halutz who led the way for the Zionist movements to follow and who created a bright multicolored tapestry of Zionism ideals, organizations, and action.

It was founded after the end of WWI. The yearning and dreams for Zion were instilled within the residents for many generations. The desire to "renew our days as in the past" was deeply rooted in consciousness, to the point it did not really require motivation from the Zionist movement. Such organic Zionism, or "love of Zion," was taught to all since childhood, beginning in elementary education and continuing into old age. Each resident continued to study the texts, pray three times a day, and find solace in the history of Jewish national self–determination, a kingdom rich with awe and bravery, and prophets fighting for moral justice. Still, it was thought the yearning for Zion was enough and a visionary of Herzl's kind was not needed. Of course, the deeply rooted and organic yearning for Zion was joined by the pressure stemming from the dire circumstances which affected Jews in Polish exile and their hearts cried for redemption.

[Page 182]

But the opposite was true. The organized Zionist movement came to practically achieve the wishes of many generations. It proposed a solution and a way out from the degrading state of exile. That movement did not find an ally among most of the town Jews who were devoted to tradition and innocently believed that such an activity is the role of the messiah whom "even if he stalls, he will arrive." They did not recognize the messiah as a movement and idea which must be intensively worked on. Additionally, there were non–believers among the leaders and members of the movement. With such a history, it is no wonder that, until that time, in town there was yet to be any Zionist organization. That changed when the diligent activist Avraham Boymfeld arrived.

In one of the issues of *Hamizrachi* published in Warsaw (Issue 41, Tishrei 7, 5680), we find a short notice: "At the effort of Mr. Boymfeld of Krashnik, Hamizrachi Union was founded in Turobin (Lublin region) and a council was elected and various committees were chosen." Who was that Mr. Boymfeld? Why did he leave his birth town and settle in Turobin? I do not know the details. What I do remember are his many actions in public matters. He was an observant Jews but progressive in his views. He owned a grocery store but could be found there only rarely. Activism was in his blood. He took part in every matter concerning the public. He was a member of the community council and served, among other notables, as a representative on the town council. In the big dispute between the chief town rabbi and the sects of Gur, Alexander, Trisk and others, he sided with Rabbi Weissbrod. By the way, the father of that rabbi, as is told elsewhere in this book, was the former chief rabbi who became a Hassidic rebbe and settled in Krashnik. For some reason, local Hassidim did not recognize him as a rebbe ("no man is a prophet in his hometown") nor recognize his son as a rabbi and the dispute was great and persistent. It is possible that Boymfeld had some connection with the Rebbe from his time in Krashnik.

Only a man of Boymfeld's character could achieve such a turning point and found a Zionist movement in the town at the time.

The post–war period was a low point. The war had caused much ongoing suffering and left many injured and impoverished. It is possible that, too, contributed to a change in the conservative mindset, causing the founding of the organization.

Credit is given to the Hamizrachi movement for making the Keren Kayemet[2] and Keren Hayesod[3] boxes a fixture in many homes. Despite their poverty, the Jews of Turobin were very generous and contributed to every constructive cause. I do not know what became of that movement since I left the town at age 13. I studied for several years in Radom and Warsaw, and returned home at 17. I could not find my place there, and it was clear to me here was no point in remaining in exile. It was also clear to me that the only place I would consider is Eretz Israel, but how does one reach it? Thus, the idea of founding a branch of Hapoel Hamizrachi. In a town such as ours there were no shortcuts. One does not jump from one extreme position to another. There were already pioneering movements in town but they were secular and I would not at all consider joining one of them. I therefore gathered my strength and enlisted the help of a few bet midrash attendees. They trusted me for, in their eyes, I was considered a worldly person and must know what should be done. We founded the local chapter and the accompanying items.

[Page 183]

Turmoil in town was great. Among the Hassidim and the scholars of the bet midrash, my move was seen as an attempt to remove good men from the righteous path. Among those who assisted me, I fondly remember Baruch Katz, son from a local noble traditional family. All the members of his household were "infected" by the Zionist bug. The eldest son, Lemel of blessed memory was extreme, the leader of Beitar in town. Mr. Dov Zuntag who is with us now also assisted with the formation of that revolution.

A while later, I went for kibbutz training for three years. In 1935 I was fortunate to receive an emigration permit. I heard that during my absence the branch's activities were somewhat weakened but the members were loyal and dreamed of reaching Israel. When I arrived here I constantly received letters full of longing and anxiety from my friends, especially from Baruch Katz, peace be upon him.

The Holocaust which occurred a while later ended everything and "solved the Jewish problem" in that town.

I often think that if a Jew like Mr. Boymfeld would have arrived in our town 50 years earlier, Hitler would have had nothing to do in our town as most of the residents would have come here to safety.

Editor's Footnotes:

1. Hamizrachi – According to Wikipedia, Hapoel HaMizrachi was a political party and settlement movement in Israel and is one of the predecessors of the National Religious Party, which later became the modern–day Jewish Home Party.

2. Keren Kayemet – Jewish National Fund

3. Keren Hayesod – United Jewish Appeal

The Revisionist Movement in Turobin
By Yosef Kopf
Translated by Meir Bulman

Among the various movements in Turobin was also the Revisionist movement which occupied an important role in town. The movement served as an attraction point for youth who wanted to be educated in a Zionist Jewish environment and be among friends. It found supporters in Turobin and began to sound its voice boldly through Zionist activism and during the dispute among various Zionist sects.

As I recall, the Revisionist movement began to develop in 1930. The formation began in the general Pioneering–Zionist movement hosted by Moshe the tailor. A while later, the movement rented its own place from Hershel Lichtman. The administrators of the organization were Lemmel Katz, Yaakov

Yaakovzon, Simcha Eidleman, Moshe Greenberg, and Chava Freiberg. The number of members in the movement reached 60 to 70. There were four members in training: Aharon Gewertz, Mordechai Pearlman, Yosef Lerrer, and Shmuel Royzner.

Activities were widespread and included establishing training grounds for Revisionist pioneers. It was in the Zhavno village, 3 km from town. The training spot included 32 members.

[Page 184]

The point (training point) received the aid of Mr. Pesach Diamand, the forest merchant[?].

There was cooperation between the training point and the branch in Turobin. There were classes teaching Hebrew, general and Jewish culture, chronicles of Zionism, Bible, military–style training, education, and lectures on various topics. The youth absorbed ideals of liberation which were expressed in song and hora dancing and the like.

The main goal for all members was to immigrate, legally or illegally, to Eretz Israel. All wished to liberate the land from the rule of the British mandate. As is known, the movement opposed the politics of obtaining a certificate.

At this occasion I recall that when there were evenings devoted to the remembrance of Dr. Herzl and Trumpeldor[1], 12–year–old girl Leah'che Friedler appeared and bravely declared: "With blood and fire, Judea fell and with blood and fire Judea will rise."

I find it appropriate to record some events of members at the training point. To go through training, members had to bear the financial burden and contribute to the best of their abilities. It was a large and complex task to get the training point on our own. Especially noteworthy are members of the Diamond family: Pesach, Shlomo, and Muttel, who helped a lot. However, unfortunately we were unable to maintain the promising training point.

I recall that my mother baked bread every day for the members at the training grounds and supplied clothes. Once two members had severe angina and stayed with us. My mother treated them until they made a full recovery.

By the way, all my brothers and sisters were members of the Revisionist Movement to the point that my mother also automatically belonged to it. For her care and her devotion to the movement, it was said in town that "Chaya Fishlova is Jabotinsky's[2] grandmother."

The Revisionist movement continued until the start of WWII in 1939.

The satanic murderous Hitler agents stormed Turobin and cruelly destroyed everything, including the once lively and glorious youth. Among all of my friends in the movement, I was the only one to survive. Fate determined that only one would remain so he could commemorate members of the movement in the memorial book written by remnants of the community.

Those beloved and delightful people were committed with heart and soul to the ideal of resurrection and rebuilding the land. It is very unfortunate that they could not make aliyah and participate in redeeming the land. Their spirits are with us here in the resurrected Israel. At every opportunity, we will remember those who worked alongside us for the life of the nation and the land in Zion, the land of our Ancestors. It seems that they are always here with us and working alongside us here, too. Bless their memory.

———

Editor's Footnotes:

1. Trumpeldore – Joseph Vladimirovich Trumpeldor, an early Zionist activist and war hero.

2. Ze'ev Jabotinsky, MBE, was a Russian Jewish Revisionist Zionist leader, author, poet, orator, soldier and founder of the Jewish Self–Defense Organization in Odessa

———

[Page 185]

The Eternal Wandering Jew

By Itamar Hopen

Translated by Meir Bulman

In memory of Mendel Yudel's and Devorah Bergman

Mendel Bergman

Devorah Bergman

The nation of Israel was destined to wander. The wandering chain
continued since the forefathers of our nation. "And Abraham took Sarai and
Lot, his nephew, and all of their belongings and came to the land of Kanaan."
"And Isaac went to Abimelech, king of the Philistines, to Gerar and God said to
him, "Do not go to Egypt.'" "And Jacob raised his feet and went to the land of
the ancients." "Exodus." "Return to Zion." "Roman exile." "The Spanish
expulsions from Portugal, England, France." And wandering during wars of
nations.

WWI erupted at the end of July 1914. As is done in times of war, the
warring parties occupied towns. Towns exchanged hands and more than once,
residents were told to leave before the town was set on fire. That happened in

234

Turobin. Before the Russians retreated, they ordered the Jewish population to leave And the town was set on fire. (The non–Jewish population was small and concentrated in the surrounding villages.) Some of the refugees wandered to other places in Poland while others wandered inward to Russia.

Among the refugees who wandered to Russia was the Bergman family, a household of 9. The patriarch Yehuda (Yiddel,) his son Mendel, his daughter-in–law Devorah (my paternal aunt,) and his grandchildren Chaya, Yaakov, Rachel, Gittel, Zipporah, and Esther. The eldest daughter, Chaya, was courted by Avraham Vechter, brother of Yitzchak Vechter. Avraham was drafted into the military as the war began. It was heartbreaking to witness the loving couple separate. Their goodbye was accompanied by a commitment to meet after the war and marry. I will return to the couple's story later. Anyway, Chaya, or as she was known, Chaya'leh, was the oldest and the rest of the children who were quite young were dependent in every aspect.

[Page 186]

Under those circumstances and the war conditions of the time, one can imagine the suffering of a Jewish family wandering a large country like Russia, on rough roads on foot or vehicle. The family wandered for years. I cannot tell of the storms, rain, and frost which the family encountered while wandering. What is a year or two among 2000 years? I *can* detail the suffering while they wandered. It was a sea of suffering. The stations on the way to Siberia were many. At one point they reached Troitsk and settled for a while and continued to Irkutsk, but there, too, they did not last long. During the Bolshevik Revolution, the Bergman family relocated to Harbin, Manchuria. After WWI, Harbin became a Jewish center. The population was comprised of Russians and Chinese. It had high schools and higher education. The Bergman family then decided to settle and cease wandering. The girls attended school and devoted some of their free time to work to help feed the family. Their family life began taking shape of normal human life.

As mentioned above, a pact was formed between Avraham Vechter and Chaya Bergman. Avraham was sent to the front, injured, and captured multiple times. Around 1918, he was released from captivity. His first move was towards Turobin to meet his sworn lover Chaya'leh. When he reached Turobin, he learned that the Bergmans had left and wandered to Russia and there was no chance they would return. After short inquiry, he learned the last known location of the Bergmans according to letters sent on the road to my father. Avraham followed in Chaya's footsteps. Wherever he went, he was told that the Bergman family had departed a short time ago, headed to "x" town. Avraham wandered from place to place in that time rife with tragedies. The country was in the midst of wars and revolutions, all–out–war and chaos of regime changes. He followed every stop until he reached Irkutsk on the Siberian border. He could not continue. There, he obtained the Bergmans' address in Harbin.

The border between Russia and Manchuria was sealed a week before Avraham reached Irkutsk. The authorities would not allow Avraham to cross the border on his way to Harbin. No matter how much he tried to prove with letters and pictures that he was to marry Chayaleh, he could not obtain a pass, even for the purpose of reentering Russia with his bride. A detailed correspondence between the lovers continued for many weeks, maybe months. After the authorities were willing to allow Chaya to cross the border to Russia, the Bergman family began considering that Chayaleh would part ways with the family and join her beloved Avraham.

Truthfully, it was difficult for Mendel, Devorah, and the rest of the Bergman family to decide about Chayaleh's departure. Chayaleh was very loved by her family and the discussion caused heartbreak for Chaya and her loving family. It became a full–fledged tragedy after the parents would not express an opinion about her betrothed. Thus, since Chayaleh was so connected to her family and was a woman of discipline, she would not leave the home until the family would express a clear opinion. The reasons for Chaya's suffering could be easily understood. Her heart was torn. On one hand, she loved her family and on the other hand, she loved her dearly cherished Avraham. From the depths into which Chaya's tragic life was woven, one day she decided to read Avraham's letters to her parents.

236

[Page 187]

Chaya, her husband Avraham Vechter and their three children

The content of Avraham's letters can be imagined. He did not write them with a trained hand. He plainly described how he suffered in the war, the scars which would never fade, his deep desire to reunite with her in his lifetime, and that she was the only hope which gave him the strength to survive all the misfortunes. He described his dramatic search for her across Russia, the tortured troubles on his journey and how he reached the border with his beloved awaiting right out of his reach. He described his deep yearning to see her. He mentioned the pact they entered on the day he was drafted.

Avraham's letters were not written in simple ink, but ink mixed with tears. The paper and the words on it were sympathetic and generous. Avraham's pleas shook laws and borders. When Chaya finished reading Avraham's letters, the house fell silent. The family sighed deeply, their sadness mixed with joy. The verdict was according to the handshake agreement they entered.

Chayaleh traveled to Irkutsk and married Avraham. The joy of their meeting and the wedding are indescribable and exceeded expectations. In the years that followed they had children and relocated to Samarkand and later Tashkent.

[Page 188]

As their life headed down the right path, the family departed Harbin and headed to Shanghai, China. In Shanghai, the family probably decided to set roots. There must be a final destination. From Turobin to Harbin, from the Baltic Sea to the big ocean, to pass through such a journey must have been intensive. The names alone indicate it was quite lengthy. An expert wanderer knows that each movement necessitates careful planning, since such a journey needs a significant amount of time and labor. The Bergmans' journey is unimaginable in terms of suffering and the obstacles along the road.

Yaakov, Mendel, and Devorah Bergman's only so, immigrated to Canada and settled in Calgary, Alberta where he established a family. In 1950, right after his daughter Yehudit (Yuness) was married, he died of a heart attack. He was succeeded by his wife Sonia and his daughters. As bitter fate had it, his daughter Yehudit also passed away in 1963, leaving three children behind.

The second daughter, Rachel, married, and established a family in Manila, Philippines. In 1950 she arrived in Israel on aliyah with her young daughter Gila. Her two older children, Ziggy and Riesel, immigrated, too, and settled in the US. The young daughter, Gila, has a family in Israel and is a mother to a boy. Rachel did not find satisfaction during her life. A year and a half after Aliyah, luck did not smile on their families' integration. The spreading of her family all over the world caused her much pain. She could not bear her loneliness and absorption pains; in 1951 she died of a heart attack in Tiberias. Her husband in Manila died around the same time.

Mendel and Devorah had two more daughters. Zipporah (Fanyeh) and Gittel settled in Israel. Zipporah arrived on aliyah in 1963. Gittel arrived on aliyah in 1949 when China became communist and most of the Jews of Shanghai chose aliyah. Gittel was widowed before she left Shanghai and cared for two children. One was Eliazar and the other Zalman (Ziami). Both served in the Israeli Defense Force. Zalman received a medal among the 8 participants of the battle on the Nohelia, his picture is included [?]. Mendel and Devorah's youngest daughter, Esther, immigrated to the US and settled in Los Angeles.

238

That is the story of the Bergman family and their descendants. I do not know the date of patriarch Yidell's passing. All I know is that he was buried in Harbin. While the family stayed in Shanghai, Mendel was a well–known figure in the Jewish community and was considered an honest and honorable man. I think that for some time he also served as a gabbai[1] of a synagogue in Shanghai. I assume there were a number of synagogues and Yiddel probably served where they lived in the International Zone (the name of the place). The description of the wandering family teaches us that the sons have not returned to their land. From among the large family, only two daughters and their descendants reside in Israel (and Gila [?])

Bless the memory of the absent.

––––––––

Editor's Footnote:

1. Gabbai – a person who assists in the running of synagogue services in some way

––––––––

[Page 189]

The Bund Party in Turobin
Translated by Meir Bulman

At the end of the 19th century, working class Jews in Czarist Russia began to awaken when they realized they were subjected to double torment as both laborers and Jews. The Bund arose and created a Jewish socialism with its own characteristics. In greater Russia, spirits were in turmoil and many shouted out for liberation and improvement of life conditions. The voice of Jacob, that of the Jewish proletariat, was heard as well. The appearance of the Bund made an impression on Jews as a liberation–seeking movement, the first which aimed to repair reality for Jews. Its aim of Jewish liberation within Russia and it dismissed the Zionism for Zionism rejected exile. The hope for a close redemption by the revolution attracted the masses to lend a hand to the Bund.

The Bund movement arrived in Turobin only after Russian forces left Poland. The late creation came after several years of uneasy hesitation by the initiators. In Turobin, there was no proletariat in the larger sense of the term.

The workers for the most part were craftsmen (carpenters, tailors, cobblers, etc.) who employed apprentices. The craftsmen did not want to aid a revolutionary movement that would actually move against them as employers although they themselves lived under difficult social conditions. In contrast, their apprentices were attracted to the Bund after Poland was liberated and gained independence from the occupying Austrian military which they had (previously) placed their hopes in – in terms of fixing their situation and their lives.

From right to left top row: **Yosef Pik, Moshe Wolf Tregger, Peretz Frank, Chaya Sarah Fleisher, Mordechai Elzon, Feigele Tregger, Abush Blotman**
Seated: **Leah Geyer, Rachel Feldman, Chaim Leib Pik, Nacha Fleisher, Hershel Shtreicher**

240

[Page 190]

After the founding of the Bund in liberated Poland and the awakening of socialist activists, new horizons were opened for the movement in various fields. The Bund program incorporated other ideals such as Yiddish and culture which became the central focus. The Bund attracted many from the working class who saw the Bund as their home. The movement ascended to an influential position within the towns and cities of the country. In Turobin, Bund members were not engaged in large–scale activism although they did hold debates concerning unending tactical and pragmatic questions with members of other parties, e.g. the Zionists, the "S.S." [?].

The Bund greatly sinned in its war against Zionism in the initial years of Polish exile. If not for that, it is possible that dozens more Jews, especially among the youth who innocently believed in the Bund and its "solution," would have found their way to Zion.

Bais Yaakov School for Girls
Translated by Meir Bulman

After WWI (1914–1918), the Jewish youth of Poland strove to join and belong to youth movements following ideological party lines. Also, their will increased to gain knowledge and education. This time around, Jewish girls also began to attend to public and private schools en masse.

**A *Bais Yaakov* Class
Teacher: Rivka Zilberklang**

[Page 191]

In response to the trend, Orthodox groups also decided to create schools for religious girls. The aim was to deter them from joining secular youth movements and grant them traditional religious education. Thus, the push to form a chain of *Bais Yaakov* schools for girls.

One of the women who was very active in the educational movement of the *Bais Yaakov* school was Sarah Schenirer of Krakow. Much of the credit goes to that activist, known by students at the school as "Mother Schenirer."

After difficult deliberation and with much financial difficulty, a *Bais Yaakov* branch also opened in Turobin. Despite the Jewish tradition of not teaching Torah to girls, in accordance with the argument "teach them diligently to your sons and not to your daughters," the institution was founded based on the passage, "It is time to act, God, for the law was voided[1]" [Psalm 119:126]. The organization constructed an important component in the town through the education of the younger generation in the spirit of tradition and Torah, which was their guiding light.

The name *Bais Yaakov* was designated by the creator and founder, Sarah Schenirer, who was familiar with the words of our sages, "'Say thusly to the House of Jacob' – refers to the women." The girls who were educated at *Bais Yaakov* acquired knowledge of Torah, foundations of halakha[2], and traditional religious life. The education of those girls was productive; from their ranks later came devoted activists who participated in various activities, be it regarding contemporary matters or for Eretz Israel.

A Class of Jewish Students at the Polish Public School During a Jewish History Lesson with Mrs. Shapira

[Page 192]

Manis Figgel the Tailor's in the Workshop with His assistants

From the left: **Manis, Chaim Tregger, Gotwilling, Perez Fink, and another person**

Avraham Frumer and Family Workshop
Avraham, His Son, and Two Apprentices

Editor's Footnotes:

1. Another translation is "It is a time to Act for G–d. ... for they have violated Your Torah."

2. Halakha – Jewish law

[Page 193]

5. Figures and Types

[Page 194]

The Four Generations of a Turobin Family

By Avraham Boymfeld

Translated by Meir Bulman

The Boymfeld–Krakoyer family was a legacy family in Turobin, even if not one of the oldest. The patriarch, David Boymfeld, came from Krakow. Krakow was the initial host of Jewish refugees who escaped persecution in Germany, Austria, and Czechia, later spreading across Poland. R' David initially passed Turobin on business and eventually decided to settle there during the first half of the 19th century. His business was furs, for which he sometimes traveled to Russia for months at a time. R' David Boymfeld was the head of the Boymfeld family in Turobin and other Jewish communities. Now, after the destruction of the Jewish community of Turobin, two members of the fourth generation of Boymfelds wanted to review and describe as much as possible the ancestors of the first generations in Turobin. Let us now turn (our focus) and hear the words of family members.

The Origin of the Boymfeld Family

A.

I had heard that Irgun Yotzei Turobin in Israel was about to compose a Yizkor book which will serve as the memorial candle for the Jewish community that perished in the Nazi war of destruction. I too, as one of the surviving members of Turobin, approached the editorial board and asked to devote a respectable portion of the book to commemorate the first members of my family in Turobin. I especially wanted to explore the image of an honorable man, R' David Boymfeld – Krakoyer (so known for his town of origin, Krakow) and his tombstone which was in the cemetery in Turobin, now part of the past.

Our generation met a bitter fate. Along with that, the memory of the previous generation, etched on the tombstones in the outstanding cemeteries of the Jewish communities in Poland, was destroyed. Teary–eyed, we join the entire Jewish people to mourn six million Jews who lived lives of purity and tradition. It is difficult to come to terms with the reality that even the old cemetery of Turobin was destroyed in the Holocaust. It was the resting place of rabbis, *rashey yeshivot*[1], community leaders, and activists from various periods. It was considered by community members as the Jewish pantheon, along with well–known centrally located cemeteries and ancient communities whose names are written in gold in the chronicles of Polish Jewry.

During my time residing in Poland, every year I visited my hometown, Turobin, and I visited the cemetery a number of times. I wandered among the tombstones and gained the impression that the Jews of Turobin had a wisdom that valued art, evident from the varied tombstones, from which the scent of history arose. But the German murderers of cursed name were merciless and destroyed the cemeteries, uprooted the tombstones, and desecrated the tombs and all that was beloved and holy. The cemetery included many tombstones beginning with the founding of Turobin centuries ago. Also emerging from the ground were grey stones, holy tombstones bowing to one another in old age, as if whispering and conversing with one another about the next world. Eulogies and memorial ceremonies took place at the entrance gate.

[Page 195]

Among those many tombstones, alongside those of rabbis with celebrated titles, a beautiful tombstone stands, praise etched on it. I will quote it here:

Here Lies
An honorable, beloved, righteous, compassionate man, honor
Torah, pursuer of charity
Who was very active in maintaining Torah and charity institutions
Always charitable towards the poor, his Tzedakah[2] known by
many
R' David Krakover of blessed memory

Those were the words etched on the tombstone of the founder of the Boymfeld family in 1906 at the start of the 20th century. His family finds it appropriate to commemorate him in the Yizkor book of the grieving Turobin community.

His settlement in Turobin can be explained by the fact that he married a local woman. He established a family and was accepted by all as a pleasant person. He had brought the fur–processing profession with him from Krakow. He maintained business contacts in Russia and spent years away from his home.

R' David was a source of blessing to the town. The town elders say that he was a man of many good deeds, a sometimes public and sometimes anonymous contributor to charity. In the center of town, he built the first large two–story house. At that same time, he devoted efforts to establishing a *hekdesh* (shelter) for poor folks who required lodging and (created) an annual budget to maintain it. He loved Turobin, nicknamed "miniature Eretz Israel," and its scholars. It is also said that he gifted the land on which *Yeshiva Chachmei Lublin* was founded. I note that during WWI when the Jews from all the towns surrounding Lublin escaped front lines there, my family stayed for a long time in the yeshiva building. The yeshiva administration appreciated the head of the family (R' David Krakover) and offered his grandsons residence there in their time of need. I, too, resided there temporarily.

R' David was very successful and wealthy. He was a successful forest merchant, which included managing some private estates owned by Tsar Nikolai. My grandfather, R' David, was an agent and contractor [?] and thus he was away from home most of the time. Banks in those days were yet to find a footing in trade and finance. Instead, he always carried with him a small metal chest containing money. In our family it was said that once R' David forgot to take the box with him; he had left it at a synagogue in a Russian town where he had prayed. He found the chest the next day when he arrived for afternoon services.

It is said that once my great–grandfather, holding the chest, traveled in a wagon operated by a Christian. When they passed the cross behind the town, R' David noticed the coachman had not taken off his hat as was the Christian custom. R' David, as a man of tradition, convinced the gentile to return him to town. A while later it was said in the town that the coachmen had robbed and murdered a man in his company.

248

[Page 196]

In Turobin and the surrounding area, R' David was known as a model of a man who was very traditional. Even the Christians very much respected "Fan Krakovski" as he was named by them. His absence from town due to business most of the year did not at all impact his traditional practices. Similarly, wife Pessa'leh was also honored and respected by society.

It is no wonder that the Boymfeld–Krakoyer family filled a leadership role in town. Many efforts were made by young men and women from near and far to arrange marriages with members of our family. My grandfather knew which jewels to add to his crown. He had three girls and one boy, Berrish. His first son–in–law, who married his eldest daughter, was Rabbi Shekhna. He was a great Torah scholar and teacher. It was enough for Rabbi Shekhna to recommend a man for him to be ordained a rabbi. Among the Christian population, the large–eyebrowed and wide–bearded Shekhna was known as "Jewish Moses" and the Christian scholars and nobles called him "the Jewish chief justice." He was a pro bono arbitrator and the noblemen on both sides respected his opinion.

There were many legends about Rabbi Shekhna and his family. The actual man turned into a legend during his lifetime. He was always met with respectful awe when passing on the street. In his character, he demonstrated Judaism and its noble traits. I recall three of his sons. One was a *dayan*[3] in Lublin. (I studied with his son Shlomo'leh in R' Mendeli's group and we were considered the top students.) R' Chaim Yarmlkh [spelling unknown] of Lublin was of majestic appearance and was met with respectful awe. It became a custom in Turobin that if someone from Turobin was in Lublin, he stopped by Rabbi Chaim's for *Mincha*[4] and to greet him. I, too, observed that custom.

Rabbi Natan ben Shekhna was similar, internally and externally, to everyone in his family. Rabbi Natan was also considered a "Jewish chief justice" by the Christian noble intelligentsia in his town of Shebreshin, [also not for profit?]. To this day, I recall his image clearly with the sharp look in his eyes and the pure expression on his wide face. His wife, Esther, was different from him. She was a woman praised by all, a righteous person whose deeds were completely for God. She was lame in one foot and, more than once, I was surprised by the contrast between Rabbi Natan, who was very tall and upright, and his wife. The family told stories about the history of that couple. Esther Miriam came from a bright family and, in Rabbi Shekhna's view, she was the most fitting in terms of lineage. R' Natan saw Esther Miriam for the first time at his wedding. He responded innocently, unlike a chief justice, "If father chose her for me, she must be the right match for me, and may we be blessed." One of their daughters survived and is in Israel.

[Page 197]

I know less about R' David's second son–in–law, R' Aharleh and his part in the social and active life of Turobin. My younger brother Aharon was named for him. I researched his life and endeavored to learn more details about his life and manners, personality, and doings. Many of his generation gave me a cryptic answer, "May the young Aharon not shame R' Ahraleh." I can say more about uncle Yosef, Ahraleh's son; his daughter is in Israel. He was the town menakker[5]. He was also my teacher and all he wanted was to prepare me for teaching and the rabbinate. There is no doubt he would have succeeded in that if not for the eruption of World War I. We had to escape the town which suddenly found itself at the front lines between the Austrian and Russian forces. We found shelter in Lublin which became a town of refuge for Jewish residents from towns near and far.

It is an honor and I am perhaps even proud I was destined to commemorate such a beautiful and noble time in the lives of residents of our town for future generations. I need to devote another small portion to a brief description of R' David's final son–in–law, R' Moshe Hillel. He was considered a man of action as a Turobin envoy. [?] He stands before me as if in a dream, sitting wrapped in his tallit among the notables sitting at the front row by the eastern wall. Although R' Moshe's tombstone in the Turobin cemetery was desecrated and destroyed, his royal spirit and holy image will continue to remain before our eyes.

B.

Until now I have more or less described the head of the family and its founder in Turobin, R' David and his three sons–in–law. I will now expand on the life of his only son, my grandfather Berrish, who married Chaya Rivaleh, a Turobin native. The young couple lived with the parents and their business was fur processing, a family inheritance.

Grandfather Berrish managed to maintain the value and honor with which the town residents regarded his father R' David; this was due to both due to his good deeds and the respect granted to his father. My grandmother was a short–statured woman, 1.4 meters in height. She had 10 children, among them five boys named Kalman, Zundel, Mordechai, Meir, and another whose name I forgot. One daughter was named Pessah. The Boymfeld family developed nicely for another generation and the founder, David, knew to carefully guard it and guide it. But all good things end. After R' David passed away, so did the success of the family businesses and a downward trend was then experienced. AS time passed, the forests deteriorated. The second generation was not loyal to Turobin and some relocated to other towns in Poland.

Sheva–Chana's family with the Itchi'lach, [?] the city butchers who had regularly supplied meat to the family, began to decline. Grandfather Berrish was unsuccessful in his business, which eventually ended. Grandfather Berrish concentrated his remaining money and placed it under his pillow, determined to no longer continue his business and instead live off cash. He left his youngest son, my father, and his daughter Pessa'leh to run the household. However, she was probably bored by that role and, when grandfather was in synagogue, she gathered her friends in grandfather's large room for dancing lessons. The next day, Grandfather was surprised to discover that the funds placed under the pillow had vanished. That event harmed grandfather's mood and caused a general shock at the house in addition to substantial financial loss. It was easy to uncover the tracks of the suspect who denied everything. There was still some hope of summoning the suspect to the town rabbi and forcing him to return the money. But Grandma Chaya Rivala interjected with the full force of her 1.4 meter stature. Despite the potentially difficult existential threat the family might be facing, she demanded that Grandfather not deviate from tradition and violate the name of God with a false oath. Her persistence was decisive and Grandfather had to sustain the loss.

[Page 198]

Today, after I have examined the details of the incident and the documents that I found in the family archive, I saw evidence of the strict observance of tradition and the financial decline of our family.

Several years later, we left Turobin and relocated to Warsaw. A short while later, Grandfather decided to leave Warsaw and return to Turobin or the general area. He reasoned that in Warsaw, the dead are not buried according to the tradition that four people must carry the coffin but are instead transported by wagon to the cemetery. He was ashamed to return to Turobin proper, fearing what would people say. Instead, he settled in a small own near Turobin where he purchased a home large enough for us all. Since then, my grandfather counted the money under his pillow every morning. The theft had negatively impacted Grandfather's health and he began walking in sloppy steps, unlike his usual manner. The event had caused his wife to burden him further.

My mother often served him tasty meals. Grandfather loved borscht with fatty bones. Once, while chewing on a bone at lunch, he began to cough and a bone was lodged in his throat. I immediately called mother. The town did not have a doctor and one had to travel by horse–carried wagon to neighboring Zholkeivka, 20 km away. Meanwhile, my mother brought neighbor Sarah'leh who was known to have medical knowledge and she shoved her long hand down grandfather's throat to retrieve the bone and he choked. I recall after the initial scare, Grandfather took out the "treasure" from under the pillow and went with me to the town rabbi. He left the money with the rabbi to distribute the inheritance according to tradition. The rabbi was a young man, a grandson of the Sfas Emes of Ger[6]. He opened a drawer in the book closet in the community courtroom and placed the money there.

We traveled to Zholkeivka and telegrams were sent to all siblings to come quickly to the funeral. Immediately after the Shiva, we went to the rabbi to sort the distribution among the inheritors. The oldest brother, Kalman, received two parts, and the rest of the brothers received an equal part.

Readers can make up their own minds on the influence of tradition and its results.

[Page 199]

I maintain, considering the past and reality, when tradition clashes with the realities of life, tradition must clear the path for life. It is a time–related commandment [Kiddushin 29a].

The Boymfeld Family

Top row from the right: **Avraham, David, Chaya Riva, Aharon**

Seated: **the parents, Mordechai and Pesya**

Editor's Footnotes:

1. Rashi Yeshivot – Jewish institutions that focuses on the study of traditional religious texts, primarily the Talmud and the Torah. Rashi was a medieval French rabbi and author of a comprehensive commentary on the Talmud and commentary on the Tanakh.

2. Tzedakah – a Hebrew word literally meaning "justice" or "righteousness," but commonly used to signify charity

3. Dayan – Hebrew word for "judge"

4. Mincha – the afternoon prayers in Judaism

5. Menakker – In kosher certification, the removal process (of animal parts) is called nikkur and the person who does it is called a menakker

6. Sfas Emes of Ger – Yehudah Aryeh Leib Alter, also known by the title of his main work, the Sfas Emes or Sefat Emet, was a Hasidic rabbi who succeeded his grandfather, Rabbi Yitzchak Meir Alter.

————

Influence of the Boymfeld Family Outside of Turobin

By Aharon Boymfeld

Translated by Meir Bulman

My brother Avraham did the hard work by briefly describing the life of the founder of our family, R' David, and his sons–in–law. He did not expand much about R' David's only son, Berrish. There is no doubt that during their lifetimes there were also various developments in Turobin and its Jewish community. There were many aspects which my brother could not describe since so many facts were lost. My brother did well in his effort of retrieving memories as much as possible from the life of the family patriarch.

[Page 200]

Even within a single family, each generation differs. Sometimes one generation changes form. Relationships change, economic and cultural factors change. I will continue where my brother left off. The truth is that my brother is more knowledgeable than I am

about the history of our family founders. I would like to thank my brother for opening the door to memories from our father's home and allowing our peers to observe. The Boymfelds were not confined to Turobin alone. Since the second generation, they began to spread throughout the immediate area. They were present in many towns and cities, and the current generation succeeded in sending a fresh seeding to the ancient homeland Eretz Israel. We took root here and were able extend a bridge between Turobin and the renewed Israel.

Since my brother has laid the foundations for our family history in decrypting the first two generations, I am tasked with continuing to describe the two generations which followed. I will not claim to uncover much, but the few details I uncover will add volume to the history of both the Boymfeld family and Turobin. The need grew after the Holocaust in which the Nazi Germans dealt their wrath against remote towns such as Turobin through which not even the train tracks passed. The Boymfeld family spread even further and today members interested in genealogy can be found in Europe and Latin America.

Let us begin with the third generation, without dealing with the end of the second generation. The second generation included our grandfather Berrish who founded a family in Turobin. He had five boys named Kalman, Zundel, Mordechai, Meir, and another, and the daughter Pessa. Since the financial downfall of the Turobin family, some began searching for a better place. Kalman traded textiles in the town of Ostrovza. He opened a textile factory there and became wealthy. His granddaughter Mira'leh Koppelman was rescued from the Holocaust by a local Christian family. After the war, she arrived on aliyah. Despite proposals from relatives in South America to join them, her oldest son's proposals to go to Eretz Israel took precedence. Zundel also formed a connection with Ostrovza, where he married and made a living by drafting official requests on behalf of various institutions. His father viewed that profession negatively, as if his son had joined an evil culture.

In 1901, my father Mordechai married his niece Pessa, daughter of his brother Meir Boymfeld of Turobin. I do not recall many details of my Turobin family members. I do recall that during my visits in 1936, some of the longtime residents visited with me in order to inquire about my experience in Israel. They also told me about my family history. Among other facts I learned that my grandfather Berrish decided to relocate from Turobin to the small town of Wysoki, 10 km from Turobin, where he resided for two years. Business was not good. Eventually, after WWI broke out, he relocated to Lublin after the Russians decreed all Jews within the Lublin District must leave their homes. He remained homeless in Lublin and was cared for by the American organization, *Joint*[1]. The women told me that my mother was a beautiful girl and my parents' wedding in town was very impressive. They also told me about the Boymfeld family which was one of the most respected in town. After the war ended, my parents returned to Piaski near Lublin; in Yiddish it was called Piyusk; it was similar to many other towns which received Jewish names.

[Page 201]

My parents had three boys and one girl: Avraham, Aharon, David (named for the family founder,) and Rivka. Avraham studied in yeshiva and enlisted in the Polish army. My father was a study–house dweller (frequenter) and was not interested in financial matters; mother and the children provided for the household. I joined halutz[2] training in Bilgoray at the Dror Kibbutz where I stayed for nine months. There were fifty members at the camp, mostly from small towns. We did road work. In 1929, the year of the Arab riots, I arrived on aliyah.

I favored Piaski as a second hometown to the point it was difficult for me to choose between Turobin and Piaski. As I resided in Piaski, I liked to often visit Turobin but could not find people there who understood me, although I had relatives there. In Piaski, I was busy with cultural matters. There were various parties and cultural institutions; a theater company; Zionist Organization, Poale Zion[3]; Mizrachi; Bund; and zealous Orthodox. I was active in Hakhalutz[4]. It pained me when I saw my hometown Turobin at such a low point of social neglect. I found that youth in Turobin were still distant from the Zionist ideal and did not have activists or guides as did other towns that would raise the flag of culture and organization, the Nation and ascend to Zion. I proposed to some acquaintances to form a drama section and assured my help, and thus I could approach the youth. Indeed, a drama section was founded in Turobin led by local activist Itamar Hopen. After the theater company was founded, political development began to take form as parties and culture in the spirt of progress and enlightenment which drifted from the occupied lands of Austria and Germany. It was a difficult task; more than one organization suffered a gap in activities due to a lack of activists. I was happy that, during my visit in Turobin, I helped activate the youth involvement in cultural activity. However, Piaski remained at a higher cultural level than Turobin.

Turobin attracted me more, perhaps because it was my birth town and therefore I occasionally enjoyed visiting Turobin and learning what was taking place there. I especially liked conversing with local craftsmen, carpenters, cobblers, and other interesting figures. I took interest in their spirit, livelihood, lives, and issues; I learned they were pure of heart, kind, Jews loyal to tradition and honest, despite their primitiveness. Thus, I found a bridge to the local youth and encouraged them culturally.

I was the first halutz in my family who made aliyah and gradually brought my parents and other family members to Israel. But then, various factors interfered with aliyah. I corresponded with my brother from Warsaw where he was studying. After he heard the situation in Israel was poor and I had yet to get settled, he attempted to persuade me to return to Poland. I refused to heed his advice. Eventually, his attitude towards Israel changed, probably after he witnessed the acts by the Polish anti–Semites in their war on the Jews, and after the intensifying of the Nazi torment of Jews in Germany. All that had influenced him, and he wrote in his letters that he, too, desired to immigrate to Israel. He arrived in 1931. Until that point, I sent funds to my parents in Turobin and there was a rumor in the town that I was rich. In 1932, I brought my parents on aliyah and my sister Pessa arrived in 1935. A year later, I brought over my brother, David, and with that we completed the aliyah of the whole family. I was ecstatic.

[Page 202]

A famous poet said once, "My heart is in the east and I am at the edge of west." I, too, struggled in my approach to my town Turobin. I became a citizen in Israel, brought my family, and yet felt incomplete. The love for my step–homeland Poland had not yet vanished from my heart. Therefore, in 1936, I decided to travel to Europe and visit Turobin. I remained in Poland five months. I visited many towns but mostly I stayed in Turobin. There I found some things which reminded me of the state of the Jews in their suffering under the Pharaoh in Egypt, "they did set over them taskmasters to afflict them with their burdens." (Exodus 1:11). I am not comparing myself to Moses who was greater than all his peers, but I, too, went to my brethren and, like Moses, witnessed their sorrow. I saw the disposition of my brethren in Turobin under the burden of *Galut*[5] and the servitude of unlimited taxes, denial of equal rights, libel, and incitement. Turobin had a lot of poverty and its economic situation was catastrophic. They were already accustomed to it and continued that poor existence without a choice in the matter. I came from the outside, especially Eretz Israel where we lived a life of freedom and hope. So, it was difficult for me to come to terms with the deeds of the Evil Angel and accept with the unbearable state of the Jews in Poland. I, the pioneer from Eretz Israel, was seen as if I came from a big city in a dream, a cultured man with whom everything could be discussed.

Eretz Israel, despite its distance from Poland, remained close in the hearts of the Jews, not just in prayers. After the gates to the land were opened in a limited capacity after the Balfour Declaration, Eretz Israel came even closer to the hearts of Polish Jews and bestowed its light and spirt on them. The Jews of Turobin were like the remainder of Polish Jews. A feeling formed among them that Eretz Israel was close to becoming a reality for Jews. Every Jewish resident of the town dreamed of sending a son or daughter to Eretz Israel, be it through marriage or halutz training, just to form a hold in Eretz Israel. They were especially interested in sending a son or daughter through marriage to a pioneer or craftsperson going on aliyah. In nearly every home, members discussed Eretz Israel in a practical sense. The opposition by the zealous Orthodox dissipated, and they, too, joined in the effort of aliyah. On the other hand, I witnessed the Poles inciting a boycott on the Jews. I saw signs saying "do not buy from Jews," and various threats. I saw youths from Nationalist Polish organizations blocking Christians from entering Jewish businesses. I had a feeling that the Jews of Turobin and other towns felt some tragedy looming. Among religious and Hasidic sects, they said that various rebbes in Poland were conducting spiritual efforts to cancel bad decrees by the heavens, and there were tsaddikim[6] who imposed fast days, foreseeing the future in which a tragic heavenly decree was unfolding. In Turobin, too, the Jews felt themselves disposable and began considering Eretz Israel as a sanctuary for Jews, although they were not aware of specifics. "I am the man that hath seen affliction" on my visit to Poland from Eretz Israel.

[Page 203]

I was especially drawn to the towns in which I spent my youth and most of all drawn to the Jews of Turobin. Yet, I barely recognized the folks of my town in their outlook in general and on Zionist questions. It was as if the Jews had opened their eyes and saw the harsh realities. I, who came from Eretz Israel, was seen by them like Moses who "descended to his brethren in Egypt and witnessed them in hard labor." It was difficult advising them on Aliyah because of the difficulties in obtaining certificates from the British authorities. Still, I advised them to gain technical knowledge and skills if they could.

Of course, I did not stay in one spot, even my hometown Turobin. Once, as I traveled from Turobin to Warsaw, I met some relatives and we went on a walk through the Zachs park. As we walked, we discussed various topics, mainly the new life in Eretz Israel which, despite difficulties, was becoming easier with experience. Suddenly, my relatives saw a group of Christian university students and began to escape fearing attack. Fearlessly, I remained standing. The relatives yelled to me to quickly escape since I was risking an assault by the students but I did not budge. The students were surprised to see a Jew who did not fear them like the rest of the "Moshkes." They approached me and asked who I was and what I was doing there. I told them that I was indeed a Jewish native of Poland but had exchanged citizenship for a British one and was from Eretz Israel. The students immediately changed their approach to me and we discussed various issues. I told them we Jews were building a state of our own and the Jews were doing various labor. They listened attentively and we parted ways in a friendly manner.

When I visited halutz training camps in Grodno, I again witnessed the horror plaguing the Jews as we traveled on the train. Everyone wanted to concentrate in a single car and not fear (wanted to be away from) the Poles. I, with my British passport, returned their confidence to them.

On my final visit to Poland, it could be seen that the Jews everywhere were uneasy, as if they felt some unknown force approaching which would be manifested in a terrifying figure who would change matters and mercilessly devour them. However, they relied on the verse, 'The Strength of Israel will not lie nor repent' and, despite the tragic visions before their eyes, continued in their ordinary lives as though there was no choice. It is unfortunate the millions of Jews of Eastern Europe are not only absent in their countries of birth, but here, too, in the old–new Israel where their absence is felt with every step. With the renewed occupation, the West Bank and the old cities of Hebron, Bethlehem, Ancient Jerusalem, Nablus, Jericho, and others could have been home to wonderful towns and strengthen the Jewish force in Israel. The Jews of Turobin could have contributed even through illegal aliyah. It would have been a wonderful contribution of value and manpower and we would not have had to make do with a few dozen families who survived the Holocaust.

Editor's Footnotes:

1. Probably the American Jewish Joint Distribution Committee

2. Halutz – a Jew who immigrated to the region of Palestine, especially as part of a movement in the years after World War I, to work the land and create Jewish settlements

3. Poale Zion – a movement of Marxist–Zionist Jewish workers founded in various cities of Poland, Europe and the Russian Empire around the turn of the 20th century

4. Hakhalutz – a Jewish youth movement that trained young people for agricultural settlement in the Land of Israel

5. Galut – expresses the Jewish conception of the condition and feelings of a nation uprooted from its homeland and subject to alien rule

6. Tsaddikim – the righteous

———

[Page 204]

Figures and Experiences

By Itamar Hopen

Translated by Meir Bulman

A. The Convert

Shmuel Zinvil Shtarker[?], was the son–in–law of Ovadiahu and the brother–in–law of Yosef Corndrexler. He lived in his father–in–laws' muddy yard, the entrance to which was through an alley bordering the houses of Yaakov Moshe Hopen and Yosef Corndrexler. When Shmuel Zinvil [S.Z.] decided to relocate from the village of Otrotcha [?] to Turobin, he built a home with his own hands, with wooden planks and a straw roof. The house had two rooms; one was finished, in which the family lived, and the other remained a foundation because Shmuel did not have the means to complete it and seal its opening. So, it served as a hallway and a "summerhouse."

Shmuel was blessed with two boys and three girls. The oldest was married and lived elsewhere. To this day, I do not know how they managed to fit 7 people in that room. The room served other functions: as a veterinarian laboratory, a bookbinding workshop, and a sewing workshop for their daughter, Gittel.

When SZ was asked what he did for a living, he jokingly said, "many jobs with few blessings." The more work he did, the poorer he was, he would say, and he was impoverished as long as I knew him. I recall that Shmuel was not trained and certified in only one field but had a knack for physiological and mechanical research. It is unfortunate that most of his ideas were unsuccessful due to his primitive views.

The bulk of his income came from selling cut straw to coachmen. With the help of his oldest daughter Chana–Rosa, he would cut straw with an industrial cutter. As he expanded, he purchased a centrifugal machine, "Carat" [?], and operated it with a horse who was blind in one eye. SZ covered the horse's second eye with a cloth, probably because the horse objected to going around in circles for hours on end or so as not to dizzy the horse. His other source of income was bookbinding which he did mainly at night through the early hours of the morning. Another source of income was his hobby, healing animals.

The medical knowledge with which Shmuel was blessed came to him naturally and instinctively. That was evident from the manners and methods he used when giving medical attention to ill animals. Most often, sick horses were brought to him. Sickness occurred when a horse overate barley or rye without prior blending and a water soak. That happened after the animal managed to free itself and access the grain. There were also other illnesses such as colds, stomach issues, etc. The diagnosis SZ would reach when a cold was concerned was drinking cold water as the animal perspired in the heat. He would give such explanations for any disease. As soon as SZ was summoned to care for a sick animal, he immediately packed his medical equipment: an awl with a precise hole of 2.5 centimeters, a special rope to stretch[?] the horse's neck for blood–letting, a hook shaped utensil with a sharp 1.5 cm length edge through which he would find a vein to let blood, some sharpened pocket knives, and a bottle of vodka. SZ began to examine the horse by touching its ears through which he could measure fever. He continued to examine the horse's skin to see if it was bloated. If it was, he immediately began stabbing it with the awl, through which, he claimed, he decreased swelling. He continued to examine the stomach with a voice enhancing device and reached the conclusion the horse's stomach must be cleaned. He had several means of doing so. The first device was plucking a single hair from the horse, looping it, and inserting it into its anus, causing stimulation and release. If that remedy was of no use, he had other devices. For an illness he dubbed "stomach typhus," he prescribed a new diet and a bottle of vodka for the horse to drink. In most of the cases he treated, he saved the animal from death for which he was praised as a miracle worker, affirmed by all those who required his services.

[Page 205]

As mentioned above, SZ had three girls. The youngest, Sarah–Beila, married a convert to Judaism, the lawyer Avraham Ben Avraham (formerly Ratchinski) Marriage to a convert in a small town, in an environment rife with anti–Semitism afflicting all walks of Jewish life, became an important event and led to relentless conversation among people at all levels of the community. The existing environment and the treatment by Christians toward Jews left their mark on such a social event, which would (otherwise) be quite simple in an enlightened country. But that was not so in a small community like Turobin. Many aspects of the event bothered community leaders, for many reasons.

According to Halakha and in practice, the rabbinate posed difficulties to someone who wanted to convert. There was a fear of the reaction by gentiles: "The Jews are recruiting Christian children for apostasy" (in propaganda.) The Christians were not aware of that aspect of Jewish law and even if they were, it was of no use. A conversion necessarily caused a wave of anger and blind hatred which was not always hidden from the Jews.

According to A. Goldfarb, Avraham Ben Avraham was born in Warsaw. He was the son of devout Catholics and a long noble lineage. His brother was interior minister in the Lublin government and an activist in the National Party (Sanacja.) The party was a fanatic, nationalist, anti–Semitic party whose main platform was to expel the Jews from their economic positions and eventually from Poland. Rachinski was raised in such an environment. He first studied theology and later trained as a lawyer. He often appeared in the court in Turobin and thus opened an office in town and divided his time among the towns, eventually settling in Turobin.

Rachinski was a tall man with a pleasant external appearance and Jewish-like behavior. Some said he returned to his past life. In his spiritual life, he did not find his place in Christian society. For some reason, he found no understanding in the society in which he was raised, and he was lonely and disillusioned. Under those circumstances, he came across the kind young woman Sarah Beileh and she tipped the scale and brought him to her religion. They had a child and their family life was non–Christian. The mother, Sarah–Beileh, shaped the lifestyle of the family. The saga was completed then for Sarah–Belieh, but for Aba the trouble had just began with his marriage to his beloved Sarah–Beileh. His previous social circle isolated and boycotted him. He prayed at the Krashnik Rebbes' synagogue from a prayer book translated into Polish.

[Page 206]

As I mentioned, he did not fit into Christian society but maintained contact with his colleagues, the judges, lawyers, and clerks. They all banded against him after he left their community. Opposition to him took practical shape in the form of tormenting the Jew. The lawyers, for instance, dissuaded clients from giving him cases. The court clerk mocked him during proceedings. It was a pity to watch him resisting his tormentors; more than once the question was raised, did the Jews not have enough troubles that he had to add to them? The Jews were decreed by heaven to suffer, but he accepted unimaginable suffering of his own volition. That is a lesson for the spiritual life of a person – he is most joyful while he suffers. Aba would say, "the more I am persecuted, the more I am filled with joy." It is customary for Jews to boycott a meshumad[1], so it can only be imagined how Christians treat a convert to Judaism. The persecution of his family was relentless and they were undoubtably subjected to the Nazi horrors. To this day no sign of life has been heard from them. Sarah Beileh's oldest sister, Gittel, survived and resides in Warsaw.

B. Turobin's Pandre

R' Zalman Fleisher was a butcher. His home and butcher shop were near the study house. (He had a nickname, Zelmele Scrop.) R' Zalman's wife, Sheva–Chava, was a sharp– tongued woman of valor. She was the commander, the person who pointed to the passage recited by the prayer leader. Because of the distance between the cantor's stand and the women's section, it was difficult to hear what passage he had reached. Woe is a person who was unfortunate enough to be subjected to her wrath. Sparks flew from her "holy" mouth and G–d save us from her blessings. It should not be assumed that she was a bad woman seeking conflict, quite the opposite. She was naturally righteous, anonymously gave to charity, was a wonderful hostess. In short, she was a proper Jewish mother ("a Yiddisha mama.)

R' Zalman and Sheva–Chava were blessed with many sons and daughters. His oldest, R' Shmuel, was short–statured with a small black beard; he had a quick tongue, spoke fluently, succinctly and to the point. Due to his quick tongue he was often interrupted during a sentence. But it was nothing out of the ordinary; he was pleasant and walked a pure path. Like his father, R' Shmuel was a butcher. Like the other butchers, he would purchase cattle for slaughter on market day. One day, R' Shmuel [bought?] a cow from a large farmer. The farmer regretted the price and R' Shmuel countered that after handshaking, a sale is irrevocable (it was customary to shake hands when trading animals.) The farmer pulled the cow towards him, and R' Shmuel pulled it to the other side. In short, they brawled. At first, it seemed like a fight between a bull and a chicken but soon it became clear that Shmuel had the upper hand. The giant farmer lay helpless in the mud, and they seemed like David and Goliath. Truth is that Shmuel's story is not the one that should be told; rather, the story that should be told is the one about lion of the two, Yosef "Pandre" Fleisher, Zalman's second son. The readers should not think that someone is attempting to plagiarize Pandre (Noah), the hero from the wonderful novel written by poet Zalman Shneur. He wrote about Pandre in the 1930s; our Pandre was born during the Russo–Japanese war in 1904. While still in his crib, he was called Pandre. Allegedly, that is clear proof that the true Pandre was a native of Turobin. It was very daring of Shneur to come to Turobin and steal the hero in broad daylight and publicize him. In protest to Zalman Shneur, we declare that the true Pandre was a figure stolen from (people in) many towns, but *our* Pandre is the one true Pandre, the archetype.

[Page 207]

Was Yosef Pandre a true hero? Of course! He was a hero yet did not fight in many wars. A hero must know when to fight, when to threaten, and when to contain himself. The main point is that the adversary does not know about the secret weapon his heroic rival possesses. Such was Yosef; his outward appearance was not particularly manly, and he was not wide or very tall. If shkotzim (young Christian men) mockingly called him or any other Jew in his presence "Jew" (Yid), then Yosef pounced on his prey and fought against two or three at a time and mercilessly broke their bones. The shkotzim who tasted his wrath no longer insulted Jews.

In the warm summer days, the young men bathed in the river. On the south side of the bridge, the river widened in a section called Slizhba. The shkotzim[2] expelled the Jewish boys from that section of the river, threw their clothes in the river, and assaulted and tormented them in various humiliating ways. Those events continued uninterpreted until Yosef appeared, and then the shkotzim escaped like mice to save their lives. If a few dared stay behind, a look from the corner of Yosef's eye was enough to have them disappear, too. Yosef would jump into the river from the bridge barrier, 4 meters high, dive under the river, and appear in a distant spot. The Slizhba was emptied of shkotzim and Yosef felt like a fish in the water. With expert hands he performed a "klefter" (a swimming method), a wonderful sight. All the young men stood and proudly breathed a sigh of relief. A strong man! Samson!

On the way home, he encountered a peasant with a calf for sale. Between each question, Yosef began to haggle. Yosef tested the calf's weight by lifting it; it must have been 100 kilograms. He lifted it like a toy and it was as if, at the same point, the calf owner was also lifted. Yosef probably proposed a low price for the calf and the peasant called him a "dirty Jew." Nu, nu, you should have seen Yosef in his glory. He threw the farmer to the ground, grabbed his throat, and threatened to suffocate him if he would not take back the Jewish insult. The farmer flailed, begged, apologized, and said that all Jews were good. He also agreed to a discounted price of the calf, just to release himself. Yosef the hero scolded him and said, "You and your calf will be repentance for the Jews. I want your calf free of charge and for your own good I suggest I never (see) you here again." Such was Yosef Pandre, the hero of Turobin.

[Page 208]

C. Yehoshua Liberbom

Like all Jews, he was known by a nickname. He was known by his father's name, "Shialeh Moshe Chaim's." Yehoshua was a tall, lanky man with a typical long Jewish nose, a long face and slanted burning eyes. He was a horse trader and had a pub in his home on the Courts Street. The pub was run mainly by his wife, Tzviya. He had two boys and one girl. One of his sons, Moshe, was saved from the Holocaust by escaping to the Soviet Union. He now lives in the United States. Yehoshua was the son–in–law of Pinyeh [?] Gevertz [?] ("Pinyeh Goy".) By his nature, Yehoshua was a good man, a lover of the Jewish people to the point of risking his life. He respected all parties in town and all respected him. He was not a member of any Hasidic sect but took part in various events to which he was invited. His presence there was very well felt because of his singing talent. He would also delight those in his presence by dancing. He had a high alto voice and when he reached a C note became a soprano; his high voice was well heard. The other choir members said that Yehoshua said Kiddush over liquor and so his singing was so pleasurable.

I do not recall Yehoshua ever having a dispute with a Jewish resident. In contrast, he took part in disputes between Jews and Christians and among the Christians. Most quarrels ended after his intervention. He broke the bones of the party he recognized as guilty and then invited the rivals for a drink (of course paid for by the rivals.)

As I mentioned, he was a pub owner. Most of his income was on market day. On that day, Yehoshua helped his wife. He knew most of the local farmers, knew the names of their fathers, their family events, and the villages where they resided. He treated the honest and pure with complete sympathy and helped them with good advice, a loan, etc. The farmer would say to that Jew, "You are like one of us. If only all Jews were like you, we would not hate you." In truth, he hated that same Jew with whom he was breaking bread.

On market day, the Christian farmers ate and drank at the pubs, including Yehoshua's. There were incidents when the drinking reached intoxication and they were unable to pay. In that state of lack of control, some uttered insults towards Jews, refused to pay the tab, or could not pay. That behavior would enrage Yehoshua and he would tell them, "If you had only refused to pay, fine, but for your curses and insults towards the Jews, I will break your bones!" And he did. He grabbed an empty beer bottle and smashed their heads and threw them out. When Yehoshua got into a rhythm, although he was thin, the farmers could not take him on.

[Page 209]

Those who had experienced head injuries appeared the next day and requested peace, since they could expect a trial for excessive noise and damaged property. After pleading, Yehoshua agreed to reconcile, the oversized bill for the shattered furniture was paid, and they began to treat Yehoshua respectfully.

I recall riots by some Christian military recruits from local villages. It happened one Shabbat in the 1930s. On the way back home, the new military recruits parked their vehicles at the center of the market and began rioting against the Jews. Yehoshua ran through the alleys to my father's house and decided to rescue the Jews from the rioters. They both took positions at the corner of Shimale Moshke's (across from the great synagogue) and battled from there. Thanks to that intervention and the intervention of some brave people on the other side of the market, and thanks to the Zionist youth who acted, the town was spared victims.

Bless his memory.

D. R' Alter Sherf (Tzaddik Nistar)

R' Alter Moshe Shayeh Leib was not known by his last name but instead by the names of his father and grandfather. Many were named not by their last name but by their ancestors, but not as a pejorative, God forbid. R' Alter's wife name was Chippa, and there were some who joined her name to his and called him R' Alter Chips. Many town residents whispered rumors that he was one of 36 Tsaddikim Nistarim[3]. Few knew his secret. There were few among the scholars at the study house who knew the secrets of his ways. Since they attributed to him that title, they treated him with special respect. And if such notables treated him so, the common man, of course, did so as well. The 36 Tsaddikim were a legend among all exiles. After the destruction of the Temple, the Shechinah[4] had abandoned the Jewish people. As the years of exile progressed, a legend came to be told that within the nation there were 36 righteous men who were messengers from the heavens who knew Kabbalah and performed miracles. They were mortals and manifested as common men such as water–drawers, beggars, and the like, to distract people from their true identity.

R' Alter was not aware of the secret. He was an honest man, humble, modest, and never raised his voice. He was tall and thin, with a dark yellow beard and merciful blue eyes, and wore simple clothes. He lived near the Bet Midrash[5] but he rarely went home to sleep. He spent most of his nights and days at the Bet midrash, where he would isolate and study kabbalah. In early morning, he would recite *Tikkun Chatzot*[6], take a short nap on a bench at the bet midrash, and before daylight, a new man was created for prayer and praise. He earned a living by fixing kitchen utensils. Housewives brought to him copper, tin, and steel utensils for repairs. R' Alter would weld the holes and do general repairs. The women knew R' Alter did not name a price for repairs and each woman paid according to her abilities. He worked between 2:00 and 4:00 in the afternoon. He worked briefly, earned little and did not eat much. He only ate meat on Shabbat, and on weekdays he returned home for lunch at 2 in the afternoon.

He fasted every Monday and Thursday.

[Page 210]

Eventually, though handsome, he appeared pale and exhausted, from bodily and mental suffering. It was not long before R' Alter became ill. It was said he had tuberculosis. The scholars at the bet midrash took turns caring for him daily. They mostly helped him with putting on his tefillin, and with his last remaining strength, R' Alter would ensure the hand and head pieces were in their lawful spot according to the Shulchan Aruch[7]. He slowly thinned and became a pile of bones. It was said that he died a painless death. Not one resident was absent from R' Alter's funeral, and in this lies the secret of his

E. Alter Shneiderberg

It was said of R' Alter that he was a *Ba'al Teshuvah*[8]. "In the place where penitents stand, even the full–fledged righteous do not stand."

R' Alter Bork [?] was a Torah teacher. Since that was not enough to provide for him, he had another role as cantor at the shtibel[9] of the craftsmen. He had another role for which he volunteered, summoning the residents to recite Psalms at dawn on Shabbat . He led the recitation. So, another nickname was added, "Zugger" (speaker[?]). Snow or shine, R' Alter walked slowly through the streets of town and called the homeowners to say Psalm; he did not simply call them but did so in a pleading song.

Everyone remembers the nights of frost and snow on Shabbat night after a long week of work. The more it snowed or rained, the more enjoyable sleep was. Right at the height of the quality sleep under covers in the warm bed, when it would be a pity to expel a dog from the doghouse, R' Alter's voice was heard. At first it seemed that this announcer came only to upset calm people sleeping the sleep of the honest. His voice fluctuated, intensified the closer he came; as he moved farther away it weakened and grew silent. R' alter would call and plead, "Israel, oh holy nation! Until when will you slumber? Shtyt oyf, shtyt oyf! Awaken and serve your Creator! Awaken, please! Rise, please! And report! To pray to Hashem! For that is your purpose!" R' alter would repeat those passages and add more, walking the streets of town, his voice echoing and entering every Jewish home. Israel, a holy nation!

He was a good Jew. May he rest in peace.

Moshe's sons, Grandchildren of Alter

Shneiderberg

Editor's Footnotes:

1. Meshumad – an apostate from Judaism, especially a convert to Christianity

2. Shkotzim – a term used especially by a Jew to refer to a boy or man who is not Jewish

3. Tsaddikim Nistarim – refers to 36 righteous people, a notion rooted within the more mystical aspects of Judaism.

4. Shechinah – the presence of God in the world, as conceived in Jewish theology

5. Bet Midrash – a Jewish study hall located in a synagogue, yeshiva, or other building

6. Tikkun Chatzot – a Jewish ritual prayer recited each night after midnight as an expression of mourning and lamentation over the destruction of the Temple in Jerusalem

7. Shulchan Aruch – the most widely consulted various legal codes in Judaism

8. Ba'al Teshuvah – literally means "master of return," one who has "returned" to G–d.

9. Shtibel – a place used for communal Jewish prayer

[Page 211]

Figures from our Town
In memory of the people of Turobin, the plain, pure, men of labor
By Israel Amir (Isaac Solkis)

Translated by Meir Bulman

Who does not remember Shalom Hafeh? And who does not remember Hemya Momek and his heroic sons? They were truly the heroes of town to the point that all the mishzins [?] (city folk) feared them like death! Hemya Momek's oldest son, Herrish, fell in battle at the center of the market while the Austrians retreated and the Polish were gaining control. It is said that, in his death, he saved the town Jews from a real pogrom.

270

They are worthy of remembrance. And while we are mentioning good men and heroes of Israel, why not remember Zelmaleh and his family? His wife Sheva–Chava saved people who were on death's doorstep by storming the synagogue during prayers and running to the holy ark. It was said that her prayers were always heard by the heavens and thus she saved many dying people. The sons of Zelmaleh Shmuelik, the short- statured, healthy man, and Yosef Pandre, the bravest among them. You think that only in Salman Schneour's Shklov there was a Pandre?

Zelmaleh Scrab [Shrab ?] had it all; he even had a son that became a shochet[1]. If we are already mentioning pure and kind people, we should remember many other people like Leibish Baruch the baker. He had so much folksy humor and wisdom.

[Page 212]

Leibish's father, R' Baruch Shemesh: what a beloved, happy Jew. He was always content, he never needed anything.

Moshe Chaim Yonlis also had it all. He earned a nice living but it was enough for him so he went to Shmelki Drimler's shop and began telling jokes to Rachel Leah. She was so busy listening to Moshe that she forgot the store and her husband Shmelki was angry. But how can one be upset with Moshe while he tells jokes and Torah tidbits? Rivakh Leah served Moshe Chaim Yonlis another cup of tea and he continued his tales. Can it be imagined that Moshe would not tell more jokes? Moshe Chaim also did not believe it would end like that.

Do you remember Alter Borik? [?] He awoke at dawn to summon the residents to worship the creator with Psalms and Selichot during the Days of Awe. He then went home and continued to sew. Jews need to make a living! The Hasidim would wait for the kippahs (yarmulkes) Alter sewed for them.

And who did not know Yerachmiel Shechnils [?] A gentle Jew. He always sat at his kiosk, waiting for customers, humming a Hassidic tune. On holidays and Shabbat he was the cantor at the Trisker shtibel[2]. He had a wonderful voice which was a true pleasure to hear. We will no longer hear the voice of that songbird.

And the Tzaddik Nistar[3] Rabbi Alter Sherf, husband of Tzippi the baker? He retired from his family life and moved to the Turobin rebbe's bet midrash where he slept by the fireplace and, in the corner, organized somewhat of a workshop to fix eating utensils, by which he would live [make a living?]. He did not want much and did not want any help; he was content with his lot.

And Shmuel Zanvil Shtarker! Der Shetshki Shnyder, the one who knew how to sign his name with his right foot. [?] He had such nice handwriting, a true graphic artist. His son–in–law the convert, Avraham ben Avraham Rachinski, the lawyer, nephew of the Polish interior minister. All Jewish residents went to see Shmuel and his son–in–law walk to the synagogue carrying the large Polish language prayer book. The gentiles exploded in jealousy. He stood in his courtroom with such Jewish honor.

We will remember all the craftsmen: the cobblers, tailors, hatters, carpenters, and coachmen.

Yaakov Lub [?] Gels [?] the shfilter [?] who, on holidays and Shabbat, led prayers at the Turobiner's bet midrash and sounded the shofar on the Days of Awe. He rehearsed while traveling from Turobin to Lublin. He prayed as he prepared for Rosh Hashanah and sounded the shofar, as the horses knew the road and did not need a coachman. The other passengers were joyful and did not sleep the whole night, as the journey from Turobin to Lublin was done during the night. We will remember them all forever.

In their death, they commanded us to never forget the Nazi party which caused the malicious loss of half of our nation.

Editor's Footnotes:

1. Shochet – a person who has been specially trained and licensed to slaughter animals and birds in accordance with the laws of shechita.

2. Shtiebel – a place used for communal Jewish prayer. In contrast to a formal synagogue, a shtiebel is far smaller and approached more casually.

3. Tzaddik Nistar – refers to 36 righteous people, a concept rooted within the more mystical dimensions of Judaism.

[Page 213]

In Memory of the Departed: Mother and Son
By Mordecai Hopen (Yoskovitz)
Translated by Meir Bulman

Among all of his friends was also the young woman, Tamar (Tammy) Feder, R' Moshe Feder's daughter. I still remember her as she passed by our house headed to the clinic; she was a strong woman full of youthful energy and a loud laugh which echoed through the air. The friendship ties between the two increased until one day we learned that soon they would marry. They married and a year later had a boy named Uriel. I, as their friend and a frequent visitor to their home, knew him well and often [sat] by his crib and carried him. Before he could experience Galut[1], his parents managed to make aliyah. Here, the boy grew, was raised in the homeland and absorbed dedication at home and at school. In his childhood, he was playful and in his youth had pleasant traits and qualities; he was always honest and in solidarity. He grew until he became a man of valor and a soldier. When he enlisted – doubtful if even 16 springs had passed – he was already in battle. As he provided cover for his friends on the battlefield, his life was given [sacrificed].

Tamar Goldfarb, Wife of Leo and Mother of Uri

[Page 214]

The pain was immense, especially for his mother who could not be consoled. The pain of losing her son ate away at her heart for years until one fateful day she passed away.

Their spirits serve as examples and their memory remains in our heart.

Bless their memory!

Family Portrait
Pictured: **R' Isaac, Silka, Niece Sheindel, Nephew Yisrael Amir**

274

[Page 215]

R' Isaac the Town "Soltis"

R' Isaac Oberweiss [Aubrois?] was a leader in town. The residents called him by his title, R' Isaac Soltis ("leader" in Polish).

R' Issacs's role was to serve as a middleman between the authorities and the Jewish population. R' Isaac accompanied government officials during their regular activities within the Jewish community. He handed out notices for various taxes, court summons, military enlistment summons, fines, etc. Every Jew who sensed a financial trouble looming, for example a garnishment, approached R' Isaac for help. More than once, R' Isaac saved many members of the Jewish community from trouble while risking his standing and knowingly violating the law, yet he still acted on behalf of Jews.

His wife was named Silka. The halutzim called her "Aunt" due to her support and kindheartedness.

The home of R' Isaac and Silka was used as a meeting spot for Zionist youth activities. There, the youth found a warm, pleasant atmosphere and a full understanding of their activities.

R' Moshe Leib Silberklang's Family

R' Mohse Leib Ben Asher was a respected member of the community. He was a tall man with a trimmed beard, high cheekbones, and blue eyes. He was pleasant, spoke calmly, and had a sense of humor. His garb was Jewish-traditional: a long coat with a slit in the back, a nice tie, and a short jacket near the house. (Devoutly Orthodox men were forbidden to wear short jackets.) He was considered progressive and indeed he was. Youth issues were near and dear to him and he treated the Zionist movements with admiration. He was a generous contributor, and alert to the problems between the authorities and the Jewish community. He was a Jew who held his head high and his appearance was respectful. If I recall correctly, he served in the Czarist Russian army and was among the royal regiment which especially selected strong, tall young men.

His lucky stars summoned to him as a counterpart to his wife Zelda (Zelda'le), a woman who was blessed with all the great qualities of a Jewish mother. She was an energetic and bright woman. The couple had 3 boys and 7 girls who were raised and educated in the spirit of Jewish tradition full devotion.

On Pilsdoski Street there was a large house with many rooms. The house was owned by R' Moshe Leib's family. The family resided there and in it formed the vessels [created the vessels?] which made up the Jewish family in those days. Additionally, part of the house served as a pub and home–restaurant. The restaurant was established and run by Zelda. She did not make do with her husband's earnings, fearing they would not suffice for her large family. She tastefully prepared the food; gefilte fish, roast, and dumplings were famous, especially known by the Christian intelligentsia who often dined on Zelda's gefilte fish.

[Page 216]

The house was also a meeting spot for girls. The girls were divided in their opinions. Most girls were Zionists. One of them, Bluma, was active in Hakhalutz[2]. She is with us in Israel. (The son Yahushua who was active in Hapoel Hamizrachi[3] is also with us in Israel). Some were members of Bais Yaakov (an extremist religious movement). When girls were recruited for Flower Day on behalf of Keren Kayment[4], or for emptying KKL boxes and the like, the Silberklang girls were always considered. The oldest daughter, Chaya'le, was a volunteer librarian at Tarbut. The house also served as a school, as one of the daughters, Hinda, was a teacher. The Silberklang house was dubbed "The Girl Swarm" by the young people (due to its structure). There was multicolored dance, the center of lively youthfulness. It closely followed the political discourse within the Zionist movement or elsewhere, and often centered debates on literary issues or socializing. All of those created the image of the young men and women in town, breathed life into it and gave it content. I remember the frequent singing which echoed from that home, songs of Zion or youthful laughter, caressing [?] as the door opens.

276

The Silberklang Family

Father Moshe Leib; Mother Zelda'le; the children Chaya, Hinda, Blumah (now in Israel), Heshel (Yehoshua Ben–Ari, in Israel,) Sarah, Rivkah, Pinchas, Asher Zelig, Mattill, Rachel Leah
In the right–side corner: **Chaya and her daughter, of Blessed Memory**

[Page 217]

That house was closed and silenced forever. Did those young folks imagine they would be quashed by the Nazi boot?

Bless their memory!

Family Parting from Yehoshua Ben–Ari Upon His Aliya

From the right: **Avraham Kopf, Lemmel Katz, Chaya Silberklang, Y. Ben–Ari, Miriam Levin**
[Caption in Photo: "To our dear friend Heshel, good luck!]

278

Editor's Footnotes:

1. Galut –expresses the Jewish conception of the condition and feelings of a nation uprooted from its homeland and subject to alien rule.

2. Hakhalutz – a Jewish youth movement that trained young people for agricultural settlement in the Land of Israel. It became an umbrella organization of the pioneering Zionist youth movement.

3. Hapoel Hamizrachi – a political party and settlement movement in Israel and one of the predecessors of the National Religious Party which later became the modern–day Jewish Home Party.

4. Keren Kayment – Jewish National Fund.

[Page 218]

A Lovely Family

By S. Barkai

Translated by Meir Bulman

In memory of the Hopen family, cruelly murdered by Poles in Tevet, 5704, January 1943

R' Yaakov Moshe Hopen Ben Pinchas HaCohen; his wife Esther Rivkah bat R' Shlomo Yanover; their daughters Golda, Devorah, and Perl; their son Elazar; their grandchild (Golda's child; and Golda's husband of the Gutwiling family of Goraj were all martyred by Polish murderers.

In 1905, R' Yaakov Moshe married Esther Rivka, the only daughter of R' Shlomo and Tisha Yanover. The Yanover family was from a great lineage, Orthodox and educated rooted in Turobin and the surrounding towns. R' Yitzchak Yanover, son of Shlomo Yanover, was a leader in the Turobin community for a few years in the 1930s.

R' Yaakov Moshe was accepted into the Yanover family. The marriage was a combination of Torah and the Way of the Land. The opinion in town was that the considerations for the combination of the linages (aside from fate) were that the son–in–law, Moshe Hopen, was a wealthy and skilled tradesman as well as a handsome man with a well–combed long black beard, full eyebrows, and burning eyes under his long lashes. After the wedding, the couple settled in Hinda's house. The apartment on the second floor which overlooked the Great synagogue

The Hopen Family Home

[Page 219]

was furnished and decorated generously and tastefully, according to the standard of the time.

R' Yaakov Moshe's business was leather, fur, and hair, an inherited trade. His business ties spread across a large territory from Bilgorj–Janów–Krasnik in the west and Tomashov–Zamosc–Krasnistav– Izbicia in the east, including local towns and villages. He bought the merchandise in that area and sold it in Mezric or Leipzig. Mezric was considered a center of the trade. R' Moshe was subscribed to a paper named *The Mezritsher Vachenshrift* or a similar name. That paper mainly contained the prices of various furs. R' Moshe spent most of the week traveling and he returned home as Shabbat approached. At home, family life developed, children were born, and life flowed calmly until WWI erupted.

Following WWI, the town was burned and the family wandered to Ludmir (Waldimir–Wylinsk.) Most of the Hopen family resided in that town so R' Moshe and his family settled in it. It was wartime and in Volyn and Ukraine, gangs of murderers of Jews like Petlorvzi, Bolkhovz, Helrzikim, and plain Cossacks roamed. The trains and their schedules were disrupted but Yaakov Moshe still travelled as was his custom. One night, as Yaakov Moshe returned from Shepetivka or the Rivne area, one of the gangs attacked the Jewish passengers. At the time, Jewish life was considered abandoned. But not Yaakov Moshe. He fought them as long as his strength would allow him. When he saw there was no other way, he jumped from the train, and after many troubles, reached his destination. Another night, two Heller gangsters attacked him and all they wanted was to cut his beard. But for Moshe, his long, carefully kempt beard was both a priceless possession and a symbol. Anyone who wanted to shave such a beard violated the commandment against waste. And so he fought them, risked his life, and hit them with the blows of the son of Phineas. He was one against many but could withstand them. After a dramatic chase, the barber[?] at the train station in Lutsk rescued him, and also ensured his return to Ludmir. He returned home injured and exhausted, his head full of wounds and a scarred body. His wife, Esther Rivkah, dressed his head with a cold compress for long hours. R' Moshe was consoled by one thing: "They did not cut my beard." He would claim "The beard is a symbol of human dignity," and that man "was created in God's image." He fought for Jewish honor; other ktzafim [word unclear?] were also bearded but the rioters did not attack them. Yaakov Moshe was a proud Jew and did not accept anti–Semitism and responded against anti–Semitic acts. If he witnesses a Jew in trouble among gentiles, he would always help and never leave him. He was a kind man with unlimited love of Israel. After the many troubles war had brought, and after advice from the Belzer Rebbe, the family returned to Turobin in the late 1920s.

After the move, a problem arose concerning the education of the children. In Ludmir, the children studied at the cheder and the Tarbut school. But in the small town, there was only a Polish school. Despite being a Hassid and devoutly religious, Yaakov Moshe worried first about professional education and immediately upon return brought a Hebrew teacher. He required Torah with [that Torah be taught according to] the Way of The Land but could not find agreement in the religious town. The opposite was true; his concern for educating the younger generation met resistance from Orthodox circles, especially Gur Hassidim[1]. As anyone familiar with the town and towns like it knows, going to war for a Hebrew teacher is suicide. Such a moment could bring about a boycott of the initiator. But Yaakov Moshe did not surrender and was wise to not battle with words but with actions. Immediately after one teacher left, he replaced him with another.

[Page 220]

The Hopen Family

Top row from the right: **Mordechai, Golda, Yehoshua, Devorah, Itamar**
Second row: **Elazar, Y. Moshe, A. Rivka, Perl**

Years passed, the children grew, and Yaakov Moshe expressed his concern about the idle youth of town. He recited to his sons, "What could the son do to avoid sinning?[2]" and "Inactivity is an unforgivable sin." He often told his friends that the community must see that a professional school of quality was

282

needed, rather than [spending money on] the many expenses caused by the disputes in town. Yaakov Moshe took no part in the fights between the various sects in town. That fight among brothers consumed everything and there was barely anyone not caught up in those disputes. Yet, it could not capture Moshe. He would claim, "What difference does it make what sect the ritual slaughterer belongs to (Trisk or Gur)? Will his blessing, the recitation before the slaughter, be different?"

[Page 221]

Still, the Gur Hassidim did not eat meat slaughtered by the Trisk slaughterer and vice versa. Truthfully, nobody knew the cause of the dispute (it must have been the result of a nation without a homeland.) During those days Yaakov Moshe, with the help of some town notables, founded the Bais Yaakov[3] school and the Bnos Yaakov[4] union. He oversaw the smooth operation of those institutions. He devoted his free time to those institutions, in part because his three daughters were members.

Despite the different political or movement affiliations of R' Moshe's sons and daughters, their home served as a center for Zionist activities brought in by the boys. The girls initiated meetings of Bais Yaakov activists who held fierce debates against Zionism. The atmosphere in that home was unlike other Orthodox homes where a conversation about Zionism or Zionist activity was the same as straying off the righteous path. Moshe and his wife Rivka treated with love and understanding [those who shared] the political affiliations of their sons and daughters and helped them. The home was open to all. Many came and went, came in hungry and left full.

As luck would have it, their three sons Mordechai, Yehoshua and Itamar made aliyah. At the height of WWII, Itamar maintained correspondence with them through the Red Cross and negotiated with the Swiss government (with the help of relatives and friends in the U.S.) to receive temporary visas for the family, based on mutual guarantees, etc. It cannot be said the Swiss government treated the request warmly, and if not for their delays in their responses which dragged across months, there is no doubt the family could have been saved. We hereby bring copies of two letters from the Red Cross. One of them is dated March 6, 1942 and states the daughter Golda is married, highlighting that the family is still in place. The second letter is dated March 30, 1943 in which it was requested that all family members sign. The most painful and shocking response was received, "The family has not been found at the recorded address and their address is unknown."

Different versions exist as to the extermination of the family. One version is that they were murdered in the woods near Otrotsha [?] Village. A second version claims they were murdered between the villages of ChÅ,aniów and Chirnichin [Czarnocin?] while they escaped the final clearing unit on the way to Izbica. All versions agree that the abomination was done by Poles. May the next generation know what that nation has inflicted upon us and judge why they were not condemned in the same manner [in which] the people of Hitler were condemned.

Bless the memory of our martyrs.

284

[Page 222]

Write in Block Capitals ✚ In grossen Druckbuchstaben auszufuellen.

From :

WAR ORGANISATION OF THE BRITISH RED CROSS AND ORDER OF ST. JOHN
Postal Message Scheme

To :
Comité International
de la Croix Rouge
Genève

P.O.B. 1085,
David Building,
Jerusalem,
PALESTINE.

ENQUIRER
Fragesteller

Name ___ Hopen

Christian name ___ Esumar
Vorname

Address ___ Eizor Taasya Beit Haftler

Nathanya

PALESTINE
PASSED BY
CENSOR
H.3

Message ___ Mitteilung.

(Message not to exceed 25 words, family news of strictly personal character).

(Nicht über 25 Worte, nur persönliche Familiennachrichten).

Odpowiedz otrzymalismy.Winszujemy Goldzie.U Szyji uro-

dzil sie syn.My wszyscy zdrowi i dobrze nam.Doniescie

o waszem zdrowiu i podpiszcie sie wszyscy.

Mordechaj Jehoszua Esumar

POLSKI CZERWONY KRZYZ
Biuro Informacyjne
10 GRUD. 1942

Date 15.9.1942

PALESTINE
PASSED BY
CENSOR
H.8

ADDRESSEE
Empfänger

Name ___ H o p e n

Christian name ___ Jakob Mojsze
Vorname

Address ___ Turobin Lub.

Pow.Krasnystaw

(Lublin)   G.G.

[Page 223]

Formularz niniejszy nie został dorę-
czony, ponieważ adresat nie przebywa
już pod podanym adresem i obecnego
miejsca pobytu nie można ustalić,

3 0 MARZ. 1943

✚

POLSKI CZERWONY KRZYŻ
Warszawa

Editor's Footnotes:

1. Gur Hassidim – a Hasidic dynasty originating from Ger, the Yiddish name of Góra Kalwaria, a small town in Poland.

2. "What could the son do to avoid sinning?" – from the Talmud.

3. Bais Yaakov – a name for Orthodox full–time, Jewish elementary and secondary schools for Jewish girls from religious families.

4. Bnos Yaakov – Girls for Life.

The Gutbertz Family

By A. Ginaton

Translated by Meir Bulman

R' Eizik the shochet was a well–known personality in the community. In addition to being a ritual slaughterer and examiner, he was honest and studious and so he was beloved by the community. Additionally, R' Eizek was blessed with musical talent and so he served as cantor, not just a cantor but THE cantor. To please the audience with song and conduct the choir, R' Eizeik used musical notes (using notes 50–60 years ago in such a small community was rare). Apparently, that musical gift passes in part by inheritance to his sons and grandsons. When his son–in–law, Chaim Gutbertz, lived in Warsaw, his sons participated in the choir of the Grand Synagogue on Tlomtski Street.

R' Eizik was blessed with many daughters. One of them, named Iyta Bluma, married Chaim Gutbertz. After WWI began, the Gutbertz family relocated to Warsaw where they resided for a few years. After the war ended, the Gutbertz family with its five sons returned to their hometown Turobin.

The national awakening in those days in Poland, especially in Warsaw, affected the Gutbertz family as well. The national consciousness, i.e. the desire for a return to Zion, was brought by the family as an inseparable as the physical load. The family constructed a small home which served three purposes: a workshop (the boys sewed for leather shoes); a center for Zionist activities; and living. The oldest son, Shmuel Abba was one of the founders of the Tarbut librarian.

[Page 224]

There are no means to describe how small the apartment was. To this day I do not understand how that space was able to contain so many people and form such a colorful life tapestry. A person who has not witnessed the size of the place, the life within it, and the emotional experiences in all their forms will not ever believe it. As I mentioned, the place served as a workshop and so the cobblers gathered there, some to drop off work and others to pick up work. They enjoyed gathering there to hear news and converse. The workmen's organization was big and was influential in community life. The organization did not officially declare an affiliation with the Zionist movement. The Gutbertz family used their professional status to instill Zionist consciousness in the industrious Jewish group. That is praiseworthy because of the impact and its mark on the Zionist youth movements. As time progressed, the workmen became admirers of the Zionist movement. At the same time and place where work matters took place, active Zionists gathered to plan activities regarding Tarbut, Keren Kaymet, aliyah, flower day, etc. At the same time, Yakov–Leib Yaffe, (a music student who returned from Warsaw) and an energetic, avid Zionist, engaged and argued with those present about issues Including Zionism. The debates took on serious form and Yaffe wanted to respectfully conclude them; then he would declare, "Shmuel Abba, please give me your violin!" Yaffe then beautifully played a Chopin piece which he had prepared for Herzl's Memorial Day.

The Gutbertz Family

Standing: **Shmuel Abba, Yosef, and Moshe**
Seated: **Uri and his son Yisrael and wife Esther, and the parents,
Iyta Bluma and Chaim**

See what can be accomplished in such a narrow space: a workshop, a choir with an orchestra and a stage, a wonderful cheerful sight. Iyta Bluma, the mother, pleasantly greeted the arrivals and during the winter offered a hot cup of tea. Chaim, the father, was an honest and humble man, living from the fruits of his labor and respected by all. R' Chaim was often involved in debates taking place in his home and his words were given credence. During the Days of Awe, the Gutbertz family filled an important role: they stood by grandfather Isaac's side and sang in a choir at the synagogue.

Such was the Gutbertz family home until the bitter Nazi enemy came and destroyed those good and pure souls. Bless their memory forever.

One family member survives. Moshe made Aliya as a halutz, was among the activists of the Borochov Organization and among the first conquerors of Hanita.

289

[Page 227]

About the Murdered Jewish People

By Itzhak Katzenelson

See: Excerpt from the longer 15 chapter mourning poem "The Song of The Murdered Jewish People."

———

[Page 228]

Our Town Burns

By Mordechai Gebirtig

See: *We Are Here* edited by Elanor Mlotek and Malke Gottlieb, pp 12
https://ia801902.us.archive.org/35/items/nybc214888/nybc214888.pdf

———

[Pages 229-253]

List of Turobin martyrs
May God avenge their blood

The Holocaust brought destruction and annihilation upon entire families, without leaving even a trace of their names, to be recorded in this Book. **May their Souls be Bound in the Bond of the Living Souls** of the residents of our town, together with the names that have been identified.

An everlasting memory to the martyrs of the Community of Turobin and Surroundings

Please stop! We do not know where our dear and beloved, murdered by the Nazi murderers, were brought to burial. May these memorial pages be their gravestone and memorial. Look, orphan and mourner, look with your own eyes and read these names, as if you were walking in the Cemetery among their graves. Here they rest, your mother and father, your children, your sisters and brothers, your grandfather and grandmother – shot, violated, choked, burned. Walk slowly, tread quietly. In your imagination, relive at least some of what they have experienced. They are looking at you, their look is demanding to remember. Remember them, remember! Engrave their holy memory, like the inscription on a gravestone, on your soul, in your memory.

DO NOT FORGET!

Translation by Yocheved Klausner

Page numbers refer to the pages of the original Yizkor Book, not this translation.

Surname	Given name	Spouse's name	Wife's maiden name	Father's name	Mother's name	Remarks	Page
א Alef							
AUBROIS	Eizik	Silka				town leader	229
EIDELMAN	Yisrael Mordechai	Perl					229
EIDELMAN	Mendel			Yisrael Mordechai	Perl		229
EIDELMAN	Avraham	Lieba		Yisrael			229
EIDELMAN	Liba (male)			Avraham	Lieba		229
EIDELMAN	Chaim			Avraham	Lieba		229
EIDELMAN	Tova			Avraham	Lieba		229
EIDELMAN	Sarah			Avraham	Lieba		229
EIDELMAN	Laybel	Ita-Rakhel	MAIMAN	Yisrael			229
EIDELMAN	Chant'che			Laybel	Ita-Rakhel		229
EIDELMAN	Esther			Laybel	Ita-Rakhel		229
EIDELMAN	Chaim			Laybel	Ita-Rakhel		229
EIDELMAN	Pin'che	Esther		Yisrael			229
EIDELMAN	David			Pin'che	Esther		229
EIDELMAN	Yosef			Pin'che	Esther		229
EIDELMAN	Zelda			Pin'che	Esther		229
EIDELMAN	Dina			Pin'che	Esther		229
EIDELMAN	Chanoch	Esther Leah	STERNFELD	Yisrael			230
EIDELMAN	David			Chanoch	Esther Leah		230
EIDELMAN	Simcha	Sarah		Yisrael			230
EIDELMAN	Reuven			Simcha	Sarah		230
EIDELMAN	Channah			Simcha	Sarah		230
EINSBERG	Yitzchak Eizik					ritual slaughterer	230
EINSBERG	Esther Beila			Yitzchak Eizik			230

EINSBERG	Mindel Leah			Yitzchak Eizik			230
EINSBERG	Feiga			Yitzchak Eizik			230
EINSBERG	Rakhel			Yitzchak Eizik			230
EINSBERG	Chava			Yitzchak Eizik			230
EINSBERG	Chaya			Yitzchak Eizik			230
EINSBERG	Sarah			Yitzchak Eizik			230
[EINSBERG]	Moshe					son in law of Yitzchak Eizik EINSBERG	230
[EINSBERG]	Yechezkel					grandson of Yitzchak Eizik EINSBERG	230
[EINSBERG]	Kreindel					daughter of Chaya EINSBERG	230
EINWAND	Yakov Itz'eh	Esther Leah					230
[EINWAND]	Chava			Yakov Itz'eh	Esther Leah		230
[EINWAND]	Pinchas					husband of Chava	230
[EINWAND]	Riba			Yakov Itz'eh	Esther Leah		230
[EINWAND]	Hershel					husband of Riba	230
[EINWAND]	Gitel			Yakov Itz'eh	Esther Leah		230
[EINWAND]	Yakov					husband of Gitel	230
[EINWAND]	Channah			Yakov Itz'eh	Esther Leah		230
[EINWAND]	Yisrael					husband of Channah	230
EINWAND	Feiga			Yakov Itz'eh	Esther Leah		230
EINWAND	Rakhel			Yakov Itz'eh	Esther		230

			Leah			
EINWAND	Moshe Yosef	Zelda	Yakov			230
EINWAND	Dov		Moshe Yosef	Zelda		230
EINWAND	Sarah		Moshe Yosef	Zelda		230
EINWAND	Berl	Brana	Yakov Itz'eh			230
EINWAND	Meir		Berl	Brana		230
[EINWAND]					16 grandchildren of Yakov Itz'eh	230
ALBOM	Mordechai	Henia				230
ALBOM	Channah		Mordechai	Henia		230
ALBOM	Shaye Leib					230
ALBERT	Avraham	Channah				230
ALBERT	Sarah					230
ALBERT	David					230
ALBERT	Berl					230
ALBERT	Chava					230
ALBERT	Esther					230
ESTRAJCHER	Yitzchak Yechiels	Perl Esther				230
ESTRAJCHER	Brandel		Yitzchak	Perl Esther		230
ESTRAJCHER	Yerachmiel		Yitzchak	Perl Esther		230
ESTRAJCHER	Golda		Yitzchak	Perl Esther		230
ESTRAJCHER	Benem	Sarah	Yitzchak			230
ESTRAJCHER	Aharon		Benem	Sarah		230
ESTRAJCHER	Yechiel	Leah	Yitzchak		2 children	230
AF	Zelig	Etcl				230
AF	Gershon		Zelig	Etel		230
AF	Yitzchak		Zelig	Etel		230
AF	Beila		Zelig	Etel		230
AF	Luba		Zelig	Etel		230

294

AF	Zelig	Sarah					230
AF	Laybeleh			Zelig	Sarah		230
AF	Yisraelik			Zelig	Sarah		231
AF	Yankel	Hinda					231
AF	Dina			Yankel	Hinda		231
AF	Tzviya			Yankel	Hinda		231
AF	Hersch			Yankel	Hinda		231
AF	Yosef			Yankel	Hinda		231
AF				Yankel	Hinda	another son	231
AF	Paltiel	Leah					231
AF	Ita			Paltiel	Leah		231
AF	Chaim			Paltiel	Leah		231
AF	Leibel			Paltiel	Leah		231
AF	Esther			Paltiel	Leah		231
AKERMAN	Shlomo	Channah		Eliahu			231
AKERMAN	Tzvi			Shlomo	Channah		231
AKERMAN	Aryeh			Shlomo	Channah		231
AKERMAN	Sarah			Shlomo	Channah		231
AKERMAN	Yechiel			Shlomo	Channah		231
AKERMAN	Tova			Shlomo	Channah		231
AKERMAN				Shlomo	Channah	another daughter	231
AKERMAN	David	Etel		Eliahu			231
AKERMAN	Channah			David	Etel		231
AKERMAN	Rivka			David	Etel		231
AKERMAN	Eli			David	Etel		231
AKERMAN	Shimon			David	Etel		231
AKERMAN	Sarah			David	Etel		231
AKERMAN	Yechiel	Etel		Eliahu			231
AKERMAN	Moshe	Sarah		Eliahu			231
AKERMAN	Nechama						231
AKERMAN	Genendel						231
AKERMAN	Tzvi	Dina				2 children	231

ב **Bet**

BACH	Yakov	Feige				231
BABET	Yisrael	Chaya				231
BABET	Aharon	Chaya		Yisrael	Chaya	231
BABET	Binyamin	Malka			brother in law of BABET	231
BABET	Chaya			Binyamin	Malka	231
BABET	Sarah			Binyamin	Malka	231
BABET	Rivka			Binyamin	Malka	231
BABET	Charna			Binyamin	Malka	231
BAUMFELD	Avraham	Sarah				231
BAUMFELD	Shimon			Avraham	Sarah	231
BAUMFELD	Feiga			Avraham	Sarah	231
BAUMFELD	Perl			Avraham	Sarah	231
BOMSTEIN	Scheindel				the mother	231
BOMSTEIN	Aharon	Reizel			Scheindel	231
BOMSTEIN	Gershon			Aharon	Reizel	231
BOMSTEIN	Binyamin			Aharon	Reizel	231
BOMSTEIN	Chaya			Aharon	Reizel	231
BOMSTEIN	Fraidel			Aharon	Reizel	231
BOMSTEIN	Tzvi			Aharon	Reizel	231
BOMSTEIN	Bluma			Aharon	Reizel	231
BOMSTEIN	Avraham	Devorah			Scheindel	231
BOMSTEIN	Basha			Avraham	Devorah	231
BOMSTEIN	Gitel			Avraham	Devorah	231
BOMSTEIN	Chava			Avraham	Devorah	231
BOMSTEIN	Eliahu			Avraham	Devorah	231
BOMSTEIN				Avraham	Devorah	3 other children	232
BITERMAN	Yitzchak Leib	Roza		Leizer		232
BITERMAN	Chaim	Rivka		Leizer		232
BITERMAN	Leizer			Chaim	Rivka	232
BITERMAN	Chaya			Chaim	Rivka	232

BITERMAN	David			Chaim	Rivka		232
BILERMAN	Shmuel	Channah					232
BILERMAN				Shmuel	Channah	their child	232
BLUTMAN	Sene	Feige					232
BLUTMAN	Feiga					daughter in law	232
BLUTMAN						grandchild of Sene and Feige	232
BLUTMAN	Nachum	Zelda					232
BLUTMAN	Alta			Nachum	Zelda		232
BLUM	Shaul	Basha					232
BLUM	Mendel			Shaul	Basha		232
BLUM	Mireleh			Shaul	Basha		232
BLUM	Dina			Shaul	Basha		232
BLUM	Channah			Shaul	Basha		232
BLUM	Miriam					mother of Shaul	232
BRAVERMAN	Gershon	Tzviya					232
BRAVERMAN	Serl			Gershon	Tzviya		232
BRAVERMAN	Nechama			Gershon	Tzviya		232
BRAVERMAN	Yakov Leib	Basha		Gershon			232
BRAVERMAN	Avraham			Yakov Leib	Basha		232
BRAVERMAN	Yitzchak			Yakov Leib	Basha		232
BRAVERMAN	Seril			Yakov Leib	Basha		232
BRAVERMAN	Welwel	Sarah		Gershon		and their 2 children	232
BRONSPIEGEL	Yerachmiel	Chaya Sarah					232
BRONSPIEGEL	Perla			Yerachmiel	Chaya Sarah		232
BRONSPIEGEL	Rivka			Yerachmiel	Chaya Sarah		232
BRONSPIEGEL	Rakhel			Yerachmiel	Chaya Sarah		232
BRONSPIEGEL	Pesya					their cousin	232
BRONSPIEGEL	Leibel	Leah		Yerachmiel		their 2	232

						children	
BRILLANT	Shlomo	Rivka					232
BRILLANT	Channah			Shlomo	Rivka		232
BRILLANT	Efraim			Shlomo	Rivka		232
BERENSTEIN	Mordechai	Sarah					232
BERENSTEIN	Yakov			Mordechai	Sarah		232
BERENSTEIN	Yisrael			Mordechai	Sarah		232
BERENSTEIN	Yoel	Sarah		Mordechai		their 2 children	232
BERENSTEIN	David	Sarah					232
BERENSTEIN	Shimon			David	Sarah		232
BERENSTEIN	Rakhel			David	Sarah		232
BERENSTEIN	Simcha			David	Sarah		232
BERENSTEIN	Basha					their relative	232

ג Gimmel

GUTBERTZ	Chaim	Yita Blima		Yitzchak			232
GUTBERTZ	Shmuel Abba	Yaffa	ROZENFELD	Chaim	Yita Blima		232
GUTBERTZ	Uri			Shmuel Abba	Yaffa		232
GUTBERTZ	Esther					daughter in law; maiden name GIBERTZ	232
GUTBERTZ	Yisrael			Shmuel Abba	Yaffa		233
GUTBERTZ	Yakov			Shmuel Abba	Yaffa		233
GUTBERTZ	Yosef			Shmuel Abba	Yaffa		233
GUTBERTZ	Yitzchak					grandfather	233
GUTWILING	Moshe	Seril		Yakov Yitzchak ha Levi			233
GUTWILING	Channah			Moshe	Seril		233
GUTWILING	Tzvi	Devorah	LEHRER	Moshe			233
GUTWILING	Sarah			Tzvi	Devorah		233

298

GUTWILING	Avraham			Tzvi	Devorah		233
GUTWILING	Frida			Tzvi	Devorah		233
GUTWILING	Chanan	Channah		Yakov Ya"hal			233
GUTWILING	Yakov	Golda		Chanan			233
GUTWILING	Moshe Zev			Yakov	Golda		233
GUTWILING	Tzvi			Chanan			233
GUTWILING	Channah Kayla			Chanan			233
GOLDSTEIN	Yitzchak	Peril					233
GOLDBLIT	Zeinvil						233
GOLDBLIT	Feiga			Zeinvil			233
GOLDBLIT	Sarah			Zeinvil			233
GOLDBERG	Chanoch	Rivche				3 children	233
GOLDRING	Yosef	Sheva	LIBERBAUM			2 daughters	233
GIVERTZ	Chaim	Rivka		Pesach			233
GIVERTZ	Aharon			Chaim	Rivka		233
GIVERTZ	Berl			Chaim	Rivka		233
GIVERTZ	Leibel	Rakhel		Chaim		2 children	233
GIVERTZ	Avraham	Scheindel					233
GIVERTZ	Yakov			Avraham	Scheindel		233
GIVERTZ	Berish	Channah					233
GIVERTZ	Avraham			Berish	Channah		233
GIVERTZ	Tzviya			Berish	Channah		233
GIVERTZ	Berish						233
GIVERTZ	Scheindel			Berish	Channah		233
GIVERTZ	Feiga			Berish	Channah		233
GIVERTZ	Frim'che			Berish	Channah		233
GIVERTZ						2 more children	233
GIVERTZ	Chaim					son in law of Berish and Channah, husband of Frim'che	233
GIVERTZ						2 children of	233

						Frim'che	
GIVERTZ	Rakhel						233
GIVERTZ	Ben Tzion					3 children	233
GIVERTZ	Michael	Leah	GOLDBLIT			their child	233
GIVERTZ							233
GIVERTZ	Pinchas	Chaya					233
GIVERTZ	Yechiel			Pinchas	Chaya	2 additional children of Pinchas and Chaya	233
GIVERTZ	Yitzchak	Rivka					233
GIVERTZ	Moshe			Yitzchak	Rivka		233
GIVERTZ	Ben Tzion			Yitzchak	Rivka		233
GIVERTZ	Rakhel			Yitzchak	Rivka		233
GIVERTZ	Gitel			Yitzchak	Rivka		233
GIVERTZ	Channah			Yitzchak	Rivka		233
GEISGUT	Yitzchak	Chava				the melamed (teacher)	234
GEISGUT	Yakov	Feige	GRINFELD	Yitzchak			234
GEISGUT	Sarah			Yakov	Feige		234
GEISGUT	Necha			Yakov	Feige		234
GEISGUT	Efraim						234
GEISGUT	Zeinvil			Yitzchak		and his wife and 3 children	234
GEIER	Shimshon	Liebe		Beirech	Pessil		234
GEIER	Feigele			Shimshon	Liebe		234
GEIER	Rakhel			Shimshon	Liebe		234
GEIER	Beirech					the father	234
GEIER	Pessil					the mother	234
GEIER	Meir	Lieba					234
GEIER	Itsche			Meir	Lieba		234
GEIER	Saraleh			Meir	Lieba		234
GEIER	Genendel			Meir	Lieba		234
GEIER	Fishel			Meir	Lieba		234
GEIER	Perl			Meir	Lieba		234

GEIER	Berl	Chava				234
GEIER	Hadis			Berl	Chava	234
GEIER	Tzirl			Berl	Chava	234
GEIR	Peretz	Feige				234
GEIR	Yidel			Peretz	Feige	234
GEIR	Esther			Peretz	Feige	234
GEIER	David	Channah				234
GEIER	Esther			David	Channah	234
GEIER	Perl			David	Channah	234
GEIER	Khone				son in law of David and Channah	234
GEIER	Moshe	Tzirl				234
GEIER	Zev			Moshe	Tzirl	234
GEIER	Zalman			Moshe	Tzirl	234
GEIER	Peretz			Moshe	Tzirl	234
GEIER	Yakov			Moshe	Tzirl	234
GEIER	Perl					234
GEIER	Yitzchak				Perl's husband	234
GEIER	Leah			Arish		234
GLATBERG	Yakov	Shosha Leah		Meir		234
GLATBERG	Meir			Yakov	Shosha Leah	234
GLATBERG	Moshe			Yakov	Shosha Leah	234
GLATBERG	Chava			Yakov	Shosha Leah	234
GLATBERG	Paltiel	Miriam				234
GLATBERG	Meir			Paltiel	Miriam	234
GLATBERG	Binyamin			Paltiel	Miriam	234
GLATBERG	Dan	Nechama		Meir		234
GLATBERG	Avraham			Dan	Nechama	234
GLATBERG	Leib			Dan	Nechama	234
GLATBERG	Esther			Dan	Nechama	234
GLASS	Shmerl	Malka				234

GLASS	Yakov Leib	Channah			2 children	234
GELBART	Moshe	Ita	It'che Leib			234
GELBART	Moshe Leib		Moshe	Ita		234
GELBART	Matel		Moshe	Ita		234
GELBART	Channah		Moshe	Ita		234
GELBART	Azriel		Moshe	Ita		235
GELBART	Yitzchak	Rivka				235
GELBART	Avraham					235
GELBART	Yakov					235
GROBERMAN	Michael	Scheindel				235
GROBERMAN	Chaim		Michael	Scheindel		235
GROBERMAN	Sarah		Michael	Scheindel		235
GROBERMAN	Scheindel		Michael	Scheindel		235
GROBERMAN	Pesya		Michael	Scheindel		235
GROBERMAN	Berl		Michael	Scheindel		235
GRINAPEL	Chaim	Miriam				235
GRINAPEL	Sarah		Chaim	Miriam		235
GRINAPEL	Rivka		Chaim	Miriam		235
GRINAPEL	Etel		Chaim	Miriam		235
GRINAPEL	Hersch Leib		Chaim	Miriam		235
GRINAPEL	Moshele		Chaim	Miriam		235
GRINAPEL	Avraham		Chaim	Miriam		235
GRINBERG	Leibish	Chaya				235
GRINBERG	Falik		Leibish	Chaya		235
GRINBERG	Chava				daughter in law of Leibish and Chaya	235
GRINBERG	Esther		Leibish	Chaya		235
GRINBERG	Tzipora		Leibish	Chaya		235
GRINBERG	Peritz		Leibish	Chaya		235
GRINBERG	Moshe	Sarah				235
GRINBERG	Meir		Moshe	Sarah		235
GRINBERG	Mordechai	Rakhela			son in law of Simcha LEVIS	235
GRINBERG	Sima		Mordechai	Rakhela		235

302

GRINBERG	Necha			Mordechai	Rakhela		235
GRINBERG	Chaim			Mordechai	Rakhela		235
GRINBERG	Eliahu			Mordechai	Rakhela		235
GRINBERG	Shlomo	Channah	WECHTER				235
GRINBERG	Efrat			Shlomo	Channah		235
GRINBERG	Leah			Shlomo	Channah		235
GRINBERG	Efraim			Shlomo	Channah		235
GRINTUCH	Avraham	Rivka					235
GRINTUCH	Feivel			Avraham	Rivka		235
GRINTUCH	Moshe			Avraham	Rivka		235
GRINTUCH	David			Avraham	Rivka		235
GRINFELD	Chaim Yosef	Rakhel					235
GRINFELD	Welwel			Chaim Yosef	Rakhel		235
GRINFELD	Tzadok			Chaim Yosef	Rakhel		235
GRINFELD	Avraham			Chaim Yosef	Rakhel		235
GRINFELD	Nechama			Chaim Yosef	Rakhel		235
GRINFELD	Yehoshua	Rivka		Chaim Yosef			235
GRINFELD	Eliezer			Yehoshua	Rivka		235
GRINFELD	Channah			Yehoshua	Rivka		235
GRINFELD	Sima			Yehoshua	Rivka		235

ד **Dalet**

DIAMANT	Aharon						235
DIAMANT	Pesach	Channah		Aharon			235
DIAMANT	Mordechai			Pesach	Channah		235
DIAMANT	Feige			Pesach	Channah		235
DIAMANT	Shlomo	{wife}		Aharon			235
DIAMANT	Aryeh	Channah		Aharon		2 children	235
DIAMANT	Chaim	Scheindel	GIVERTZ	Aharon			235
DIAMANT	Sarah			Chaim	Scheindel		236

DIAMANT	Mirel		Chaim	Scheindel	236
DIAMANT	Aharon		Chaim	Scheindel	236
DRIMLER	Shmuel (Shmelke)	Rivka Leah			236
DRIMLER	Moshe		Shmuel (Shmelke)	Rivka Leah	236
DRIMLER	Pereleh		Shmuel (Shmelke)	Rivka Leah	236
DRIMLER	Yitzchak Meir	Nechama	Shmuel		236
DRIMLER	Channah		Yitzchak Meir	Nechama	236
DRIMLER	Guta		Yitzchak Meir	Nechama	236
DRIMLER	Dov		Yitzchak Meir	Nechama	236

ה Hey

HALPRIN	Henya				236
HALPRIN	David			Henya	236
HALPRIN	Chaim			Henya	236
HALPRIN	Yon'che	Rakhel			236
HALPRIN	Sarah		Yon'che	Rakhel	236
HALPRIN	Channah		Yon'che	Rakhel	236
HALPRIN	Leah		Yon'che	Rakhel	236
HALPRIN	Chaim		Yon'che	Rakhel	236
HALPRIN	Akiva		Yon'che	Rakhel	236
HALPRIN	Dina		Yon'che	Rakhel	236
HALPRIN	Berl	Gila			236
HALPRIN	Rivka		Berl	Gila	236
HALPRIN	Mirel		Berl	Gila	236
HALPRIN	Feige		Berl	Gila	236
HALPRIN	Elkeleh		Berl	Gila	236
HOFF	Yehoshua	Tzviya			236
HOFF	Mirla		Yehoshua	Tzviya	236
HOFF	Eliahu	Leah			236
HOFF	Chaya		Eliahu	Leah	236

HOFF	Feivel	Sarah				236
HOFF	Efraim			Feivel	Sarah	236
HOFF	Feige			Feivel	Sarah	236
HOFF	Aryeh	Chaya				236
HOFF	Moshe			Aryeh	Chaya	236
HOFF	Eizik			Aryeh	Chaya	236
HOFF	Rakhel			Aryeh	Chaya	236
HOFF	Sheva			Aryeh	Chaya	236
HOFF	Nachman	Scheindel				236
HOFF	Sheva			Nachman	Scheindel	236
HOFF	Beila			Nachman	Scheindel	236
HOFF	Feiga			Nachman	Scheindel	236
HOFEN	Yakov Moshe	Esther Rivka	YANOVER	Pinchas		236
HOFEN	Golda			Yakov Moshe	Esther Rivka	236
LICHTER					husband of Golda; their young baby	236
HOFEN	Devorah			Yakov Moshe	Esther Rivka	236
HOFEN	Perla			Yakov Moshe	Esther Rivka	236
HOFEN	Elazar			Yakov Moshe	Esther Rivka	236
HOIZDORF	Benem	Roch'cha (Roch'che)	LIBEERBAUM			236
HOIZDORF	David			Benem	Roch'cha (Roch'che)	236
HOIZDORF	Iteleh			Benem	Roch'cha (Roch'che)	236
HOIZDORF	Rivka			Benem	Roch'cha (Roch'che)	236

ו Vav

VEINGARTEN	Tzadok	Fai'che	LIBEERBAUM			236
VEINGARTEN	David			Tzadok	Fai'che	236
VEINGARTEN	Channah			Tzadok	Fai'che	237

VEINGARTEN	Rivka			Tzadok	Fai'che		
VEISBROD	Mordechai Meir	(wife)				Rabbi	237
VEISBROD	Devorah		Mordechai Meir			and her husband, son in law of Rabbi Mordechai Meir	237
[VEISBROD]						husband of Chaya, daughter of Rabbi Mordechai Meir	237
[VEISBROD]						husband of Reizel, daughter of Rabbi Mordechai Meir	237
[VEISBROD]						husband of Rivka, daughter of Rabbi Mordechai Meir	237
VEISBROD	Berl		Mordechai Meir				237
WEBER	Gedalyahu	Malka					237
WEBER	Rakhel		Gedalyahu	Malka			327
WEBER	Rivka		Gedalyahu	Malka			237
WEBER	Yisrael	Masha					237
WEBER	Devorah		Yisrael	Masha			237
WEBER	Leib					brother of Minov	237
WECHTER	Yitzchak	Malka					237
WECHTER	Mirla		Yitzchak	Malka			237
WECHTER	Yakov	Rakhel	Yitzchak				237
WECHTER	Saraleh		Yakov	Rakhel			237
WECHTER	Chen'che		Yakov	Rakhel			237
WECHTER	Meir		Yakov	Rakhel			237
WECHTER	Pinchas	Chen'che	Yitzchak				327

WECHTER	Gitel			Pinchas	Chen'che	and a child	237
WECHTER	Aharon	Sarah					237
WECHTER	Alter			Aharon	Sarah		237
WECHTER	Sarah Leah			Aharon	Sarah		237
VACKS	Chaim	Basha					237
VACKS	Feige			Chaim	Basha		237
VACKS	Yitzchak			Chaim	Basha		237
VACKS	Nechemia						237
VACKS	Chava						237
VACKS	Scheindel (Shunka)						237

ז Zayin

SONTAG	Frimit					wife of Yerachmiel	237
SONTAG	Moshe	Bluma		Yerachmiel			237
SONTAG	Pinchas			Moshe	Bluma		327
SONTAG	Golda			Moshe	Bluma		237
SONTAG	Yosef			Moshe	Bluma		237
SONTAG	Tzvi			Moshe	Bluma		237
SONTAG	Avraham			Moshe	Bluma		237
SONTAG	Shachne			Yerachmiel			237
SONTAG	Shachne	Chava				and their four children	237
SONTAG	Abba						327
SONTAG	Reuven	Freida				and their two children	237
ZEIDEL	Eli David						237
ZEIDEL	Moshe			Eli David			237
ZEIDEL	Baruch			Eli David			237
ZEIDEL		Etka	ARMAN				237
ZEIDEL	Binyamin				Etka		237
SILBERSTROM	Yosef	Channah				"manaker": ritual slaughterer who removes veins	237

SILBERSTROM	Leibel	Chava		Yosef			237
SILBERSTROM	Alter			Leibel	Chava		237
SILBERSTROM	Channah			Leibel	Chava		237
SILBERSTROM	Zindel	Golda		Yosef		Ritual slaughterer and examiner	237
SILBERSTROM	Alter			Zindel	Golda		237
SILBERSTROM	Tova						238
SILBERBERG	Wew'che	Ziese					238
SILBERBERG	Chaya			Wew'che	Ziese		238
SILBERBERG	Neche			Wew'che	Ziese		238
SILBERBERG	Aharon			Wew'che	Ziese		238
SILBERBERG	Moshe	Esther					238
SILBERBERG	Shmuel			Moshe	Esther		238
SILBERBERG	Sarah			Moshe	Esther		238
SILBERBERG	Azriel	Gitel	KUPER				238
SILBERBERG	Chaim			Azriel	Gitel		238
SILBERBERG	Moshe			Azriel	Gitel		238
SILBERBERG	Yechiel			Azriel	Gitel		238
SILBERBERG	Yitzchak			Azriel	Gitel		238
SILBERBERG	Berl			Azriel	Gitel		238
SILBERBERG	It'che	Nechama					238
SILBERKLANG	Moshe Leib	Zelda		Asher			238
SILBERKLANG	Chaya			Moshe Leib	Zelda		238
SILBERKLANG	Hinda			Moshe Leib	Zelda		238
SILBERKLANG	Sarah			Moshe Leib	Zelda		238
SILBERKLANG	Rivka			Moshe Leib	Zelda		238
SILBERKLANG	Pinchas			Moshe Leib	Zelda		238
SILBERKLANG	Asher Zelig			Moshe Leib	Zelda		238
SILBERKLANG	Rakhel			Moshe Leib	Zelda		238
SILBERKLANG	Matel			Moshe Leib	Zelda	(daughter)	238
SILBERKLANG	Yosef	Channah Breindel		Asher			238
SILBERKLANG	Yehoshua			Yosef	Channah Breindel		238

308

SILBERKLANG	Sima			Yosef	Channah Breindel		238
SILBERKLANG	Etel			Yosef	Channah Breindel		238
SILBERKLANG	Yitzchak	Chen'che		Asher			238
SILBERKLANG	Gershon Henich			Yitzchak	Chen'che		238
SILBERKLANG	Scheindel Leah			Yitzchak	Chen'che		238
SILBERKLANG	Breindel			Yitzchak	Chen'che		238
SILBERKLANG				Yitzchak	Chen'che	their two additional children	238
SILBERKLANG	Shmuel	Devorah		Yosef			238
SILBERKLANG	Chaya			Shmuel	Devorah		238
SILBERKLANG	Scheindel			Shmuel	Devorah		238
SILBERKLANG	Asher			Shmuel	Devorah		238
SILBERSTEIN	Leibel	Yocheved	ALTMAN			and their two children	238

ט **Tet**

TREGER	Yona	Reizel		Chaim			238
TREGER	Yocheved			Yona	Reizel		238
TREGER	Lipa			Yona	Reizel		238
TREGER	Yitzchak			Yona	Reizel		238
TREGER	Yechiel	(wife)		Yona		their children	238
TREGER	Berish	Sarah	FRIEDLER	Yona			238
TREGER	Gitel			Berish	Sarah		238
TREGER	Sonya			Berish	Sarah		238
TREGER	Leah Roza			Berish	Sarah		238
TREGER	Avraham						238
TREGER	Feigele					her two children	238
TREGER	Avraham	Feige					238
TREGER	Chava			Avraham	Feige		238
TREGER	Malka			Avraham	Feige		238
TREGER	Chaim	Nechama		Avraham	Feige		238

TREGER	Yakov			Chaim	Nechama	238
TREGER	Riba			Chaim	Nechama	239
TEVEL	(Tewe)	Sarah				239
TEVEL	Chaya			(Tewe)	Sarah	239
TEVEL	Aharon			(Tewe)	Sarah	239

י Yod

YEGERMAN	Leibish	Sarah				239
YEGERMAN	Chaim			Leibish	Sarah	239
YYE	Berl			Leibish	Sarah	239
YEGERMAN	Sarah			Leibish	Sarah	239
YEGERMAN	Yenta			Leibish	Sarah	239
YEGERMAN	Tova Scheindel					239
YEGERMAN	Moshe	Etka			Tova Scheindel	239
YEGERMAN	Rivka			Moshe	Etka	239
YEGERMAN	Batya			Moshe	Etka	239
YEGERMAN	Tzadok			Moshe	Etka	239
YANOVER	Yitzchak	Devorah		Shlomo		239
YANOVER	Yisrael	Batsheva		Yitzchak		239
YANOVER	Gitel			Yisrael	Batsheva	239
YANOVER	Yechiel			Yitzchak		239
YANOVER	Batsheva			Yitzchak		239
GRINBOM	Tzvi				husband of Batsheva YANOVER	239
[GRINBOM]	Zehava			Tzvi	Batsheva	239
[GRINBOM]	Sarah			Tzvi	Batsheva	239
[GRINBOM]	Yechiel			Tzvi	Batsheva	239
YAFFE	Gitel					239
YAFFE	Yitzchak				Gitel	239
YAFFE	Binyamin				Gitel	239
YAFFE	Moshe				Gitel	239
YAFFE	Yakov Leib	Yitta			Gitel	239
YAFFE	Chaim			Yakov Leib	Yitta	239

YAFFE	Etil			Yakov Leib	Yitta		239
YAFFE	Michael	Channah	DRIMLER		Gitel		239
YAFFE	Dina			Michael	Channah		239
YAFFE	Beila			Yitzchak			239
YAFFE	Chaya						239
YAFFE	Rivka						239
YAFFE	Binyamin	(wife)			Gitel		239
[YAFFE]	[Binyamin]					wife and his 3 children	239
YAKOVSON	Sarah Rachel					the mother	239
YAKOVSON	Channah			Zeinvel			239
YAKOVSON	[Channah]					her husband and her two children	239
YAKOVSON	Pinchas	Feige		Zeinvel			239
YAKOVSON	Yakov Ber			Pinchas	Feige		239
YAKOVSON	Matel			Pinchas	Feige	(daughter)	239
YAKOVSON	Miriam			Pinchas	Feige		239
YAKOVSON	Dan			Pinchas	Feige		239
YAKOVSON	Yakov	(wife)		Zeinvel			239
YAKOVSON	Chaya Tzviya			Zeinvel			239
YAKOVSON	Necha			Zeinvel			239
YAKOVSON	[Necha]					her husband	239
YAKOVSON	Zeinvel			(husband)	Necha		239
YAKOVSON	Lieba			Zeinvel			239
YAKOVSON	Eliezer					husband of Lieba	239
YAKOVSON	Zeinvel			Eliezer	Lieba		239
YAKOVSON	Berl			Eliezer	Lieba		239
YAKOVSON	Tzadok			Eliezer	Lieba		239
YAKOVSON	Efraim			Eliezer	Lieba		239
YAKOVSON	Serel			Eliezer	Lieba		239
YAKOVSON	Yosef	Pesya					239
YAKOVSON	Tzvi	Zlata		Yosef			240

YAKOVSON	Dov			Tzvi	Zlata		240
YAKOVSON	Necha			Yosef			240
YAKOVSON	Basha			Yosef			240
YAKOVSON	Mottel			Yosef			240
YAKOVSON	Moshe	Malka					240
YAKOVSON	Chaya			Moshe	Malka	and 2 children	240
YAKOVSON	Necha			Moshe	Malka		240
YAKOVSON	Tzviya			Moshe	Malka		240
YAKOVSON	Levi	Yentel					240
YAKOVSON	Berish			Levi	Yentel		240
YAKOVSON	Yocheved			Levi	Yentel		240
YAKOVSON	Nechemia			Levi	Yentel		240
YAKOVSON	Leah					wife of Nechemia	240
YAKOVSON	Shlomo					husband of Yentel	240
YAKOVSON	Chaim			Shlomo			240
YAKOVSON	Etil			Shlomo			240
YAKOVSON	Sarah			Nechemia			240
YAKOVSON	Esther			Nechemia			240
YAKOVSON	Chaim	Chaya					240
YAKOVSON	Levi			Chaim	Chaya		240
YAKOVSON	Yenta					wife of Levi	240
YAKOVSON	Perl			Levi	Yenta		240
YAKOVSON	Yakov			Levi	Yenta		240

כ Kaf

COHEN	Moshe						240
COHEN	Leah			Ozer			240
COHEN	Dina			Moshe	Leah		240
COHEN	Efraim			Moshe	Leah		240
COHEN	David			Moshe	Leah		240
KATZ	David						240
KATZ	Perl Dovri			David			240
KATZ	Avraham			David			240

KATZ	Rakhel			David			240
KATZ	Perl			David			240
KATZ	Roza			David			240
KATZ	Moshe			David			240
KATZ	Shlomo			David			240
KATZ	Malka			David			240
KATZ	Azriel Lemel			David			240
KATZ	Baruch			David			240
KATZ	Malka			David			240
KATZ	Azriel Lemel			David			240
KATZ	Moshe			David			240
KATZ	Shaya			Moshe			240
KATZ	Karshel			Moshe			240
KATZ	Eli	Feige				and their 3 children	240
KATZ	Yehoshua						240
KATZ	Rivka Perl						240
KATZ	Yisrael Yitzchak						240

ל Lamed

LUSTIGMAN	Moshe	Perl		Mordechai			240
LUSTIGMAN	Chaya			Moshe	Perl		240
LUSTIGMAN	Mordechai			Moshe	Perl		240
LUSTIGMAN	Chaim			Moshe	Perl		240
LUSTIG	Zelig			Mordechai			240
LUSTIGMAN	Perl		ROZNER			their 2 children	240
LEDER	Chaim	Rivka		Eizik			240
LEDER	Yosef			Chaim	Rivka		240
LEDER	Eizik	Rakhel		Chaim			240
LEDER	Scheindel			Eizik	Rakhel		241
LEDER	Yosef			Eizik	Rakhel		241
LEDER	(daughter)			Eizik	Rakhel		241

LEVIN	Channah					241
LEVIN	Leibel					241
LEVIN	Tova					241
LEVIN	Yitta					241
LIBERBOM	Welwel	Menucha				241
LIBERBOM	Chaim Meir	Fradel	Welwel			241
LIBERBOM	Rivka		Chaim Meir			241
[LIBERBOM]					husband of Rivka; and their 2 children	241
LIBERBOM	Beila		Chaim Meir			241
LIBERBOM	David		Chaim Meir			241
LIBERBOM	Devorah		Chaim Meir			241
LIBERBOM	Sheva		Welwel			241
[LIBERBOM]					husband of Sheva, and their children	241
LIBERBOM	Moshe	Roza	Chaim			241
LIBERBOM	Yisrael		Moshe	Roza		241
LIBERBOM	Sarah				wife of Yisrael; and their 2 children	241
LIBERBOM	Channah		Moshe Chaim			241
[LIBERBOM]	Avraham				husband of Channah	241
LIBERBOM	Efraim		Avraham	Channah		241
LIBERBOM	David		Avraham	Channah		241
LIBERBOM	Serel		Avraham	Channah		241
LIBERBOM	Shalom	Tzina	Moshe Chaim			241
LIBERBOM	Chaim		Shalom	Tzina		241
LIBERBOM	Din'che		Shalom	Tzina		241
LIBERBOM	Esther		Shalom	Tzina		241
LIBERBOM	Yehoshua	Tzviya	Moshe Chaim			241
LIBERBOM	Yisrael		Yehoshua	Tzviya		241

314

LIBERBOM	Dina			Yehoshua	Tzviya		241
LIBERBOM	David			Yehoshua	Tzviya		241
LICHTMAN	Yakov	Leah					241
LICHTMAN	Gitel			Yakov	Leah		241
LICHTMAN	Necha			Yakov	Leah		241
LICHTMAN	Shlomo			Yakov	Leah		241
LICHTMAN	Golda			Yakov	Leah		241
LICHTMAN	Shmuel			Yakov	Leah		241
LICHTMAN	Leib	Sarahle					241
LICHTMAN	Chava			Leib	Sarahle		241
LICHTMAN	Golda			Leib	Sarahle		241
LICHTMAN	Asher			Leib	Sarahle		241
LICHTMAN	Herschel	Beila					241
LICHTMAN	Rakhel			Herschel	Beila		241
[LICHTMAN]						husband of Rakhel	241
LICHTMAN	Nechemia			(husband)	Rakhel		241
LICHTMAN	David			(husband)	Rakhel		241
LICHTMAN	Chaim	Sarah					241
LEICHTER	Moshe						241
LEICHTER	Avraham			Moshe			241
LEICHTER	Ozer			Moshe			241
LEICHTER	Miriam			Moshe			241
LEICHTER	Chuma			Moshe		(daughter)	241
LANDOVER	Shalom	Yeteleh					241
LANDOVER	Yosef			Shalom	Yeteleh		241
LANDOVER	Tova		LEVIN			daughter in law of Shalom and Yetele	241
LANDER	Yakov						242
LANDER	Necha						242
LANDER	Channah						242
LANDER	Aryeh						242
LANDER	Sheva						242
LANDER	Rivka					and her	242

						daughter	
LANDER	Sarah Leah						242
LANDER	Guta						242
LERER	Simcha	Zelda		Lipa			242
LERER	Sarah			Simcha	Zelda		242
LERER	Yakov			Simcha	Zelda		242
LERER	Hadassah			Simcha			242
[LERER]	Yitzchak					husband of Hadassah, and their 2 children	242

מ Mem

MEYERSDORF	Benem	Rakhel	LIBERBOM				242
MEYERSDORF	Yehoshua			Benem	Rakhel		242
MEYERSDORF	David			Benem	Rakhel		242
MEYERSDORF	Feige			Benem	Rakhel		242
MANDEL	Avraham	Yoshpa					242
MANDEL	Mordechai			Avraham	Yoshpa		242
MANDEL	Esther			Avraham	Yoshpa		242
MANDEL	Mordechai (Motel)	Rakhel	ZUBERMAN				242
MANDEL	Yitzchak			Mordechai (Motel)	Rakhel		242
MANDEL	Esther			Mordechai (Motel)	Rakhel		242
MANDEL	David			Mordechai (Motel)	Rakhel		242
MANDEL	Dina			Mordechai (Motel)	Rakhel		242
MANDEL	Feivel	Silka	DRIMLER				242
MANDEL	Channah			Feivel	Silka		242
MANDEL	Gitel			Feivel	Silka		242
MANDEL	Yitzchak			Feivel	Silka		242
MANDELKER	David	Scheindel	ROSENFELD			and their children	242
MORGENSTERN	Avraham	Chaya					242

MORGENSTERN	Hersch			Avraham	Chaya	242
MORGENSTERN	Sarah			Avraham	Chaya	242
MORGENSTERN	Channah			Avraham	Chaya	242
MAIMON	Chaim	Esther				242
MAIMON	Yisrael			Chaim	Esther	242
MAIMON	Sarah		FREIBERG		daughter in law of Chaim and Esther	242
MILGROM	Avraham	Sarah	BABET		and their two children	242
MITZNER	Yosef	Channah				242
MITZNER	Malka			Yosef	Channah	242
MITZNER	Henya			Yosef	Channah	242
MITZNER	Manis	Chava				242
MITZNER	Mordechai	(wife)		Manis		242
MITZNER	Alta			Mordechai	(wife)	242
MITZNER	Sarah			Mordechai	(wife)	242
MITZNER	Channah			Mordechai	(wife)	242
MITZNER	Frida			Mordechai	(wife)	242
MITZNER	Henya			Mordechai	(wife)	242
MITZNER	Yitzchak					242
MITZNER	Malka					242
MITZNER	Sarah					242
MITZNER	Yakov				Sarah	242
MITZNER	Yitzchak				Sarah	242

נ Nun

NA	Shlomo Shaya	Shifra				243
NA	Hersch	Hinda		Shlomo		243
NA	Aryeh			Hersch	Hinda	243
NA	Asher			Hersch	Hinda	243
NA	Gitel			Hersch	Hinda	243
NA	Simcha			Hersch	Hinda	243
NA	Sarah			Hersch	Hinda	243
NA	Pin'che	Finkel		Shlomo		243

NA	Zelig			Pin'che	Finkel		243
NA	David			Pin'che	Finkel		243
NA	Perl			Pin'che	Finkel		243
NA	Chaya			Pin'che	Finkel		243
NA	Esther			Pin'che	Finkel		243
NADLER	Leibel	Leah	ROSENFELD				243
NADLER	Sarah Leah			Leibel	Leah		243
NADLER	Chen'che			Leibel	Leah	(daughter)	243
NEIHOIZ	Frida						243
NEIHOIZ	Sarah				Frida		243
NEIHOIZ	Frim'che				Frida		243
NEIHOIZ	Devorah				Frida		243
NEIHOIZ	Chava				Frida		243
NEIHOIZ	Moshe	Scheindel			Frida		243
NEIHOIZ	Nechama			Moshe	Scheindel		243

פ Peh

PAPIR	Berl						243
PAPIR	Tova						243
FEDER	Moshe	Mindeleh					243
FEDER	Yakov			Moshe	Mindeleh		243
FEDER	Avraham			Moshe	Mindeleh		243
FEDER	Golda			Moshe	Mindeleh		243
FEDER	Yitzchak	Chen'che		Moshe		and their two children	243
FEDER	Moshe	Channah		Leizer			243
FEDER	Gitel			Moshe	Channah		243
FEDER	Aharon	Rakhel		Moshe			243
FEDER	Tzviya			Aharon	Rakhel		243
FEDER	Avraham			Aharon	Rakhel		243
FOGEL	Nisan	Gitel					243
FOGEL	Mottel			Nisan	Gitel		243
FOGEL	Yoshpa			Nisan	Gitel		243
FOGEL	Pesya			Nisan	Gitel		243

318

FOGEL	Rakhel			Nisan	Gitel		243
FOGEL	Yidel			Nisan	Gitel		243
FOGEL	Channah			Nisan	Gitel		243
FOGEL	Roza		FOGEL			and husband of Roza	243
FOGEL	Hersch	Malka					243
FOGEL	Miriam			Hersch	Malka		243
FOGEL	Welbish	Sarah					243
FOGEL	Yerachmiel			Welbish	Sarah		243
FOGEL	Avraham			Welbish	Sarah		243
FOGEL	Meir	Leah					243
FOGEL	Bunim			Meir	Leah		243
FOGEL	Reizel			Meir	Leah		243
FOGEL	Shmuel	Devorah					243
FOGEL	Channah			Shmuel	Devorah		244
FOGEL	Scheindel			Shmuel	Devorah		244
FOGEL	Nicha			Shmuel	Devorah		244
FOGEL	Nachman	Leah		Shmuel			244
FOGEL	Yerachmiel			Nachman	Leah		244
FOGEL	Gitel			Nachman	Leah		244
FOGEL	Channah			Nachman	Leah		244
FOGEL	Yechiel			Nachman	Leah		244
FOGEL	Manis	Leah					244
FOGEL	Yerachmiel			Manis	Leah		244
FOGEL	Channah			Manis	Leah		244
FOGEL	Miriam			Manis	Leah		244
FOGEL	Hersch	Malka				was blind	244
FOGEL	Miriam			Hersch	Malka		244
FOGEL	Wolf	Raikel					244
FOGEL	Yerachmiel			Wolf	Raikel		244
FOGEL	David			Wolf	Raikel		244
FOGEL	Roza						244
FOGEL	Batya						244
FUKS	Avraham	Esther					244

		Channah				
FUKS	Mottel			Avraham	Esther Channah	244
FUKS	Chaim			Avraham	Esther Channah	244
FUKS	Aharon			Avraham	Esther Channah	244
FUKS	Malka			Avraham	Esther Channah	244
FUKS	Mindel			Avraham	Esther Channah	244
FUKS	Tova			Avraham	Esther Channah	244
FUKS	Pesya			Avraham	Esther Channah	244
FUKS	Welwel	Channah		Menashe		244
FUKS	Necha			Welwel	Channah	244
FUKS	Malka			Welwel	Channah	244
FUKS	Eidel			Welwel	Channah	244
FUKS	Zelig			Welwel	Channah	244
FUKS	Josef	Tzviya				244
FUKS	David			Josef	Tzviya	244
FUKS	Simcha			Josef	Tzviya	244
FUKS	Herisch			Josef	Tzviya	244
FUKS	Berl			Josef	Tzviya	244
FUKS	Avraham			Josef	Tzviya	244
FUKS	Michael			Josef	Tzviya	244
FIGLER	Welwel	Frida				244
FIGLER	Necha			Welwel	Frida	244
FIGLER	Sarah			Welwel	Frida	244
FIGLER	David			Welwel	Frida	244
FINK	Sarah					244
PIK	Natan	Scheindel				244
PIK	Josef			Natan	Scheindel	244
PIK	Sima			Natan	Scheindel	244
PIK	Chaim Leib	Rakhel		Natan		244

PIK	Mendel		Chaim Leib	Rakhel		244
PIK	Sarah		Chaim Leib	Rakhel		244
FEIERSTEIN	Tzvi	Chava				244
FEIERSTEIN	Yoshpa		Tzvi	Chava		244
FEIERSTEIN	Etel		Tzvi	Chava		244
FLAKS	Bentzion	Basha				244
FLAKS	Shaul		Bentzion	Basha		244
FLAKS	Meir		Bentzion	Basha		244
FLAKS	Rakhela		Bentzion	Basha		244
FLAKSER	Chaya				the mother	244
PLAKSER	Leibel	Tzviya		Chaya		245
PLAKSER	Sarah		Leibel	Tzviya		245
PLAKSER	Chava		Leibel	Tzviya		245
PLAKSER	Mottel	Devorah		Chaya		245
PLAKSER	Rakhel		Mottel	Devorah		245
PLAKSER	Zerach		Mottel	Devorah		245
PLAKSER	Scheindel				wife of Shepsel	245
PLAKSER	Avraham			Scheindel		245
PLAKSER	Devorah			Scheindel		245
FLASCHNER	Yitzchak	Sarah Ita				245
FLASCHNER	Shaul		Yitzchak	Sarah Ita		245
FLASCHNER	Scheindel		Yitzchak	Sarah Ita		245
FLASCHNER	Necha		Yitzchak	Sarah Ita		245
FLEISCHER	Nechemia	Rivka				245
FLEISCHER	Zelda		Nechemia	Rivka		245
FLEISCHER	Nachum				husband of Zelda	245
FLEISCHER	Shmuel	Sarah	Leibel			245
FLEISCHER	Devorah		Shmuel	Sarah		245
FLEISCHER	Arish		Shmuel	Sarah	and another child	245
FLEISCHER	Shalom	Necha				245
FLEISCHER	Michael		Shalom	Necha		245
FLEISCHER	Mali		Shalom	Necha		245

FLEISCHER	Feige		Shalom	Necha		245
FLEISCHER	Sarah		Shalom	Necha	and another son	245
FLEISCHER	Berl	Chen'che	Nechemia			245
FLEISCHER	Shmuel		Berl	Chen'che		245
FLEISCHER	Sarah		Berl	Chen'che		245
FLEISCHER	Yakov		Berl	Chen'che		245
FLEISCHER	Sarah				wife of Shlomo	245
FLEISCHER	Chaya			Sarah		245
FLEISCHER	Necha			Sarah		245
FLEISCHER	Roch'che			Sarah		245
FLEISCHER	Chanoch (Henech)	Rakhel				245
FLEISCHER	Avraham	Frida	Chanoch			245
FLEISCHER					son in law of Chanoch	245
FLEISCHER	(daughter)		Chanoch			245
FLEISCHER	Berl		Chanoch	Rakhel	and two other daughters	245
FLEISCHER	Mendel	Chaya	Nechemia			245
FLEISCHER	Hersch		Mendel	Chaya		245
FLEISCHER	Hinda		Mendel	Chaya		245
FLEISCHER	Rivka		Mendel	Chaya		245
FLEISCHER	Zalman	Sheva-Chava				245
FLEISCHER	Mordechai		Zalman	Sheva-Chava		245
FLEISCHER	Eliahu		Zalman	Sheva-Chava		245
FLEISCHER	Moshe		Zalman	Sheva-Chava		245
FLEISCHER	Shmuel	Serl	Zalman			245
FLEISCHER	Aryeh		Shmuel	Serl		245
FLEISCHER	Leah		Shmuel	Serl		245
FLEISCHER	Tzviya		Shmuel	Serl		245
FLEISCHER	Yosef	Sarah	Zalman			245

322

FLEISCHER	Chaya			Yosef	Sarah		245
FLEISCHER	Rakhel			Yosef	Sarah		245
FLEISCHER	Yakov			Yosef	Sarah		245
FLEISCHER	Heschel			Yosef	Sarah		245
PELTZ	Netel	Menucha					246
PELTZ	Avraham			Netel	Menucha		246
PELTZ	David			Netel	Menucha		246
PELTZ	Fradel			Netel	Menucha		246
PELTZ	Shmuel	Rivaleh					246
PELTZ	Moshe			Shmuel	Rivaleh		246
PELTZ	Fishel			Shmuel	Rivaleh		246
PELTZ	Yosef			Shmuel	Rivaleh		246
PELTZ	Chaya			Shmuel	Rivaleh		246
FEFFERKICHEN	Zelda			Hersch Leib			246
FEFFERKICHEN	Leah				Zelda		246
FEFFERKICHEN	Chen'che				Zelda		246
FEFFERHOLTZ	Moshe	Sarah				son in law of Avraham GIVERTZ	246
FEFFERHOLTZ	Beila			Moshe	Sarah		246
FEFFERHOLTZ	Channah			Moshe	Sarah		246
FRUMER	Feige					the mother	246
FRUMER	Yosef	Perl			Feige		246
FRUMER	Tanchum			Yosef	Perl		246
FRUMER	Yitzchak			Yosef	Perl		246
FRUMER	Avraham	Fradel	SHMOREK	Yosef			246
FRUMER	Chava			Avraham	Fradel		246
FRUMER	Shimon			Avraham	Fradel		246
FRUMER	(son)			Avraham	Fradel		246
FRUMER	Yakov	Nechama		Yosef		daughter of Yosef	246
FRUMER	Yehoshua			Yakov	Nechama		246
FRUMER	Rivka			Yakov	Nechama		246
FRUMER	Tuvia	Chava		Yosef			246
FRUMER	Sarah			Tuvia	Chava		246

FRUMER	Gitel			Tuvia	Chava		246
FREIBERG	Aharon	Hadassah	TEPER	Avshalom			246
FREIBERG	Chava			Aharon	Hadassah		246
FREIBERG	Perla			Aharon	Hadassah		246
FREIBERG	Malia			Aharon	Hadassah		246
FREIBERG	Leibel			Aharon	Hadassah		246
FREIBERG	Shlomo	Reizel		Avshalom			246
FREIBERG	Leibish	Malka		Avshalom			246
FREIBERG	Sarah			Leibish	Malka		246
FRIEDLER	Mordechai	Sarah		Yirmiyahu			246
FRIEDLER	Feige			Mordechai	Sarah		246
FRIEDLER	Miriam			Mordechai	Sarah		246
FRIEDLER	Henya			Mordechai	Sarah		246
FRIEDLER	Yirmiyahu			Mordechai		wife and their two children	246
FRIEDLER	Hen'che			Mordechai			246
FRIEDLER	Avraham	Hinda		Yirmiyahu			246
FRIEDLER	Aharon			Avraham	Hinda		246
FRIEDLER	Levi			Avraham	Hinda		246
FRIEDLER	Meir			Avraham	Hinda		246
FRIEDLER	Beila			Avraham	Hinda		246
FRIEDLER	Alter			Avraham	Hinda		246
FRIEDLER	Henya			Avraham	Hinda		246
FRIEDLER	Yirmiyahu			Avraham	Hinda		246
FRIEDLER	Matel			Shlomo		(daughter)	246
FRIEDLER	Rivka		LICHTENSTEIN				246
FRIEDLER	Eliezer	Hinda		Yirmiyahu			246
FRIEDLER	Mindel			Eliezer	Hinda	and her two daughters	247
FRIEDLER	Yisrael			Eliezer			247
FRIEDLER	Sima			Eliezer			247
FRIEDLER	Chaim	Sarah					247
FRIEDLER	Riva			Chaim	Sarah		247
FRIEDLER	Shlomo			Chaim	Sarah		247

324

FRIEDLER	Mordechai Leizer			Chaim	Sarah		247
FRIEDLER	Gitel			Chaim	Sarah		247
FRIEDLER	Zelda			Chaim	Sarah		247
FRIEDLER	Yitzchak			Chaim	Sarah		247
FRIEDLER	Daniel						247
FRIEDLER	Mordechai			Daniel			247
FRIEDLER	Shmuel	Fradel		Yirmiyahu			247
FRIEDLER	Yirmiyahu			Shmuel	Fradel	wife and their two children	247
FRIEDLER	Baruch Yitzchak			Shmuel		and his wife	247
FRIEDLER	Sarah Gitel			Shmuel			247
FRIEDLER	Avraham Hersch						247
FRIEDLER	Shlomo			Avraham Hersch			247
FRIEDLER	Fradel			Avraham Hersch			247
FRIEDLER	Shlomo	Devorah		Yirmiyahu			247
FRIEDLER	Shlomo			Shlomo	Devorah		247
FRIEDLER	Fradel			Shlomo	Devorah		247
FRIEDLER	Henya			Shlomo	Devorah		247
FRIEDLER	Frida						247
FRIEDLER						wife of Baruch Hersch	247
FRIEDLER	Yirmiyahu						247
FRIEDLER	Frida				Hinda		247
FRIEDMAN	David	Mindel					247
FRIEDMAN	Channah			David	Mindel		247
FRIEDMAN	David			David	Mindel		247
FREITIK	Welwel	Chaya					247
FREITIK	Ita			Welwel	Chaya		247
PERLMUTTER	Shlomo	Sarah					247
PERLMUTTER	Yakov			Shlomo	Sarah		247
FERSHTENDIK	Binyamin						247

FERSHTENDIK	Yechezkel			Binyamin		247
FERSHTENDIK	Yechezkel			Binyamin		247
FERSHTENDIK				wife of Yechezkel		247
FERSHTENDIK	Tzvi			Yechezkel		247
FERSHTENDIK	Elkana			Yechezkel		247
FERSHTENDIK	Dina			Yechezkel	and her husband	247
FERSHTENDIK	Moshe			Yechezkel	and his wife and Moshe's children	247
FERSHTENDIK	Batya					247

צ Tzadik

TZWEKIN	Avraham David	Esther				247
TZWEKIN	Etel			Avraham David	Esther	274
TZWEKIN	Channah Sarah			Avraham David	Esther	247
TZWEKIN	Tzviya			Avraham David	Esther	247
TZUKERMAN	Min'che					247
TZUKERMAN	Scheindel				Min'che	247
TZUKERMAN	Esther				Min'che	247
TZUKERMAN	Sarah				Min'che	247
TZUKERFIN	Tzadok	Perl	LIEBERBOM			247
TZUKERFIN	Yehoshua			Tzadok	Perl	247
TZUKERFIN	Yakov			Tzadok	Perl	248
TZUKERFIN	David			Tzadok	Perl	248
TZITRENBOM	Yokel	Rivka				248
TZITRENBOM	Shmuel	Etka		Yokel	Rivka	248
TZITRENBOM	Chaya			Shmuel	Etka	248
TZITRENBOM	Yosef			Shmuel	Etka	248
TZITRENBOM	Welwel			Yokel		248
TZIMBERLAD	Chaim Yisrael	Rakhel				248

326

TZIMBERLAD	Shimon			Chaim Yisrael	Rakhel		248
TZIMBERLAD	Perla			Chaim Yisrael	Rakhel		248
TZIMERMAN	Matot (Mates)						248
TZIMERMAN	Leah						248
TZIMERMAN	Sarah					their daughter	248
TZIMERMAN	Nachum	Yenta		Matot (Mates)			248
TZIMERMAN	It'che			Nachum	Yenta		248
TZIMERMAN	Chaim			Nachum	Yenta		248
TZIMERMAN	Yitzchak						248
TZIMERMAN	Miriam						248
TZIMERMAN	Avraham						248
TZIMERMAN	Yakov						248
TZIMERMAN	Gitel						248
TZIMERMAN	Sarah						248
TZIMERMAN	Matel						248
TZIMERMAN	Moshe	Chaya					248
TZIMERMAN	Alta			Moshe			248
TZIMERMAN	Michael					husband of Alta	248
TZIMERMAN	Berl			Michael	Alta		248
TZIMERMAN	Chaim			Michael	Alta		248
TZIMERMAN	Bracha			Michael	Alta		248
TZIMERMAN	Uri (Aharon Shlomo)	Gitel					248
TZIMERMAN	Baruch			Uri (Aharon Shlomo)	Gitel		248
TZIMERMAN	Dina			Uri (Aharon Shlomo)	Gitel		248
TZIMERMAN				Uri (Aharon Shlomo)	Gitel	another daughter	248
TZIMERMAN	Dov (Berl)	Channah					248
TZIMERMAN	David			Dov (Berl)	Channah		248

ק Kof

KAMINSKY	Yechiel	Devorah				ordained Rabbi	248
KAMINSKY	David			Yechiel	Devorah		248
KOFENBOM	Chaim			Tuvia			248
KOFENBOM	Yisrael			Chaim			248
KOFENBOM	Shlomo			Chaim			248
KOFENBOM	Reizel			Chaim			248
KOFENBOM	Leibish	Kayla		Chaim			248
KOFENBOM	Neta			Leibish	Kayla	(son)	248
KOFENBOM	Avraham			Leibish	Kayla		248
KOFENBOM	Dina			Leibish	Kayla		248
KOFENBOM	Tzvi			Tuvia			248
KOFENBOM	Leibish			Tzvi			248
KOFENBOM	Moshe			Tzvi			248
KOFENBOM	Yehudit			Tzvi			248
KOFENBOM	Rivka			Tzvi			248
KOFENBOM	Sarah			Tzvi			248
KOFENBOM	Noach					husband of Sarah	248
KOFENBOM	Ruth			Noach	Sarah		248
KOFENBOM	Efraim			Noach	Sarah		248
KOFENBOM	Eizik						248
KOFENBOM	Basha						248
KOFENBOM	Yehoshua					his son	248
KOFENBOM	Hillel					his son	248
KOZHUKH	Chaim David	Gitel				ritual slaughterer and examiner; and two children	249
KOPF	Chaya					the mother	249
KOPF	Avraham	Chaya		Fishel			249
KOPF	Rakhel			Avraham	Chaya		249
KOPF	Reizel			Avraham	Chaya		249

328

KOPF	Efraim			Avraham	Chaya		249
KOPF	Zelig	Hadassah		Fishel			249
KOPF	Moshe			Zelig	Hadassah		249
KOPF	Fishel			Zelig	Hadassah		249
KOPF	Sarah			Zelig	Hadassah		249
KOPF	Peretz	Rakhel					249
KOPF	Moshe			Peretz	Rakhel		249
KOPF	Efraim			Peretz	Rakhel		249
KOPF	Dina			Peretz	Rakhel		249
KOPF	Sarah			Peretz	Rakhel		249
KOPF	Welwel	Bracha					249
KOPF	Sarah			Welwel	Bracha		249
KOPF	Sima			Welwel	Bracha		249
KOPF	Chaim			Welwel	Bracha		249
KOPF	Leizer	Serl					249
KOPF	Dan			Leizer	Serl		249
KOPF	Moshe			Leizer	Serl	and two additional daughters	249
KOPF	Yechiel	Sarah					249
KOPF	Dina			Yechiel	Sarah		249
KOPF	Rakhel			Yechiel	Sarah	and two additional children	249
KOPF	Yona	Miriam					249
KOPF	Sarah			Yona	Miriam		249
KOPF	Chaya			Yona	Miriam	and two additional children	249
KOPF	Mordechai	Rivka					249
KOPF	Efraim			Mordechai	Rivka		249
KOPF	Dan			Mordechai	Rivka		249
KOPF	Bella			Mordechai	Rivka		249
KOPF	Dina			Mordechai	Rivka		249
KOPF	Leibish	Masha				from Chernichin;	249

					and their two children	
KOPF	Yosef	Tova		Leibish		249
KOPF	Shlomo	Yita		Fishel		249
KOPF	Fishel			Shlomo	Yita	249
KOPF	Gitel			Shlomo	Yita	249
KUPER	Leibish	Reizel		Baruch		249
KUPER	Eidel			Leibish	Reizel	249
KUPER	Yechiel	Rakhel		Leibish		249
KUPER	Baruch			Yechiel	Rakhel	249
KUPER	Dina			Yechiel	Rakhel	249
KUPER	Seril			Leibish	and her husband and children	249
KUPER	Zlata			Leibish		249
KUPER	Yechiel				Zlata's husband from Goray and their two children	249
KUPER	Tova			Leibish		250
KUPER	Chaim				Tova's husband and their 4 children	250
KORN	Yisraelke	Hadassah			son in law of VACHTER, and their child	250
KORNDREKSLER	Shimon					250
KORNDREKSLER	Berl			Shimon		250
KORNDREKSLER	Moshe			Shimon		250
KORNDREKSLER	Chaya			Shimon		250
KORNDREKSLER				Shimon	another daughter	250
KLEINER	Chanoch	Reizel				250
KLEINER	Shlomo			Chanoch	Reizel	and his wife and child	250
KLEINER	Yisrael			Chanoch	Reizel	250
KLEINER	Ozer	Chaya				250

330

KLEINER	Gitel			Ozer	Chaya	and her husband Nachum	250
KLEINER	Chaim	Sarah		Ozer			250
KLEINER	Efraim			Chaim	Sarah		250
KLEINER	David			Chaim	Sarah		250
KLEINER	Yishayahu-Nute	Yita	SCHLESINGER	Ozer			250
KLEINER	Sarah			Yishayahu-Nute	Yita		250
KASTENBERG	Avraham	Chaya	YAKOBSON			and their 2 children	250
KRITMAN	Reuven						250
KRITMAN	Daniel	Golda		Reuven			250
KRITMAN	Perl			Daniel	Golda		250
KRITMAN	Dina			Daniel	Golda		250
KRITMAN	Efraim			Daniel	Golda		250
KREITMAN	Yosef Leib	Zlata		Reuven			250
KREITMAN	Chaya			Yosef Leib	Zlata		250
KREITMAN	Serl			Yosef Leib	Zlata		250
KREITMAN	Dov			Yosef Leib	Zlata		250

ר **Resh**

ROSENBERG	Nachum	Shprintze					250
ROSENBERG	Fruma			Nachum	Shprintze		250
ROSENBERG	Mirel			Nachum	Shprintze		250
ROSENBERG	Frimit			Nachum	Shprintze		250
ROSENBERG	Leibel			Nachum	Shprintze		250
ROSENFELD	Yehoshua	Chaya		Yanis			250
ROSENFELD	Leah			Yehoshua		and her husband and child	250
ROSENFELD	Yakov			Yehoshua			250
ROSENFELD	Yechiel			Yakov			250
ROSENFELD	Elimelech			Yakov			250
ROZNER	Chaim	Gitel					250
ROZNER	Zeinvil			Chaim	Gitel		250

ROZNER	Yitte			Chaim	Gitel			250
ROZNER	Masha			Chaim	Gitel			250
ROZNER	Avraham			Chaim	Gitel			250
ROSEN	Yitzchak							250
ROZNER	Moshe-Meir	Bren'che						250
ROZNER	Shimon	Rivka		Shalom				250
ROZNER	Shoshana			Shimon	Rivka			250
ROZNER	Shalom			Shimon	Rivka			250
ROZNER	Efraim			Shimon	Rivka			250
ROZNER	Avraham	Shprintze		Shalom				251
ROZNER	Gitel			Avraham		and her husband		251
ROZNER	Kayla			Avraham				251
ROSENBERG	Shalom Moshe			Avraham				251
ROZNER	Shmuel	Liebe	YAKOBSON	Shimon				251
ROZNER	Chaim			Shmuel	Liebe			251
ROZNER	Sarah			Shmuel	Liebe			251
ROZNER	Feige			Shmuel	Liebe			251
ROSENSTOCK	Avraham	Rakhela						251
ROSENSTOCK	Tzviya			Avraham	Rakhela	and her husband		251
ROSENSTOCK	Rivka			(husband)	Tzvyia	and her husband		251
ROSENSTOCK	Yitzchak Meir			(husband)	Rivka			251
ROTBLAT	Yosef	Channah Giteleh						251
ROTBLAT	Reikel			Yosef	Channah Giteleh			251
ROTBLAT	Shprintze			Yosef	Channah Giteleh			251
ROTBLAT	Pesya			Yosef	Channah Giteleh			251
ROTBLAT	Chava			Yosef	Channah Giteleh			251
ROTBLAT	Ratza			Yosef	Channah Giteleh			251

ROTBLAT	Hersch			Yosef	Channah Giteleh		251
ROTBLAT	Shaul	Feige		Yosef		their 2 children, and 2 grandchildren (Yosef's)	251
RIEDER	Malka						251
RIEDER	Yosef	Rakhel			Malka		251
RIEDER	Yehudit			Yosef	Rakhel		251
RIEDER	Yakov			Yosef	Rakhel		251
RIEDER	Leah			Yosef	Rakhel		251
REIDLER	Yehoshua	Sima	KOPF				251
REIDLER	Batya			Yehoshua	Sima		251
REIDLER	Roza			Yehoshua	Sima		251
RINSILBER	Zalman	Rakhel	MANDELKER				251
RINSILBER	Charna			Zalman	Rakhel		251
RINSILBER	Yosef			Zalman	Rakhel		251
RINSILBER	Yeshayahu			Zalman	Rakhel		251
RENTNER	Zindel	Miriam				and grandchildren	251
RENTNER	Rivka						251
RENTNER	Moshe						251
RENTNER	Yitzchak						251
RENTNER	Freidel						251
RENTNER	Leibel						251
RENTNER	Yakov Shlomo						251
RENTNER	Yisrael						251
RENTNER	Nechama						251
RENTNER	Brendel						251

ש Shin

SCHULSINGER	Berish	Mirel					251
SCHULSINGER	Chaim			Berish	Mirel		251
SCHULSINGER	Rakhel			Berish	Mirel		251
SCHULSINGER	David	Chaya					251

SCHULSINGER	Shmuel		David	Chaya		251
SCHULSINGER	Hersch		David	Chaya		251
SCHULSINGER	Matel		David	Chaya	(daughter)	251
SCHULSINGER	Yita		David	Chaya		251
SCHULSINGER	Sarah		David	Chaya		252
SCHULSINGER	Avraham	Riva	Hersch			252
SCHULSINGER	Herish		Avraham	Riva		252
SCHULSINGER	Leah		Avraham	Riva		252
SCHULSINGER	Mendel		Avraham	Riva		252
SCHULSINGER	Shmulik		Avraham	Riva		252
SCHULSINGER	Yakov		Avraham	Riva		252
STREICHER	Leizer	Perla			Perla a midwife	252
STREICHER	Yakov		Leizer	Perla		252
STREICHER	Esther		Leizer	Perla		252
SHTREKER	Shmuel Zinwil	Bran'che				252
SHTREKER	Roza		Shmuel Zanwil	Bran'che		252
SHTREKER	Ovadia		Shmuel Zanwil	Bran'che		252
SHTARKER	Mordechai Hersch	Chava				252
SHTARKER	Ovadia		Mordechai Hersch	Chava		252
SHTARKER	Kayla		Mordechai Hersch	Chava		252
SHTARKER	Channah		Mordechai Hersch	Chava		252
SHTERNFELD	Yeshayahu					252
SHTERNFELD	Moshe	Golda	Yeshayahu		and their children	252
SHMUREK	Mendel	Shprintze				252
SHMUREK	Menucha		Mendel	Shprintze		252
SHMUREK	Welwel		Mendel	Shprintze		252
SHMUREK	Rakhel		Welwel			252
SHMUREK	Golda		Welwel			252

SHMUREK	Esther			Welwel			252
SHMUREK	Tzirl			Welwel			252
SHMUREK	Chaim	Etel		Mendel			252
SHMUREK	Efraim			Chaim	Etel		252
SHMUREK	David			Chaim	Etel		252
SHMUREK	(son)			Chaim	Etel		252
SHMUREK	Avraham	Miriam	SONTAG				252
SCHNEIDERBERG	Alter						252
SCHNEIDERBERG	Moshe	Chaya	LIBERBOM	Alter			252
SCHNEIDERBERG	Sarah			Moshe	Chaya		252
SCHNEIDERBERG	(son)			Moshe	Chaya		252
SCHNITER	Yechiel	Sarah Leah					252
SCHNITER	Moshe			Yechiel	Sarah Leah		252
SCHNITER	Mordechai			Yechiel	Sarah Leah		252
SCHNITER	Charna			Yechiel	Sarah Leah		252
SHAPIRA	Welwel	Yita					252
SHAPIRA	Frida			Welwel	Yita		252
SHAPIRA	Duba			Welwel	Yita	(daughter)	252

List transliterated by Judy Petersen

Martyrs whose surname was not recorded

Page numbers refer to the pages of the original Yizkor Book, not this translation.

Given name	Spouse's name	Wife's maiden name	Father's name	Mother's name	Remarks	Page
Elimelech	Chaya				the carpenter, and their adopted daughter	252
Gedalyahu	(wife)	BACH			nicknamed "the yellow", and their 3 children	252
David			Moshe			252
Perl Dabre						252
Leibish					my father	252
Chaya Hinde					my mother	252
Welwel					my brother	252
Moshe					my brother	252
Yosef					my brother	252
Dina					my sister	252
Geula					my sister	253
Sarah					my sister	253
Moshe	Necha				the tailor, the lame	253
Aryeh			Moshe	Necha		253
Feivel	Necha				the shoemaker; and their five children	253

Yitzchak-Meir	Zlata		Ritual slaughterer; and their four children	253
Wolf-Ber	Rakhel		Ritual slaughterer; and their child	253
Aharon	Pereleh		Ritual slaughterer, son in law of BRONSHPIEGEL	253
Levi			from Zhrebitch	253
David			from Zhrebitch	253
It'che			from Zhrebitch	253
Hersch Ber	Genendel		water carrier	253
Moshe	Feige		Reamer. And their 3 children	253
Yisrael	Channah		Reamer. And their 2 children	253

Unveiling of the monument in Martef HaShoah, 5724

[Page 254]

German extermination camps in Poland
Translated by Meir Bulman

This map are marks 10 main extermination sites which the Germans erected in Poland starting with the occupation 1940–41. Many labor and concentration camps are not mentioned here, including large ones like Janówska in Lwow, Kraków–Plaszów, and others, which were also camps for systematic extermination, and in all the Germans massacred local Jews.

1. Chelmno. A village on the shores of the Bar [Wila...?] approximately 12 km from the town of Koło between Warsaw to Posen. Probably the first large extermination camp in Poland, established in 1940. Exterminated in it were the Jews from the Western districts of Poland from the Lodz and Kalisz. The method of extermination was poising by gas in specially designated freight trucks in which the

338

expelled [?] Jews were carried to the nearby forest. It is estimated that in that camp a million people were exterminated, mostly Jews.

2. Auschwitz – Birkenau. Oswiecim, approximately 60 km west of Krakow. The camp is infamous for its cruelty and the immense destruction toll. Jews from all over Europe were imprisoned there. In 1944 the Jews of Hungary were majority of those exterminated. Non–Jews were also imprisoned there, relatively many in comparison to other camps. Birkenau, (the Polish village of Brzezinski [?]) 4 km from Oswiecim. Expelled to it were the Jews of Slovakia, Czechia, Greece, Italy, Holland, France, Poland, and Russia. 6 crematoria operated in it non–stop.

3. Szebnie. A village in the Jaslo county in Western Galicia, on the Yashalka [?] River, at the bottom of the Carpathian mountains. The murders began there in March of 1941 as Soviet prisoners were executed. In fall 1942 extermination of Jews began in the woods near the village of Warzyce. Murdered there were the Jews of Tarnów district and other places in Galicia.

4. Sobibór. A village in Wlodawa county, on the way from Brisk to Chelm. 77 km from Brisk and 41 km from Chelm. The origin of the camp was in April 1942, and spanned 2 square km in the woods. There were times when every day five trains arrived carrying men, women, and children from various European countries. A majority of those exterminated in the camp were Jews from towns and cities in the counties of Lublin, Zamosc, Krasnystaw, Chelm, Izbica, Zolkiewka, Turobin and more. The camp operated nonstop until 1943 and was supervised by SS Hauptsturmfurhrer Stangl. A few days after Yom Kippur in October 1943, a nicely prepared uprising took place in it by 600 Jews who destroyed the camp. Among the organizers of the uprising were natives of Turobin, Zolkiewka, Izbica, and others. Only 400 of the rebels managed to leave the camp's territory, and only 50 survived. As this book is being printed it was reported that the criminal Stangl was captured in Brazil and facing trial.

5. Treblinka. The infamous extermination camp in which a majority of Warsaw Jewry was destroyed, and many hundreds of thousands of

Jews from all over Poland and Europe. It is a small village, 4 km from Małkinia halfway between Warsaw and Bialistok. The Camp was liquidated after the Jewish uprising in August 1943. Jankiel Wiernik and others have published detailed description of the camp.

[Page 255]

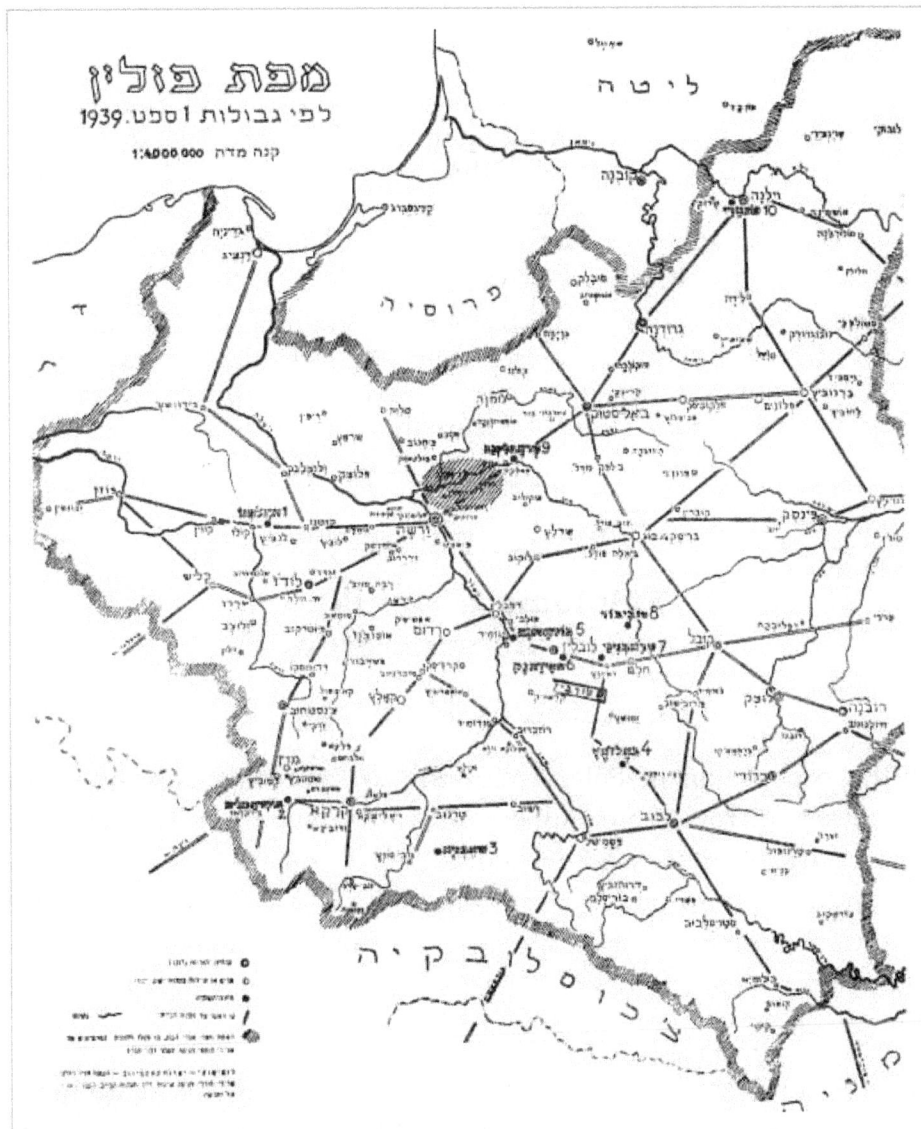

6. Ponary. Approximately 9 kilometers from Vilna in a forested area. The extermination of Jews in that site began at the end of 1941 and then about 50,000 of Jews from Vilna and the area were murdered there.

340

7. Belzec. A town in the Rava–Ruska district in Eastern Galicia, about 90 kilometers from Lwow on the way to Warsaw. Swedish paper *Aptntidnign* from February 11, 1944 reported that there were days when 10,000 people were eradicated daily.

[Page 256]

8. Poniatowa. A small village in Opole County near the Wisla... River in the Lublin area. At the start of November 1943, the remainder of Warsaw Jews expelled there after the uprising was quashed were exterminated there.

9. Majdanek. The infamous concentration and extermination camp near Lublin on the way to Chelm. It spanned 25 square kilometers and was built according to the model of the German concentration camp Dachau, but much larger. Its construction began in the winter of 1941. Jews were brought there for extermination since April 1942 starting with Jews from Slovakia, Germany, Austria, and others.

10. Trawniki. A village and industry point, 35 kilometers east of Lublin, a concentration station between Lublin and Rejowiec. In the beginning of 1943, remnants of the Jews of the Warsaw Ghetto were exterminated there after the quashing of the uprising.

The Dark Days

Shlomo Zissmilkh
(man of the underground)

Translated by Meir Bulman

After the occupation of Poland and the Russian–German agreement, the Russians retreated from the occupied Polish territory from the western side of the Bug river, with the fixed border along the river. That was in October 1939. In that month, on the holiday of Simchat Torah, the Russians left Turobin. They were immediately followed by Nazi forces, and as soon as they arrived they conducted a weapons search. There was not a home where they did not present themselves.

I remember an interesting event from that day: in our home we housed five refugees from Krakow. The German soldiers entered our homes and instructed, "stand still with your hands up." (Upstehen Händen in den noch) The refugees, who spoke German, froze in place and remained in their beds

341

without grasping what they were told. Only after the soldiers began hitting them with their rifle butts they recovered and understood the situation.

At the start of 1940 the population had to sustain itself economically. There were weak business ties. A few merchants brought products from nearby villages to export to Lublin in wagons (buses were not operating.) They purchased products that were unavailable in town and brought them back. The Germans treated that trade like smuggling, and due to the ban one could not move merchandise to and from Lublin in the daytime. There was also a nighttime curfew. The import and export from Lublin were done at night anyway. In one trip to Lublin, I joined six passengers, one of whom I remember, Chan'che wife of Avraham Liberbom the hatter. Before we reached Wysokie, the Germans captured us and imprisoned us in the Wysokie jail. We did not sleep that night because we feared our end. There were precedence for that fear as the Germans simply shot captured smugglers. As morning approached an officer entered and asked where we were traveling to at night, and we replied honestly and told him we were traveling to Lublin to purchase necessities. Based on that he freed us and we continued our journey to Lublin. In Lublin we bought food items, sewing instruments, leather, etc. The stores in Lublin were already half shuttered, but one could still obtain merchandizes. Under those condition Jews traveled to Lublin two–three times weekly to shop and on their way, there brought produce from villages. The situation continued the entire winter of 1940.

[Page 257]

The German army was stationed at the outskirts of Turobin. According to their plan they worked the Jews in clearing snow, ditch digging, trash removal, and other services for the military. In place of a salary the Germans gave beatings, and more than once caused grave injury. One day, I walked through street in Lublin and heard "snatchers" and until I managed to escape to Kowalski Gate number 3 I was captured by an SS man who brought me to Shvinta–Doska [?] where there were many detainees and we were all led to a farm near Maydan. We were worked clearing the territory of mud and clearing trash from the stables. The bearded Jews among us were shaved [?] using lit candles. Suddenly, they gave an order to run and began shooting, to injure or kill. I worked diligently and tried to avoid any reason for assault. The whole day an SS guard with a lash passed by and hit the workers. Toward evening the SS passed by me and I asked if I can go home. He replied, "yes, you worked diligently. Go home." As I was walking away I walked back and saw the same SS talking to a Jew, who possibly also asked to go home. In response he took out his gun and shot him on the spot. After I saw that I left quickly and traveled home to Turobin. Such a day was called, "snatching day."

In the summer of 1940 there was a forced labor quota which had to be fulfilled by the *Judenrat*. In one convoy, 150 Jews were sent to work in Zamosc, and I was in that group too. The job was to building walls using pedestals and wood by the river bank. The workers slept in barracks and received a little food through representatives of the community. Each community supplied food to its members. At the same time the representatives of Zamosc brought food they extracted me from the work camp thanks to family members I had in Zamosc. My younger brother remained in that Zamosc camp that whole summer. In addition to the worker quotas there were also snatching days in Turobin.

At the start of 1941, anti–tank ditches were being dug along the Bug River. Many people were snatched for that job. In Turobin 16 people were snatched. The snatched Jews from Turobin were sent to the Rava–Rus'ka area. The arrangement was that each community was permitted to bring food and clothes for its people once every two weeks.

In one day in May 1941, in early evening, as the community people walked through town to gather clothes and food for the forced laborer, a car with 4 Gestapo men. One of them One of them guarded Velvel Birnbaum's home so that the people in it would not leave, and the other entered. We immediately heard an explosion and understood a hand grenade was thrown. Mottel Yakovzon heard the explosion and struck the SS man to the ground and escaped outward, and I followed him and escaped too. Yakov Feder survived because he fell to the ground and the murdered laid on top of him. That day, those SS men passed door to door and killed every Jew they came across. 130 people died that day. That was the first big day of slaughter. People began to grow accustomed to those horrors. The fear continued and occasionally some were killed and others were snatched and shipped. It continued until the winter of 1942.

[Page 258]

In the winter of 1942, the Jews continued to work for the Germans. The synagogue was converted into a warehouse for the German army. At That same time, some compulsory laborers returned from Zamosc. They told of a short SS supervisor who rode a white horse and every day had to find some victims and shoot them.

Most expulsions were done in the summer of 1942. I was in the group last expelled, dubbed "*Judenrein*" during the holiday months in October 1942. On Saturday morning, an order was issued that no Jew may remain in town by 7 in the evening. The Germans brought several wagons, and the expulsion began.

I remember that among those expelled the second time was my mother OBM, and they were brought to the Trawniki train station. All those expelled were placed in freight carts. After the train n began to move in the evening, my mother jumped through the slit in the car. She sprained her foot and made her way home leaning on a stick, dozens of kilometers.

The final expulsion was towards Izbica. The procession, numbering inn the thousands (there were some refugees from Lodz among us) made its way slowly to Izbica. I remember that when we reached Kleparz Yakov Moshe Hopen OBM turned to me and said, "these are the final hours of our lives. Let us escape from the procession towards the woods." I proposed that to my father who replied that the same fate of all Jews will be his fate too. But Yakov Moshe, his wife, and two daughters departed the convoy, headed to the villages. I have not seen that family since. They must have been murdered by Polish villagers after hiding for some time in the woods.

Before the expulsion of the Turobin community there was also an expulsion from Modliborzyce and Janów. At the same time, a few young men from Janów and one from Modliborzyce. He proposed to the *Judenrat* to purchase weapons and we will be accepted into a group of partisans hiding in the Godziszów woods. A payment was made, but we did not see that man since.

Along the route of expulsion some 30 young men organized and we escaped to the woods. Near the forest which splits Zolkiewka, we encountered a German army unit which opened fire on us. We dispersed. Along with a large part of that 30–man group, we returned to the expulsion procession. Part of the group regrouped and entered the Godziszów woods, where a group of 90 people convened. That group negotiated with a group of murderous Polish partisans, who took their money to purchase weapons and then murdered the

344

whole group, except for two, one of whom I later met. I of course returned to the convoy and my family. The family continued to walk all winter [?] It was a cold day accompanied by pouring rain throughout all hours of the night. The rain added to our bad luck of the destruction and permeated the bones of the expelled. The convoy arrived wet and exhausted in the evening to Izbica [?]

The Turobin expellees were split up and placed in Jewish homes. That night, I was approached by Shalom Shabtai, a member of the Turobin *Judenrat* who told me the town was approved to be turned into a (judenstaat) Jewish town. Most of the local communities from Zamosc to Lublin were concentrated In Izbica. It was said that from each community 40 people will survive and comprise the Jewish city. That was probably the German scheme, which demanded a large payment for Turobin to be included in that plan. I paid a large sum to the *Judenrat* as did many others. The *Judenrat* had to pay that ransom to a German villain who I think was named Abeyer. Yakov Feder and I then constructed a bunker in Altman's leather workshop.

[Page 259]

The form of the scheme was that all those who paid the ransom and placed on a list would remain in the field and then returned to town. Early on Monday morning, the expulsion of the Jews from Izbica began to the train station outside of town. The expellees were commanded to sit on the wet and muddy grass. The victims sat there all day. In the afternoon, a command was issued to board freight trains. They began to recite the last names of those on the list to return home and instructed them to pass to the other side of the tracks. But many people not on the list followed those families and chaos ensued. The guards did not like that and they began assaulting the victims and shot some them. The SS men present shot those who tacked to distinguish between those on the list and others. That situation continued until it was announced that all Jews without distinction must board the train. After everyone boarded, they commanded that all young, healthy men exit the train. Truthfully, they did not want to leave the train so the SS entered the train and aided by blows from rifle butts.

The whole day of waiting, many commands were issued. Once it was commanded that all must hand over their money, and another command to hand over silver and Gold, and then that all craftsmen cobblers, carpenters, tailors move to a special section. That same time Shalom Shabtai offered me to become a carpenter but I refused and entered the train car. 1200 young men who were removed from the cars. We were gathered in a field and commanded to clean the area. Gold, dollars, other currency, and jewelry could be seen spread across the territory. Afterwards, the guards faced a machine gun at us and fired for 10–15 minutes. The screams reached high heaven. Those who fell, fell and those who remained were told to return to town.

On the way back to Izbica, the Ukrainian camp guard stopped me and ordered me to give him my boots which he liked. In their place I was given shoes with wooden soles which could not be walked in. I reached town and encountered Shmerrel Gells and Yakov Lev. They told me they had built themselves a bunker. Since I did not have shoes, I entered one of the Jewish homes to find shoes. In that house I found murdered Jews. I searched and found a pear of boots. But when I wore them I saw they had no soles. Shmerrel told me there was a cobbler not far from there who would repair them for me. Shmerrel gave me some money since I remained penniless. I told them of the events by the train station and they did not reply, since they did not know what could be done and where to turn. On the way to the cobbler, an SS man grabbed me by the neck and led me to a freight truck.

Among those on the truck was Avraham Kopf from my town. We were driven to a mixed village of Poles and Germans near Wysokie–Zamoyski. The Poles were cleared from the place and the farms were repurposed for the Germans. In place of two–family farms, one farm was constructed for a single German family. New homes were being constructed and we were tasked with construction. We were housed in a camp of small houses with kitchen. Of course, no food was given for cooking. Among the kitchen workers I met a friend from Zamosc. The construction manager arrived the next day and designated me as a roofer. I was trained and began work. Avraham worked in building walls with heavy wooden planks.

[Page 260]

The home we were constructing was for a German farmer. At lunchtime he called us and told us to eat from the potatoes cooked for the swine. Potatoes were already priceless at that time. I filled my appetite and kept some potatoes in my pockets for dinner. The farmer's wife was in Germany. One day, we entered the home and before we could taste the potatoes we met the farmer's wife. I heard her say to her husband, "you're letting those dogs eat? I will have you ordered shot," and left the house. As I recall, the farmer turned white as snow after he heard his wife's words and was more nervous than we were. I did not forget to take advantage of the opportunity and stuffed some potatoes in my pockets. The German told us to leave quickly and we returned to work. I remember that everyone began crying about the potatoes we were barred from eating. At that chance I took out the potatoes from my pockets and we ate. One day as I returned from work I saw that Avraham suffered a face injury and his teeth were shattered. He explained that while working he lifted a heavy wooden plank which fell from his hands. The construction manager of the SS approached him and kicked him, breaking his teeth.

For a few days, Avraham repeatedly told me that we must escape the camp. But in order to escape we needed food, so we waited for the 800 grams of bread we received weekly. We received the bread portion, and I managed to steal some of the beets on their way to a sugar factory. On a stormy and rainy night, Avraham and I began to cross the camp fence. As we began to tread the muddy route, the camp guards noticed us and began shooting. Avaram's hand was injured, but we had gotten away. We walked all night. In the morning, we reached an area which Avraham did not recognize. We feared continuing traveling in the daytime so we took position in the fields, among the piles of wet hay. We began walking in the evening and walked through the night and reached a village. In one farmer's house we received food and then moved on to different acquaintance and stayed for the night. He also fed us, but then said we could not stay longer. We continued walking and reached a farm where we fond large piles of crops before harvest. We hid in those piles. We had one loaf of bread, which we lived on for three days. We heard noise near our hiding spot and thought we were discovered, But we saw people approaching a neighboring pile and extracting from it a young man named Velvel Kashizki. We did not know he was there, but the farmers knew. They extracted him and led him to the Gestapo in Turobin. After we had witnessed that, we left quickly that night, and continued walking towards the village of Czernięcin.

In Czernięcin, we encountered Yosef Kopf who supported us. I knew it was difficult for him to do so as the farmer must have demanded a high payment. I then decided to go to the front yard of my house in Turobin where my family had hidden gold and silver. One night, after I arrived in the yard and began digging, I saw a German was living in our house who awoke when I began digging. When the German came out to the yard I quickly left. The German saw me and shot after me, but I miraculously survived. As I ran I heard the guards in the town also began shooting and chasing me. I ran towards Czernięcin through the swamps, and the dogs they sent after me could not track me. After I returned to my former spot, I told Avraham I would return to Izbica, and Avraham stayed put. Yosef, who said he wanted to know what we would do there, joined me on my journey to Izbica. We reached Izbica after a long night of wandering. We then saw that the remaining Jews in Izbica were being gathered in the movie theater for one last expulsion. After Yosef and I saw that we left Izbica and returned to Czernięcin. A few days later, Avraham and I went to obtain food form a farmer who Avraham was acquainted with. On the way, we encountered Germans who shot at us. I left Avraham and escaped on my own.

[Page 261]

I was headed to a work camp in Trawniki where my brother worked. I followed the route of the tracks of the freight train. I headed the wrong way and entered a lit village house, where there were five Poles. I asked for directions. The Poles were very happy to meet a Jew and invited me home, joyful they had found a "treasure" since for every Jew captured for the Gestapo they received several kilos of sugar and a bottle of Vodka. The farmers locked me in a room. At night, of course, I did not sleep. I contemplated an escape because I knew my end was approaching and my will to live overpowered everything. I began searching and found an axe in the fireplace. I was not sure I could battle five men with that axe, but they were sound asleep. I broke through the window with the axe and escaped. I reached Tarnow, where there was a guard inspection. They saw me and began shooting. I escaped into the woods.

I wandered the woods and survived off sorrel leaves and hackberries. A few days later I dared and approached a lone home near the forest. I knocked on the door. A tall farmer opened the door and said, "Jew, what do you need? Are you hungry? Please come in." My frightful experience had impacted me, and I was too afraid to enter. The farmer fed me and said that in the nearby forests thee were Jews I could find. After a few days of hunger and cold, I swallowed the food to quickly and after I finished eating I could not move and my legs swelled immediately. The farmer was like an angel to me, he brought me to the attic laid me down and rubbed my legs with clean ethanol which was priceless at the time. That continued for 4–5 days and I then left to the woods with food the farmer had given me. For a few days I wandered the woods, unable to find the group of Jews the farmer had gestured toward.

One night, I heard braking branches. I moved towards the noise, and immediately fell into a pit. After I managed to leave the pit, I saw a campfire with a pot of chicken cooking. I sat, took the chicken, and began eating. Suddenly I realized I was surrounded by people. Those people were Jews who lived in a bunker. They feared me, scattered, and after they saw me up close returned. Those Jews did not have weapons. I stayed with that group several weeks until the snow period began. The group would purchase food in nearby Białki[?] village.

At the edge of the village I came across a farmer's house, whose granddaughter came from France and could not return. The grandfather and his granddaughter, a young woman of about 20, ran the farm. I occasionally received food from them and then disappeared into the woods. The snows began then and we constructed bunkers to hide in.

[Page 262]

One Saturday evening I went to the farmer to ask for food. The French woman told me, "Why would you return to the forest while it snows and freezing? Sleep here and in the morning return to the forest." Of course, I stayed. Early in the morning she said, "I will cook some food for you. Eat and then return to the forest." In the meantime, she borrowed scissors from a neighbor and cut my hair, since it was overgrown like a savage. The grandfather carried milk back from the barn. After the grandfather returned he said gunfire was heard from the forest. After it snowed, farmers had noticed footsteps and understood a group of Jews was hiding in the woods. It was told to the Germans who executed the group of Jews. Some managed to survive. I stayed with the farmer for the entire winter of 1943.

One night, I wanted to breath fresh air and stretch. I found two people laid on the snow, dying in the cold. They were brother and sister. I carried them to my spot in the attic but was afraid to tell the French girl about the event. Since that day, I shared my food with them, and of course we suffered hunger. One Sunday the French woman heard us conversing and she became aware of her new neighbors. She was not pleased by it. But she was simply an angel. After she learned of their presence, she constructed a bunker in the yard, and every time she learned Germans were to visit the village she notified us, and we scattered to the woods. One day, the French woman told us the Germans were on their way, and the pair and I left for the woods. We stayed there all day. I understood our friends would check on us and bring us food, since we were hungry. We stood guard and waited at the edge of the forest. In the afternoon she appeared and brought food.

We received notice that a group of Jewish partisans was hiding in the nearby forest section. That information was correct, since Germans placed a blockade on them and they relocated to our section. When they saw a stranger, me, wandering the area, they surrounded me, and brought me to their commander. It was a mixed group of Christians and Jews. There were 30 armed young men and some women and children. They hid in the forest without bunkers, as it was the spring (1943). They brought me to their camp and introduced the commander, a Jew from Kraśnik. His pseudonym was Adolf and his real name was Avraham Braun. He assembled that partisan unit. He was very active and organized, and thanks to him many survived. He was a talented leader, with a great sense of smell. He always recognized ahead of time when the Germans were approaching and hid the women and children ahead of time. In the span of months there were several clashes with Germans or Poles, also during food obtainment missions.

In midsummer, a Polish man arrived from France, formerly a volunteer fighter in Spain. He was sent to us to organize the partisans. He assembled 50 Poles and joined them with our group. Thus, we became a group of close to 90 men. Our first mission was to derail a freight train and obtain the weapons loaded on it. It was according to a notice we received that the train was carrying weapons to the Russian front. We did not have explosives nor tools to disassemble the tracks. We approached a point guarding the tracks. We overpowered the guard, obtained the keys, and disassembled the rails. We lacked experience, so we left the keys between the tracks so when the train approached the conductor noticed them and managed to somewhat stop the train, so from 30 cars, only 18 derailed. There was also an additional surprise: in place of a freight train with the weapons headed for the Russian front, it was a passenger train carrying officers from the German front headed to vacation. As we were in the middle of a mission we shot at the officers and killed 700 [?] of them. We lost one fighter, Yehoshua Klinbaum of Shestucka [?], the only one among us who operated a light machine gun.

350

[Page 263]

Our hopes of obtaining weapons in that mission were in vain. Therefore, we attacked lone Germans, killed them and took their weapons. A war could not be waged with all that light weaponry, as we lacked the minimum necessary machine gun. That situation continued until the end of summer. Then our headquarters obtained contact with Moscow, and they sent us a commander named Vatzek (he reached us by paratroop) who brought with him a radio with a receiver, and a pair of Jewish radio operators, a husband and wife. Immediately after their arrival, we were supplied sufficient arms and ammunition. The Partisan group began to take the shape of an army, divided by roles and areas of operation. Our group spanned across a 50–kilometers–long territory. Our role was to destroy rail tracks, bridges, and police stations. I was given the role of communicator and received a horse for transportation.

That activity continued until the start of winter 1944. In that winter, we did not construct bunkers. Firstly, because we were accustomed to the unusual conditions, and secondly because we were always prepared for battle. In that winter we would construct protective nests from bushes and branches. Those huts were built only for protection from the snow, and we slept lightly standing up. The hut was built in such a way that our feet were immersed in the ground so they would not freeze. We lived that way and more than once we awoke covered in snow. Every morning, there was someone tasked by rotation to build a fire. We lit the fire at least 100 meters from where we lived. There were those who wanted to take off their boots to straighten out their feet but could not wear them in morning because the boots froze. If such a remover's turn to build a fire arrived, he had to walk barefoot in the snow. I was accustomed to bathe half my body in cold water. Almost every morning, I would open a frozen puddle with an axe and bathe.

I remember a mission we were on in that winter. Near Czarnocin there was a farm, owned by a man named Hoskowski. The farm was confiscated by Germans who placed in it a German manager. Our plan was to attack the farm. But as we approached Olszanka, a suburb near Turobin, we discovered a German police station. The Germans in the station held a long battle with us. We did not lose any men, but we had to retreat. We battled German forces almost daily.

In the winter of 1944 we battled Polish gangs, like the "O–Ka," and ordinary gangs of robbers. We battled them more in the winter of 1943. That year we suffered much from those gangs, mainly the O–Ka. I remember an event when three other Jews and I traveled in a sled while returning from a mission. On the way we met a larger group of O–Ka who also traveled in two sleds. They blocked our path, and we jumped from the sled, prepared for battle. We were some distance away and the first to ask them to identify themselves. They replied they were O–Ka, and we asked what group they belonged to, as we recognized their names. If we were the first to identify, they would have easily beat us since they had more manpower and firepower. We replied we were also O Ka. "If so," they replied, "we will send a representative and you will too, for we are brothers." The second their representative left we sent our representative who killed him with a Russian PPSh machine gun, and we retreated. We battled the Andki [?] groups for most of 1943 ns the winter of 1944. There were more groups like that in Janów and the Turobin area, but they did not dare fight us because they were few and at that time we numbered 6000 Partisans.

[Page 264]

The Germans would siege certain areas of the forest, because they could not surround a larger territory as they did not have the necessary manpower. Thus, when we learned of a siege of one area our group would leave for a different spot. If the Germans were a small group, we went to battle. Usually in battles within the forest the Germans suffered losses because we hid in certain spots and sniped at them.

In 1943, we received no help from the Russians, because the Russians in those woods were mostly thieves and murderers. They were even worse than the O–Ka and were overtaken by a complete spirit of anti–Semitism. They were mostly Ukrainians. until the Russian captain arrived from Moscow, we knew the nature of a Jewish partisan in the woods. The captain's first order was that he did not want to hear "Jew" used as an insult as we all fight as one against a common enemy. Truly, since the day he arrived, we ceased to feel persecuted as Jews.

I recall than when the Polish envoy arrived from France, we were tasked with liberating a labor camp names Janisow. We stormed the work camp, killed the guards and offered the workers in the camp to follow us. We suffered heavy losses. In the end, the people in the camp did not want to leave, for many reasons, and only few followed us. They had lost faith in man, and

352

feared that the Poles would murder them, since they heard many such stories and so preferred to stay in the camp.

After liberation, I met Yosef Kopf who said that after we parted ways near Izbica he still managed to hide for some time in the villages, and then returned to Izbica and was sent from there to the extermination camp Sobibór. He told me how he and his friend Leibel, son of the rabbi of Zolkiewka led the uprising in Sobibór. They arranged for the craftspeople to invite the SS men in relation to issues with the work they had ordered and killed them when they arrived. Yosef and Leibel and another group then killed the guards and breached the fence. Some prisoners managed to escape and survived. After the war ended, Yosef Kopf returned to Turobin to recover his property and the Poles murdered him. The Poles murdered Leibel in broad day light on Kowalski Street in Lublin.

Our battles in the forest continued in the winter of 1944 until the French was front was opened. Then the Germans relocated two divisions from the Russian front to the west, and those divisions were tasked with exterminating the Partisan troops along the way.

[Page 265]

In the summer of 1944, we were surrounded in the forest for three weeks and fought the Germans during the day and by night retreated to a different area, then continued to fight. We received aid from the Russians who airdropped food and resources, in view of the German soldiers. In the three weeks of that battle, the German casualties reached 6000. We received those figures through the Polish press. During those battles, German headquarters was in a village surrounded by woods. We were located three kilometers from them. One clear day, a general went to tour the area in a caterpillar track vehicle accompanied by other vehicles. One of our men began to make his way towards the sled, but we could not understand what he was doing (at that time many lost their mind from exhaustion and war). The man approached the car and took the general's hat and briefcase. The general dared not move, and the man returned to us in good health. There were plans in the briefcase, and thanks to the intelligence recovered by the young man on his private mission we knew what was to take place, which prevented much suffering and victims.

After the battle we split into smaller groups. At that time, a fascist Polish group from the O–Ka approached us by messenger near Józefów. They proposed their help with an attack on the Germans. We agreed, and they received a designated strip. A few hours later, they surrendered without our knowledge. Suddenly, the Germans were on our backs and we decided to retreat by breaking the German line [?] Our group comprised 50 Jewish fighters. We had 23 wounded in that battle and we retreated to the Szczebrzeszyn area. While returning to the Otrocz woods we fought in one day nonstop from 6 in the morning to 9 in the evening. The SS had already penetrated our ditches [?] At that moment, an order was given for 40 Stalinowtzs [?] to go to battle. We were unaware that group existed. They had a Yeaktrow [?] machine gun with special plates [?] The group began a counter-attack and the Germans retreated. In that battle we obtained cannons. Until then we only had machine guns and submachine gun like the ZKM [?].

I remember that after that battle in Józefów we came across the forest keeper's house in the Szczebrzeszyn area. The guard housed us in the pavilion and left. We stayed to sleep. The next morning, he returned with two Poles. I knew one of them well; his name was Mokha and he was a pronounced Jew-hater, a leader of the O–Ka. The second he said, "hello, Mr. Zissmilkh," I turned cold. I knew that in total we numbered 30 men and among us were 18 wounded and exhausted. Mokha the Pole approached me and said, "I see you are slightly disappointed to see me. But I must thank you and tell you that on your mission you have stopped the Germans from advancing for three weeks and killed many of them, for which you deserve praise." He ensured we were brought food and drink and everything we needed, and supplied us transportation to the Otrocz woods. A group of fifty men formed and were given instructions to go on a mission in the Pławo area near Warsaw. A short while later, we returned to the woods in the Janow–Turobin area. We operated like that until the end of summer 1944.

[Page 266]

At that time, Lublin was already liberated by Russian forces. As the Russians approached our area, we stayed put. The Russians continued towards Germany. Most of the partisans were joined with the allied forces. I was enlisted in the Russian air force in a camp that formed near Kraśnik. A large number of partisans joined the Polish forces led by Wanda Wasilewska. Many were sent to the first battle on the Wisla River. Few survived that battle. The Wisla was red with the blood of the fallen who fought in that cruel battle. I served in the Russian military until liberation in 1945.

I was released from the Russian military in Lodz. Immediately after liberation, I married, and we traveled to Berlin. From Berlin we traveled to Munich. I stayed in Germany until 1949, when I made aliya.

The Town and Neighboring villages
Yehoshua Ben–Ari
Translated by Meir Bulman

One cannot speak of the Jews of the town without noting the Jewish families which lived in the neighboring villages and were an inseparable part of the Jewish community in town.

Many matters linked the two. There were family ties, business ties, and most importantly, there was the crucial attachment in spirituality; to the rabbi to rule on a question, the Rebbe to sit by his table and enjoy the presence of the Shechinah near him. The synagogue for prayers on holidays, the slaughterer, the circumciser, the matchmaker, the wedding comedian, and the wise Jew for advice, etc.

Thanks to that attachment and the warmth of Judaism, which accepted the rural Jew in his visits to town, he could keep going, at times as a lone man in a sea of gentiles; to trade with them, to have a home, and raise generations while preserving one's Jewish image.

Wondrously, despite the antisemitic condition which the Poles were afflicted with for generations, those village Jews managed to place roots among them, live respectfully, and for the most part were not harmed until the Holocaust. During the Holocaust the blind primitive hatred of gentiles towards Jews resurfaced. In a short time, one forgot everything, ignored friendship and good neighborly ties which were formed and improved for years. Aside from few Righteous Among the Nations, most of the rural population was hostile to Jews, be it actively or passively. The hatred towards the Jew was proportional to the danger he faced.

As one converses with a remnant of those beloved Jews, the impression is that the tragedy those rural Jews faced was mostly due to the Polish population which they lived within. While they were being aggressively targeted, the Poles were those who handed them to the Nazis or executed them on their own. For the sake of historical accuracy, it is noted there was also financial motivation: the riches of the Jew gathered by hard work could be gained only through physical extermination. A store, house, and sometimes land could be possessed. It can be said with near certainty that in theory the rural Jew, as opposed to the more urban Jew, would have a higher chance of survival if not for his neighbors who did everything in their power to fail him.

[Page 267]

A while ago, we, a group of friends, realized the Yizkor book we are publishing would be incomplete if it did not include the beloved rural figures, only few of whom survived.

We were told of one man who lives among us and comes each year fir Yizkor who could tell many details, but feared divulging them publicly. At first, I did not understand that, until one night, we came to his house unannounced and explained the reason for our visit. He had no escape. For the sake of manners, he could not kick us out but it was clear he was doing everything to pass the visit without substance.

We did not relent. We enlisted his wife so she too would influence him to speak to us. Slowly, he agreed to speak to us on condition of anonymity. It was clear to us he was doing everything he could to forget the horrific events he witnessed, which likely will never let him rest. He has founded a new home, is admired, and has successful children. He is invested mostly in hard work to support his new family and ensure the children's future. But when he recalls the horrors, he separates from the present reality and returns to a dark world, all struggle for life without knowing why and for what.

He is from the village of Zdzilowice, about seven kilometers from our town. Unusually, that village had many Jewish families who worked in many fields: agriculture, trade, and crafts. They had their own synagogue and holy utensils. Almost like a little town. They had good neighborly relations with the gentile population, and suddenly, the Holocaust arrived. At first, they made do somehow. Until 1941, no drastic events occurred. People continued their lives and businesses with very few changes. The troubles began when the Russians began to battle the Germans. At that time, the Nazi plan for extermination of Jews was in place. Occasional horrors and killing took place.

In urban areas, decrees, limitations, and assaults increased. It was nearly impossible to travel freely. One night, he snuck into Turobin to visit his

356

mother and other family members. He stayed the night. The next night, he dreamed his family back at the village was in danger. He awoke and snuck out without parting with his family and began running through the fields to the village. His dream became a reality, but he arrived after the tragedy. He found that a day before, a Gestapo unit came to the village, and in one fell swoop cruelly murdered 90 village Jews including his wife and two young sons. Those who remained escaped. In that state, unaware of the tragedy, he appeared in the village and sensed a deadly silence. A gentile friend he came across told him the horrible news and warned he must leave quickly. He could not.

[Page 268]

What does that mean, "leave quickly?" Until a few days prior he was a respected man, admired by his neighbors, safely living on his land, a husband and father, a man of certain wealth, how can he leave? Are his wife and children, to whom he said goodbye only yesterday, no longer living? No, it cannot be. He knocked on his neighbors' door. They feared to let him in, feared speaking to him. He met a young gentile who told him the place he can find the victims. He reached the kill field in the village, a large grassy field soaked with blood and scattered severed bodies immersed in the puddle. He had to find his wife and two sons. But how could he find them in such a valley of death? He suddenly noticed two hats he recognized belonged to his little children. That was sufficient proof for him. He took the hats and began to run quickly.

He returned to Turobin, and was kidnapped or handed over for compulsory labor. He was brought to the sugar factory in Klemensów near Szczebrzeszyn. He was not given food. He was commanded to sing [?] and work. He escaped from there too. With him were also Yakov Leib, Shmuel Itza'le, and Berrish Tregger. They ran under cover of night and hid in the fields. One day in the early morning, they were noticed and shot at. Shmuel was killed. Our man managed to reach Turobin (where else would he run to?) and stayed for a bit. The situation in town was awful. The restrictions worsened. It was difficult to leave and enter town. The local Polish gentiles already gave their opinion and guarded so that nobody escape his fate. Our hero managed to leave anyway, in the open, through the bridge. He was stopped by gentiles by the bridge. He fought them. They shot after him, but he already managed to escape and reach his village. He found there the same terrible graveyard. It was a year and a half following the slaughter. His mission was to find his brother who had also resided in that village from whom he had not heard since the killing.

There were a few more kind gentiles in the village and he managed to hide and survive through them. At the same time, he discovered that 36 others from the village survived and have returned to the village, or more accurately to the forest near the village, hiding and surviving with the aid of friends. It was rumored his brother was among them, but how would he confirm that and contact him? It was a difficult mission, but he succeeded. They began to discuss employment and life together in the underground. He needed a scale to weigh grain. He recalled he once loaned the scale to a gentile friend. He came to him after dark and requested the scale. At first, they were frightened by his sight and asked "Are you still alive?" after they saw he was not dead he was told to wait a bit. They began to prepare to exterminate him. He sensed it. He had no other way but to climb to the roof via a ladder and an entrance in the house. He was followed. He fought and could not be overcome. He was strong and fought for his life. That after he had been through nine circles of hell. The gentile was tired. He went to call for help after he locked all the doors in the house. He saw from a distance a murderer approaching holding a gun, a neighbor. A girl, probably a member of the household probably took pity on him and showed him a window through which he escaped. He ran and was chased until he reached the woods. He hid there a while until he joined a group of Russian partisans which he joined and survived.

That man could fill volumes with what he went through. Where is the talent that could faithfully describe those tragedies, the thoughts, feelings, and dilemmas?

[Page 269]

One wonders when seeing how strong the will to live is, and how strong a person is when facing danger and tragedies strongly inflicted one following another, and still finds the mental strength to build a new life upon the ruins of his first life which was exterminated so tragically.

Indeed, man is a hero and nature is so indescribably mighty, human language cannot describe it. A while later, we reached another survivor of the villages. He is Yitzchak Lander of the village Tokary [?], in the same area of the previous village. He is not interested in anonymity, but you feel that a broken man sits before you, who has been affected by time and the events in his external appearance as well. He is all white and elderly. He is quite old, suffers from illness, and in his eyes one can see a certain degree of apathy. He still lives in his world of memories, which likely do not relent. It is of no wonder after you hear his life story and the tragedy he experienced in the Holocaust.

Apparently, even after he succeeded, survived, and came to Israel, ready to build a new life, he married a second time and fell into the hands of a woman who tormented him until he managed to part with her. She and her family maximized the man's suffering threshold so that the natural strength of the villager we had come to know could not withstand and he shattered. He is now married a third time and our impression is that he has finally reached peace, even if minor, in the sense of "If he has found a woman – he has found good." They live in silent harmony.

The man's story is not very different from the previous story. He was also a respectable homeowner in his village, was rooted in his land and the surrounding population whom he coexisted with for years. He frequented Turobin, and residents of Turobin visited him. He witnessed the horrors and tragedies of his family and others which will not be novel if I detail them here, and who can even describe all of it?

The main part of the story is the life of the escapees – those who hid in the forest near Otrocz. Otrocz was also a local village in the area where Jews resided. The Otrocz woods were known in the area as a thick forest and at times dangerous with robbers. I recall that from my childhood. Poland does not lack forests and the beauty of its natural scenery is contrasted with the human scenery.

The human scenery served to spoil the natural scenery. Those enchanting forests hid among their trees many big tragedies which will never be uncovered. There, survivors found refuge. There, they dug in the ground like mice or moles and lived in the ground in mold and fear of tomorrow. There, one had to suppress any sound of a moan, groan, or cry so not be discovered. There, people did not converse because the voice is traitorous. There they leaned a language of signals like they learned a lowly way of life. Nobody dared emerge from the ground in the daytime. In the beginning, 300 people lived in that manner in the Otrocz woods, spread across a territory of a few square kilometers. At night, people snuck to the nearby village or a close field in search of something to survive by.

The local gentiles sensed it. Even under such conditions, the movements of 300 people cannot be ignored. Occasionally they appeared in the woods accompanied by Gestapo. Or local murdering blackmailers and exterminate one *kriovka* or another. *kriovka* was the Polish name for such a dugout. Our witness said that in a relatively short time almost of the previous survivors were executed. 6–8 survivors remained, he among them.

[Page 270]

It is difficult to describe what those few survivors encountered. More than once they desired the fate of those who were exterminated. How can a person live like a mouse in a hole, in the cold of winter, in the snow, the rain, without food and in fear of disclosing any sign of life? It is of no wonder that Yitzchak and the unnamed hero from the previous story became strong believers in God and religion and to this day live a stringent religious life, and raise their children in that spirit.

They find one explanation for their survival under such terrible conditions; the hand of God. With the help of God they survived and by his mercy they continue to live. Not long ago, our hero Mr. Lander contributed a Torah scroll to his local synagogue. He funded the writing of the scroll which he led in a glorious ceremony to the synagogue.

He lived like that in the dug–out for three years and saw little of his surroundings. He remembers a gentile named Thomas Shchofk who was the fire commander in the village and saw him lead the Germans to the *kriovka*s in the woods and helping in exterminating those living within them. According to his testimony, that same gentile also had a hand in exterminating the Hopen family, the family of Itamar, Mordechai, and Yehoshua who are here with us.

Those woods were also the den of combatants who were defectors from the Russian military or those who had not managed to retreat when the war between the Russian and Germans erupted. They lived as nomads and murdered for survival. They did not have Jews in their ranks, unless they could aid their war for survival.

Mr. Lander recalls that among those hiding in the woods were the families of Shalom Fleischer, Zalman Fleischer, and other families whose names he cannot recall or did not know their names.

360

The extermination in Tokary[?] began on the first night of *Selichot* in 1942. 57 Jews were murdered then. In Otrocz, 20 people were murdered on the 1ˢᵗ of Elul that same year. In Zdzilowice village on the second night of *Selichot*, 75 people were murdered as well as in Dzielce [?] and the other villages. Those were the villages to the north of Turobin. On the road to Janow–Lubelski there were many villages throughout the whole area where many Jews lived such as Tarnawa Szewnia [?] and more.

The town was in that sense the tree trunk from which the villages branched. The Germans in their diabolical plan began with cutting those branches, and only later cut the tree down and exterminated the Jews of Turobin. According to Mr. Lander's testimony, the extermination in town began when 12 *Judenrat* men were forcefully removed from the town and murdered in cold blood near the brick mill. Eight days later, the final extermination of Jews plan began, and others testify as to that.

May the souls of the martyred victims, the pure and honest villagers, be bound in the bond of life, in the bond of the pure souls of Turobin from which they drew their strength.

361

[Page 271]

These pictures were found in the ruins of the Jewish town after the Holocaust.

By all indicators this was on the eve of the third and final expulsion.

Memories

Itte Fass (Zweken)

Translated by Pamela Russ

The owner of the memories was born (1921) and raised in Turobin. She went through the tragic experiences of the Jews of the town, beginning on September 1, 1939, when the Nazi invasion of Poland reached Turobin, and the Nazis' brutal behavior towards the Jews began to be noticeable. Miraculously, she was fortunate enough to save herself – jumping off a marked, running train, and after all kinds of roaming and inhuman suffering she managed to survive. She arrived in Israel and set up a home in Jerusalem, near the very border of *Ever HaYarden* [Transjordan, the other side of the Jordan].

[Page 272]

Her descriptions are filled with exact details, chronological memories of the expulsions and destruction of the entire Jewish population of the town.

1.9.1939

Very early, airplanes appeared on the Turobin horizon. We thought that these were Polish planes doing manoeuvers, but tragically, by midday, it was evident that these were German airplanes, and that by 5 AM, Germany and Poland were already at war. This is how our tragedy began. Already in the second day of the outbreak of war, many Turobiner Jews already ran away from the town to the surrounding villages. At the same time, the town became filled with Jewish refugees who had fled from the cities and towns that bordered Germany. Among the refugees were all kinds – the rich and the poor. The wealthier came by car, others by wagon or on horseback, and then many on foot. It was so pitiful to see these people's pain. Many of them were exhausted and then stayed with us in town, waiting until the Germans would take over the town, and then they would be able to return to their homes. We also noticed a great tumult in the Polish army. They were marching (retreating) without end. On September 18, 1939, after some small fighting, the German murderers marched into town. They were there for a few days, and soon there came a report that Russia and Germany had divided Poland into two parts: until the Vistula it belonged to Russia, and beyond that – in the west – to Germany. There was great joy, and in the first days of Sukkos 1939, the Red Army marched in. I remember how Reva Briliant knocked at the door and happily called out that we should come out into the street. Volvish Vassertreger [water carrier] was carrying a gun, as well as Chaim Treger and others whose names I no longer remember. The Jews breathed in relief, and raised up their heads a little. But sadly, not for long. A few days later, our Polish neighbors put out a rumor that the Red Army was leaving, and the Germans were coming back to replace them. A confirmation of this came quickly from the Zhilkevker military command, that the Russians were moving in only until the Bug River. The youth began fleeing from the city in the direction of the other side of the Bug River. Not all of them were able to decide whether or not to leave their home. The elderly who were so closely tied to their small piece of land from their great–grandparents could not come to terms with this fate of voluntarily leaving the town.

This picture was found among the ruins of the city, after the destruction

364

[Page 273]

I remember a fact: On *Simchas Torah* [last day of Sukkos holiday], Aizik Oberweiss, of blessed memory, was just leaving the synagogue after prayers and he was holding his *talis* [prayer shawl] in his hand. Towards him came riding a Russian Jewish officer. The officer stopped the Jew and asked: "What sort of valuables do you have?" So Aizik took him to his home. The officer burst out laughing and told Aizik to leave the house and run away.

There were also many people who fled to Russia and then came back. For example: Motel Diamant and some other *bochurim* [young men] went to Michałowo, but seeing that there was no place better than one's own home, he returned. Then the Turobiner Christians fabricated a story that on the way he had shot some Polish officers. Motel remained in hiding in a Jewish home from 1939, because the Christians wanted to take their revenge.

*

[Page 274]

The terrible winter of 1949 arrived. The cold was fierce. They began to capture people for work. What kind of work could there have been in a town like Turobin? They snatched up elderly Jews and ordered them to carry rocks from one place to another. This was only a ploy to denigrate the Jew; to mock him in the neighborhood of our Polish friends... At that time, Turobin had a population of 8,000–9,000 residents. Jews from nearby towns that had been burned down came to Turobin – towns such as Frampol, Janów, Biłgoraj. There were also evacuated Jews who came to us, from Łódź, Kalisz, Kutno, and other cities. They gave the people half an hour to leave their homes and 20 marks for each person, and then sent them out to the General Government. We too had the merit of taking in some unfortunate people. The town became very crowded. Every family had to take in one or two people. People were also quartered in former Jewish stores. All Jewish stores were locked up, and the *Batei Midrashim* [Study Halls] were overcrowded with refugees. A typhus epidemic broke out from the overcrowding and hunger. There were houses where all the people were sick and there was no one to take care of them. There was no doctor to be had. Jews were not permitted to be taken care of by a Christian doctor. At the demand of the local Christians, they sent us a Jewish doctor by the name of Hendler from Kraków. He also put up a hospital in the Polish school. They organized courses for the nurses, but the Angel of Death still took his portion. There were about 40 deaths a day. The frost was so bad that we could not dig into the ground deeply enough to bury the bodies. The fear of illness was so great that people were afraid to cross the street so as not to be in contact with other people. But the Gestapo did very little about this. They stole everything they could from the Jews.

One afternoon, Gestapo men from Lublin arrived. There was no *Judenrat* [Jewish Council] yet, so they went to the Council Head Pik and demanded a list of the rich Jews. He treated them well, and answered that in such a small town there were no rich Jews. Then they demanded a list of community representatives. He gave the list of names to them, and soon thereafter they invaded the home of my parents. They separated the women into one room and men into another, and then they began their beatings, demanding that they be given money. They cut off the men's beards along with some flesh. They did this in a few houses. Then they invaded the town's synagogue, broke the lamp and the Holy Ark; they took out the *seforim* [religious books] and burned them, ordering the Jews to dance. After that, naturally with more beatings, they asked: "Where is your God?" This type of incident happened many times.

In this atmosphere, months passed. Then the order came that all Jews, without exception of type, 12 years and older, had to wear armbands on on their right arms, 12 centimeters wide, with a Star of David sewn on. Jews were also not allowed to be outside except from 7 am to 7 pm. At the same time, the Council Chief Pik received notice that he no longer was in charge of the Jewish population. He must select 10 appropriate Jews who belonged to the Jewish community before the war and were also active socially in Jewish life. So he chose ten men, who were:

[Page 275]

1. Shmelke Drimler
2. Avrohom Boimfeld
3. Yechiel Kuper
4. Moishe Shternfeld
5. Berl Halperin
6. Avrohom Zweken
7. Az'ye Kopenboim
8. Tuviah Frumer
9. Sholom Shabtai
10. Shloime Akerman

Doctors' notes were of no help, and neither was money. Pik said that he too would gladly remove himself from his position, because in wartime it was no good to represent a people, but he had no choice, and so they too had to accept this. This is how the Turobiner *Judenrat* was created. At the same time, an aid committee in the *Judenrat* was set up, for clothing and food.

In spite of all these difficulties, there were Turobiner residents who risked their lives and smuggled merchandise, traded whatever was possible, and with that became wealthy. The majority of them ended up in prison, but the refugees ended up the worst. They were also the first to be sent away to the camps because they had nowhere to hide.

In January 1940, the Germans sent an order to the *Judenrat* that by the end of three days the Jews had to pay a tax, a very large sum of money, and if not, all the Jews would be evacuated. There was a great commotion, and no one believed that there was such a large sum of money in Turobin. The *Judenrat* went to the *Landrat* [civilian official] in Krasnystaw. He deducted only a few tokens from the sum, 50%, and somehow they escaped the Angel of Death. At about the beginning of 1940, another order came once again to the *Judenrat* that they must appoint their own policemen. These too were not selected of their own will. The names of the policemen were:

1. Motel Jakobson
2. Hilel Leder
3. Yitzchok Bernstein
4. Avrohom Feder
5. Yonchu Feder
6. Moishe Kopenboim

And the other five were from those who had arrived [newly arrived].

For all kinds of reasons there was a great hatred between the Turobiner Jews and those newly arrived. First, because the Turobiner were better situated and those newcomers were always the ones who were needy. The jealousy, more than once, led to fights and informing. The people became very demoralized. This was also an enemy of the *Judenrat* because they lent money, they sent them to work, they were the messengers for everything bad.

[Page 276]

Months passed like that with hopes for a better situation. One hope everyone had, was that they would outlive them. The Jewish children were not allowed to go to school. They were neglected by their own parents because there simply was nothing for them. You could see how the children played in the Gestapo, how one child treated another if he was a "Jew." A few young girls got together at the home of Zeldele Zilberklang, and there, in secret, they taught children to read and write. The girls were: 1) Rivka Zilberklang, 2) Rivka Veisbroit, 3) Etel Zwekin, 4) Rikel Eidelman, 5) Malka Fuks, and two Kalisz girls.

It was the holiday of Shavous, 1940. The city of Zamosc needed 500 men in a labor camp. There was a tumult in town. No one wanted to go voluntarily. The *Judenrat* collected gifts and went to Zamosc. They negotiated down to 200 men and they drew up a list of young men, age 18 and over. There were those who "bought" people for money to go instead of their son. Shmelke Drimler, Bunim Mayerson, Avrohom Boimfeld, Dovid Bernstajn, Shloime Akerman, and others, got people to go instead of their sons going. The youth suffered greatly there. They worked for many months and were starving and beaten at the same time. Twice a week they received food from the *Judenrat* and received beatings at the same time, and also risked their lives by delivering the food supplies of the Gestapo–gendarmerie.

Months passed in hunger and need, and spring 1941 came with the outbreak of the German–Russian war. The repression of the Germans towards the Jews increased. It was forbidden to eat white bread, meat, and so on. They could also not leave the town, that meant [go only] until the bridge, from one side until the garden and the other until the suburb. They shot Bashele Kopenboim at the bridge. It was evening, and they saw a taxi coming with Gestapo men. Four men got out and began shooting the people in the street. After that, they likely decided that a bullet is a luxury for a Jew so they collected about 30 Jews, herded them into the house of Velvel Liberboim, threw in a few hand grenades, and that's how they went from house to house and killed 112 people, among them young children and elderly. They slaughtered without mercy, anything that came into their hands. The following day they collected the blood and flesh, because ... the bodies were not recognizable, and they made two communal graves. Some weeks later, an order was given that the Jews should remove the tombstones of their families and put them together in the Jewish cemetery. Soon the Councilman Pik arrived and with trucks, drove the tombstones to several places. He paved the road from his home to the municipality with Jewish tombstones. His friend Fliss paved the road from his home to the mill, and they also paved the roads with Jewish tombstones. The Germans asked in mockery: "Where is your God?" That's how the residents became more dejected. They felt that this was not yet the worst thing they had experienced.

[Page 277]

One Friday night, screaming was heard: "Open up, Jews!" Whoever did not have a place to hide was taken into cars. Some were taken to Bełżec where later the gas chambers were built. And some were taken to a sugar factory near Szczebrzeszyn. Then they took only men. The second Shabbath morning, the Gestapo–gendarmerie and the city *Wehrmacht* [armed forces] arrived and they also wanted men in the same sugar factory. But they did not find too many men. This *Judenrat* also hid itself, because if the Germans caught a *Judenrat* member they forced him to search out Jews along with them. Then they decided to take women as well. I too was among those taken for work. They took us to the railroad station and told us to wait there. If they would bring men from Wisoki, then they would let us go free. Making a mockery of us came to an end. Late in the night, when the Wisoki Jews arrived they let us go home, naturally being beaten en route.

The people who were taken to Belzec suffered very much. They also had to be brought food. This was very risky because they shot more than one person who came close to the camp. Nevertheless, every two weeks the *Judenrat* chose two people of these ten and they were regularly brought food and clothing.

Day in and day out, in fear of the future, with beatings and starvation, the summer of 1941 passed. We Jews saw our terrible fate in front of our eyes. Winter 1941 arrived. And at that same time, an order from the German authorities that all Jews must give in their fur coats and fur collars and everything that is made of fur. Anyone who did not obey this order would be punished by death. Anyone they spoke to said that they would rather burn the furs rather than give them up. But life was too dear than to lose it over fur, so within three days there was not a piece of fur owned by any of the Jews, as a piece of pig with a religious Jew. You saw people carrying coats and collars made of stiff linen. They also carried summer coats, and then they had nothing to wear, but they were happy now that the murderers had to become dependent on Jewish fur.

[Page 278]

News came at the beginning of the year 1942, that Turobin must be evacuated. Only craftsmen [physical laborers] would be allowed to remain in Turobin. We did not yet know at that time that evacuation meant death, but we were told that all the people would be going to the Poleszczi forest. It was the Council Chief Pik who carried out the evacuation with the "assistance" of the *Judenrat*. There was chaos in town. Who wanted to leave Turobin? Turobin had a few hundred craftsmen, but primarily Turobin had small merchants. In such a situation, how can a small merchant become a glazier or a shoemaker? But it happened anyway. For money, the Council Chief Pik turned a merchant into a laborer. Lists were compiled, and according to the lists, you had to stay in Turobin. You sold your last things in order to remain on the list, but this also came to naught. The Germans did not stick to the list, it was only an excuse to squeeze out more money from the Jews. Rumors came from other cities that people were being snatched up in the streets. They were being taken away by train and no one knew where they were going. This happened in Krasnystaw and in Izbica, because there were train stations there. Every Jew began to build bunkers for his whole family because they knew that Turobin would not be an exception, and that is exactly what happened.

On July 17, 1942, the first evacuation took place. After the evacuation, everyone came out of the bunkers. They still did not know that evacuation meant death. How the evacuation took place, I sadly cannot describe because I myself was in hiding. But one thing I can say, that the noises of the shooting during the evacuation carried into the deepest cellars as from a horrible slaughter. The largest number of Jews who were evacuated were from the refugees who lived in the *Batei Midrashim* [Study Halls], former Jewish stores, and they had nowhere to build the hideouts for themselves and for their families. During the evacuation, they also shot some people, and since our Polish neighbors informed on us, the destruction increased. On that very same day, Christians from the city and from the village already moved into the Jewish homes. Jewish *seforim* [religious books], and all kinds of Jewish items, *besomim* [spices] boxes [to use as part of the blessing at the close of

370

Shabbat], from which our parents took a sniff at each *havdalah* [blessing at the end of Shabbat], candelabra, prayer shawls – you could sell all that for a few pennies. But who needed all these kinds of things at that time? The rest of the Jews lived in terror. They felt that the worst was coming closer. They thanked God that the Germans were accepting the gifts from the Jews. And what tumult it was. People were asking the *Judenrat* to take money from them, when a year earlier these very people did not want to give them any money. They shivered from each movement and every loud cry. People became simply discouraged, and this was the worst. No one cried anymore and no one reacted when terrible things happened.

[Page 279]

This is how the Rosh Hashanah and Yom Kippur arrived in 1942. There were rumors that the *Judenrein* plan [cleaning out the Jews] was to be enacted in some cities and towns. The German newspaper "*Der Velkischer Be'abachter*" ["The National Watch"] reported that the *Judenrein* action was approaching from the Lublin district, but no one could imagine that such a thing could happen. It was the first Friday after Sukkos, and very early a taxi arrived with Gestapo men. They stopped at Motel Shenker's building. His tavern was owned by a *Volksdeutche* [an ethnic German]. From there they summoned the whole *Judenrat* and the Polish municipal citizens. They took some addresses from former wealthy Jews. When all of these were already in the community center, they did not allow anyone out of there, except for Yechiel Kuper, so that he would bring them some things. I myself was the runner to get all kinds of things, because not everyone wanted to obey the *Judenrat*. And also that time, Yechiel Kuper came to me that I should get him leather for women's boots, two suits, soap, coffee, and a nice diamond ring. I bought all of these and when I gave these things to Yechiel I...

[One line missing in original Yiddish]

they will likely leave immediately. It did not take long, and we saw Yechiel leaving with Feigele Boimfeld and Yitzchok Yaffe in a taxi on the side of Olszanka. A half an hour later the taxi returned without the people. That is how, slowly, they took 14 Jews out to the Olszanker forest and shot them there. The only one who wanted to run away was Shimon Boimfeld. But the Polish police captured him and as a punishment they held him until three o'clock and locked him in chains in the community center. When they took him out, with a raised head he called out in Polish to the Polish policeman and to the Germans, in German: "You'll never get all the Jews out, and then the revenge will be tremendous!" They beat him and threw him into the taxi. They took him on the same route as the other 13 Jews. There was a tumult in town, and by the time everyone gathered their thoughts about what had happened news came from the Zhulkiewer *Judenrat* that until the next day at 8 AM – this was Shabbat morning – no Jew was allowed to remain in Turobin. Looting of our neighbors began immediately. Naturally, this did not get to the point of beatings. We were helpless. They beat Chaim Meyer Lieberboim, and other Jews who worked with leather, so that they were not in any condition to go with the transport in the morning. Before dawn, they prepared wagons for baggage, children, and the elderly, and all the Jews had to go to Izbica.

[Page 280]

That's how, on October 14, 1942, we left our town of Turobin forever. We traveled all of Shabbath accompanied by a heavy rain. We arrived in Izbica in the evening. My father, may he rest in peace, was from Izbica, so we had a place to hide. We went directly to that family. In Izbica there were Jews from all the surrounding areas of Turobin –Zolkiewka, Gorzkow, Wysokie, Zamosc, Tomaszów. Izbica became a Jewish city, meaning that from there, there were daily transports to Belzec and Sobibór.

Then came a notice in the morning that anyone who could pay a certain amount of money could remain behind. The sum was very high and not everyone had that amount. There were also no more places to hide because each Jew had built his own mouse hole for his own family, and Monday, very early on, they began to snatch up people and everyone was assembled at the train station. Those whose names were on the list went to the right, and the rest were sent to the left and then sentenced to death. There was chaos. Everyone pushed his way to the right. Then they encircled everyone and packed everyone into the wagons. The Izbica Jews call this day "Black Monday." Also, 90% of our holy Turobiner were also taken out to Belzec at that time. This was the first Monday after *Shabbos Bereshis* [first Shabbath after Sukkos, beginning of a new Jewish year], October 16, 1942.

In this manner, my place of birth, Turobin, was destroyed, and along with the city, my dearest ones. The only survivors of those who suffered Hitler's hell am I, Chana Pulk, Tzivia'le Einvoiner, Hilel Leder, and Moishe Roizner.

*

Now, about my experiences of October 16, 1942, until the end of the war.

As I already related, we had a large family in Izbica. When we came there on the tragic Shabbath night, we divided up our family. I and two of my sisters stayed with one uncle, my parents and my youngest sister – with another uncle, and my grandfather and grandmother – with their family, because my grandmother also came from Izbica. We all hid in cellar holes. We heard shooting all day. Overhead, where we were hiding, was a tavern, and we heard the laughter of the Christians. There were about 50 people in this cellar.

[Page 281]

We could not sit because it was very low, and it was very wet. Izbica rested on swamps. That's how we sat until people came and said that the wagons were already sealed, and they already saw people, that is Jews, outside. I went up to see what was happening with my parents. Then I saw my mother wounded, and crying, she told me that the head of the *Judenrat* of Izbica arrived, and he was a neighbour of my grandfather in Izbica, and he said that an order had been given that whoever had paid and was on the list, and if they called his name and he was not here in this place, then he would not have the right to live in Izbica after that. Everyone believed them, even though each time their bluffery was obvious. That's how my father took my mother and my youngest sister and they went to the train station. My mother's head was split open with a truncheon, and the women who were standing near her protected her so that she would not be shot. She likely fainted because when she revived, the train with the transport had already left. The ones on the list had also left. That transport that left had 10,000 Jews. There was no more place in town, there were no more people lying in the streets. But everyone knew that those who had remained would have the same fate.

There were men who fled into the forests and there the Poles captured them and turned them in to the Gestapo, or they themselves killed the fugitives. A cousin of mine made a deal with an Izbica Christian who worked in the Izbica magistrate, to get documents in Polish names. And my mother, may she rest in peace, bought these for me and my sister Etche, may she rest in peace, and they were supposed to bring these papers to us. But they could not do this, unfortunately, because on Shabbath night [Saturday night] the evacuation of *Judenrein* began. Once again we were separated from my mother and youngest sister. They were at the home of one uncle, and I along with my older sister and the middle one – were at the home of another uncle. Also, my grandmother and grandfather were hidden somewhere else. We went down without any food, without any water. And that is how we sat until Wednesday afternoon. When they took us out, we could not even stand on our own feet. They beat us fiercely and took us to the theater where thousands of people were dying of thirst. They put us outside around the theater with guards all around – firemen, Polish policemen, German gendarmerie, and Gestapo. There was also my aunt's sister with us, she was from Zamosc and she already had a Polish identification. She bribed a Polish fireman, so that he should get her out along with me. She did not know Izbica, she was from Zamosc. I too was not so familiar with the surrounding areas of Izbica.

[Page 282]

One of the guards approached me and gave me a bucket, and also gave one to the girl from Zamosc, that we should go bring water for the Jews at the theater. I take the bucket, and on the way the girl says to me that she had bribed the Christian and that he would let us escape. I was opposed to doing this because I did not have any Polish documents. Everyone knew me, because I was black, filthy, and had not eaten since Shabbath. This was already Wednesday night. The Christian understood that I was opposed to this and he began to beat me. He was afraid that I would inform on him that he had taken a bribe. So he took us out of the city. We traveled all night. In the morning we heard shooting. We met a Christian woman on the road and asked her where we were. She said that this was Izbica. It was miraculous that we actually came to a village that was three kilometers from Izbica. There, we went into a house where there was an elderly woman, a stranger to us. She gave us some means to wash up a little and some food. The Zamoscer girl said to me that I should not call her Gutche any longer, but Irena, then she gave me her passport into my hand so that I should learn the details written on her passport, that is the names of her mother and father, and so on. As I was holding the documents, I saw a transport through the window. Among those in the transport I saw my sisters and a few other familiar people from my city. I threw aside the documents and ran to my sisters. She also saw her parents and ran to them. On the way she told me that she forgot her passport at the home of the Christian. The transport went to Trawniki for work. That is what they were assured was to happen.

We came to Trawniki in the evening and they took us to the camp. But the camp director did not want to accept us because he said there was no room for us. Immediately, they began herding us to the train station. Jews began grabbing up their money, and whoever still had some jewellery had to give that up. Ukrainians began to chase us into the wagons, ordering us to give them everything because within an hour, we would not exist anymore. They crowded more than one hundred of us into a wagon. People stepped on the elderly and on little children. We had no air. Everyone pushed to the door, to the small sliding door, to get a little air. When the train was standing still, everyone said they would jump off. But when the train began to move no one wanted to jump because the Germans knew that people jumped from moving trains, so the arranged for trains in which the Germans rode as well. One railroad car for the Jews, one for the Germans. The conditions in the car were horrific. The screams went up to the seventh heaven, and no one tried to jump because they were shot immediately as soon as the Germans detected the slightest movement near the small window that was there. I said that I would be the first one, and discussed it with my two sisters, telling them that they should jump too. My two cousins said they would jump too. There were men there who had items with them that could be used to open the window. They lifted me up, I threw over my feet, and held onto the window with my hands. The Germans began to shoot. Then, for the last time, I heard my sister's words: "They shot her."

[Page 283]

But they did not get me. I pushed myself off the train with my feet and remained lying on the ground not far from the opening [of the train], as if in shock. But it did not take long and soon I came to my senses. I was still able to see the train at a distance. I had discussed that whoever would be the second person to jump should stay in his place. I will get to him by using the tracks. I wandered around all night and then found my cousin, no one else. He reassured me that both my sisters had also jumped train, but I never found anyone else.

We decided to go to Chelm because my cousin had an aunt there. He wanted to dress and go join the partisans. When he jumped he could not get through with this coat, so he had to leave it behind. I decided that I would buy a Polish passport and papers there. We jumped not far from Wojsławice and continued on foot to Chelm. Not far from Chelm, a Christian warned us not to continue because in Chelm they were amassing all the Jews and putting them into the church, and from there they were being taken to be gassed. We remained still like stone and decided to go back to the Christian near Izbica where the Zamosc girl had left her papers with her birth certificate. My cousin was supposed to go to Izbica and get some clothing from one of the Christians she knew. We went for eight days without food or drink. We did not have any strength left to lift even one leg. We went with the Polish route, and the second Shabbath at night, we came to the Christian. There I found the document that the girl had left behind. I could not take the passport because it had the picture of the girl. I only took the birth certificate and parted from my cousin. He returned to Izbica.

[Page 284]

He found my mother there and my oldest sister. She had also jumped from the train and wounded her head somewhat as she jumped, and she returned to Izbica. It was my uncle who told me all this, he survived the war. A few days later, they took my mother and my oldest and youngest sister, and my cousin who had also jumped from the train, and other members of my father's family. They had to dig ditches for themselves. They were then shot in the Izbica graveyard. There were 400 Jews.

From Wólka Orłowska I went on foot to Krasnystaw. There I was afraid that Christians from Turobin would find me. I went to the train station and got onto a train that was going to Zamosc. It was Sunday and the work office was closed. I went to a hotel and registered under my new name. I washed up, slept, and the next day I went to the work office. In the work office, there were Poles who worked there, and they had to assemble transports of Poles for the Germans to do forced labor. If you volunteered for this, then they were happy. They understood that these were Jews, but they were protected because they had Polish papers. The officials and the workmen's office told me that I should go to Lublin by passenger train and present myself on Krochmalna Street. Having no other way out I went to the train station again and left for Lublin. On this trip there were Christians whose entire focus was to make fun of Jews: how they are punished, and all this for our terrible sins. I could not participate in these discussions. My heart broke as I passed by Izbica again, as the train station was near the theater. Again from the train I saw Jews around the theater, and guards near them. Naturally they recognized me immediately and they wanted to hand me over to the police. But then a Christian woman who was going to see her daughter in Lublin took me under her wing. She took me to her daughter's home as well because the train arrived at 10 o'clock at night and I had nowhere to go. By now there were no Jews left in Lublin. The following morning, I bought two shirts and some food from the daughter, and then I went to Krochmalna Street. A Christian there dealt with me. "A transport is leaving now," she told me. But I could not go with him because I first needed a doctor's examination and a disinfection. I told her that I wanted to leave today. She probably understood that I was a Jewish girl, and that same day, at three in the afternoon, we left for Lublin.

[Page 285]

After I was taken in the transport, I was taken to a camp where thousands of Christians were already waiting. Among them I recognized a few Jews. There I also met Tzivia'le Einwohner and a familiar girl from Izbica. We went together with them until Dessau. We were in Dessau for a few days in a camp of thousands of Christians. There also came a director of a chocolate factory. He selected 40 girls and took them to Dölitz near Leipzig. We arrived to a camp that was specially prepared for us. That same evening, officials arrived from the labor office and took 15 of us. Twenty five of us remained. Of the 25, 11 were Jewish. There were Jewish girls among us who spoke a poor Polish. Their looks were different from the Polish girls. Also, the religious songs that the Christians sang we did not know – this betrayed us. The Christian girls wrote up a list [of our names] and gave it to the camp director and she gave it to the Gestapo. That same night three girls ran away. They had Jewish friends who worked in the labor office in Dessau with Aryan papers. They went to Hamburg and I saw them after the war.

We, eight Jewish girls, remained. The following morning the Gestapo came to the factory. Each of us was summoned individually into a designated room. I did not reveal myself. Only one of us could not withstand this and revealed herself. They let her stay another three weeks with us in the camp. We thought that they would not take her from us, but one day they did take her from work and I never heard from her again.

This is how our lives in camp began. We worked well and the directors were happy with us. We worked together with German women. After nine hours of work, we went to clean the rooms of the directors. For this, we received a little bit of thread, a pair of stockings, a shirt, because the entire time that we were in Germany we did not have the means to buy anything, and each of us came in one shirt. We were allowed to go to church every Sunday after the first. We, Jewish children, did not go because the Christian girls knew that we were Jewish, so we went to a Jewish friend who worked privately in a business and we spent two hours there. When we were met by Christian girls who did not know us, our Christian girls told them that we were Jewish, so that the entire town's foreign residents knew that we were Jewish. Each ring of the telephone made our hearts race, and we thought now they were coming to get us. We worked in the factory for eight months and when they were short some material to make the chocolate they redid the factory to make it into a waffle factory. Then they sent ten of us girls to work in a courtyard. The rest were sent to the farmers in the villages. Among these ten girls there were five who were Jewish.

[Page 286]

The work here was more difficult but the food was better. We worked in all weathers, in rain and in the cold frost. We had to work in all situations.

I worked there for nine months, and one day I received an order that I should go to the Szczecin hospital to replace a nurse. When I arrived in Germany, everyone was asked about what job they could do, and I said that I was a nurse. I had taken a course in nursing in Turobin during the time of the epidemic and later I also worked in a hospital in Turobin under the supervision of Dr. Hendler. Since the Germans had taken their nurses to the front, they were now looking for foreign nurses. That means, under the supervision of the German state hospital they had put up barracks, and there they took in Russians, Poles, and Ukrainians. The work was very difficult. I was a nurse by day and by night, I was also a cleaner, heat the ovens in the winter, and sleep in the same room as the sick women. More than once, when there was no place – I even slept in the same bed. When I had a free minute I had to work in the operating room, more than once all night, and then begin again regular work in the morning. When I was sick with fever, I also had to do this work. I often heard the argument between the landowner and the hospital director because the landowner needed me back since spring was coming. The hospital director replied that anyone could do field work, it does not have to be a nurse. The hospital won. I remained working in the hospital.

In the city hospital, one of the workers was a Christian, and she was sent to work in the foreign countries and they me to work in the German hospital. The work was easier there because I did not sleep with the sick. I was given a room with two other Russian girls in a barrack. Here, my fears were once more aroused, that they should not discover my origins. I had discussions more

378

than once with the German nurses. They were loyal supporters of the Hitler party. They hated all the races, and especially the Jews. I heard the radio every day in the hospital, I heard the defeats that took place in Russia. We also saw many women dressed in black. We saw that their end was near.

The Germans were convinced that Hitler would distribute new weapons and that would save them. There were also bombings every evening. From one side, this exhausted us physically, I had to help carry down the sick and also medical instruments into the cellar. More than once, we worked all night and in the morning, falling from our feet, and we had to go back to work again. But as to our morale, we were very excited. The Germans sat in the cellars and continually crossed themselves. We, the foreigners, continued to recount anecdotes and this broke their patience. More than once we were teased by a nurse, who was a devil herself in human form.

[Page 287]

At the end of 1944, we saw transports of people traveling in wagons. We asked them where they were coming from and they answered that they came from Silesia. They were also speaking Polish. They said that the Russians were approaching the German borders and were killing everyone of German origin. This is how every day, transports arrived with refugees. We also felt a disorganisation in Germany. For the sick, there had always been the best food and suddenly, there was a shortage of potatoes and sometimes even bread and other life supports. The stores were empty, even for Germans.

April 20, 1945, we heard shooting. The nurses told us that the Germans were shooting at American airplanes. We began to carry the sick down into the cellars. The shooting lasted all day and in the evening, we went into the hospital and they told us that the American military had marched in. I went outside into the street. We saw foreigners looting the German private homes and stores. We took revenge all night. But this did not please me at all. For me, this was the most tragic day of my life. All this time, I thought that I would not survive. I was without a home, without a family, and without the will to continue living.

I also very soon became extremely ill. For six weeks, I was in the same hospital until I discovered that Dölitz was taking over the Russians. I knew that no one from my family had survived, but I had family in America and I figured that I would make contact with them.

The Americans set up transports in the train stations and all foreigners were able to use them. I and another Jewish girl went until the Szwebis region. Over there, was a camp of only Poles. There were about 10,000 Poles there. The over crowdedness was tremendous. I decided to go work in the hospital. I worked for a few months in a hospital supported by UNRWA. Once, a Pole from Dölitz came to see me in the hospital. He was from the camp security. He said that a tall military officer had come in, an American, and asked about the Jews in the camp. He found it necessary to ask if I would speak with him, then he would wait near the police office. Understandably, I went to him right away...

[lines are missing in original Yiddish text]

———

[Page 288]

From a Living Witness – Chana Gevirtz, of blessed memory

Berl Zontag

Translated by Pamela Russ

When I left my home in the year 1939, I still had my entire family. In 1945, when I came back from the Soviet Union, I no longer found anyone. My entire family was murdered by Hitler. But it was not simple for me to find out that they were wiped out, because from our town, as I had heard, only two Jews survived: one was Shloime Fleisher, who had hidden himself in the village Tokary, not far from Turobin, with farmers; and the second, was a woman by the name of Chana Gevirtz, who had hidden herself in many different hideouts, in fields and in bunkers, and in the end, she hid herself in the home of a Polish man, in our town, by the name of Antek Teklok.

When I arrived in Lublin, my only goal was to find the two surviving Jews of my town, from which I had earlier ...

[lines are missing in original Yiddish text]

... out. He extended his hand, and greeted me. This was the first time in three years that I heard a Yiddish word. I told him about my tragedy. Then he told me that I wasn't the only one, that not far from the Szwebis area, there was a

380

camp of only Jews. He himself was a rabbi of the American Jewish military. His father was connecting families of Americans with the survivors of the Holocaust. I gave him details about my family in America and within ten days, I received a letter from my cousin.

I immediately presented myself to UNRWA as an orphan and I received the appropriate papers to go to America. Meanwhile, I found out that an uncle of mine had survived, but he was very sick, and I decided to take him to Germany, because now he was with strangers. The border between Germany and Poland was open. I went to Poland, but I was not able to take my uncle to Germany. He had become paralyzed. I was with him for four months until he died.

I was no longer able to return from Germany, because the border was now locked. A little while later, I got married and settled in Szczuczyn. My husband and I registered in the Haganah to go to Israel. I could no longer step on the cursed Polish earth. In 1948, we left Poland to go to Israel to build our new home in a secure way.

Tragically, I was one of the only people of Turobin to survive.

[lines are missing in original Yiddish text]

[Page 289]

heard that they were the "one in a thousand" in order to find out who in my family was still alive. All day I am wandering through the streets looking at every face, maybe I will find someone from my family, because there were Jews who told me I should not go to my town. From these very same people I found out that right after the liberation of Turobin the first young man, by the name of Motel Fuks, a hat maker arrived. The Poles murdered him. After him, another man by the name of Yosel Kofef arrived and he also had the same ending as the first young man. When I heard this I decided not to return to Turobin.

I decided, at any cost and no matter what to look for one of the two surviving witnesses. I and my friend Yitzkhok Leikhter, with whom I had come from the Soviet Union, walked through the one street that was sparsely populated with Jews, Lubarski Street, and we looked for the two surviving witnesses who would tell us about the final fate of our families. Yitzkhok Leikhter also left his father behind when he left home. This was Moishe

Leikhter, with sisters and brothers and also his whole family from his mother's side. This was from the Aron Diamond's dynasty.

Hour to hour, our nerves became more tense because no matter which Jew we asked about Khana Gevirtz the answer was always that she was in Lublin, but where she was living now, nobody knew. So we decided to go to the market and search among all the Jews who were there, maybe we would find her as we were looking through all the Jews from our town, because with all the Jews that we were seeing now, it was possible that we were seeing them for the first time in our lives but they were so similar to us and so close, as if they were from my own town. I feel a foreignness to every non-Jew and have a strong feeling that no matter where I turn, I am in an ocean of hatred. Every Jew is being stabbed by the Poles with their gaze. They also did not believe that they would ever see a Jew in front of their eyes and wherever the Jew would be, he would always look all around him [in nervousness]. One Pole smiles to the other, as they say: "There is still some merchandise left for us, we cleaned so many of them away, we will be able to get rid of these as well. But meanwhile, the Red Army is bothering us a little so we have to hold ourselves back, but the time will come..."

I swear to you that walking through the streets of Lublin the moral pain was so great exactly as if I would have been physically beaten. If not for the fact that I had to look for my fellow townspeople, I would never have come to these streets. If you would see how the Poles are standing in the stores where Jews used to sit for many years, and how the Poles are over-stuffed as fat pigs, and they are the ones who helped get rid of the former businesspeople by sending them to Majdanek, where all that remains is a pile of ashes – the Jew is left with only one wish [Hebrew]: " *Timkheh es kol hayikum me'adam asher al pnei ha'adamah*" [Yiddish]: "God's Hand should bring a flood to the entire world, and the world should go back to vastness and emptiness." There should be no human dominance over the world, let the wild animal be the actual leader on the earth, because that is what he was created for. He has not lost any of his animalism. But the person, who, throughout all this long time has raised his humanness, in one minute, lost his whole human form.

[Page 290]

But the wish remains only an actual wish. The world is not going under and meanwhile we have to become aware of that which is already been lost. For that goal, we continue our search, and we have found it.

382

I will always remember the moment when I went to the place where Khana Gevirtz was standing. When I saw Khana from a distance, I recognized her right away, but she asked us what we wanted. At that moment we did not answer her. I was thinking to myself that that which I wanted, no other person of another nation could want ("I came to you to get Job's news"; referring to the Book of Job and reports of all the suffering). The fact that we did not give her any answer forced her to think about us and then in a minute she recognized us. She broke out in a hysterical cry. "Is it you, Berl, the son of Yerakhmiel and Frumit Zontag?" And she immediately added, "Yes! There is a memory left of you but from me and of my nineteen souls, not one person is left." And Khana Gevirtz begun to tell me how the first pogrom came about in Turobin.

This was May 15, 1942. A troupe of Germans came into Turobin only for a few hours. Whichever Jew fell into their hands was dragged into the home of Velvel Liberboim. In that manner they herded together 33 Jews among whom was her sister Frimtche. This was the first murder in Turobin and at the same time she was the first victim in the family. The one who helped the Germans was the well–known enemy in the town, Genik Brankewycz, may his name be erased, a terrible anti–Semite and hater of Jews. Another assistant in this slaughter was a Pole who worked for Weiler as a shoemaker. When the Germans completed their murderous act and saw that all the Jews were already lying spread out on the ground, they left the city. At that moment, the above–mentioned Poles went over to see if anyone was left alive, they noticed that one person who was lying there was moving. This was Fajtche Liberboim, the daughter of Velvel Liberboim. When she lifted her head and saw that the Pole was standing next to her, she pleaded with him that if he would let her live she would give him all the possessions that she had. But the Pole answered her:

[Page 291]

"You, Jew, lie down and I am going to shoot you." Nothing helped, she lay back down on the ground and he shot her.

This was told to us by Jontche Feder, the son of Moishe and Mindele Feder, who was the thirty fourth Jew in that murder event, but he was only wounded slightly and was able to run away and recount everything that happened there. On that day, the entire Liberboim family was murdered –

from young to old with the exception of the youngest daughter Sheva Liberboim, who was not home at the time.

After that episode, Jewish life was already chaotic, bands of city Poles assembled under the direction of the Brankewyczes and the Wages. They organized the so–called firemen whose job it was to stand on the roads and not permit the Jews to run away from the city. When they captured a Jew on the road trying to run away, they brought him back to town to the German police, or they themselves did the job. In many cases, nevertheless, some Jews managed to run away to nearby villages where they thought they would be able to save their own lives. To deal with this, the Poles from the city organized the so–called firemen from among the farmers of the surrounding villages. Their job was to find the Jews who were hiding in these villages and we have to say that the Polish farmers fulfilled their tasks to perfection. When a fireman knew that a Jew was hiding somewhere, he dragged him out of there. If he wanted, he was able to kill him on the spot. In many events they would capture the Jews, tie their hands with rope and summon the farmers, and then take the Jew to town to the German police. All along the whole way, the Jew was tortured with all kinds of pains to show the German authorities how loyal the citizens were.

This is what the only surviving woman of our town Turobin, Khana Gevirtz, told us. Her children remained in hiding along with other Jewish children, in her house. Some Poles, along with Genik Brankewycz, their commander, went in there and asked her where she had hidden her children. She answered that she did not know. One can only imagine the moment when murderers come in to a mother and ask about her children and she knows that they are going to their certain death. She knows that her own children are lying hidden in her house with children of other Jewish mothers, and she must remain silent. The murderers of the Polish nation go around the whole house looking for Jewish sacrifices to slaughter on the altar, which means remove them from the nation of Israel. But this time the sacrifice will not have an altar nor a designated time, but where it is found and when it is found, the Jewish lamb can be sacrificed in any house, in any place in a city, in a village, in a field, in a forest, wherever you find it. Every soul that carries the name Jew is fitting for a perfect sacrifice, a slaughter of people who belong to other nations.

384

[Page 292]

The murderers continue to take Jewish children from the hideouts. Among these children is also her son Pinkhas. The children are taken away not far from the home and then they are shot. This is what elderly Khana tells us. This is already the second sacrifice of her children and the mother of these children sees that the situation is so bad and tells all the other children to quickly leave the house. The children go on the road that leads to the village of Czernieczyn. But on the way, the commander of the Turobiner firemen, Genik Brankewycz, may his name be erased, captures them. He takes them back to the city and the German police orders that they be thrown into prison. Tomorrow they would all be shot. The old mother knows all of this and also that her children were in the prison and that the following day they would all be shot. This mother sees that all is already lost so she herself decides to go to the prison to be with all her children. She wants to die with them but she is successfully able to bribe the Polish guard of the prison and the children manage to flee from the city. Mostly, it was men who were taken captive with the express idea that they were needed for work. For that reason she sends away her son and the daughters remains with the mother.

Chana also knows how they took out Avrohom Boimfeld with his only son Shimon, Moishe Szternfeld, Yechiel Kupfer, and Moishe Kopenboim and a few other Jews in the Olyszanker forest across Wantrubka's brickyard, and then shot them there. She also knows that my father's brother and son by the name of Shachna Zontag was shot by Germans in the village Tarnowa, together with his wife and child, and along with them, also Avrohom Boimstajn's son. They were taken behind the city on the wagon and they were shot behind the house of Sweis Miller. They were also buried there. Chantche Shmelke's was shot when she was just giving birth to a child. She also knows about each time hidden Jews were brought from the villages since there were no Jews left in Turobin. At that time, she was hiding at the home of a Pole whose name was Antek Teklok. The Jews of Turobin who knew the abovementioned non–Jew would never have said a good word about him. They would never have thought that he would risk his life by hiding a Jew in his home.

After all the evacuations, the Polish farmers brought a Jewish family from Turobin into the city. This was Daniel Krajtman with his wife Golde. Their children, it seems, had a place where they were able to hide illegally. In the end, the farmers found them and brought them to Turobin. The joy of the Poles was without bound because this happened long after there were already no Jews seen.

[Page 293]

When they were taken through the streets of Turobin, they shut their eyes tightly out of great pain so they should not see what was going on around them. Young and old from the "good Polish society" of Turobin gathered around them to greet them and see these "wild animals" that call themselves Jews. For these Jew haters, this was simply the greatest pleasure in their impure hearts, that after such a long time, after they had already sent out with the second evacuation all the Jews from Turobin, a whole Jewish family came into their hands, the family Kreitman and their children. The Poles, with a bitter irony, persisted in asking: "How were you able to hide for so long and what kind of audacity do you have to stay alive, at the time when all the Jews have already been killed?" As they were taken through the streets of the city, every Pole wanted to fulfill his *mitzvah* of wiping out the Jewish nation until the very last Jew, because it did not occur to even one of them that this was not the last Jewish family of Polish Jewry in general, and of the Jewish community in Turobin specifically. Therefore, everyone slapped them around, and the youth of the Polish thugs tore pieces of the clothing that the family had on them so that in that way they could fulfill the *mitzvah* of wiping out the last Jewish family in the town of Turobin. After taking them to the streets, they were taken to another place and all of them were shot.

All of this, the only living survivor knows to give over, as she herself saw all of this. After that, since she was in hiding, she knew that she would give this over as an actual witness. As was mentioned above, Khana was in hiding by Antek Teklok in the attic, and when the man of the house came at night he told her everything that happened in the town all day. One thing I cannot find out from her is the exact dates of events, for example the month or the day, and that is because of her gruesome experiences. There were 29 people in her family, her own children and grandchildren, and with her own eyes she saw how each one of them was bestially murdered. Fate had it that the old mother and grandmother should be the only one remaining alive of her entire family. No wonder she is completely broken and cannot give over exact dates. She does know that all of this took place in the year 1942, meaning that all the killings began in the year 1942. The first evacuation was at the beginning of

1942 when the Jews of Turobin were taken to the train station to go to Izbica, to the Lublin circle, and where they arrived after that, nobody knows. But according to the survivors they were taken to Bełżyce. The second evacuation took place in the month of Cheshvan [October] 1942.

[Page 294]

Memoirs

Yechezkel Boimstajn, Kibbutz Alonim

Translated by Pamela Russ

In memory of my perished father and mother, sisters and brothers, along with all the Jews of my town, I am writing my tragic memoirs. It is not simple to write these memoirs, particularly of such a gruesome era. But I wish to add my own memoirs to that which is now being written here in Israel.

There was a small town named Turobin, in the Lublin province, where every Jew had worries about earning a livelihood, worries about children, and fears of the tomorrow, and it still had to be good, because this was our destiny.

My parents had a bakery, in partnership with my father's brother. There was never any peace there. There were always arguments. One always had complaints of the other. They say that when there is no peace, there is no blessing. They argued for so long until they finally split. They made two bakeries from one. Each one considered himself to be on top of the other. Even if he was on the bottom, still he wanted to be on top.... They were enemies until each cursed even their father. When I turned twelve, I had to help in the bakery. When I got older, I had to go work elsewhere. This was in the year 1937: I left my mother and father, young sisters and brothers. My heart ached. I worked for a year and amassed some money, then went back home and gave my earnings over to my parents. I resumed working in my father's bakery. But this did not go on for long, because the war broke out; Germany invaded Poland. The war did not last long. Even before the Germans invaded our town, I decided not to stay there because we heard and knew that when the Germans would come it would not be good. I decided to go to Russia. I went over to my father when he was standing and praying. This was Hoshana

Raba [during the days of *Sukkot*] in the morning. He was wearing his *talis* [prayer shawl]. I told him that in my opinion it was better for me to go to Russia. My father said that he did not want to go to the Communists and also told me not to go. Afterward, when I went to say goodbye to him, he said that he was sure he would never see me again. I said my goodbyes to everyone and left.

And now new challenges began. Alone, without any family, I roamed with other refugees. We came to Lemberg, and it was black before my eyes. There was nowhere to stay, even for one night. There was nowhere to buy any food. In this way, we wandered for some time until I found out that the Russians were registering people to go to Donbass in the mines. You had to enlist to work for two years in the mines. There was no other choice. The Russians took our Polish documents and the following day we arrived in the train station. We had to be ready by ten in the morning. As we were standing and waiting at the station, and a commander arrived with a list in his hands, and began to call out names. For each name he called out, that person had to go into a car [of the train]. In this way, all the wagons filled up. The doors were locked, and we did not see anything at all during the entire time the train was moving.

[Page 295]

When we arrived in Dobnass it was already dark, but here everything was prepared. We were divided into blocks of fifteen men. It looked like barracks because there were only men there. It was already cold but it was much better than in Lemberg. Here we had food and a place to sleep. They gave us a few weeks of rest after which they told us that we would go and become familiar with the work. They gave us work clothing and when they let us down into the mines it became dark in front of our eyes. They took us to the mines for three days and divided us into work groups. The labor was very difficult and also life-threatening. Almost every day one of our Jews became a victim. Some stopped going out to work because their energies were depleted. Some started to try to escape. Everywhere there were fewer and fewer men for work. When I looked around the barrack, I saw that more and more beds were empty and so I went over to the supervisor of the mines and in the name of all the others I asked him to use us according to our physical abilities because were no longer able to work in the mines. He said that there were no factories for us here [in which to work]. We asked him to let us go, and once again he did not consent. He told us that we had to work for two years and after that he would free us

388

from the work in the mines. But we did not wait for him to free us and we started to free ourselves. We simply ran into the nearby small towns. I ran with a friend of mine to Satzi; it was not very cold there; the surroundings were nice and the city was pleasant for us. We went to enlist so that we were able to work but we were declined first because we did not have any Russian papers, and second, they noticed that we were deserters because we did not have any documents to show.

[Page 296]

The Turkish border was close by and there was also a port (Namal) not far away. The police ordered us to leave the city within twenty–four hours or we would be arrested. When we heard that, we returned to Meinkop. In that city they let us get work, but we had to report to the police once a month. This lasted for a half a year until finally we received Russian passports. I left Meinkop and went to Krasnodar and my friend stayed there. He worked as a shoemaker and once again I began to work in a bakery.

But this did not last long. The Germans invaded Russia. I could not figure out what to do with myself because the Russians ensured that the Germans would not come here. I remained working in Krasnodar.

One beautiful bright day when I came home from work, I received a notice that I had to appear for military service. I went and reported. There I found a good many people. It did not take long and they took us to the cargo station where the cargo wagons were already prepared for us.

When the train began to move, we had absolutely no idea where they were taking us. But when the train stopped, we asked the conductors where we were and they told us that we were behind Kiev and that the Germans were shooting to the other side of Kiev. When we got out of the wagons there was no one left to ask because the commissioners had fled like mice. The Germans continuously bombed Kiev. Masses of people fled from there, and I was also among the fugitives. Everyone wanted to save themselves from death. The Russians wanted to give us over to the Germans. We knew that we were not considered military because among us there were also undesirable people. Running like that, I do not know how after a month's time I came back to Krasnodar. By that time, the Germans were already behind Rostov. I went to present myself before the commissioner, but as soon as he saw me, he asked how did I get back, then ripped out the gun from his belt and shouted at me:

"I am going to shoot you, Jew! You don't want to fight in the war!" I stood like that before him shaking with fear. I told him that everyone in our train had fled, and that included all the commissioners. He continued to scream and I thought he would kill me any second. But he finally understood that I was not the only one who had fled. He knew that the commissioners had committed sabotage and he became a little gentler towards me and gave me permission to go work in the same place. But it did not last long.

[Page 297]

In a short time, once again we were summoned to the military. And then they chased us on foot out of Krasnodar to Rostov because there were no trains going there.

We travelled at night, because the Germans were bombing all day. And so we came to Bataysk, ten kilometers from Rostov. There was nowhere else to go because the Germans were everywhere. We wandered around the area of Rostov. Suddenly, in the middle of the night, we were ordered out and told to march, where to – we did not know. But one thing was clear: wherever we would go, we would fall into the hands of the Germans. But orders are orders. It was a cold, snowy night, and we heard that not far from here were Germans. We arrived in a village where all the houses were empty. There were no people. Here, they told us that we should form into a unit. We knew that something here was false. They told us to lie on the bare earth, but we could not sleep because of the cold. We huddled together and it was a little warmer. Everyone began to snore. I hardly slept that night. But from time to time, I napped for a few minutes and trembled with fear. In my dreams, my father and mother came to me and said: "Do not be afraid, everything will be fine." And that is how it was.

Soon it began to dawn. Those who were asleep barely awoke themselves, and soon there was an order that we had to evacuate the village because the German tanks were approaching. Everyone fled as quickly as possible. I came to Rostov and began thinking about how I was going to rescue myself.

I went into a courtyard, but I did not know if there were any Jews there. I spent the entire night there. I went into a wooden hut and slept there all night. When daylight began, I left because I could no longer tolerate the cold. I left the hut even before it was light and I did not know where to go until I saw a ray of light through the splits of shutters. I went over to the house and

390

knocked on the door. They told me to come in. When I entered the house, I saw they were packing up their things. They asked me if I was Jewish, so I began to speak Yiddish to them. They told me that they hoped I would stay with them, and then told me to go to the train station. There were masses of people already there, mostly Jews. I remained close to the Jewish family and together with them we went to Kavkas [Caucasus]. We arrived not far from Tiflis [Tbilisi] and went to a village. There they sent us to work. I said that I was a baker, so they sent me to work in a bakery. After I had worked there for an entire year, they gave me a new passport. I understood from this that I was now able to leave so I went to Tiflis [Tbilisi]. I worked there until the end of the war.

[Page 298]

It was now 1945. When I heard about this on the radio I began to think about going back to my home in Poland. But how could one go to Poland? I began to take the trouble and consider this. I prepared all the legal papers for traveling until Lemberg. I did not want to wait longer so I caught a train and arrived in Lemberg unencumbered, as someone freed from the war. You were not able to travel further, you had to wait until the Jewish committee would organize all of it. I had to wait a whole month until there was a train to Lublin. When we arrived in the Lublin station, we got out of the cars [of the train] we heard the Poles talking amongst themselves: "Where are these Jews coming from? Hitler said that he killed all the Jews." When I heard this I was very frightened and since I had nowhere to go I only went where my eyes led me, thinking about how I would get to the town of Turobin, and that maybe I would find someone there from my family. Nobody could have imagined such terrible destruction. As I was walking around, I came to a market where people from the area were gathering together. One person from my town, a Christian, recognized me. He came over to me and began to interrogate me asking where I had been during the time of the war. I also asked him about my town Turobin.

The Christian told me that the Germans had murdered all the Jews in Turobin and he convinced me to go into the town with him. I agreed. Just as I was going to go with this Christian into my town, an angel came to save my life. This was a woman from my town, by the name of Khana Bazilis. The woman grabbed my hand and dragged me down from the wagon where I was just about to leave with the Christian. The woman began to tell me what had happened to her and how she was the only one left alive because a Christian that knew her had hidden her. So I went with her to her place and then she told me that I was lucky that she had arrived just as the Christian was trying to trick me to go to Turobin, because they would have killed me there.

Two Turobin Jews, Josef Kopf and Motel Fuks, met their death that way when they came to the town in order to get the things from their homes that they had hidden before they fled from there. For one week we sat there and cried for all those who had been killed. After that, she remembered that an uncle of mine from Bulgaria was alive, but she had no idea where he was at this time.

[Page 299]

She told me to stay with her until my uncle would come because whenever he came to Lublin, he usually came to her house. I obeyed and slept and ate in her home, because I really had nowhere else to go. In a few days, my uncle appeared. But when he came into the house, I did not recognize him: He was dressed completely differently. I knew him from before when he used to dress as a *chassid*, but he did recognize me. We embraced each other, kissed each other, and cried terribly about the great tragedy that had happened to us. When we released each other, with tears in his eyes he told me how he and his son had saved themselves and how his wife and all his other children were found by the German murderers in a stable of horses where they were hiding.

We stayed in the town overnight, eating and sleeping at her home. The following morning, we left her, and my uncle and I went to Bitam (in German: Beiten). Before the war this was a German city but after the war this city belonged to Poland. Here, my uncle managed to get a few rooms right after the war and here I stayed alone for a few weeks because my uncle and his son would travel around for trade. When I saw that my uncle had left me alone and did not leave me any money, and I had nothing to eat, I found a community where they took me in. When my uncle came back home and did not find me, he found out from the neighbors where I had gone. When my uncle found me and asked why I had left, I said to him, understandably, that I had no choice. By that time there were already a few settlements in the Lublin area. In a short time they sent me over to Sosnowica. I stayed there until the whole settlement left Poland and went to Israel.

392

Meanwhile, my uncle came to visit me in the settlement and of course I welcomed him very nicely, better than he welcomed me when he took me into his home. At that time, he offered that I go with him to America, but I naturally declined because I was afraid to travel again. He parted from me upset, and he went on his way. Meanwhile, I stayed and worked in the bakery of a Christian until I had to leave the city with the Aliya [group immigrating to Israel] and they I no longer went to work. They made me get drunk so that when the baker would come and call me to go work, I would not be aware of it. They would tell him that I could not go to work because I was drunk. When my boss came and called me, unfortunately, he left with a bad impression of me and of Jewish workers in general.

[Page 300]

In about a few days' time, we were ready to go to Israel. We were told not to take any heavy bags with us because we would have to pass through several borders on foot. Since we did not have much to take with us, we were able to follow this order. The next night we came to the Czech border. There was a small town there, it was called Krinitz [Hranice]. We had to wait here for several weeks before we could "*shwartzen*" [sneak out at night]. Soon, in the middle of one night, they awoke us to get moving. We did not have to wait long, we were all prepared. We went into a forest until light began to dawn, and by then we were in Czechoslovakia. Everyone's heart beat in fear. The entire way, we were not allowed to breathe loudly. We were not allowed to hear a sound from anyone. That is how we crossed the first border from Poland to Czechoslovakia. It was not a simple thing to steal across a border in those times and in those places. Meanwhile we stayed there for a few weeks until we had to move on.

The second border was from Czechoslovakia to Austria. Once again, we took to the road at night. We crawled across the mountains and in the forests in the dark where you could not even see the stars in the sky, that's how dense the forests were. When we came to the Alps, it was extremely difficult to climb. We had to go on all fours, until we arrived, midday, in an Austrian village. We rested there for a few hours until cars arrived and took us to Vienna. They took us into a house where people were already waiting. The house was Rothschild's hospital. We remained in Vienna for a few months, until we were able to continue onward. This border was already easier to cross. Only the first two were difficult to cross – from Poland to

Czechoslovakia, and the German–Austrian border. Now we crossed into Germany. They sent us into a camp by the name of Lopreis. Here we also found many Jews who had come before us. We remained in this camp for half a year, until we had to cross the Italian border. This was also a difficult border to cross, because we had to protect ourselves from the British. Once again, we traveled all night, and early in the morning we arrived in small village in Italy. They hid us there until dark. Then cars came and took us to Milan. Here they took us into a vocation school that was called Codvarela School. From there they took us to Rome. There they took us to a Caesar's villa in an Italian village that was called Grotta Ferrata. Here we also remained for half a year. While we remained in each of these places for a long time, we studied Hebrew.

[Page 301]

From some individuals, we already heard that we would be going directly to Israel. That is why they kept us far from a port, so that the British would not suspect that we wanted to sneak away to Israel. In that village, our directors assembled a lot of people, and they had to take us in secret, because there were English spies that moved around there, and they guarded all the ships. We had to leave there also at night. They took us from the camp to the seashore. From a distance, we saw a ship weaving in the waves, but we still did not know how we would get to that ship.

But our directors had already prepared everything beforehand. We were taken to the ship in small rubber boats, then one side of the rubber boat was tied to the large ship, and from the other side they pulled a rope to the seashore. That's how we were pulled to the ship, and there was a ladder already set there for us. That's how we climbed onto the ship. There was no other way because there was no port there. They filled up the ship as they pack up a barrel with herring. The crowding on the ship was so dense that since there was no room for each person to stand on his feet, you had to lie down. This was an old cargo ship. They packed in about 1,500 refugees until the middle of the night, and when the ship began to move, we felt as if we were wavering just as small children feel when they are being rocked inside. The heat inside the ship was so terrible that we could not stand it. So people went on deck to get some air. When we were already a distance from the shore and the waves began to hurl at the ship from all sides, we began to vomit. Those who lay on top, vomited onto those who lay underneath. You cannot describe the agonies of these inhuman conditions in which we had to live on the ship. It was an illegal journey in all regards.

When we were already fifty kilometers from Haifa something happened to the ship. Water began to flood into the mechanical part of the ship. The ship stopped floating. Now there was no choice but to call the British for help. Soon airplanes appeared and very quickly two large ships appeared alongside our ship. They began to pump out the water from the rooms of our ship and our ship straightened itself out on the surface of the sea. Some of the British who had boarded our ship began to ask where we were going. Understandably, everyone answered that we were headed to Israel. They laughed at us and said: "Your ship will not be able to go there," and they disembarked from our ship. They were summoned again, and they came to us and told us to get onto their ship. So the elderly and the pregnant women boarded the other ship. They were taken to Cyprus. Then, through a loudspeaker, we were once again asked what we wanted. We answered that we wanted to go to Israel on our ship. So they tied up our ship with ropes on either side to two of their ships, and we hung up our blue–and–white flag. And that is how we arrived in the Haifa port. Then they ordered us to board their ships so that they could take us to Cyprus. Of course, we did not want to do so. A fight broke out. Whatever fight we had left in us, they received over their heads. But it did not help. We battered them; this was our thanks to them for saving us from drowning. I remember that I threw a package of butter into the face of one of them and he started to lick his face with his tongue. But nothing helped. They were stronger than us. With force, they carried us over to their ships and took us over to Cyprus into a detention camp.

[Page 302]

This took place on the eve of Passover 1947. Here in the camp, we also went through terrible experiences: We slept in tents, and we suffered from thirst because they did not give us enough water to drink. When some of us began to demonstrate, and we approached the gates, the British began to shoot at us. Soon, two of our people were killed. The others fled, nothing helped. We remained in that camp the entire summer, and after that we were taken into a winter camp where there were no tents, only tin huts which we could not go into during the summer because the tin was scalding hot. But it was freezing cold there in the winter. This is how we suffered for all of two years, because we wanted to go to Israel. They considered us to be the worst criminals.

In 1948, when the United Nations declared Israel as a state, the British freed us from the camp, and ships came from the State of Israel and began to take us over there. I arrived in the Land of Israel only in January 1949. From the ship they took us to *Beit Leyad*. Here everyone had to pass through a military commission who selected those who would have to go immediately into military service. Those who were freed were taken to *Beit Olim* in *Pardes Chana*. From there we were sent to *Ma'aborot* [where there were refugee and absorption camps] because they wanted to make sure we had somewhere to sleep. They took us into a place where there were beds and mattresses, but there was still nothing with which to cover ourselves. The supervisors said we had come too late, and there was no one to talk to.

[Page 303]

This was after four years of wandering. I saw what was going on here. I collected my few rags and left to one of my cousins. He welcomed me warmly. He too was a new *Oleh* [immigrant to Israel]. After, he told me to go to Haifa. There was a *Beit Olim* [residence for new immigrants] in *Bat Galim*. But you needed to have connections to be permitted entry. It was very difficult for me to get this, but they did let me in. Shortly after that, I began to think: "How is this going to work? I have to find a job. But I am a baker!" I went to a bakery and asked for a job. They sent me to the *Histadrut* [General Organization of Workers in Israel]. I went to the *Histadrut* and the secretary of the bakers said that he did not believe that I was a baker. So he sent me to a bakery for an examination. He gave me a note. I did not know what he had written there. I could not read Hebrew. I worked in that bakery for an hour and they sent me back to the secretary with a note saying that I was a baker. He started asking me where I lived, whether I had a family, and of course, I answered that I had just come from Cyprus, and that I had no one, and for now I was living in *Bat Galim*. So the secretary said to me that he could give me work for a day or two but he really had to take care of those who with a family and children. He said I must come twice a week to register, and each time he sent me to another bakery. I asked him, did he not think that a single person needed to earn money to survive? He answered that there was nothing he could do to help.

396

Life became terrible for me. I thought it was very important for me to come to my own country after such a war, but even here I was suffering. I thought that for now I would stay in the *Beit Olim* and after a day's work, I would go there and rest. But they did not allow me to do that. The *Beit Olim* was in a large barrack of British people. The house was crowded, and not all the residences would get together at the same time. Some left to work, and meanwhile others arrived. It was impossible to rest there after work. Now it was different. Many new *Olim* were arriving. They were being brought to Israel on cargo ships, and here in Israel, they were being provided with everything: money, work, and with housing. That is how it is in this world: One person cries and another is successful. For me, it was not good at that time. I saw there was no other way out, other than to get married. But how could I allow myself to do this? I had no money, no place to live, I could not even get any work. But I actually did get married, with the help of my uncle. Then my wife gave birth to a girl, and I gave her a name after my dear mother, Raizel. Then came another daughter, and my uncle who was just in Israel at that time for a pleasure trip, asked me to give the name after his mother Serel. This was my mother's mother. I looked around at that time and saw that it was not good to live here with two children because the walls were peeling. This was an old Arab house – so I left to Kibbutz Alonim. I am living here now for ten years. My young daughters have since grown up and they are studying well along with the other children of the kibbutz. I am working here in my vocation, in a bakery. Here in the kibbutz there are other families from my hometown Turobin.

[Page 304]

To close my memoirs, I want to wish that our children have a happier future than we had, that they honor all those who died, whose names should never be forgotten.

Under the Murderous Regime

Tzivia (Einvohner) Blutman

Translated by Pamela Russ

On Friday, September 18, 1939, in the afternoon, the Germans marched into Turobin. They came through the Lublin road. The town was filled with homeless people who had fled the Germans, beginning in the Posen area – Kalisz – Lodz. Many had hoped to find their secure place of refuge in this burdened town of Turobin. Everyone hid in cellars and other places in fear, and waited in terror and anguish for the cruel fate that awaited them.

One day passed, and then another in calmness, and we did not feel the [presence of the] Germans. They did not bother us. A week passed like that. As life goes, people began crawling out of their hiding places and everyone went to do his work – some to business, some to their own vocation. People began to believe that the treatment by the Germans was not as terrible as the homeless had related, and that it was so–called gruesome propaganda.

One fine morning, we saw groups of tens of Gestapo men coming from the direction of the municipality. These men went from house to house snatching up girls for work that required them to wash the main road to Turobin with rags and buckets of water. The torture began. They poured buckets of water onto those who were thought not to be working quickly enough. They also beat [the girls] mercilessly. This is how the daily work went until the winter, when the snow began to fall. They also snatched up people to peel potatoes for the military. At the beginning of the winter, they also took men for work, regardless of age. They were led into the forests around Turobin to chop wood and to clean the snow off the roads around Turobin. At the beginning of the year 1940, a group of Gestapo men came to Shmelke Drimler with an order to create a *Judenrat* [Jewish Council] that would be responsible to carry out all orders that they would receive for the Jews in Turobin.

[Page 305]

Meanwhile, many more refugees from the surrounding cities arrived. These were people whom the Germans had chased out from their living places. They were placed in the Batei Midrashim [Study Halls], synagogues, and even in the large synagogue, because all the houses were already overcrowded with the homeless who had come earlier. The objectives of the *Judenrat*, among others, were:

1. to provide food for the refugees, medicine, and a roof over their heads

2. to put Jews into forced labor

3. to maintain order in the town

Shmelke created the *Judenrat* with the following people:

1. Shmelke;
2. Baumfeld Avrohom;
3. Zweken Avrohom;
4. Kuper Yekhiel;
5. Halperin Berl;
6. Shneider Shulem (Shabtai Golan);
7. Frumer Tuviah.

The departments of the *Judenrat* were as follows:

The committee to provide Jews for forced labor was comprised of: Berl Halperin, Schulem Schneider, Tuviah Frumer; and the committee to take care of the refugees was comprised of: Shmelke Drimler, Yechiel Kuper, Avrohom Zwekman. They hired police to keep order in the town, comprising of: Hillel Leder, Mottel Jakobson, Yitzkhok Bernstajn, Yakov Frumer, Shmuel Roizner, Avrohom Feder, and a few of the refugees. The goal of the police was to capture people and put them into forced labor; to search out bunkers where people could be hiding to avoid being sent into forced labor, and so on.

During this time, a typhus epidemic broke out among the refugees as a result of poor nutrition and lack of medical help. Daily, 15–20 people died. The help that was provided by the American Red Cross from Switzerland through American Jewry somehow secretly disappeared. Only little bits reached the refugees. As the epidemic began to take over the town, the *Judenrat* took drastic measures. They created an isolation point for the sick in the *Beis Medrash* [Study Hall]. This was under the supervision of the city paramedic Leizer Shtreicher, and a women's committee assisted him: Miriam Zweken, Khana Bezis, Henye Hersh–Leyb's, Tzivia Zimmerman, Rokhel Fuks, Frimtche Milkhman, Tzipe Miriam Moishe's, and so on.

As soon as the typhus epidemic broke out, the Germans closed off all the roads to Turobin and secured each road into and out of the city. They severely punished those who did not follow these orders. Disregarding the regulations that ruled with hunger, some Jews – among them Shimon Glass, Hersh Jakobson, and so on – risked their lives and smuggled in flour and other life necessities into the town, and in that way somewhat appeased the hunger which, along with the typhus epidemic, reigned over the Jews in Turobin.

[Page 306]

The First Evacuation

One Thursday, in the month of May 1941, between three and four in the afternoon, a group of SS men tore into the secured ghetto, under the direction of SS men Bauer, Shindler, Riger. They grabbed up people in the streets and took them into Pinye Gewurtz' store, and into Velvel Liberboim's store, and into Yitzchok Goldberg's home, and saying that it is a shame to waste a bullet on a Jew, the SS men threw grenades into the above-mentioned places. In that way, with terrible anguish, more than 100 Jews were killed. Among them were: Soroh Dvoire Lender, Shaindel Braverman, her mother Golde Reva Braverman, Khantche Drimler, Perele Drimler, Mottel Shenker, Shaindel Tzukerman, Khume Kraitman. As they ended their bestial work, the Nazis ordered wagons to be brought, and under their watch and escorted with beatings, they placed the bodies, which were so beaten up that they were beyond recognition, onto the wagons and took them to the cemetery and buried them in a mass grave.

At the first evacuation, I, along with a large group of Jews, was sent to Krasnystov the following morning. We arrived in Krasnystov in the evening, exhausted and drained. We were detained in a water field, and that is how we spent the entire night – in water and in the cold. In the morning, we were set out in rows, and then ordered to march in the direction of the train station. When we arrived there, each of us received a piece of bit of bread and some black coffee from the Krasnystover Jewish police. Soon a rumor began to circulate that we were not being taken to work but that they would make soap out of us. From whom and from where we heard this news, I do not know until today. Very soon, I decided to save myself, that means to run away, and soon there came a good opportunity for this. A group of Christian women passed close by to us. They had come from the village to Krasnystov to go to church. Soon, unnoticed, I joined the group, went along with them, and when we approached the church I quickly turned away from them and went back in the direction of Turobin. A farmer's wagon was coming up this road.

[Page 307]

The farmer, from the village Kozienici near Krasnystov, stopped and asked me where I was going. I answered him that I was just discharged. He believed me because I looked like an Aryan, and he took me into his wagon.

War Tragedies
Aryeh Goldfarb
Translated by Pamela Russ

A. The Tragic Murder of Arohom Peltz and His Wife Necha

When they were in the Sobibor camp, Avrohom Peltz and his wife Necha were among those who organized the uprising of the camp. He himself murdered two SS guards with a simple pair of scissors, and he was able to flee from the camp with his wife. They hid in the forests for a long time until they were able to come to the village of Wierszewina. In that village, the farmers surrounded the two [husband and wife] and cruelly murdered them.

B. Yakov Feder, may his memory be blessed

When Yakov was in the camp Majdanek, Yakov told an SS man that there was a lot of money and foreign cash hidden in his house in Turobin, and he was prepared to show the SS men the hidden place on the condition that he was to be freed from the camp. The SS men accepted this, and they drove to Turobin. He showed him the place and they actually did find the entire fortune there. They took it all and then immediately returned Yakov Feder to Majdanek, where they murdered him.

Experiences
Yerachmiel Fogel
Translated by Pamela Russ

In Memory of My Murdered Family

I am relating my brief memories which I am writing here – printed for the holy Yizkor Book of the Turobiner community, with the intention to perpetuate the memory of my family and my town for the children's children, and for generations. They should know about the most bestial deaths which were used by Hitlerism on our parents, brothers, and sisters.

happened to her and how she was the only one left alive because a Christian that knew her had hidden her. So I went with her to her place and then she told me that I was lucky that she had arrived just as the Christian was trying to trick me to go to Turobin, because they would have killed me there.

Two Turobin Jews, Josef Kopf and Motel Fuks, met their death that way when they came to the town in order to get the things from their homes that they had hidden before they fled from there. For one week we sat there and cried for all those who had been killed. After that, she remembered that an uncle of mine from Bulgaria was alive, but she had no idea where he was at this time.

[Page 299]

She told me to stay with her until my uncle would come because whenever he came to Lublin, he usually came to her house. I obeyed and slept and ate in her home, because I really had nowhere else to go. In a few days, my uncle appeared. But when he came into the house, I did not recognize him: He was dressed completely differently. I knew him from before when he used to dress as a *chassid*, but he did recognize me. We embraced each other, kissed each other, and cried terribly about the great tragedy that had happened to us. When we released each other, with tears in his eyes he told me how he and his son had saved themselves and how his wife and all his other children were found by the German murderers in a stable of horses where they were hiding.

We stayed in the town overnight, eating and sleeping at her home. The following morning, we left her, and my uncle and I went to Bitam (in German: Beiten). Before the war this was a German city but after the war this city belonged to Poland. Here, my uncle managed to get a few rooms right after the war and here I stayed alone for a few weeks because my uncle and his son would travel around for trade. When I saw that my uncle had left me alone and did not leave me any money, and I had nothing to eat, I found a community where they took me in. When my uncle came back home and did not find me, he found out from the neighbors where I had gone. When my uncle found me and asked why I had left, I said to him, understandably, that I had no choice. By that time there were already a few settlements in the Lublin area. In a short time they sent me over to Sosnowica. I stayed there until the whole settlement left Poland and went to Israel.

Meanwhile, my uncle came to visit me in the settlement and of course I welcomed him very nicely, better than he welcomed me when he took me into his home. At that time, he offered that I go with him to America, but I naturally declined because I was afraid to travel again. He parted from me upset, and he went on his way. Meanwhile, I stayed and worked in the bakery of a Christian until I had to leave the city with the Aliya [group immigrating to Israel] and they I no longer went to work. They made me get drunk so that when the baker would come and call me to go work, I would not be aware of it. They would tell him that I could not go to work because I was drunk. When my boss came and called me, unfortunately, he left with a bad impression of me and of Jewish workers in general.

[Page 300]

In about a few days' time, we were ready to go to Israel. We were told not to take any heavy bags with us because we would have to pass through several borders on foot. Since we did not have much to take with us, we were able to follow this order. The next night we came to the Czech border. There was a small town there, it was called Krinitz [Hranice]. We had to wait here for several weeks before we could "*shwartzen*" [sneak out at night]. Soon, in the middle of one night, they awoke us to get moving. We did not have to wait long, we were all prepared. We went into a forest until light began to dawn, and by then we were in Czechoslovakia. Everyone's heart beat in fear. The entire way, we were not allowed to breathe loudly. We were not allowed to hear a sound from anyone. That is how we crossed the first border from Poland to Czechoslovakia. It was not a simple thing to steal across a border in those times and in those places. Meanwhile we stayed there for a few weeks until we had to move on.

The second border was from Czechoslovakia to Austria. Once again, we took to the road at night. We crawled across the mountains and in the forests in the dark where you could not even see the stars in the sky, that's how dense the forests were. When we came to the Alps, it was extremely difficult to climb. We had to go on all fours, until we arrived, midday, in an Austrian village. We rested there for a few hours until cars arrived and took us to Vienna. They took us into a house where people were already waiting. The house was Rothschild's hospital. We remained in Vienna for a few months, until we were able to continue onward. This border was already easier to cross. Only the first two were difficult to cross – from Poland to

I was born in Turobin in the year 1922 to my parents Shmuel and Dvoire Fogel, of blessed memory. My father Shmuel, may he rest in peace, was a tailor. Many respectable people did their tailoring with him, and many knew him as an honest and decent person. He had a beautiful face, with a long wide beard, and followed the *mitzvos* [Torah commandments] religiously. He prayed every day and was very pious. My mother Dvoire, of blessed memory, wore a wig and was very religious. They ran a religious Jewish, refined home, and had a peaceful life. My mother gave birth to six children, but five remained: three sisters and two brothers. But now, with great sadness, I am the only orphan remaining.

[Page 308]

I remember when I went to *cheder* [early religious school] and later to the Polish school, I heard more than once anti–Semitic remarks from the Polish students. When I was older, I joined *Beitar* [Zionist Movement]. After that, my friend Yisroel Aberweiss convinced me to join *Hechalutz* [Youth Movement trained in agriculture in preparation for immigration to Israel]. I remember well the expressions of the *Chaverim* ["comrades"] at the time, that "our only future is in the Land of Israel."

On the eve of the outbreak of World War Two, in the year 1938, my father, of blessed memory, died, and I was left an orphan, at not even 16 years old. The entire responsibility of supporting the family rested on me. It is easy to understand how difficult it was for me then.

The war broke out in the year 1939. Hitler's fascist army shot and bombed, and in just a few days, marched into Poland. They grabbed people for work, beat them, and murdered them. My mother cried and worried all the time about what would happen to her children. One morning, we saw the Red Army marching into Turobin. Happy faces appeared, but this lasted only a few days. It was Simchas Torah [last day of Sukos holiday]. They said that whoever wanted, should go with them to Russia because they were leaving us and they did not encourage the Jews to remain with the Germans. I decided to go along with the Red Army. The time was short, so much so that I did not have time to say goodbye to my family. When I was already in the military car, my youngest sister Necha'le brought me a piece of the cake that my mother had baked for Simchas Torah. From a distance, I saw my mother, brothers, sisters, all waving to me. At that time, I thought this was temporary, and that in a short time I would see my family. To my great sadness, that was the last time I saw them.

In the year 1941, when I was in Russia, Hitler's army invaded Russia. They moved forward, and the Russians receded. Bitter reports were heard, that just as the Hitlerists captured a town, the first victims were the Jews. I began to worry about the fate of my family.

In the year 1944, we heard that Hitler's army was beaten, and on a certain day, I heard on the radio that the city of Lublin was liberated by the Red Army. At that time I was in Bataysk, in the region of Gruzye. At that time, communication was very difficult. You also had to have permission to travel, but I took a chance and went from town to town on the roofs of trains. I traveled like that for two weeks, until I arrived in Lublin just for *Kol Nidrei* [Yom Kippur prayers]. In Lublin, I found Jews from the Polish military, and in the Peretz–House [shelter for refugees] I found Jews who had saved themselves. Then I found out that from my big family, there was not even one survivor. I also heard that several Jews who had saved themselves, were murdered by the Polish bandits.

[Page 309]

After these bad reports, I decided that I would no longer stay on these soiled Polish grounds that were drenched with Jewish blood. I went back to Russia, the war was still going on. But the end of the Nazis was already close.

In the year 1945, I was in Moscow, and heard that Hitler's downfall had come. I decided to marry and start a new branch of the family.

In the year 1957, I decided to go to Israel. For that goal, I first went to Poland. When I was in Poland, I decided that I wanted to visit the town of Turobin. I remember that when I was on the bus with my cousin, the Poles looked at us contemptuously, and as we passed the cities of Piaski, Krasnystov, Wysokie, all were *Judenrein* [cleansed of Jews]. When I arrived in Turobin, a shudder overtook me. Not one Jewish soul, the houses destroyed. I asked a Christian, where is the courthouse? He asked me if I had come to sell my house. I recognized the house where I had been born and knocked at the door. "Please come in," someone answered. I entered and saw that there were Poles living there. So I left to the municipality to get my birth certificate. On the way, I noticed, and my cousin noticed that suspicious Poles were following us. Suddenly, a Christian approached and said that we had better leave the city quickly because they were getting ready for us, and as a "friend" he suggested that we "leave" [run away quickly]. The Christian helped us get onto a bus, but the thugs wanted to break into the vehicle. Miraculously, we were able to escape. When we arrived in Lublin, the preparations did not take long, and my family and I soon left for Israel.

———

[Page 310]

In Memory of the Holy Martyr Mendel Szmarak, of blessed memory

Dov Zuntag

Translated by Pamela Russ

Without a doubt, many people remember Reb Mendel from our town, Reb Mendel Szmarak, an Orthodox, modest, refined Jew, with his majestic beard and his thick, overgrown eyebrows, through which his eyes looked with difficulty. In his home – they looked high up, and when he was outside – they humbly looked down on the ground.

He always used his free time to study a page of *Gemara* with great affection. On Shabbat, after the *cholent* [hot meat and potato stew served on Shabbat], he always sat in his designated place in the *Beis Medrash* and studied. If someone had taken his seat before him, he did not make a big deal of that; he found his own corner where he would be able to do his holy work. In contrast, there were other scholars who were egotistic with "glorious ancestry" and they [the scholars] demanded their own place even if others had come before and their seats had no numbers. Mendel did not belong to that category.

[Page 311]

His wife was called Shprintze, of blessed memory. This woman was a Cossak Jewish woman. She took it upon herself to support the family just as other women of her sort did, those who wanted to be a "footstool" to their husbands in the next world. She used to go to the village, do trade with the farmers and especially on market days, when that was the day, she took a

404

sack of products over her shoulders and when she found it necessary, she shouted out to whichever farmer. Of her own husband, she said that he was an idler.

Mendel Szmarak, Shprintze, daughter, son, and the children

It is understandable that this sort of *Eishes Chayil* [woman of valor] took care of the family and this also meant that the husband had the distinct opportunity to continue his religious studies.

This is how the family Szmarak lived calmly and quietly, not wealthy but comfortable. The one thing that created disturbance and serious worries for them was that in their elderly years they still had a daughter who needed to be married. Their daughter Fradel was already not such a young girl according to the criteria of the times: When a girl was already over twenty, she was no longer considered a young girl, and Fradel belonged to this category of an older girl. One has to be careful to note that when a girl of these years was still in a refined home this was a great tragedy and a source of constant pain. The religious Jews, however, believed that a destined spouse comes from heaven and if God has no mercy and does not send the match, maybe that daughter was judged to be passed by. In such a situation, you had to take every opportunity to make a match, no matter what.

In these situations the custom was that when a sort of girl such as Fradel did not find her mate and her parents were financially comfortable, generally "money is the answer to everything," and they would already find an appropriate young man. But since Reb Mendel was not a rich man, it was actually difficult to find a match. To find just any mate does not even enter anyone's thought and there was a great conflict between two serious choices: either this daughter would heaven forbid, remain single, or she would have to be displaced from the great tree of ancestry and marry into a family that was a little beneath her. Only Elijah the Prophet was able to discard the hierarchy of the ancestry and measure this by the pound and by the gram. To this day, it is impossible to explain how certain people maintain an index of each individual family, how great their ancestry extends, actually according to every period and comma.

[Page 312]

And for these very reasons a potential mate for Fradel was not so quick to happen. However, Reb Mendel successfully found a wonderful spouse for his son Chaim, of blessed memory, and for his daughter Menucha, he found a wonderful son in law, Reb Yakov Fogel, may he live long. And why should we not continue the tradition?

The women who occupied themselves with making matches were not professional. They did this more so for the sake of God rather than for the sake of making matches. Usually, these women, on a regular Shabbat day or on a holiday would visit one side of the potential in-laws and soon the secrets of the discrete dealings of the match would be carried across the entire town.

406

If the event would end in a fortunate outcome then this would be carried out with a large dowry and then they would write up a contract, and from the time of drawing up the contact until the wedding would take a bit of time. This "bit of time" had no boundaries. To do this quickly meant about half a year. It could also have taken a year or two. The reason for these conditions depended on the speed in which the bride's side was able to prepare her dowry and the outfitting [all other home necessities], and sometimes tragically, the match was dissolved, and the bride and groom had to forgive one another (for the terrible shame that they had caused the other person).

Since we know how a match was done, the matchmakers and their assistants took themselves to Shprintze, Reb Mendel's, and they presented a potential groom for their daughter Fradel. The potential groom was Avrohom Frumer, Reb Yosef Frumer's son. Even though the ancestry of Reb Yosef Frumer was not as great as that of Reb Mendel Szmarak's (as we know it was weighed by grams), but because the bride did not have a wonderful dowry, and the groom Avrohom had his own workshop and assistance, and he also earned a good living, Shprintze said that if her Mendel would say amen, then the match would go through. Despite the fact that Shprintze wore the pants in the family and was the wage earner, in these decisions Reb Mendel had the final word. And Reb Mendel agreed with his wife and his daughter Fradel. He did this because he was a good man and he saw their impatience. Therefore, he gave his blessings of amen and good fortune.

In truth, Fradel and Avrohom already knew each other from the *Tarbut* [Hebrew culture center] library. They used to meet there. But Heaven forbid that either of the in–laws should know about this because the institution of the *Tarbut* was "totally non–kosher," and every father denied that his child visited such a place.

[Page 313]

And so there was an engagement and then a wedding, and then grandchildren were born.

This couple was happy and Reb Mendel and his wife Shprintze had even more joy and more pride. As was his habit, Reb Mendel would go to the *Beis Medrash* every day. His house was at the edge of town and the *Beis Medrash* was located at the opposite end. His *mechutan* [son–in–law's father] Yoske, did not live far from the *Beis Medrash* where the young couple also settled. It was as if it had been written in Heaven that where Reb Mendel passes every day, that is where his daughter would live. Reb Mendel had to pass through the entire marketplace until he reached the *Beis Medrash*. As we know, Reb Mendel did not lift his eyes off the ground [in modesty], but when he passed the home of his daughter, he intentionally lifted his head and looked. Who were his eyes looking for? Obviously he desired to look at his grandchildren to embrace them and to say with his lips "these are my offspring" and these are His "holy ones" and "future generation" but, "man thinks and God laughs." Hitler's slaughter arrived and he took all the best.

May their memories be blessed!

Khone Blutman – House Brother Avrohom Treger
Translated by Pamela Russ

Khone Blutman, son of Sone and Faige, born in the year 1918. After the death of his father, he was raised by Yitzkhok and Faige Treger. Because of the difficult economic situation in the home, in his younger years he had to work as a shoemaker's associate for Sholem Shabtai, and help the elders with his income. In spite of his hard work, he was full of energy and a lust for life, loved by all his friends and acquaintances.

As a youth, he joined the Bund party [Jewish labor/socialist party] where he actively worked, and by nature he was gifted, and he successfully took part in the Turobiner dramatic circle.

When the war broke out, he and other Turobiner fled to Russia and he settled in the town of Boguslov, near Kiev, and there he met his future wife Zhenny Lukow and he also established himself there with his skills in the local drama circle. At the outbreak of the war between Russia and the Nazis he voluntarily enlisted in the army, and in the bloody battles at the main station of Voronezh, he died a heroic death in 1941. His memory remains deep in the hearts of his surviving brothers and all his acquaintances.

Avrohom Treger – Born in Turobin in the year 1919. With the outbreak of the war, he fled to Russia with the Red Army's retreating train from the Lublin district. He settled in the town of Ortov, near Vinytza (in Ukraine). In that town he got married and set up a family.

[Page 314]

With the outbreak of the Russian–German war, he voluntarily enlisted in the Red Army to fight against Hitler's military. He died as a hero in the slaughter of Rostov in the year 1941.

From right to left: Khone Blutman, Avrohom Treger with his child

Memorial Calendar
Jewish Communities in Turobin and the Surrounding Area
Translated by Meir Bulman

Zolkiewka — Expulsion to Izbica, 5 Cheshvan, 5703.

Goraj — Expulsion to Belzec, 8 Elul, 5703.

Turobin — Expulsion to Izbica, 20 Tishrei – 20 Cheshvan, 5703.

Janów Lubelski — Transfer to Zaklików, 20 Tishrei – 20 Cheshvan, 5703.

[Page 315]

Józefów — Final [?]liquidation 20 Iyar 5702
Expulsion to Bełżec, 22 Cheshvan, 5703
Ghetto Liquidated Spring 1942

Modliborzyce — Expulsion to Krasnik 20 Tishrei – 20 Cheshvan, 5703.

Krasnobród — Aktion, 19 Elul 5702 – 20 Cheshvan 5703.
Local murders (Judenrein) 15 Cheshvan, 5703.

Krasnystaw — Expulsion to Izbica, 22 Iyar 5702, 20 Tishrei – 20 Cheshvan, 5703.

Krasnik — Final liquidation 21 Cheshvan – 21 Kislev 5702.

410

Rejowiec   Final Aktion, Tishrei –
Cheshvan 1, 5703
and Elul 5703

Dates from designated book at Yad VaShem, Har ha-Zikaron, Jerusalem

Holocaust Survivors from Turobin. Some battled alongside Partisans in the forests, some found refuge in the Soviet Union. After the war, they gathered in Ulm, Germany.

Top row: **Peretz Fink, Shlomo Ziss Melekh [?], Yosef Yegerman, Avraham Fuks**
Second row: **Abish Blitman, Yosef Kopf, Yisrael Zeidel, Chana Givertz, Hillel Ledder, Gitel Tzitrenbom, Yakov Mitzner, Yakov Gutwiling, Hersh Biterman. Children of Yakov Gutwiling (Avituv)**

[Page 316]

Family Zimerman Moishe

Top standing from right: **Eliezer Zimerman, Berel Zimerman, Yenta his wife, Yitzkhok Zimerman, Dovid Zimerman**
Seated from right: **Mikhoel, Alte his wife, Moishe Zimerman, Khaya his wife, Eidel his daughter, Arish his son, and Shloime his grandson**
[Note: The two women in the picture seated next to each other – Alte and Khaya – may be reversed, since the daughter Eidel looks younger than wife Alte, so the note in the caption may be in error.]

412

[Page 317]

The Town in Its Life

[Page 318]

The Town of Turobin

Itamar Hoffen

Translated by Pamela Russ

Turbin or Turobin, that's what the city was called. From a geographical point, the town was located in the Congress [Kingdom] of Poland in a lower region of black terrain. The town belonged to the Lublin administrative division [province], surrounded by near and far towns and cities, for example: 50 kilometers from Lublin on the south side; 40 kilometers from Zamosc, 20 kilometers from Szczebrzeszyn, 20 kilometers from Frampol, 35 kilometer from Biłgoraj, 10 kilometers from Wysokie, 10 kilometers from Zholkiewka.

The city was cut by a river into the shape of a parabola. The river came in from Targovisk (northwest) and ran in the direction of Szczebrzeszyn. The river also had a name. If the river would have had no name then no divorce would have been possible in Turobin, and since there were divorces, the river was called "Fohr."

To describe the years of establishing the Jewish community in Turobin, we have no historical documents to show and exact details. We only have the opportunity to enlighten the past with a few facts:

Reb Nechemia Fleisher (with the nickname of "Momek"), a Jew of about 90 years old, one Shabbat day, when he was standing in a corner of the Lublin–Malinkowa Street, near Avrohom Motzke's house, related a little bit of history, and this was in the year of about 1930.

When he was a young boy, he remembered a little about the rebellion, and his grandfather told him that he remembered how people would speak with fear when they mentioned Bogdan Chmielnicki's name. He recounted:

When Chmielnicki and his Cossaks marched into Poland and they were already near Rove–Roske, several Jewish families came to settle in Turobin. They spoke a German Yiddish and sang a song "Bogdan, Bogdan, you are a traitor," and so on. It has not yet been confirmed that the city was established in the 17th century, but you can deduce that this was about in the 16th or 17th century.

[Page 319]

Also, as it appeared, there were one or two profiteers who were like that by inheritance [ancestry], and these profiteers approached the Turobiner Jews, with the good will of the princes who were very wealthy and lived in the area, and were rich because of the blessed natural agricultural conditions. The princes rented the fish ponds, the fruit orchards, etc., from the Jewish farm lessees. And this goes back to the royal rule in the 17th century.

As was customary, that each town and city convinced itself that it was the central point of the surrounding area, each one used this fact to show that it was surrounded by other cities, and each town and city was able to use this fact and hold itself as the actual "center." But each city that was actually at the ocean and not surrounded by other cities was not able to say that it was a "center." Well, this city was a port city.

This is how the city of Turobin characteristically argued, that it is a little bit of a "center," just not a geographic one, but a spiritual one.

In the town there were baths, ritual baths, a *Beis Medrash*, a synagogue, three *chassidic stieblech* [smaller, informal synagogues belonging to the *chassidim*] and a stiebel for working people, and the *Rav* [main rabbi] had a special synagogue that served the Kraśnikower Rebbe and his *chassidim* [followers].

The financial institutions and sources of food were: a cooperative bank, a general cooperative fund, and a non–profit aid fund. There was a handworkers' union of all trades, about 100 people, that took in all kinds of handworkers: carpenters, tailors, shoemakers, gaiter makers, rope makers, belt makers, hat makers, and other handworkers.

Other than these abovementioned productive forces that provided the necessities for the population of the town and for the farmer population of the surrounding area, there were no other provisional bodies.

There were two flour mills with power stations, which ran in partnership with the Christians. The rest of the Jewish population worked in trade. Some were shopkeepers – small and larger stores, which sold everything for people's needs; and some were small merchants, who lived from trade on the market day. The traditional market day was on Thursday, and the earnings from the market day sustained a large part of the population. If the market day was not too successful, there were some merchants who would ride around and sell land products to the farmers of the surrounding villages, as well as on the other days of the week.

During the year, there were several organized fair days. Merchants from the surrounding cities came to these types of fairs: from Zamosc, Szczebrzeszyn, Krasnystaw, Piaski, and so on. The workers sold all their merchandise at these types of fairs.

[Page 320]

In a few short lines, in order to understand the economic constraints in which the Jewish population of the city existed, you can say that the farmers in the surrounding areas produced and sold the agricultural life–products, and the Jews bought and acted as middlemen for the farmers' products. They also sold back to the farmers the products which they [the workers] had acquired, and other non–agrarian needs, for example: better goods, manufactured goods, food, and other household needs, all of which the merchants imported from the largest cities such as Lublin, Zam Zamosc osc, Łódź. The portion of Jews that did not have business with the farmers lived off the other Jews. These jobs were involved with religious life: ritual slaughterers, sextons of the synagogues, beadles of the synagogues, rabbis, teachers, widows, orphans, and so on. There were also some Jews who worked with the land, families who worked with meat. The other jobs of the population were: butchers, wagon drivers, bakers, booksellers, bookbinders, and so on.

Educational and cultural institutions were: a Polish public school, a Beis Yakov school [religious girls' school], a "*Tarbut*" school [secular Zionist] which was busy with several breakdowns [of their work] because of the challenges of maintaining their budget. There was a *Tarbut* library, a Polish library, and a culture–league library of the Bund; there was a *cheder* [religious school] for young children (three–year–old beginners with the "yellow teacher"); three teachers of young children; a *cheder* that prepared the students for *Beis Medrash* [higher learning in the Study Hall]; some studied with Reb Mordche and others studied on their own.

The political, social and religious organizations comprised of the following: the Zionist organization; *Hechalutz Hatzair* organization; revisionist organization (*Beitar*); *Agudas Yisroel* [religious organization]; *Bnos Yakov* [religious organization for women and girls]; the Bund [Jewish labor movement]; Gerer *chassidim*; Alexanderer *chassidim*; Kraśniker *chassidim* and Trisker *chassidim*.

The general population of Turobin in the year 1939 counted 5,000 souls, included here were about 40–45% Jews. In 1929, the Jewish population totaled about 50%. Then the city council was comprised of Jews and Christians from the center of the city and also of the Christians from the suburbs. Because of the fear of "if they will increase," the governor of the province decided to extend the borders and to include the Christian population from Olszanka and Zalawcze into the council of Turobin. The end result of this was that the Jewish population remained at 40%. It is worth noting that the greatest taxpayers for the city council budget came from the Jewish population, not proportional to their numbers and not proportional to their earnings. The use of the budget was not implemented for the Jewish population according to their numbers, and even more inconsistent with the Jewish taxpayers' numbers.

[Page 321]

In general, the services of the city council for the population were minimal, and even less so especially for the Jewish group. The wooden sidewalks were only around the city on the streets where the Christians lived. Also, the planted trees were not in the Jewish quarter. The large, round marketplace, in the center of which stood a large wooden cross, was empty and poorly lit.

The highway that led to Lublin, cut through the town through Pilsudski Street and stretched across the bridge of the river "For." The rest of the streets were not paved, and there were no other sidewalks. When spring arrived, the snow melted and the rains came, and all the streets became filled with mud. There was like an actual river of mud, and in some places the depth was as

416

much as half a meter. On a moonlit night, the mud river looked like a large, fine mirror. As mentioned, the city rested on low, black terrain, and the waters had nowhere to recede. The periods of the mud stretched into many weeks until a strong sun came and dried it all up. Until the time that all of this dried, there was movement of many wagons, and the pools of mud were so worked through by the wheels of the wagons that they became as a type of clay out of which you could even build houses. These pools of mud presented terrible discomforts for those youth who liked to go out early mornings in fancy boots. They jumped like spry deer from stone to stone and from one veranda to another. Many times fortune was not with them and they would fall with one boot into deep mud. But if his kaftan was not a modern one with a traditional length, then his kaftan also got immersed, add to that his *Tzitzis* [fringed garment worn under kaftan, over shirt]. This is how the young man entered into the *Beis Medrash*, an embarrassed person, mumbling to himself as if to say: "This is how the street looks!"

The houses around the large marketplace were built as a closed *khes* [eighth letter of the Hebrew alphabet, ח]. On both sides of the streets there were two long passageways that were built along with the houses. Along the length of the passageways there were shops. The passageways served for the people as a protection from the rain, snow, or sun, such that any business was not disturbed by the weather. More than once, on a rainy day, these places served as a gathering point for the merchants, for the gossipers, and also for political debates.

[Page 322]

The larger number of houses were built one level high, and some buildings had two or three levels. These larger buildings and several smaller ones were built of red brick. All the other houses were built of wooden boards, twenty to thirty centimeters thick, with shingled roofs. Other houses, primarily those belonging to the Christians, had straw roofs. The external appearance of the houses gave a poor beggar's impression. The houses were calcified [old], painted, also bare, blue, white, green – in one word: an eclectic group of colors. On a cloudy, rainy, miserable day, the streets with these houses looked very depressing and the drops of rain rolled off the poor shingles of the roofs, and they actually cried as the Jews did by the rivers of Babylon [when the Temple was destroyed].

This is how the small provincial, poor, town of Turobin looked, where there was a community of 3,000 Jewish souls. They were born there, they were raised there, and they lived there until their death.

As we mentioned earlier, each town thought of itself as the center, and that is how Turobin thought of itself as well, and proudly expressed that it was the real center but not the geographical one, only the spiritual one. These were not simply comments. The town of Turobin demonstrated factually that it served as the well of exporting spiritual energies. The Turobiner Rav, Reb Mordekhai Meyer Weisbrod, and his father Yankele, a teacher and a brilliant scholar of Torah, who sat with honor on his rabbinic seat in Turobin. On a bright day, the city Kraśnik cast an eye on Reb Yankele Weisbrod and the Kraśniker community was prepared to pay comfortably to the Turobiner community. This is how the transaction wad decided and the city of Kraśnik welcomed the Turobiner Rav. It did not take long and soon the Kraśniker Jews crowned him as Rebbe [spiritual leader] (not the chief teacher of Jewish rulings), and he was surrounded by 1,000 *chassidim*.

The Frompoler Rav, Reb Eliezer Feder, Moishe Feder's brother, was a student in the Turobiner *Beis Medrash*. Zolkiewka needed to have a Rav, so they turned to the Turobiner scholars and they took on a young scholar, a Torah scholar from the Turobiner *Beis Medrash*, Reb Simkha Felhendler, his brothers–in–law were Yerakhmiel Broinszpigel and Reb Yisroel Mordekhai Eidelman.

The Szczebrzeszyner Rav (unknown name) was also born in Turobin and was a student in the *Beis Medrash*. The old Rokhower (Annapol) Rebbe was also involved in Torah learning in Turobin. Reb Bunim Estreikher, Reb Yitzkhok Yekhiel's son, was taken on as *Morah Hora'ah* [instructor of Jewish legal rulings] in the *Yeshiva of Khokhmei Lublin*. Reb Yeshaya Nuteh Treger, the son of Ozer the wagon driver, was hired as the Rav in a certain city in Greater Poland. This is how the chain stretched from the Torah scholars and teachers. Are these not sufficient facts of which the Turobiner Jewish community can be proud? These are only a few facts, but the truth is that if you looked at or thought about the Turobiner Jews, you would have had to use a candle to find an ignorant person.

[Page 323]

The Jews of Turobin lived with Torah and trade, and some with crafts. Many Jews lived with Torah alone. Oh, but how can that be? That's how it was! The women did the trading in the market or sold in the stores, and the men sat and studied Torah. There were Jews who were completely removed from material, daily things. All, from the Rav to the water carrier, were able to study a page of *Gemara* and commentary with ease. Everyone had a Book of Psalms in his pocket, and in their free time, or when someone was on the road, he managed to get in a few chapters of Psalms. The Turobiner wagon driver was not an ordinary wagon driver as in other cities. They were all learned men in Torah. When they would go to Lublin – during the times of the great mud marshes – and the wagon would be stuck deep in the mud from which the horses were unable to extricate themselves, they would use the Name of God [for help]. They would feed the horse and then go to the nearest town into the *Beis Medrash*, and there they would study a page of *Gemara*. When they returned, they would say to the horse: "In the name of our patriarchs Abraham, Isaac, and Jacob!" And soon the horses would drag the wagons out of the mud, and they would fly like eagles. So, you see God's wonders? Ha!

The *Beis Medrash* was the support for Jewish spiritual life – a star in Turobin, just like a huge smithy's steel. Day and night, both in summer and winter, it could be thundering and lightning, in rain or snow – the musical tones did not stop for a while to resonate with the beautiful echo of the *Beis Medrash*. Thin resonant voices, base resonant voices, and simply students' voices and chants. Those who were studying, swayed and sang. As they were swaying, the thick wooden tables and benches became so rubbed out, that they shone as if having been polished. If someone had a *yarzeit* [the anniversary of someone's death], he collected a *minyan* [quorum of ten men] and together they studied a chapter of *Mishnayos* [Talmud; as is traditionally done on a *yarzeit*]. The first letter of the chapter had to be the same first letter as the deceased's name. At another table, they were studying the designated daily page of *Gemara*. Others were busy studying verses of *Yoreh De'ah* [Jewish law]. There were also a few who studied Kabbala [mysticism]. Everyone was studying Torah for its own sake, not expecting any reward for that. There were also simpler categories of learned ones, When the younger students had any questions they asked the second category, and when the others had a question they asked the higher category of scholars. When the response was not so simple a discussion with great debate took place, with simple explanations and with interpretations, and each of the learned ones wanted to demonstrate his energy. One brought up Rambam [Maimonides], another brought up the Rashban [Rabbi Shlomo ben Natan; commentary]. Many hours went on like that, and often there was no resolution! You have to ask greater scholars! There were also very learned young students who prepared the answers, even before the question came about. But they kept the answer as a "hidden kiss"; and that's how they produced an improvised answer. At the end of the scene, "by chance" they found the answer. That's how the entire spiritual life of the Jews in the *Beis Medrash* played out. The *Beis Medrash* was a warm home for anyone who came in. If someone, sadly, had no income, or had no peace in his home and so on, he found comfort in the *Beis Medrash*. The *Beis Medrash* also served as a trade center, and business transactions were done there between the afternoon and nighttime prayers. A handshake held more value than a signature on a contract. On the long winter nights, the *Beis Medrash* was lit up with the large lanterns, and the oven was burning so hot that you could not touch it. The stronger the cold in the streets, the closer everyone drew to the oven. They encircled the oven as bees to honey. Some had pleasure simply to warm their hands. Those who were there stayed for many hours and they wanted to eat as well. So there were young boys who brought for sale *bonyekeren*, frozen apples, hot potatoes, cigarettes, cakes – to sustain these souls. At the same time, these young children learned how to do business.

[Page 324]

The following morning, Reb Mottel the beadle had a lot of work. The face of the *Beis Medrash* looked as if it was after a pogrom of *bonyekeren* and other peels. He, may he rest in peace, was a raging Jew, particularly when he found such a dirty floor. When he was sweeping up the area, he always mumbled that he had never seen such pigs in all his life. He said this after 20 years of sweeping. Someone said to Reb Mottel the *shamash* [beadle]: "This is nothing. This doesn't matter, it's just holiness during the week. But look here, Reb Mottel, look at what is going on outside, around the walls and at the entrance of the *Beis Medrash* where everyone who was coming in would first go stand at the wall ... but then if they would come into the *Beis Medrash* , understandably they would first wash their hands *netillas yadayim* [according to the required ritual of handwashing]." Reb Mottel looked at him and did not know what to say. All he did was mumble: "We are in *galus* [exile]."

420

This is how the religious Jews of Turobin lived out their spiritual lives. The *Beis Medrash* was like a university for them, and in their lives it was the "eternal light." From this came wisdom, philosophy, morals, the specific Jewish characteristics, and this was inherited from generation to generation until Hitler's destruction.

[Page 325]

Erev Shabbat [Shabbat Eve] in the Town

Friday afternoon before sundown, every Jew, no matter what his job was, was enveloped in a holy Fear of God. If he was not able to finish his six days of labor in time, he was overtaken by a shiver. He hurried to complete his work and to complete his preparations for the Shabbat Queen. The wagon driver who was delayed in arriving into town was whipping his horse and urging them: Shabbat! Shabbat! Hurry up! The storekeeper was hurrying his last customers that they should buy less and move more quickly because the Shabbat was coming. Several times he also decided that it was late and that the only thing he would do now was sell candles in honor of Shabbat and nothing else. The worker ceased his work on time and went to the bathhouse. Some were going to the baths and others were already coming back. Everyone was rushing, hurrying, and everything was being done quickly.

When the sun was already beginning to set, Reb Borukh the *shamash* quickly ran through town with a special hammer and knocked on all the shutters and summoned everyone to come to synagogue.

The Jews were streaming into the *Beis Medrash* that was lit up with large Shabbat candles. All the candles of the chandeliers were lit. The congregants come to the synagogue on time, took a seat and began to recite *Shir Hashirim* [Song of Songs, composed/authored by King Solomon] with a beautiful melody, and those who came later began with *Minkha* [late afternoon prayer].

The leader of the prayers, Reb Yerakhmiel Shakhnales, approached the lit-up podium and opened with a thunderous voice the "*Lekhu neranena*" ["*Let us go and praise*"; the two opening words of the Shabbat evening prayer], such that the walls shook. The congregation followed him and his helpers supported him, singing beautifully. This is how we prayed until "*Mizmor shir leyom haShabbat*" ["A song for the day of Shabbat"; continuation of Shabbat evening prayers], and when we reached the verse of "*Veshamru bnei yisroel es haShabbat*" ["And the Nation of Israel heeded the Shabbat"], the congregation was aroused and prayed loudly, because in the merit of heeding Shabbat the Jews would be redeemed. The prayer ended and the congregation rushed home. Near the door at the exit of the synagogue several poor people were waiting to be invited to private homes for the Shabbat meal. And what do you think? They are brothers of Israel; you can be assured that there was not even a single person remaining without a Shabbat meal. Rushing home from the synagogue on a Friday night really had only one motive: first, they were afraid that the candles would burn out and not be lit throughout the meal. Second, that the children would already be asleep; and the most important, third, that the food should not get cold because you were not permitted to light a fire.

[Page 326]

When the Jew would come home from synagogue he began with "*Shalom Aleikhem*" ["Welcome"; opening two words of prayer preceding the Friday night *Kiddush*] and he would invite in the Shabbat Queen. He recited the *Kiddush* [prayer over wine] and they conducted the meal which was prepared as if for a king, meat and fish and other delicious foods, since it is a mitzvah to eat on Shabbat.

The echoes of *zemiros* [Shabbat songs] were heard in every Jewish house, "*Kol mekadesh shvi'I ko'rui lo...*" ["He who sanctifies the seventh day is called..."]. More than once, a Christian would stop outside a Jewish home and ponder in amazement, what kind of lives do these Jews have? These Jews are so strange. Try to explain to a Christian how the Shabbat fish tastes. This is how the Shabbat eve concluded in "Jacob's tent" [a Jew's home, referring to the patriarch Jacob].

The appearance of the street was also different from the other evenings because the Jewish Shabbat made a distinct impact even on the Christians' lives.

There was practically no transportation seen in the streets. Occasionally, a wagon would be moving slowly. Trade was at a standstill, stores were closed, because the Christians were not able to do business with themselves, they needed to have the Jews.

422

The Christian homes went on as usual but the Shabbat candles were shining out of every Jewish home and the songs were heard beautifully. The Shabbat festivities were sensed in the air, and the "*Neshama Yeseira*" ["additional soul" that traditionally Jews receive on the Shabbat] rested on each Jewish soul.

The boys and girls who had just completed their Shabbat meal went to the youth clubs and to the different organizations and this youth went for a stroll in the streets. The Jews of the older generation went to sleep with complete faith in their hearts and with "*krias shema*" [bedtime prayer] on their lips.

The youth went strolling through the streets of the town, taken with new ideas, with new world outlooks, and views towards a different future.

The debates that took place in the clubs did not end there but also took to the streets. The youth that was strolling through the streets divided into groups and because of that, in different corners there were always heard loud voices of the presenters and of their opponents. The topics were known by everyone so there were no winners or losers. The agenda for the day was: Does the lover of Zion have to be a function of the lover of the Jews? Can a socialist such as Karl Marx be a lover of the Jews? Was *Moshe Rabbeinu* [Moses] a socialist? Can a liberal be nationalist Jew? And so on. The group split into pairs that snuck into the Christian side streets, strolling on the wooden sidewalks. The couples sat on the Christian balconies – there the "*maciejka*" (fragrant evening flower in the mustard family) intoxicated the air with its smell. They sat there until the morning star came out, and then one wished the other "good Shabbat" and then they disappeared.

———

[Page 327]

The *Admor* of Turbin,
Reb Yakov Veisbrod, of blessed memory

Shimon Schlaferman

Translated by Pamela Russ

There were all kinds of Rebbes in the Polish congress. Some of them had the custom of going around to the towns where they had *chassidim* [followers], and there they conducted *tishen* ["tables"; festive and scholarly events around a "table" served with elegance and reverence for the Rebbe]. During these events, the Rebbes accepted *kvitlech* [notes from their followers requesting blessings or salvation from specific hardships] that were accompanied by some monies [contributions]. Others, and these were the largest numbers, who did not leave their rabbinic courts, conducted their rabbinic rule in their courts, and the *chassidim* brought the *kvitlech* and monies to them personally. There were also Rebbes who accepted the *kvitlech* but did not accept any monies. For this, the *gabbai* [beadle] went around to the *chassidim* and he recounted the Rebbe's miracles and wonders, and then, at that opportunity, they would collect monies for the Rebbe's court. During the High Holidays, the holiday of receiving the Torah [Shavuot], and Shabbat of Channuka, all the Rebbes were in their own courts, and there the *chassidim* delivered their requests that he help them in personal, material, and spiritual matters, and just as a Tzaddik [righteous man] requests, then God fulfills. Therefore, all you had to do was ask of the Rebbe. There were also *chassidim* who, other than on the days of the holidays, would go to the Rebbe on Shabbat (the Shabbat lasted – months until the Rebbe said his goodbye to him). During these months, the *chassid* discussed a possible marital match for his daughter, another discussed whether to plant a wound on his son to avoid the military, God forbid, another needed advice about his business, and so on.

The majority of the *chassidim* were wealthy Jews, successful men, knowledgeable in Torah. Other ordinary Jews who were workers, did not have a Rebbe in my town of Yaniv Lob. There were workers who were *chassidim* who followed a worker's Rebbe – and that was the *Admor* Reb Yankele Veisbrod –

424

the Turobiner Rebbe – who occupied the Rabbinic seat in Kraśnik before he became Rebbe. In World War One, the Kraśnik Rav, Reb Yisroel, may God avenge his blood, died sanctifying God's Name, with other working men. After creating a libel, the Czarist military enacted a decree and they [the men] were hanged.

As the city of Kraśnik remained without a Rav, they took on Reb Yakov Veisbrod of Turobin as their Rav. There were also other *chassidim* who were workers in our town, who belonged to the Rokhover Rebbe, and also to the Bekhower Rebbe – HaRav Rabinowycz – who was a warm Zionist and a member of the Mizrachi party.

[Page 328]

When the Rebbe, Reb Yankele of Turobin came to his *chassidim* to Janov Lob, this very city that was destroyed and no longer exists all the *chassidim* assembled in the Turobiner *shtiebel* [informal synagogue]. This was the tailors' *shtiebel*, and just as in the other *chassidic shtiebel*ech [plural] there was another class of *chassidim*, that's how in Janov there were many working men, and when their Rebbe came, there was a great celebration in town. There was tremendous joy and a great love. First, there was a great welcoming ahead of his arrival to the city as they escorted him into the town. There was singing and dancing in the home where he was hosted. This was the home of Reb Avrohom Velvel the butcher. Before the Rebbe arrived Reb Avrohom Velvel's household did a complete overhaul of his house so that when the Rebbe would come he would have a clean and fine and large home. There was already a precedent set that the Rebbe would stay there, and this was a great merit for him, because it was difficult to find a large home among the workers. So, every year, before the Rebbe arrived, Reb Avrohom prepared his home and put the women to the side so that the moment the Rebbe would come the entire house was prepared for the esteemed Rebbe and his family. On that day that the Rebbe came to town, all the workers and the ordinary people were dressed in their holiday finest and they did not work on that day either, because they had to welcome the Rebbe.

When they went to greet the Rebbe – they went until Godzhisow, with a special wagon (droshke) that was borrowed from the prince. The Rebbe was seated in this carriage, along with his two sons, the *shamash* and the *gabbai*. They drove and sang until they arrived into the city, then drank a *l'chaim*, and the Rebbe settled into Reb Avrohom's house. That same evening, after *minkha* and *maariv* [evening prayers], the *chassidim* urged their women forward to the Rebbe so that they would receive his blessings. The women approached the *gabbai* Reb Binyomin'el who listened to the requests and the wishes and he wrote the *kvitlech* which were given to the Rebbe.

There was total dedication to the Rebbe, and they spoke to him with an open heart. There were all kinds of requests of the Rebbe, and cumulatively and factually, the *kvitlech* showed the display of the difficulties and challenges of life in exile, of the problems that pressed on these families. These problems were presented before the Rebbe, and the Rebbe had to remove all of these issues. This is what the *chassidim* asked of their Rebbe, and the Rebbe had to comply. The requests and *kvitlech* were of all sorts, as for example: One person suffered from gallstones, another had a daughter who one year after her wedding was childless, a third asked her son to be more eager to study Torah, a fourth asked for a blessing because she had difficulties earning a living, and so on.

Once Reb Binyomin'el had written everything into the *kvitlech*, the women tossed a coin into his hand and wiped their teary eyes.

[Page 329]

With these *kvitlech*, the women went to the *shamash* Reb Eliezer the yellow one, and he also received a coin in his hand. Then the *shamash* opened the door that led to the Rebbe's presence.

With a quick heartbeat and with tears in their eyes, they placed the *kvitlech* on the Rebbe's table, along with a generous contribution. The Rebbe spread out the amassed coins across the table, he gently patted the coins, and blessed and extoled the one who contributed the monies according to the order of the *kvitlech*. He gave advice, and often he shook the hand of the women's' sons and gave them blessings. The owners of the *kvitlech* left the Rebbe like new people, filled with hope and contentment. That's how the days and nights went during the time that the Rebbe was in town.

The *gabbai* and the *shamash* would entertain the *chassidim* with all kinds of anecdotes and tales, so that the *chassidim* were filled with enthusiasm and were very proud [of their Rebbe] – even of the ordinary people involved with holy work. In order to show the *Admor* Reb Yankele the proper respect – several prestigious businessmen and scholars came to see him as well. They had discussions with the Rebbe about issues that are in the Higher Worlds,

426

and the Rebbe provided an answer to each question. The handworker *chassidim* were sitting around this discussion and had great pleasure that they, along with the others, also had a Rebbe who knew how to answer questions with wisdom.

When Shabbat eve arrived, the entire city prepared for the Shabbat day when the Rebbe would conduct his *Tish* [festive "table"]. Women placed *kugels* [pies, casseroles] into the ovens, sweet *kugels*, salty *kugels*, and all other types of foods. All the Turobiner *chassidim* ran to the ritual baths on Shabbat morning to immerse themselves in the water, and all the successful businessmen came to the Rebbe's *tish*, even the higher ups who made fun of the handworkers' Rebbe. They also came to the *tish* to hear some of the hidden thoughts of the Torah, and to grab up some of the Rebbe's leftovers [considered to be very valuable], even though they complained that the Rebbe talked a little through his nose.

On Friday night, the Rebbe prayed in the house of Reb Avrohom, where he was hosted. All the *chassidim* came to the prayers, along with their children dressed in their best finery, with their new prayer books. All sorts of other people of high standing, not the *chassidim*, came as well. Reb Mordekhai Yosef the deaf one, begins the "*Lechu nerannenu*" ["*Let us go and praise*"; opening words of Shabbat prayers], and sings "*lecho dodi*" ["Go, my beloved Shabbat Queen..."; continuation of prayers]. The congregants assisted him and the Rebbe's eyes were glistening, as he released a shout: "Our Sweet Father, help Your Nation of Israel!" When they were standing for the *Shmone Esreii* [the "*Amidah*"; the central prayer] and it was completely silent, the leader of the prayers glanced to the other congregants to see if he could now step back from the *Shmoneh Esreii* [where taking three steps backwards indicates completion of the *Amidah*]. After the end of the prayers, all the *chassidim* approached the Rebbe to wished him a "Good Shabbat" or greeted him for the first time. The crowd rushed to go home and have their meal and then to grab places at the Rebbe's *tish*, since the seats at the *tish* were filled very quickly.

[Page 330]

Everyone was guarding his few centimeters that he had grabbed for himself and he did not move, as if glued to his spot. The door opened, and the Rebbe entered along with his family. Suddenly the entire crowd rose to their feet and they gave honor to the Rebbe. Some shouted out "Make space – the Rebbe is here!" The Rebbe took his place and began to recite *Sholom Aleichem* in a mystical voice. After that, he recited the *kiddush* [over wine] and then washed his hands ritually for the *challah* [Shabbat bread loaves]. He then cut off a piece, dipped it into salt, recited the blessing, and all answered "*amein!*" The crowd tried to grab up pieces of the Rebbe's blessed *challah*. This was number one. Everyone sat tense, and tried to use tricks [every effort] so that he would successfully get a piece of the Rebbe's *challah*. The other foods arrived: fish, soup with noodles, and so on. The Rebbe did not eat any of these foods, he merely tasted them, and the rest was snatched up by the others as his blessed leftovers. All the *chassidim* grabbed some and licked their fingers. In order to get these pieces of food, the *chassidim* actually crawled over one another. The table looked like it was after a pogrom, the uproar, the pushing, the chaos was huge, without bounds. Between one course of the meal and another, the Rebbe recited "*kol mekadesh...* ["all those who sanctify"; song for Shabbat] and sang the melody. Suddenly it was quiet. The Rebbe was reciting Torah, "The voice of God throws out flames of fire..." [Psalms]; he was revealing Heavenly mystical secrets, he lamented over the Divine Presence being in exile, and concluded with "*u'vo letzion go'el...*" ["A Redeemer shall come to Zion"]. All the *chassidim* were moaning and sighing, just as if they would be hypnotized. Suddenly, all the *chassidim* came alive and began to sing and clap their hands. When they entered a state of ecstasy, they began dancing, and the entire crowd was now in the Heavenly Worlds. With the Rebbe's two sons at the head, the "soup" spun as if drunk, and the Rebbe was in the middle of the circle. He danced slowly and lifted his hands to the Heavens, and his eyes were shining as they gazed upwards, and he voiced to God: "You see Your beloved nation, how much they love Your Torah – help them, and bring them their salvation." The crowd danced and danced until they are exhausted.

The following morning, the same picture played itself out, and they read from the small Torah scroll [the portion for Shabbat] that the Rebbe brought along with himself. And they brought *kugels* to the *tish*, and there were more of the Rebbe's leftover holy pieces of food, and now the show of grabbing up the Rebbe's pieces was even more interesting. The Rebbe recited more Torah and concluded with the verse: "*Vetaher libeinu be'emes, ve'nizke le'geula sheleima, bimheira beyameinu amein*" ["may our hearts turn to truth, and may we merit the complete redemption, in our days, amen"]. There was another dance until the time for *Minkha* prayers, and then the Rebbe was escorted into his chambers, after having the "Third Meal" of Shabbat – and then after *Minkha* and *Maariv*, the people began to sense that their extra Shabbat soul was slowly beginning to leave, and that the next day they had to go back to the daily struggle for a piece of bread. This is how a week or two stretched when the Rebbe came to town. When the Rebbe left, his *chassidim* escorted him far out of town, and parted with him in the pain of separation from the holy, but the words of the Rebbe, his smile, his Torah, these the *chassidim* remembered and it gave them the strength to exist.

[Page 331]

The list that I have written is dedicated to the *Tzaddik* [righteous man] Reb Yakov of Turobin. In the generation in which he lived, he was the spiritual leader not only in Turobin where he lived, but also for other towns and cities. He completely understood the soul of the simple Jew, the worker, and he himself was a humble person. He infused a Jewish identity into the Jewish person, and if the Rebbe said "Next year in Jerusalem," all the *chassidim* were prepared to go – if only the Rebbe said so. Tragically, the Nazi murderers destroyed and erased the city and towns, and all the dear people. May these lines remain as a memory for innocent Jews who were killed, for all future generations.

Translator's Note

1. Honored *chassidic* Leader

Seven Good Years

Y.L. Peretz

Translated by Pamela Russ

This is a story that took place in Turobin. There was once a porter in Turobin. His name was Tuvia, and he was a very poor man. Once, on a Thursday, he was standing in the marketplace, with the flaps of his coat rolled up with a rope that was tied to his body, and was looking out to see where his help would come from so that he could earn something for the Shabbath. The stores all around him were empty. No one was coming or going. There was no one coming to buy any merchandise so that there would be something to earn.

Sadly, he lifted his eyes to Heaven, and pleaded that he should not have a disturbed Shabbath, and his wife Serel and his children should, Heaven forbid, not be hungry on the Shabbath.

Just as he was praying, he felt that someone was tugging at his coat flaps. He looked around and saw a young German looking like a hunter in the forest, with a feather in his cap and a green symbol on his jacket. And the German said to him in pure German, which here we are translating into Hebrew with these words:

"Listen Tuviah, you were destined for seven good years, seven years of good fortune and luck, and treasures of prosperity, but it depends on you, when you wish to have these seven good years. If you wish – your good fortune will shine on you on this very day, and before the sun that stands over your head will set, you will be able to buy the entire Turobin and its surrounding areas. But after seven years, you will once again become a poor man, as you were – or then if you wish, those seven good years will come at the end of your days and you will leave this world as the greatest rich man."

As it was, it seemed that Elijah the Prophet, as he usually does, disguised himself as a German. But Tuviah thought that this was an ordinary sorcerer, so he responded:

[Page 332]

"My dear German, leave me alone, because I am a great pauper, may this never happen to you. I have nothing for the Shabbath and have nothing to pay you for your advice and trouble."

When the German did not leave him alone and repeated the words yet again, twice, and a third time, Tuviah finally understood and answered him: "You know what, dear German, if you are serious about this with me, and are not making fun of me as a poor man, and you are asking me truthfully, then I have to tell you that when anyone approaches to me [with a question], I look to my wife Serel for a suggestion and without her I cannot give you a clear answer."

The German replied that it is a very good thing to seek advice from one's wife, and he suggested that Tuviah consult with his wife and he, the German, would wait there for an answer.

Tuviah once again looked all around, saw no possibility of any earnings, and he thought that he had nothing to lose, and he went home to seek his wife's advice. He let his coat flaps drop and went behind the city where he lived, almost in the field, in a limestone house, to talk to his wife.

When Serel saw him through the open door (it was summer) she ran out to meet him with great joy. She thought he was bringing her something to help her prepare for Shabbath. But he told her:

"No Serel, His Name [God] has not yet allotted me any earnings, but that is why a German came to me..."

And he told her this and that, described what the German said, that he is destined for seven good years and it depended on him when the good years would be coming – now, or before his death. He asked her advice – when?

Serel did not think for a long time, and she said: "Go, my dear husband, and tell this German that your good years must start this very minute!"

"Why, Serel?" Tuviah asked perplexed. "After seven years, we will become poor again, and that decline becomes even worse than just being an ordinary poor man!"

"Don't worry, my dear good friend. In this world, take whatever you can and say: Bless God for every day! Especially if you need money for *cheder* [school] for the children. They were sent home [because no school payments were made]. See how they play in the sand."

This was enough for Tuviah to run back with a clear answer, that he wanted the seven good years right away. The German said to him:

"Think about it, Tuviah. Today you are a person with strength and you can earn sometimes more, sometimes less ... But what will be later on, if you will get older and you will decline, and you will not have all your strength for working."

[Page 333]

Tuviah responded:

"Listen, German, my wife Serel wants this right away. First she says to bless God for every day, and then she says not to worry about the future, and second, they have sent our children home from *cheder*...."

"If so," said the German, "then go home and before you enter the house you will be a rich man!"

He wanted to ask him more about the seven years, but meanwhile the German had vanished.

Tuviah returned home. Tuviah, as we mentioned, lived behind the town, almost in the open field. As he approached his home, he saw how the children were playing there in the sand. He saw that the children were shovelling something away from a hole that did not look like sand but looked like pure gold. Real, pure gold... Understandably, one did not need more than that. The seven years had already begun, the seven years of good fortune...

Time went quickly, as an arrow from a bow, and seven years passed quickly. After seven years, the German came back to Tuviah and told him that the seven years had passed and that that evening, the gold would disappear into the ground – the gold in the house as well as the gold he had hidden by others...

He found Tuviah standing in the middle of the marketplace, just as seven years earlier with the same coat flaps tied up to around body, and he was trying to make some earnings. He said to Tuviah, the seven years have passed!

Tuviah answered him: "Go tell my wife Serel, because the wealth was in her hands all of the seven years."

So they both went behind the city and come to the same limestone house in the field and found Serel in front of the door. She was dressed poorly, as before, but she was smiling. The German said to her the same words, that the seven good years had passed. She responded, that they had not yet begun to have the seven good years, that they never considered all the money as theirs because that which a person earns with his ten fingers, that belongs to him. But this type of wealth that comes without sweat and hard work is only a deposit that his dear name leaves behind in the hands of people to give to poor people... All she took from the gold was payment for school. This is God's Torah, and you can use money from His gold for that, and for nothing else! And if His good name from today onwards has a better provider for His gold, then of course let Him take it and give it to someone else!

Elijah the Prophet heard all this and disappeared. He gave over all this information to the Heavenly Courts, and the Heavenly Courts decreed that

432

there was no better provider, and the seven years did not end all the while that Tuviah and his wife Serel lived.

———

[Page 334]

"A Jew Who Recites *Tehilim* [Psalms]"

Itamar Hofen

Translated by Pamela Russ

As an eternal memory of the Tzitrinboim family, may their blood be avenged

Reb Yakele or Reb Yekele – that is how he was called in the street (his real name was probably Reb Yakov) – when they said the name Yakele it was not simply a name. He was a distinct type of Jew, a unique type.

In his young years, Reb Y. worked as a shoemaker, but later when I remember him, he was already not working and was very likely being supported by his children.

Reb Y. used to come very early into the *Beis Medrash* [Study Hall] in his regular place, pray with pure sincerity and after that, he recited the entire book of *Tehilim* [Psalms] and then he went home. He kept this small book of *Tehilim* in his pocket and when he had some free time, he continued reciting a little more *Tehilim* and that is how he completed the entire book of *Tehilim* and began once again.

The recitation of *Tehilim* for him never ended. The book of *Tehilim* for Reb Yakel was exactly like a weapon for a soldier on the front. For him, the book of *Tehilim* served as a spiritual and physical protector. If, Heaven Forbid, you are hungry, you recite *Tehilim*, if Heaven Forbid, you are assaulted by hooligans, you recite *Tehilim*. The calendar [indicated at the top of each page or ahead of each chapter] of the book of *Tehilim* [chapters are designated per day, per week, per holiday, etc.] were blackened and rubbed out and the edges of the pages were all creased from turning the page so many times without end. And the more he recited the *Tehilim*, the more he wanted to continue. He practically knew the entire book of *Tehilim* by heart. Until this very day, I am amazed, how a hidden power urged him to say the same thing over and over. And each time it was very likely for him as if he was reciting the *Tehilim* for the first time, and it was not repetitive for him. It seems that he understood the meaning of each of the words, and that is why he recited all of it with such passion. Today, imagine how many times Reb Y. recited *Tehilim* during his entire life.

Reb Y. had a son in the Soviet Union, a daughter Miriam who lives in Israel, and a younger son Velvel who died in the war. His son who was in the Soviet Union, held an important position as a well–known commissioner and an active Comrade in the Communist Party. The younger son Velvel, was a very conscientious young man, and he was among the founders of the Bund [Jewish socialist movement], and the culture library. Truth be told, he was never a member of the Bundist ideology and did not support Medem [Vladimir Davidovich Medem, 1879–1923, Russian Jewish politician, ideologue the Bund].

[Page 335]

Velvel Tzitrinboim

Yakele, Miriam, and her husband

But he hid himself behind the banner, and in fact, he was an active Communist and he did the same things that other youth in his time did when the Communist organization was forbidden.

[Page 336]

It was at the beginning of the thirties, when there were rumors circulating in the town that Reb Yakele was going to leave and go to the Soviet Union. That means that his son wanted him to leave. Whoever lived in Poland at that time and remembers the strained Polish/Russian connection and the strict border guard between the two countries, knows that both refused to give visas, regardless of what kind. With that I just want to explain how difficult it was to break through the powers and to receive permission to get into Russia. Only because his son was of the first revolutionaries and then an active Comrade of the Communist Party was he [the son] able to bring over his father. And because he [the father] was a religious Jew with a beard and already an older person, indicating to the Polish government that he was not a spy, he was successful after great efforts to immigrate to the Soviet Union.

When Reb Y. left to the Soviet Union, he took along "sustenance" for the road, that means his *Talis* [prayer shawl], and his *Tefilin* [phylacteries], and his book of *Tehilim*. In his letters he had only one complaint, that the Russians did not let him pray. He would forgo their food, as long as they would let him pray. But Yakele saw that even before he would fight the Bolsheviks he would be defeated. He would remain without his book of *Tehilim*, he would not have kosher food, and no matzos – He made a decision – and within a year or two, Reb Yakele came back to the town of Turobin with the same *Talis*, *Tefilin*, and book of *Tehilim*.

He took back his position in the *Beis Medrash* and he felt as if revived "back from the dead," that is what he said. Very likely he was told not to say what he had seen in Russia, but one thing he did say was "they do not let you say *Tehilim*"; "Over there, there are non–Jews and here there are still Jews." This same Yakele, the same beard and side locks, the same voice, the same smile, the same pinch that he used to give that young boy in the *Beis Medrash* when he was in the mood. May he rest in the Garden of Eden.

———

A Guest Stays Overnight
Greenberg
Translated by Pamela Russ

In my impressions of the Polish Jewish province that I visited often, the city of Turobin remained deep in my memory. When I was in Lublin, I decided to visit Turobin for two reasons: 1) to visit my friend Leon Goldfarb who was a dentist in Turobin; 2) to visit the customers from my shoe factory in Warsaw, misters Liberboim, and P. Rotblat. When I arrived to Turobin, they told me that Mr. Goldfarb and his family had immigrated to Israel.

When visiting merchant Liberboim, his wife told me: "You came at the right time, we are making a wedding for our youngest daughter, with good fortune and blessings. Of course you will stay for the wedding and after that you will have the meeting."

[Page 337]

Not having a choice, and respecting a good and honest customer, I agreed. There was no hotel so they found me a place to stay with a seamstress, a widow with 4–5 grown children who were members of the *HeChalutz* organization [Jewish youth movement preparing for pioneering in Israel].

436

It made a real impression on me that the entire town was preparing for the wedding, even the large goat that was lying comfortably on the ground – at the entrance of several shops. In the evening, they introduced me to the parents [in–laws] of the groom's side, Jews with long beards and long frock coats, with Jewish hats, and some of them with *shtreimlech* [round, fur hats]. People sat at long tables and there was discussion, beginning with weekday matters and moving to matters of Torah, commentaries and innovative ideas for issues of the day, and so on. A messenger came and informed everyone that the Zamosc musicians had arrived. From a distance, you could already hear their sounds, and everyone went into the street. A huge crowd of Jews and Christians were already waiting for the parents and the bride and groom to appear.

The ceremony begins. Two women, dressed in wigs and with decorative pins, were holding two large braided *challos* [plural of "*challah*"; braided bread] in their hands. Other women were holding large candles in their hands. The ceremony proceeded, accompanied by dance and song with the help of the musicians, the bride and groom, parents and in–laws, guest, and the entire town, Jews and Christians, and I among them.

That's how we passed the synagogue, circling seven times [according to tradition]. Those who likely recognized me as a new face, looked at me as if throwing darts [uncomfortably] ... a "warm" welcome, but this was beyond the normal.

At the *sheva brachos* ["seven blessings"; festive ceremony of reciting seven blessings for seven nights following the wedding], the groom presented several innovative interpretations of Torah portions, and there were several sharp analyses as well, and clever thoughts expressed by several scholars, from which I took real spiritual pleasure.

For all kinds of reasons, I remained in Turobin for Shabbath. I gave a lecture to the youth of *HeChalutz* that took place outside of the city in the open air on the green grass. In my lecture I spoke about Bialik's last tale, "The Onion Champion and the Garlic Champion." The crowd listened with great attention.

During my brief visit to Turobin I found an idealistic youth, filled with a yearning for a constructive life in Israel. Before my eyes are the beautiful faces of the young friends, of the Zionist and *HeChalutz* organizations, who strived to be the leaders of the *HeChalutz* camp on the other side [in Israel].

[Page 338]

I remember the beautiful faces of the scholars, businessmen, and ordinary, innocent Jews who were bestially murdered.

A dynamic town, with a colorful lifestyle, and all types of people. Idealists, yearnings – they, along with all the Polish population were tragically murdered.

May this Memorial Book of Turobin serve as a tombstone for the holy martyrs of the beautiful and beloved town that once was and is no longer.

A Soul

Itamar Hofen

Translated by Pamela Russ

Published in memory of my mother–in–law Aliza Sirkis of Johannesburg, who died on Tammuz 14, 5727; July 22, 1967

A town has not only a name, but also a soul. A person has a name, but also has a soul. A river has a name and has a soul as well. All have names, and all have souls. A person is born with a soul, and he receives his name after eight days. A river is created with its soul first, and it receives its name later on. But a town is given its name first, and its soul is created for generations – without stop.

When a person dies, you cross off his name, but his soul remains. The soul struggles, experiences reincarnations, is caught up in a mystical manner – until it finds its right ending.

When a river dies and its name is crossed off – its soul dies too. The only thing that remains of the river is its memories of history. Living witnesses tell that after the devastation of the Turobiner Jewish community, the river "For" cried and dried up.

When a town with a Jewish community is destroyed, its name is crossed off, but the soul remains, and only then does its soul know – the need of its existence. It never dies, even when a tombstone is set for it. This is only to show that the spirit is alive. The Jewish nation is still alive after the Spanish Inquisition, 470 years later, and will continue to live as long as Yom Kippur is kept.

A name, a soul, this is a known thing! But what is that? Can we understand? Can we feel this? Can we touch this? Can we see this? Yes! And certainly yes! Each one on its own, and all together.

[Page 339]

The soul of a person, everyone knows – even those other than people. "He is a sterling person with a golden soul." "He is a person with a gentle heart, with a modest soul." "The souls of the people – you can see in their eyes." "After death, the souls will roll under the cellar... until they come to Israel." "A dear soul! A good soul! *And into your hand, I command my spirit*" [from morning prayers].

Perhaps you would like to know, you will hear that a river also has a soul: The river has overflowed! (It cried too much.) The river has dried up! The river is demanding its yearly human victims! The river is storming! The river is calm and is shining as a mirror! The river contains fish, minerals, and so on. The river has all kinds of secret places. The river also has a heart. The heart of the river – these are the wells from which it takes its vitamins. The river has a head, a center, and feet, the river takes everything in, even the sins of *tashlich* [Rosh Hashana ceremony conducted at a river, all sins are "tossed in" to purify the person]. If the town is in mourning – the river does not mourn. You can see clearly that the river has a soul, a good one, a large one, a broiling one, a creative one, a powerful one.

A town and her soul: The *shamash* Reb Boruch wakes up the town with the knocking of a wooden hammer [paddle]. If the *shamash* bangs three times – then everything is normal. If he bangs twice, that is a sign that there is a death in town.

"Into the baths!" shouts Reb Hershele. He used to smack the businessmen on the highest benches [in the baths]. If it was not hot enough, they all shouted, "a pail!" That meant that he should pour a pail of water onto the heated stones, and the stones released more hot steam into the baths.

On Shabbath morning – Reb Alter Shneiderberg, with a sing–song pleasant voice, summoned all to come and recite Psalms. Also, every Friday afternoon, Reb Alter used to go around the town and call out: "Bread for the poor!" and Reb Hershele collected the bread in a sack. The bread for the poor was distributed to the needy people, but everything was done with discretion. Everyone rushed to the synagogue. They left the synagogue leisurely. Between *mincha* and *maariv* [evening and night prayers] there was buzzing in the synagogue as in a beehive. The greatest business deals were made there.

If there was a difficult birth, for a salvation, the *cheder* boys would stretch a thread from the Holy Ark until the bed of the birthing woman.

The *Beis Medrash* had no lock because there were always people there who were studying. The resonating, melodious voices of those who were learning were heard outside.

[Page 340]

The court of the synagogue also had a purpose. All the marriage ceremonies were held there. In rain and in frost, the wedding ceremony took place in the courtyard of the synagogue under the open sky. The groom stood under the canopy and covered his eyes with a handkerchief. He waited until the bride was brought forward, and if the bride lived at the other end of the city, sometimes it took a half hour until the bride arrived. This waiting time was a very uncomfortable experience for the groom, because he surely had a rival or even a loving brother – who did not begrudge him his bride, and if it was a winter evening, the "good friends" made snowballs and "respectfully" threw the snowballs at the groom right under his eyes, since his eyes were covered anyway. If the groom would have known about this situation beforehand, then he certainly would have delayed the wedding ceremony. So you see, that you cannot even appreciate such a Jewish soul.

Friday after prayers, the Heavenly Spirit rested on the town. Everyone was dressed in their Shabbath finery. The street was quiet, calm, and peaceful. The glow of the candles was noticed in all the homes, and the Shabbath singing was heard in the streets.

The Shabbath day was busy. The congregants, the students in the *Beis Medrash*, and in the *chassidic shtieblech* [informal synagogues]. The *chassidim* with their satin frocks were demonstrating in the streets. The

Zionist *shtiebel* – and the Zionist meetings and lectures, everyone knew that it was Shabbath, and they were doing something.

Yom Kippur night, quiet and serene. A deep mood of fear. The community was standing in front of the Heavenly Court. Everyone was enveloped in a fear. Even a fish in the river trembled. They completed the prayers, ended the fast [of Yom Kippur], and Yom Kippur ended with the verse: "Next year in Jerusalem!"

Simchas Torah [last day of Sukkos holiday, celebrating with the Torah]. If the Jews completed the reading of the Torah, then of course they have to dance. And when the *chassidim* dance, the entire town dances along with them. Understandably, before dancing, the *chassidim* had made a *lechayim* [had a drink of alcohol] and ate the kugels that were prepared in the ovens. Reb Shmelke, a tall and broad Jew, was a hefty *chassid*, and somewhat tipsy, and he did not want to dance on the ground. He climbed up onto Tisha's two–meter high rooftop – and wanted to jump down. When the other *chassidim* saw this, they began to shout: "Reb Shmelke, have pity! Don't dance because you'll break Tisha's roof." Imagine how much strength it took to get Reb Shmelke off the roof. They brought a fatty kugel, and they told Reb Shmelke that he had to come down and make a blessing over this kugel. Only then did Reb Shmelke climb down off the roof.

Reb Shmekle Drimler was a Gerer *chassid*. They say about him that on a market day, when his store was filled with customers, and a familiar Jew of his same *chassidic* group came into the store, Reb Shmelke gave a broad *shalom aleichem* [greeting] to Reb Yakov, and told him that if he wanted to talk about business issues, then he would have to wait a while, but if he wants to discuss *chassidic* subjects, then he would leave behind all his customers and would come to speak with him immediately.

[Page 341]

If a Jew did not have sustenance for Shabbath, then other Jews would collect whatever he needed. If a Jew did not have the means to marry off his daughter, then there were other Jews who helped him with his needs. If a Jew was sick or had other needs, then the other Jews would help him in any way, and truthfully, should he go to the non–Jews? The Jews went to the non–Jews if there was a dispute in the town. In that case, all means were kosher, even going to a non–Jew and inform them, in order to break the opponent, that means the Jew and his side. And all this was done in the name of Torah. So? Can you figure a Jewish soul?

Reb Shaul Mendel disappeared from the town for a few months. The women discussed this secretly, and thought that maybe he was upset with his wife. What does that mean? A Jew leaves behind his wife and four young children, and his leather business, and then disappears. But the *chassidim* in town knew that Reb Shaul was yearning to see his Rebbe, so he left to visit with him for a few months. So, imagine that, a Jewish soul.

(The end is on page 391)

Memories

Avrohom Boimfeld

Translated by Pamela Russ

I do not have many memories of my town of birth, Turobin. When I was just a young child, my entire family moved away from the town. Later, I happened to visit the town a few times, and that's how I am left with a few memories. There are very few remaining survivors of the small Turobiner community. I maintain this as my moral obligation to describe it and to perpetuate all possible memories in the form of a book for the future generation. I salute the initiative of the region, even if the book will not comprehensively and completely reflect the town. The goal of this project is to sanctify, to measure the writer's qualifications, and for the reader – an apology.

As if it were today, I remember the holiday of Sukos 1932. I was waiting for the transport of the trip to go to Israel. I waited every second to receive notice from the *Misrad* [Ministry]. I gathered my courage and left noisy Warsaw to go to the small town to spend my final days in Poland with homey Jews and friends. As was usual in a small town at that time, the news that there was an Oleh to Israel [someone immigrating to Israel] swept into all corners of the town with mockery and contempt but this did not prevent me from being called up to the Torah several times for readings, and receiving warm wishes from the gabbai [beadle].

442

[Page 342]

The town could not really boast about its special architecture. There were four such streets, without names, some with shingled roofs, and some with straw roofs. In one street corner – the only two–level house in town. Incidentally, near the house where I was born all kinds of legends circulated about the house's inhabitants in the generation before me. It was a wealthy family that did business with all the neighboring aristocrats, as well as with Prince Potocki. A very respected family from pure Torah scholars and community leaders. I forget the neighboring street from the other corner house which was called the "*potchene*" ["passageway]. The entire street consisted of a row of little shops and homes. The second corner of this "*potchene*" street bordered the synagogue and the *Beis Medrash*, which I will describe further. Turobin was blessed with a large marketplace, and it was hard to see the start of the street on the opposite side. This is the impression of what Turobin looked like in my eyes.

Turobin was not very blessed with rich Jews, but thus there were many Torah scholars, beginning with the leader of the town all the way to the wagon driver. Being distanced far from the central settlements with Polish roads and no highway, the population existed in poverty. The only source of the town's income were the weekly fairs every Thursday, when the neighboring farmers would come together, buy merchandise, and sell their own products to the Jews. Only once a year was there an annual fair in town, and at that time, merchants from a distance came as well, and about 70% of the town had earnings for months from this event as well. There was only a small portion of people in Turobin who maintained a weekly trade contact in the center of town. These were the wagon drivers and the few tens of merchants who provided the town with products and merchandise, as well as with gossip and sensations from the outside world, for the people in the *Beis Medrash*. I have mentioned here my own interpretations of the economic state, according to my own appraisals.

As a Key to My Own Memories

A new era opened for the town of Turobin in general, and for the Turobiner youth specifically, with the beginning of the autobus run. As if automatically disappearing, the generations–old, rusty fanatic traditions were pushed aside. The city youth awoke as if from its slumber and freely began to inhale fresh, new air. Slowly, the youth began to leave the Trisk and Ger *shtieblech*, and began to meet in the secular meeting points. Young girls, as with a tidal wave, became swept away, and energetically, became busy and active. A deep darkness divided the two camps. With threatening clenched fists, the conservatives warned the camp of secularists, "We are excommunicating you" – the slogan went like that, "and we are also excommunicating you as husbands for our daughters."

[Page 343]

I find myself now in the official position of recounting the memories, with full respect and honor to the Turobiner martyrs, of the difference in ideologies. And I will try to remain objective with my own ideology about the situation created between the war of brothers.

Also, Khantche, Reb Shmelke's daughter, was swept into the flow of the new waves. And when Khantche, as she passed by a few times, peeked into the *HeChalutz*, she was attentively noticed by Michol Yoffe, the baker's son. As if electrified, his glance towards her totally ran through her entire body. His thirsty glance at Khantche lasted a long time. Also, Khantche tossed back a warm and meaningful glance, and then shyly dropped her eyes. With time, it appeared that Yoffe's picture had been etched in Khantche's mind from the frequent discussions between the young men and the girls. when they went swimming in the ponds. Soro'ke had already cast an eye on him long ago. Such a pleasant and proud person, and also an independent person in Turobin. Khantche really blushed every time that they spoke about Yoffe. But Khantche, having a strictly religious upbringing from her parents, could never allow herself to dream of such things... Her curious glances, as she passed by the place of *HeChalutz*, were to confirm how much truth there was to what her friends were saying. And especially Soro'ke's words. But since that time, Khantche did not hold back the warm, contented glance. He followed her as if hypnotized. Khantche's feelings quietly grew and she strongly rebuked her parents' protests against this match. A black cloud spread over the quiet, very religious, traditional family of Reb Shmelke. In order to really understand the full tragedy of this situation we have to go back a few years.

[Page 344]

The satin [religious; called satin because of the clothing they wore] youth was very popular at that time. Torah was deeply rooted in the youth. But still there were always some exceptional intellectuals in the Jewish towns who acquired the title of "satin young man." A satin young man was always rewarded with a wealthy young girl and with limitless room and board. As a young man, our Shmulek, as he was called at that time, was assured a rabbinic career because of his deep insights into the entire *Mishnayos* and even the Zohar [book of mysticism]. With his sharp view of the world's ideas, he excelled in each debate with his points right in the mark. He was strongly religious, without bounds. He immersed himself in the ritual baths several times a day, before prayers and after each prayer. Each Tomaszower mother wished that their own sons should be so accomplished. Shmulek was tall and thin, with black curly hair on his head, with his fine broad shoulders, he gave the impression of a *Kohen Gadol* [High Priest]. More than one girl hid in a corner near the Ger *mesifta* [place of study] to have a glance at the tall, handsome Shmulek, and then wipe away their warm, running tears. Turobin had nothing to be ashamed of regarding their satin [religious] youth. Many Jewish communities across the breadth of Poland were enriched by the heads of the *yeshivos* and rabbinic leaders from the satin youth of Turobin. Rabbi Yehoshua Neu's selecting Reb Shmulek for his daughter Rivka Laya must be allotted to the blind fate of "the One Who arranges all the matches." It just happened that Reb Yehoshua Neu was invited as a guest to the town of Tomaszow, as a visitor to Reb Shmulek's court. Reb Yehoshua had several conversations with Shmulek about his successful interpretations of sections of the *Gemara*. Reb Yehoshua Neu did not leave Shmulek alone and within a few days, they celebrated the engagement. A very happy person, Reb Yehoshua returned from Tomaszow and told his Shifra about the deal. "This time, I arranged for merchandise that is completely unimaginable," he proudly reported smiling to Shifra. And as Rivka Laya overheard this, she, more deeply embarrassed than ever, let her eyes drop. Very soon, a wedding was celebrated, as if for royalty. The best musicians were brought in, Reb Arish with his musicians, and from both sides, actually the cream of the crop came to the wedding. The only thing you saw there was silk, satin, and *shtreimlech* [round fur hats worn by *chassidim*] and not even the slightest exposure of skin by the women. Wine and other whiskeys flowed like water. The most brilliant, innovative analyses of the Ra"n [R. Nissim Gerondi, commentary on the Talmud] and of the Zohar. The music was heard far and wide. All the poor people and simple beggars from the area outside of the wedding, felt like poor dogs, and they came on time. Separate tables were prepared for them, and they celebrated seven days of ease. For weeks and months afterwards, the town was still feeling the impact of the wedding.

But it was only a short time after the wedding that there was a change for the young and old couple. I was unable to find out the reasons that the young couple broke the deal of unlimited room and board, and they went their own way. There were many versions. The gesture impressed me. A future spiritual custom of a community does not have to depend on the physical kindness. He closed his Rivka Laya into a shop, as was the custom, and with inner joy she threw warm glances at her departing Shmelke, as he left every morning to the Gerer *mesifta* for a Torah lesson.

[Page 345]

We will come back from the stroll we just took, to the tragedy that befell Reb Shmelke's family.

Reb Shmelke always used to discuss with Rivka Laya the possible marriage possibilities for his Khantche. Reb Shmelke greatly respected Rivka Laya. She was the real *Eishes Chayil* [Woman of Valor]. Life for them went on as if automatically. "You hear, Rivkale," he said, "I had a conversation about the tractate *Yoreh Deah* [section in Talmud that addresses laws of ritual matters] with Akiva the herring–merchant's son in Lublin. He's a real character. He coughs a little and is a little in pain with his left ear, but with the careful management of our fine, religious daughter Khantche he will be able to sit and learn Torah with great application. We will also organize all issues of their boarding. Reb Gimpel, Reb Akiva's father, would always send regards to Khantche." With great hope, Reb Shmelke tried to spin and use his long chain of ancestry. During each casual conversation of the scholars he always loved to talk about his aristocratic ancestry, and here was such a tragedy, may God have mercy.

Even the Gerer Rebbe did not give Reb Shmelke much hope for a miracle from heaven, because the Rebbe, it seems, had already had challenges in this area, and was satisfied with the wish that God should help.

We will return to the memories of *Simchas Torah* in the year 1932. Outdoors, strong, cold winds had already begun, accompanied by thin drops of rain. The two neighboring synagogues were filled with congregants. The time came for taking out the Torah scrolls in preparation of the *hakafos* [joyful dancing with the scrolls, rejoicing in completing and recommencing of the readings], and from a small dance there evolved a great dance. The crowd in both synagogues felt very squeezed for space. Without noticing, they went

446

dancing into the court with the Torah scrolls in hand, from the open gates of the court, with eyes closed in deep ecstasy, to the neighboring empty space of the Turobiner marketplace. The dance of the various groups, wrapped in their prayer shawls, presented a disheveled picture. They danced in groups, and they danced alone, in ecstasy and entranced, and some simply danced on their own feet. With lightning speed, news befell the town and it began to flow. The small groups from the Gerer and Trisker *chassidim* joined those dancing. They continued dancing through the passageway [on the sidewalk] then back to the marketplace. It was very narrow. Several times, I was almost swept into the mob of people dancing by, but I managed to turn myself away in time. Thanks to that, today I am able to write these memoirs. Or am I imagining this? No, I am not making an error. Here is Reb Dovid Merder ["murder"] (an odd name). He is flying in the air. He is not dancing – as if he is holding onto the dancing angel for a jig. More than once did I want to stick my small childish finger into his pointy beard and long face, for his perpetually disturbing my sleep as he was reciting the midnight prayers along with my father, may he rest in peace. The praying all day was not enough for them, so, every Monday and Thursday, they undertook to serve God, not considering anything about me, that they would be disturbing my sleep. There is a dance happening among the large group of congregants, of someone alone. Solo, holding the Torah scroll in his hands, he is dancing with his face just as with his feet, with all kinds of gestures. Today is his holiday, *Simchas Torah*.

[Page 346]

You all know him, this is Reb Alter Burg. All year, each Friday evening after midnight, Reb Alter Burg's voice resonated through the town as he summoned people to the service of God. This was a warm voice that embraced you softly and worked its way into all corners of your soul. All kinds of people began to stream in the direction of the synagogues towards the chapters of Psalms. They say that the echo of Reb Alter's calling reached all the way to Jerusalem. And at the very same time, they began a fresh midnight prayer in Jerusalem. There are all kinds of legends about this tailor, Reb Alter Burg. He had all the properties of a Turobiner native: honest, pious, and a Torah scholar. But still, without any family, being only by himself, his past remained really unsubstantiated. In town, people whispered that Reb Alter Burg, because of the sins he committed during his life, decided to work his exile so that it would forgive him, and went to Turobin, where a tailor was very much needed. Since then, Turobin merited to have its own tailor.

More than once, I had the thought that the writer of the expression "He who has not seen the *simcha* of drawing water has not seen a real *simcha* in his days" [referring to a water–drawing ceremony conducted during the time of the Temple, each morning of the holiday of Sukos], just like me, had to stand at that time in the large *Beis Hamikdosh* [Temple] marketplace town and enjoy the *simcha* [festivities]. The dances had almost little resemblance to the dances in the Warsaw opera theater, Wasela or Morska, actors, but they had in them a unique, enticing charm. Yesterday's lonesome, dreamy, wrinkled youth, disappeared, and in front of my eyes arose a dancing, enflamed, heroic youth, with many photos, and only the strong winds and rain put a stop to the wonderful spectacle of *Simchas Torah* 1932. The whistling wind mixed with the large raindrops, gruesomely and mercilessly dispersed the large crowd from the marketplace, but one person energetically tried to resist nature. In the foggy darkness I recognized him, the last of the Mohicans, Reb Shmelke. His prayer shawl had already flown away from him. The sections of his satin now torn frock coat were torn into separate parts. "Reb Shmelke!" I screamed to him. "Finish your dance. I understand your tragedy only too well: tradition, ancestors, but listen well to what the wind is blowing your way, such unfamiliar slogans. Even in Israel, where I am going now – different winds are already blowing, with new slogans – the ingathering of the exiles, a state, independent. It fell upon us, as fate has it, to push forward the necessary spiritual and physical operations." With an embarrassed glance, Reb Shmelke put his hand out to me and then disappeared.

———

[Page 347]

Characteristic Anecdotes and Tales

Berel Zuntag

Translated by Pamela Russ

How did Turobin become a town?

Reb Izak the *Shochet* [ritual slaughterer], may he rest in peace, used to say how Turobin became a town. As is known, in many of the towns in Poland there were no roads, and our town was also among those where roads had to be built. Large mud pools developed before *Pesach* [Passover], so much so that

448

it was difficult to leave town. Reb Izak used to say about this: "Now I understand how Turobin became a city. By chance, a few Jews came to Turobin for *Pesach*, and they could not leave here [because of the mud], so not having any choice, they wrote to their families that they should come to them [toTurobin] because they cannot get home for *Pesach*. And that is exactly how it was. The women and children came for *Pesach* and when summer came they did not feel like going back to the large cities, when all those in the larger cities went for summer respite to the province. That is how the city of Turobin was established."

The Times of *Moshiach* ["Messiah": the time of Redemption]

Hershele Rotblat, may he rest in peace, saw that Pinye Gevurtz, may he rest in peace, once burst out laughing in the *Beis Medrash*. "As it is known, Pinye Gevurtz never laughs..." Hershele said. "Jews, you should know that is the times of *Moshiach*, as it is written that when the *Moshiach* will come there will be 'our mouths will be filled with laughter' [verse from Psalms]... if not for that, then it would be impossible that Pinye would be laughing.

Hersh Farshtendig Studies Hebrew

When they opened a *Tarbut* [Zionist] school in Turobin, Hersh Farshtendig registered to learn Hebrew. When he came home from the classes, he would speak Hebrew very slowly in his home. His father, Binyamin Farshtendig, may he rest in peace, was not happy about this study because he was a *chassidic* Jew. But his mother, Khana'le Farshtendig would say, "It does not matter, children need to learn everything. It may as well be in *Tarbut* as long as he is learning." Once, sitting at the table, his mother asked that Hersh pour her a glass of tea. When he brought his mother the tea, at the same time he asked his father in Hebrew, "*Abba, ata shoteh*?" ["Father, would you like a drink?"] When the father heard this he gave Hersh a slap. "You have been going to *Tarbut* only for a few days and you are calling me a 'shoteh'ש?" He shouted out in a rage. Hersh began to shout and cry and to explain to his father that he had asking him if he also wanted to drink some tea but the expression was just the same. The father answered: "I do not want your tea and I do not want your Hebrew."

[Page 348]

Not Growing in the Width

When Shloime'le Greenberg came to Turobin as a son–in–law of Yitzchok the baker, may he rest in peace, he considered himself one of the Torah scholars that Turobin possessed. Whoever remembers, *Shiye Moreh Ho'raah* [Rabbinic leader of the city], may he rest in peace, was a proud Jew who loved to have people show him respect, and Shloime'le did not pay attention to this. For example, when *Shiye Moreh Hora'ah* would enter the *Beis Medrash* with his large *Tefilin* bag the people would make a path for him to pass through. But Shloime'le Grinberg was a revolutionary in this area, and he too would also proudly promenade through the *Beis Medrash.*

Once, *Shiye Moreh Ho'raah* called over Shloime'le and said to him: Young man, since you are new here in town, then you had better behave a little differently." "For example?" asked Shloime'le. "For example," replied *Shiye Moreh Ho'raah*, "if you consider yourself a learned person, and you say you are a Torah scholar, that does not bother me. You can make yourself as tall as you wish. But to interfere with my pathway, that not! Do not grow in the width…"

Repelling the Evil Eye

As is known, Jews believed that one person can place an Evil Eye upon another. But there was also a cure for this terrible curse. This was called "repelling an Evil Eye," and it was only singular people who were able to do this.

Understandably, Reb Izak the *Shochet* [ritual slaughterer] was one of these singular people. If something of this sort happened, they went running to Reb Izak… "Oy, Reb Izak, save my daughter!" the mother says. "She just finished eating supper and suddenly she did not feel well. Her head and her stomach hurt her very badly, and she is screaming terribly! She cannot stop!" After listening to the whole story, Reb Izak asked the mother what was her name and what was the name of the daughter, and he began to recite something quietly. When he finished, that means he repelled the Evil Eye, he said to the mother: "You can go now, you daughter will have a complete recovery."

When the person left, Reb Izak would say: "She probably overate on a bowl of *teiglech* [small pieces of dough cooked in honey] with potatoes until she

450

began to feel the pressure under her heart. But what should she do? The mother thinks I am a Rebbe'le, and if she believes that then I must help her like that."

Secrets from the *cheder* [schoolhouse]

Who knows what else is written in the Torah they but do not want to tell about it!

[Page 349]

Khaim Friedler the butcher, slaughtered an animal and the *Shochet* [ritual slaughterer] who slaughtered the animal said that the actual slaughter was not as it should be. The butchers who were standing there at the time, knew that the animal would have to declared *treif* [non–kosher]. The animal was a very fatty one and had cost a lot of money. The other butchers were quite satisfied that the animal was *treif*, because they knew that Khaim Friedler would have the best meat in town the next day, if it would come to that. And they did not like that. Many of them were secretly happy with what happened, and said: "A Jew like Khaim should not be slaughtering such expensive animals." But since there are such laws for the Jews, the Rabbis and the *shochtim* [ritual slaughterers] got together and began to ponder this situation.... Since Khaim Friedler is a poor man with young children, and the money that the animal had cost was not his but was borrowed from others, then this Jew will not have any bread for his children. So the decision was made that this animal was purely kosher so that he [Khaim] could at least be left with his pride intact.

When this verdict of the Rabbis became known, he went out into the streets and began to shout: "Who knows what else is written in the Torah that you can do .... But the thieves don't want to talk about it."

Two Things Learned from *Shechita* [ritual slaughter]

Once, they asked Reb Yitzchok the *Shochet*, may he rest in peace, when he was already in his eighties, what did he learn after his many years as *Shochet* in Turobin. He responded that he learned two things: first, how long the cake [bread] at the celebration of a circumcision has to be; and second, how heavy the Rav in town has to be so that he can rightly be called "*moreinu ve'rabeinu*" ["our teacher, our Rav"; prestigious title].

One: As was known, Reb Yitzchok the *Shochet* was also a *mohel* [rabbi who performs *bris milah,* circumcision]. Once, when he came into a village to perform a bris, all the Jews who lived there gathered together to be included in the *mitzvah* of the *bris milah.* Before setting the table the villagers asked each other if everything had been prepared so that they would not be shamed in front of the *Shochet.* And the main thing, if the cake [bread] is appropriately Jewish [is it right for this occasion]. One Jew replied to this saying that about this cake he can rightly say that one can make the *Hamotzi* blessing [the blessing recited over bread, which is more prestigious than the blessing said over cake]. He placed the cake on the table and measured the cake according to the length of his arm. When the cake reached from his hand to elbow, he announced: "Yes, this is the correct measurement. According to Jewish law, this is the right measurement of a cake that is to be used at a bris."

Two: When the butchers of Turobin would come to Reb Yitzchok for the slaughtering of the animals, before the slaughtering took place, they would talk about the activities of the day and what had happened to them during the day at the animal market – who had bought a bargain, and who was just about to make an important purchase, but it slipped right out of his hand; who lost a sale, and so on. All of this, the *Shochet* had to hear from those who gave him his livelihood. Once, in the midst of this discussion, one butcher came in and said: "Friends, I have something to tell you about today's events." "What happened," the other butchers asked. "You should know," he said, "that today I bought a *moreinu ve'rabeinu!*" "Really?" his listeners asked. "How much does it weigh?" "She weighs six pood [one pood is approx. 16.38 kilograms]," he replied. "Six pood?" say the butchers," then she really is a *moreinu ve'rabeinu.*" "From that," Reb Yitzchok the *Shochet* says, "I learned from the butchers that a Rav has to weigh about six pood so that he can be called *moreinu ve'rabeinu.*"

[Page 350]

———

Translator's footnote

1. fool; the two Hebrew terms, shoteh, are homonyms, therefore easily confused

———

Turobiner Sayings and Traditions

Yosef Kopf

Translated by Pamela Russ

The city of Turobin stands before my eyes. And all my dear ones who lived there and are no longer – my mother, brothers and sisters, neighbors, friends, and other dear Jews. The large active marketplace, Velvel Zigelboim's brown brick large store, and similar to that – Kreindel's old house which is about to cave in; the shops around the marketplace; also Yeckhiel Kuper's shop with the youth exchange that served as a place for discussions; the synagogue, the *Beis Medrash*, the youth organizations, and so on.

In memory of: Shprintze Mendel's and Khava Shkheyne's were a "couple" from heaven. Particularly on market day, they went around, hand in hand, feeling all the merchandise which the farmers had brought on their wagons. They bought everything: wheat, grains, chickens, eggs, and so on. When the two ladies, women of valor, were standing and making a purchase, no other Jew dared, Heaven Forbid, to outbid them, may God protect us, they fired such a *maaneh lashon* [prayers to be said at the gravesite of a righteous person] at him that he could not find the way out fast enough.

In memory of: Avrohom'ke and Yekele, two brothers, both summer and winter, wore two thin *olifogene* jackets (frocks). After the first frost, all the Jews smeared their boots with oil [for protection against winter], and Yekele is still going around with muddy boots. They asked him why? He answered that he is still unsure about the first frost. Avrohom'ke, on the contrary, was not lazy even for one step. One evening, when he went out of his house to close the shutters, he went to Lublin. The next evening, his wife asked him: "How did you disappear when you went to close the shutters?" He said: He remembered that he had to be at the lawyer's in Lublin.

In memory of: Khaim Meyer Liberboim, he would suddenly grab onto his beard and shout: "It's bad until Gur [until the "end of the world," but really still in Poland]. Everyone is guilty but *Moshiach* should come right away." Everyone said that he is not normal.

[Page 351]

In memory of: Yehoshua Liberboim – his burning eyes with his trimmed, pointy beard. Whenever there was an incident between a non–Jew and a Jew or among non–Jews themselves, he always found the way to straighten out the issue, and ended with some schnapps in a bar.

In memory of: Shakhna Zuntag – He always sat in the *Beis Medrash* and learned Torah, and collected money for needy brides, visiting guests' accommodations, taking care of *sforim* [religious books], and so on.

In memory of: Hersh Ber the water carrier – He was the water carrier during the day, and at night he recited Psalms, and Fridays he collected money for bread for the poor.

In memory of: Hershele the blind one, had many jobs – He cut hay for horses, turned the grain mill, and kneaded dough for bread. On Friday mornings, he heated the baths, at noon, he called all the Jews to "come to the baths," and whoever paid him, Hershele would give him a good swish with the broom across his shoulders [as is done in the steam baths], that means, he slapped him well. When Hershele poured water on the scalding rocks, the damp heat became stronger in the baths. From all these jobs Hershele still did not earn a livelihood, so he also went to each house in town to collect his percentage. In spite of all that, his wife always warned him that she would divorce him (and by the way, Hershele became blind in the Russian Czarist army).

[Page 352]

In memory of: Alter Shneiderberg (Barek). In summer and winter, in rain and snow, Reb Alter always summoned the Jews to recite Psalms, every Shabbath in the morning.

In memory of: Yerakhmiel Shakhnales, how he conducted the *shalosh seudos* ["Third Meal" of the Shabbath, on Shabbath day in the early evening] in the *Beis Medrash*, and sand the *chassidic* songs. He also used to recite the Psalms between *Minkha* [evening prayers] and *maariv* [nighttime prayers].

454

In memory of: Reb Yisroel Mordekhai Aidelman – studied *Mishnayos* [Talmud commentary] with a group of Jews every night in the *Beis Medrash*.

In memory of: all the *chassidim* who were part of the *chassidic* tables [with their Rebbe] in the *Beis Medrash* every Shabbath when the Rebbe came to visit his *chassidim* in town, seeing how the *chassidim* snatched up the leftover pieces of food from the Rebbe's plate, the Torah from the Rebbe's mouth, and the singing with ecstasy.

May they all remain as a holy memory!

———

The Cooperative Bank for Merchants and Handworkers [Craftsmen]

Aryeh Goldfarb

Translated by Pamela Russ

Turobiner Jewry experienced a very difficult economic situation after the First World War. They always suffered from anti–Semitic persecution from the local townspeople who tried with everything possible, kosher and non–kosher means, to suffocate Jewish economic life based in the surrounding villages, whose farmers would come to Turobin to sell their products for cash and buy their needs primarily on credit. This forced the businessmen from all the associations to find ways to save themselves and to help their friends who were suffering from real poverty.

The main plan was to help them with credit so that they could set aside their struggles and survive.

To that end, the Cooperative Bank was created, which supported itself by subsidies from the "Joint" and on friends' monthly donations from each friend who was interested in receiving a loan.

Understandably, everyone was interested in loans, without exception. Representatives from each association were elected to the administration of the bank. These representatives felt responsible to specifically help their friends with the loans. That's how the Turobiner Cooperative Bank filled a great need in the area of the economic and social lives in Turobin.

The founders of the bank were: from the merchants' association: Shmelke Drimler; from the handworkers – Zissel Shuster. As chairman, Shmelke was elected; Avrohom Boimfeld – treasurer; Yisroel Janower – principal financier; Avrohom Zweken – secretary.

———

The Handworkers' Society

Translated by Pamela Russ

After World War One, through the initiative of Zissel Einwohner (shoemaker), Nute Pelz, Manis Fogel (tailor), Matisyahu Tzimerman (spat maker), Yakov Itche Einwohner (carpenter), and Avrohom Fuks (hatmaker), Noson Pik, Daniel Kreitman (rope spinner), the Turobiner handworker society was founded, which joined the Warsaw Central, and with its aid organization all the handworkers who worked on their own, and those who had several workers assisting them.

The Central also invested a sum of money in the small business handworker's bank that was established at that time to help the Turobiner handworkers with loans for buying raw materials and for discount exchanges and other financial operations for the handworkers. As chairman, Zissel Einwohner was elected, and she accomplished a lot for the association.

[Page 353]

The Turobiner handworker association also had its own synagogue where they prayed every Shabbath, and it was also a meeting place for all the friends. Politically, the managers of the Turobiner handworkers belonged to the People's Party which was led by the well-known People's representative Rosner.

With time, because of friction in the administration in the abovementioned bank, the handworkers separated from them, and created a separate handworkers bank.

———

The Revisionist Organization in Turobin

Yosef Kopf

Translated by Pamela Russ

Among the various organizations that were in Turobin, there was also the Revisionist Organization that held a fine, respected place. The organization was an attractive place for all types of youth who wanted to raise themselves in a Jewish Zionist atmosphere and live as comrades.

As I remember, the beginnings of the Revisionist Party were in the year 1930. The organization began in the general Zionist *Chalutz* [preparing for immigration to Israel, with training in agriculture] location, which was held at Moishe the tailor's home. After a short time, the organization took its own separate place by Hershel Likhtman. The people of the organization were: Lemel Katz, Yakov Yakobson, Simkha Eidelman, Moishe Grinberg, and Khava Freiberg, of blessed memory. The number of members of this organization was between 60 and 70. There were four comrades in *Hachshara* [preparation for immigration to Israel]: Aron Gevurtz, Mordekhai Perlman, Yosef Leder, Shmuel Roizner, of blessed memory.

The activities were multifaceted, among them was that there was a *Hachshara* location established for the Revisionist *Chalutzim* [pioneers to Israel]. This was in the village of Zhabno, three kilometers from town. This *Hachshara* locale had 32 members. This *Hachshara* locale was supported by the forest merchant Pesakh Diamond, whose business was forestry.

Between this *Hachshara* locale and the Turobiner branch there was ongoing joint activity, such as, for example: There were Hebrew courses, general and Jewish history, Zionist history, Tanakh [Biblical studies], scouts and military lessons and education, lectures on various themes. The youth was filled with the ideology of liberation and this expressed itself in song and Hora dancing, and so on.

The principle goal of all the comrades was to make *Aliyah* [immigration] to Israel be it in a legal or illegal manner, in order to help free the country from the Mandatory government. As is known, the organization was opposed to the politics of the certificate distribution.[1]

[Page 354]

At this occasion, I remember when the Trumpeldor and Hertzel yahrzeit evening events [commemorating the anniversary of their death], once, the 12–year–old little girl Laitche Friedler declared: "In blood and fire the Jews fell, in blood and fire the Jews will rise up."

I feel it necessary to mention several experiences of the comrades of the *Hachshara* locale. In order to sustain the *Hachshara*, all the members of the *Hachshara* had to pay a tax [membership], and this was a very difficult and great task to enforce in order to uphold the existence of the location. It is important to note that the Diamond family – Pesakh, Shloime, and Motel – helped tremendously, but sadly, they were not able to upkeep the *Hachshara* location.

I remember how my mother, of blessed memory, baked bread every week for the comrades of the *Hachshara* locale, and also busied herself with their clothing and laundry issues. It happened that two comrades became sick with a difficult angina, and their "hospital place" was in our home. My mother, may she rest in peace, took care of them until they became well again.

In any case, all my sisters and brothers belonged to the Revisionist Organization, so my mother, of blessed memory, automatically did as well. For this act, there was a verse that circulated in town, that Khaya Fishelowa must be the grandmother of Zhabotinsky.

This is how the activities of the organization went until the outbreak of World War Two in 1939.

The beastly Hitlerist murderers marched into the community of Turobin, and in a brutal manner, murdered them all, as well as the rich, energetic youth. Of all my friends in the organization, I was the only one to survive. This is what fate decreed, that only one remain, so that this one remaining should have the opportunity to remember the names of the comrades of the organization, and this should serve as an eternal memory. Unfortunately, they did not live to be in the free land [Israel], but their spirit is now with us here in the Land of Israel.

May their memories be blessed.

Translator's note

1. In the 1920s and 1930s the Palestine Office distributed the immigration "certificates" issued by the Mandatory government to the Jewish Agency; dealt with *hakhsharah* (i.e., agricultural training of *chalutzim*); provided information to prospective immigrants; prepared and provided the necessary travel documents; and served as a link to the British consulates and the authorities of the country concerned. https://www.jewishvirtuallibrary.org/palestine-office

———

[Page 355]

The *Agudas Yisroel* [religious organization] in Turobin

Translated by Pamela Russ

Turobin was a Jewish community that stood out in party and cultural connections. The *Agudah* was established late in Turobin, only after Poland became independent, although in Warsaw the "Orthodox *Agudah*" was established in 1915 or 1916 and published the daily paper "*Dos Yiddishe Vort*" ["The Jewish Word"]. It was only in about the year 1922 that the *Agudas Yisroel* was established in Turobin by Reb Shmelke Drimler (chairman), Reb Zindel Rentner, Velvel Liberboim, and others, who took the responsibility upon themselves to guard the religious life in town.[1]

At the same time, a youth organization was established in town, by the name of "*Tzeirei Agudas Yisroel*" ["The Youth of Agudas Israel"], through the young men Fintche, Itche Meyer Drimler, Tzvi Kopf, Leibel Eidelman, Fintche and Hirsh Nei (brothers). The *Agudah* had about 20 to 30 members, and the *Tzeirei Agudas Yisroel* approximately the same. The *Tzeirim* [youth] had their own club (or *shtiebel*) in the home of Fishel Kopf.

Very often, speakers would come from near and far. From Warsaw, Anshel Shar would often come from Bilograj and give homiletic speeches and draw many listeners. Understandably, the local *Agudah* and the *Tzeirei* were counted as affiliates of the Center in Warsaw, and from there would come the directives for the activities. The *Agudah* was tasked with developing the Orthodox education, and thanks to them, a *Bais Yaakov* school [religious girls' school] existed for girls. The *Tzeirim* [plural *Tzeirei*] held courses of *Gemara* and *Tosefos* [Talmud and commentary] for the Orthodox youth. There were discussion evenings on all kinds of Torah topics, special lectures during the holiday times.

Turobiner delegates would travel to Warsaw and other cities for country conferences of the *Agudah*. These delegates would later provide reports. In Turobin, there was also established a *Keren Hayishuv* ["Funds for the Settlement"], and there was great activity among the Orthodox masses in Turobin.

The *Agudah* and youth movements were active in Turobin until the great Destruction.

Original footnote:

1. Reb Shmelke Drimler had a reputation of being a fine Baal Tefila [leader of prayers] and would lead the prayers in the *Beis Medrash*, and all his listeners had great enjoyment from his prayers and his melodies.

A Modzitzer *Nigun* [*chassidic* melody] in Turobin

[Modrzyce, town in Poland, renowned for its *chassidic* music]

Translated by Pamela Russ

Turobin had many *chassidic* groups and *shtieblech*, but no Modzitzer *chassidim*. The Modziter Rebbe acquired a large number of *chassidim* because of his lively and warm musical *Nigunim* [plural of *Nigun*]. Of the hundreds of *Nigunim* that the Modzitzer Rebbes had composed, one *Nigun* found its way to Turobin and grabbed the hearts of entire city.

[Page 356]

Before, in the "good days," each of the *chassidic* dynasties used to have their own *Nigunim*, either because of prestige, or for other reasons. But the ruling dynasties in Turobin, such as the Ger and Trisker *chassidim*, were not productive in music and they were forced to "import" *Nigunim* from other *chassidic* dynasties. The Turobiner *chassidim*'s desire for music was a natural one. How can you live without a new *Nigun*? And how long is the time that you have to keep singing the old songs? It's possible, that if the Turobiner *chassidim* were not so deeply involved with issues of "earning a living," they would also have been able to produce something in the "world of *Nigunim*." The Turobiner were thirsty for a new, beautiful *Nigun*. But how do you get that? Also, the Turobiner were not the "sit at home" type. From time to time they would get away and go to Ger to the Rebbe or to Warsaw to the Trisker Rebbe. But either no new *Nigunim* were heard, or the *chassidim* did not possess the "extra soul," which a *Nigun* must have. The Modzitzer *Nigunim* did not need any announcements. They had a famous name all over Poland. And here was an opportunity, and a Modzitzer *Nigun* found its way to Turobin.

Who brought over this melody? Who was this "messenger of a *mitzvah*" that provided the Turobiner with a brand new and fitting *Nigun*? There are all kinds of answers to this. The Turobiner in Israel cannot provide a clear answer. Everyone is trying to find a name, and not all the ideas seem right. But the explanation that I heard from Mordekhai Yoskowycz (Hofen) of Netanya about the *Nigun* importer, makes sense. He also remembers a date, with the name of the relevant person. He says that in the year 1928, that is in the years that the Polish Jews had already grabbed up whatever they could have grabbed up in the new Polish regime in terms of their livelihoods, Reb Yehoshua Manis, a wealthy Turobiner Jew and a lover of *Nigunim*, brought over the abovementioned *Nigun*. Reb Yehoshua himself sang very nicely, had a fine voice, and somehow he packed up the *Nigun* and carried it with him to the holy city of Turobin.

The biography of this *Nigun* was either forgotten or was not cared for. And Modzitz, as is known, had more than one Rebbe who composed *Nigunim*. There were, as in other dynasties, and the *Chabad* [Lubavitch] *chassidim* first, an Alter Rebbe ["Old"; First Rebbe], a *Mittler Rebbe* ["Middle" Rebbe], and a third. Reb Yisroel, the founder of the Modzitzer dynasty, was a composer with a "higher heart," and his *Nigunim* had fire and many "scenes," not the way other *Nigunim* were, with two or three scenes. It seems that the musical businessman wanted to create a sensation in town and show the people that a Modzitzer *Nigun* is something special... And it seems that he made a welcome reception for the *Nigun* as one would for an honored guest, and that's how he planted roots.... Is this Modzitzer *Nigun* number one?

[Page 357]

The Mittler Modzitzer Rebbe, Reb Shaul Yedidya Elezer, of blessed memory, was also a bottomless well of musical chords and voices. He himself created over 1,000 *Nigunim* and did not have to use his father's, Reb Yisroel's musical inheritance. It seems that the Turobiner musical guest came from the *Mittler Rebbe*. It seems that the Turobiner Rebbe left too much for himself. He could have chosen a more beautiful and longer *Nigun*, even though this *Nigun* is not to be dismissed. Also, he had enough good possessions as all the other Modzitzer *Nigunim*. But just as when you choose an *esrog* [citron for the Sukos holiday], a most beautiful one, with *Nigunim*, there are also all kinds of ratings of "beautiful." It's true that in Turobin there were also ... Velvel, was a very conscientious young man, and he was among the founders of the Bund [Jewish socialist movement], and the culture library. Truth be told, he was never a member of the Bundist ideology and did not support Medem [Vladimir Davidovich Medem, 1879–1923, Russian Jewish politician, ideologue of the Bund].

[Page 358]

other Modzitzer *Nigunim*, but our *Nigun* carried a strong, proudly historical stamp, that you had to consider it of the greatest importance.

Our Turobiner *Nigun* is longer than the *Nigunim* of the other dynasties. It has five scenes, and the musical quality is felt in each scene. Each scene has a different mood. An original one. The foundation of the *Nigun* is a lyrical one, as if it reminds us of the Divine Presence being in exile. Even the happier *Nigunim* have to cry a little, grab your soul, and evoke a little sigh, a traditionally Jewish sigh. The *Nigun* allows itself to be sung. And since it is not soaked with too much depth and mysticism, it gets very easily absorbed into the ears of the listeners, and everyone can sing it. The *Nigun* is a mix, sometimes in 3/4 rhythm, and sometimes in 4/4. Sometimes andante, sometimes moderato. But the *Nigun* requires singing musically, and not to commit the sin of adding or taking away anything, as the other *chassidim* are wont to do with other *Nigunim*. The *Nigun* also has a beautiful advantage in that it can be sung with an introduction of a choir or at least as a duet.

462

Recorded from the mouth of Mordechai Yoskowycz;

Modzitz *Nigun* [Melody] from the Turobin tradition

The *Nigun* became a resident and they sang it everywhere in all the *shtieblech*, to "*yedid nefesh*" ["my dear soul"; part of Shabbath evening prayers], to "*lecho dodi*" ["come, my bride" part of Shabbath prayer, referring to the Bride of Shabbath], to *shalosh seudos* [the Third Meal of Shabbath]. The

Gerer *chassid*, Reb Yisroel Mordekhai Eidelman would sing this with his son as part of the special Shabbath songs. Also, Izak Shokhet would sing it, and passersby would stop to listen at the window.

We are doing a "*chesed shel emes*" ["a real kindness"; said about acts done for the deceased] for this *Nigun,* and perpetuating it with the language of musical notes.

Rabbi Yechiel Kaminski MOTZ[1] in Turobin

Translated by Meir Bulman

The usual role of the MOTZ was to assist the ABD with trials and instruction and sometimes when the rabbinate role was vacant to serve as rabbi. But in Turobin the motive for appointing a MOTZ was different; some of the residents were not pleased by the local Rabbi, Rabbi Weissbrod, who was not the greatest Torah scholar and some thought that the Turobin Hassidim (the Kraśnik Rebbe) were the only reason for his appointment. A few dozen families decided to appoint a MOTZ to fill the gap.

It was roughly 1932 when some families in town like Welwel Liberbom, Rantner, Tzwekin, Sontag, Halperen, Bomfeld, Kofenbom, and others decided to hire and fund a MOTZ. It was decided Rabbi Yechiel Ben Rabbi Moshe Nachum Kaminski, a native of Ozorków circa 1905, would serve as Turobin MOTZ. The hire was successful on all accounts, as he was the kind of rabbi with a great, influential personality, of those shaping the spiritual character of the town. He was a great Torah scholar, God-fearing, familiar with the ways of the world, and added to all was a secret Zionist.

Rabbi Yechiel was orphaned of his mother as a child, and he and his two brothers were raised by their maternal grandmother. His father was a grocery tradesman. Rabbi Yechiel studied at the Alexander Yeshiva near Lodz where he was ordained as a rabbi. His brother Heshel also was immersed in the study of Torah, ordained, and accepted as ABD of Zduńska Wola. The third brother, Yekkel David, was the only one who did business, and the one who survived the Holocaust and currently resides in Bnei Brak. Rabbi Yechiel married Reitzeh, the daughter of a wealthy businessman from Kalisz. They

464

had three children: one boy and two girls. Turobin was his first role as rabbi and he and his wife acclimated well.

[Page 360]

He rented a nice three-room apartment in Turobin in the building which housed the craftsmen and merchants bank, including a large hall in which he would greet people. His home was open to all, was always full and the table always set. He was also very active in public life and organized many matters with the authorities to favor the community. All residents treated him honorably.

He was a great Torah scholar who studied the Torah, Mishnah, Talmud, Halakha, and Aggadah. He was quite skilled in explaining unclear parts of Sage commentary, and skillfully and tastefully clarified hard-to-understand portions of the Torah. He was well-respected by the rabbis of the adjoining towns who considered his opinion in various matters which concerned the Jewish and rabbinic world, and also asked him to mediate on difficult halakha and complex trials. His dealings with the public were conducted faithfully and truthfully, and all his words were honest. He worshipped Hashem happily and enthusiastically. He also skillfully led services with his pleasant singing voice. He led services on Shabbat and during the Days of Awe accompanied by a choir and the audience enjoyed his pleasant prayer and songs. Even plain men like craftsmen and shopkeepers were impressed by his lectures. His appearance, his facial structure projecting nobility, deep eyes, the look and the manner of speaking noting seriousness and importance left a deep impression on the listeners.

He was also involved in the matters of parties and their views and followed the disputes taking place in papers and debates. It is said that after the Bund members began to raise their head in Turobin and would organize meetings and violate the Sabbath in public, disrupting prayers and more, the MOTZ once met bold Bund-ists who were invited from some big city to lecture in town. They told him with chutzpah that he opposes the revolution and encouraging reactionism and clericalism in the town. He replied that he would provide answers once they sobered from their revolutionary intoxication, "Religion lies dead before you and one does not debate a man whose dead lies in front of him." He looked at them piercingly, and they left him, speechless.

His wife, the Rebbetzin, was respected and accepted by the town women. She always lectured the local women that one needs to dress nicely. She hosted Hanukah balls for women and attracted them for enjoyment of traditional, spiritual occasions. For clear reasons, folks would mention our Forefather Abraham and his wife Sarah, since Abraham converted the men and Sarah converted the women.

The Rabbi and his family perished in the Holocaust. They are survived by some relatives in Israel who memorialize them at every opportunity, and it is they who were motivated to memorialize him in this Yizkor book as an influential figure of the town.

Translator's footnote:

1. More Tzedek, "teacher of justice"

[Page 360]

Yehoshua Lieberboim, of blessed memory

Itamar Hofen

Translated by Pamela Russ

As is usual for all the Turobiner Jews, he was also called by his patronym, "Shiyale Moishe Khaim's." Yehoshua was a straight, thin man with a typically long Jewish nose and an elongated face, and deep burning eyes. He was a horse dealer. He also had a tavern (a beer business) near his house on the street where you go to the court. His wife Tzivia, was the main manager of the tavern. He had two sons and two daughters. One of his sons, Moishe, saved himself because he fled to Russia. Today he lives in the United States.

Yehoshua was the son in law of Pinye Gewurtz ("Pinye Goy"). Yehoshua had a fine character and was a lover of Jews to the point of forfeiting himself [doing for others]. He was connected to all the parties in town and each one cared for him, but in particular though, he did not belong to any *chassidic* circle, but he participated in several celebrations wherever he was invited. His presence was always noted because he sang and danced and celebrated with the others. He always participated in the choir of the shul, he

466

had a thin old voice and when he raised his voice until "C" his voice turned into a soprano and his thin voice was heard loudly. The rest of the choir members said about Yehoshua's singing that when he recited the Kiddush [blessing over wine] before prayers, his singing was very pleasant.

I don't remember that Yehoshua ever had a disagreement with a Jew in town, but he participated in arguments among the non–Jews, and among the non–Jews and the Jews. Whenever he got involved, he ended the fighting. He broke the bones of those that he felt were guilty and after making peace, he invited both sides for a drink [liquor], (understandably, on their tab). As mentioned earlier, he had a tavern where most of the business was done on market day. On that day he helped his wife. All his guest, the farmers from the area, he knew well, by their names and by their father's names, their family situation, and the villages where they lived. Once, Yehoshua participated in some fun with his guest because he had many friends. Yehoshua treated the honest ones and refined ones with respect. He helped them with advice, with loans, and so on.

As was usual for the non–Jew, he would express his friendship for the Jew, whichever one would drink with him, saying with flattery: "You are like one of us. If all the Jews would be like you, then we would not hate them." In truth, they hated this Jew as well. On market days the farmers would even drink in the taverns, also in Yehoshua's. It happened once, that they drank so much, almost gallons, that it was even more than they had money to pay for. When some of the farmers were very drunk, they cursed the Jews and insulted them with terrible words, and did not want to pay their tab, or they did not have any money. This awful behavior of those [farmers in Yehoshua's tavern] broke Yehoshua's patience and he said to them: "You don't want to pay your bill, fine. Maybe you don't have money, but because you cursed the Jews I am going to break your bones." Said and done! Like an arrow from a bow he grabbed a bottle of beer, cracked open their heads, and threw them into the streets. When Yehoshua went back into the tavern, even though he was thin and gaunt, the farmers could not overcome him. The wounded and bandaged heads came the following day to make peace with Yehoshua because they felt bad for having disturbed the peace and having caused damages. After many of their pleas, he made peace with them. These treated the Jew Yehoshua with great honor and respect.

[Page 361]

I remember a pogrom day of the mobilized non–Jews in the area. One Shabbath day, in a year of the 1930s, when the mobilized went home from their service, they situated their wagons in middle of the marketplace and assaulted the Jews. Yehoshua came running through a side street to my father, may he rest in peace, and told him that they have to save the Jews from those who were leading the pogrom. The two of them positioned themselves in a corner of Shimele Sholom Mashkes's building (opposite the synagogue), and from there they started their defense fighting. You can imagine, woe to the hooligan who fell into their hands. Thanks to the commitment and thanks to the other fighters on the other side of the marketplace, and thanks to the *Chalutz* youth, who also took up the fighting – they saved the city from having victims.

Family Kopf

Translated by Pamela Russ

Khaya Kopf was the mother of the great and multi–branched family. She was widowed in the year 1923. Certainly, Turobiner people remember what a sad impact was had on the town when a Pole, a murderer, killed her husband Fishel Kopf, may he rest in peace, behind the town. Khaya Kopf was left a widow with young children. She had a will, a spirit, and a good character. She did not lose herself after this terrible incident, and thanks to her strong will she was able to raise her children, giving them lessons and respect. Khaya's home was open to anyone who was needy, and anyone who entered her home hungry left satiated.

[Page 362]

Of the Kopf family, those who were saved and are now in Israel: Tzvi Kopf and his family, Yosef Kopf and his family, Shmuel Kopf is in Uruguay.

Top – Khaya Kopf. From right to left: Yitta Rokhel and her husband Tzvi; Shmuel – his wife Monye; Yosef – his wife Tzile; Zelig, Avrohom – his wife Khaya; Yehoshua Reidler – his wife Sima

[Page 363]

Turobiner *Landsleit* [compatriots] in Israel and in the Diaspora Countries

[Page 364]

Turobin Landsleit in Israel

Translated by Pamela Russ

Some Turobiner who live in Argentina

First row from right: **Khaim Kleiner and his wife; Mikhoel Gutman and his wife; Nakhman Topel and his wife**

Second row from right: **Nekhemia Apel and his wife; Mendel Topel and his wife; Moishe Eichenblat and his wife; Moishe Eichenblat**

Turobin Emigrants in Israel
at the front of Labor and Construction

Translated by Meir Bulman

The Beginning of Aliyah from Turobin

The Belfour Declaration came as an official policy notice published by the British foreign minister on February 11, 1917 and in which it was declared that "His Majesty's Government views with favor the establishment in Palestine of a national home for the Jewish people and will use their best endeavors to facilitate the achievement of this object." The Jews interpreted "the establishment of a national home" as the clear goal to establish a Jewish state. The Declaration was the first to recognize Zionism as a political player. That, in turn, intensified the belief in the possibility of being like all other nations: independent in their ancient homeland. A wave of enthusiasm swept the Jewish ghettos and many saw, in the declaration, the footsteps of the messiah. However, a majority of Jewish youth did not make do with the happiness and the celebrating masses in the streets and instead began a constructive effort which demanded ascent and sacrifices. The Declaration gave a new push to the renewal of aliyah, culminating in the 3rd Aliyah in which many young folks stood out among members of the Hahalutz[1] movement. The Olim[2] brought with them tremendous strength and human spirit, in accordance with the verse, "The eternal Israel does not lie."

The influence of the 3rd aliyah was well sensed in Turobin, too, and folks began training. The song of redemption and aliyah began to sound openly in Jewish homes. The youth of Turobin did not take part in the 3rd Aliyah. Due to the stagnation of Zionist education in Turobin, aliyah began with the 4th Aliyah. The 3rd aliyah took place between 1919 – 1923. It was optimistic, as much of the world felt about the future in those days. The line "gay and joyful, shoulder to shoulder, come aid the nation," from the Bialik poem "Tehezkna" which we often sang, summed up the spirit of the olim on the 3rd aliyah. In Turobin, too, there was unlimited love for the Land of the Forefathers and a strong desire to be a free nation. Those two motives were what caused many Jews in every town and city to leave their comfortable homes and a life of wealth and which brought them to Israel. The 3rd Aliyah was incorporated into cultural and social life. That time of building was awe–inspiring from all aspects. The olim were called to perform large acts befitting the needs of the time, actions which were larger and more encompassing than the first two aliyot. The wave of aliyah which began in 1924 received a new number, the 4th aliyah. The "Grabski Aliyah" (the Polish treasury minister who implemented a taxation system which expelled the Jewish class from their positions) left its mark on the 4th Aliyah and brought a new style to life in Eretz Israel. The first halutz from Turobin to make aliyah was Shlomo Kopf who, in 1924, opened the door to aliyah from Turobin.

The aliyah from Turobin was slow. The emigration of each person involved a major effort. The 4th aliyah took place between 1924–1932. In 1930, Aharon Bofmfeld and Yerachmiel Friberg made aliyah. The 5th aliyah (1932 – 1940) was divided into two periods. The wave of aliyah in the first portion(1932 – 1935) brought about an economic flourishing in Israel, during which Aliyah HaNoar was founded. During that time, the arrivals from Turobin included Avraham and Gila Aurbs [?], Berish Gevirtz, Yehoshua Ben–Ari, Moshe Gutbertz, Yakov Friedler, Mordechai Hopen, Avraham, Riva, and David Bomfeld and their parents (1934). Leon Goldfarb, his wife Tamar, and their son Uriel arrived in 1933. In 1935, Itamar Hopen arrived, as did Bluma Silberklang, Yaffa Shnovski [?] Hadassah Kisolowitz [?] Miriam Levin, Zvi Kopf and family, and Yechiel Friedler.

[Page 366]

The second period (1936 – 1940) was a time of riots in Eretz Israel and an economic downturn. British Mandate authorities placed limitations on aliyah for economic and political reasons, yet aliyah did not decrease. In 1935, the Corndrexler and Milkhman families arrived, as did Sarah Yanover. In 1939, on the eve of the War, Yehoshua Hopen, Yisrael Amir (Auborois), Yona Amir (Yanover), Nechama Reider, and Yechiel Liberbom made aliyah. The 6th aliyah (1941 –1947) was a constant struggle against limitations on aliyah and based in large part on illegal emigration. Following the start of WWII, the aliyah from Turobin ceased. The remnants of the Jewish community after the destruction of Polish Jewry in the Holocaust began arriving, including the Jews of Turobin.

First Olim and Halutzim in Eretz Israel

1) Scheindel Yaffe, Rivka Bomfeld, Itamar Hopen, Miriam Levin

2) Yehoshua Ben–Ari, Yakov Friedler, Hadassah Yaffe, Moshe

Gutbertz, Bluma Silberklang

The emigrants from Turobin were not a group separated from the public, but within the Yishuv[3] they were united in a special spirit, always in an "awakening from Above." The spirit was expressed as, "United as one, devoted to the ideal of action and reconstruction, security and defense, without exceptions, in the sense of 'with all of your heart and all of your being.'" There were few olim from Turobin. But that minority made an impact on Israel and took part in labor, building, defense, and plant construction. It is noted they withstood the challenge and took part in many efforts of expansion, protection and defending what existed.

[Page 367]

Turobin Fortress in Israel

At the beginning of the 5th aliyah, the World Zionist Organization conducted large settlement efforts across Israel. The Turobin folks desired a pleasant corner in Kfar Yona[4] in the Sharon plain, founded in 1932 by the Mata'ai HaSharon company, named for Yona (John) Fisher, a famous Zionist leader from Belgium. The point had strategic importance, as it was situated on the main road from Tulkarm to the Sharon. It served as an important base during the War of Independence when it was necessary to block the westward advancement of the Arabs. Kfar Yona is situated on a tall hill in the Sharon. The mountains of Sumeria can be seen to the east. The John Fisher fund granted special loans to settlers in the village, mostly workers from the towns of Judea.

Kfar Yona then had a territory of 6500 dönüm[5] with orchards. Kfar Yona also was frowned upon by the Arabs who disdained its development and the development of the whole area from Tulkarm to Netanya. During the 1936 Riots, Arabs uprooted many trees in the area and victims fell among the Jewish guards.

Kfar Yona housed Jewish workers who planted orchards in the area such as at Nahlat Shubim, so called because it was founded by a union of shochetim[6] from the United States. Kfar Yona began to serve as a sort of settlement center for Jews and a guarding fortress against enemies hostile to the expansion of the Yishuv. Settlements in moshavim[7] and kibbutzim near and far were planned in Kfar Yona. During the riots, the settlers of Kfar Yona grew tired as they worked during the day and guarded at night. Settlers claimed the situation could not continue in that way and threatened the national institutions they would leave if not assisted with work and guarding. The Borochov settlement organization which included a significant number of members from Turobin [and?] received a directive from the security institutions to come to the aid of the residents of Kfar Yona. The organization would set up camp in the village until they would relocate to the designated territory – the land of Wadi Cubani [?] as the institutions promised at that time. Meanwhile, they participated in the conquering [?] of Hebrew labor in the moshav, participated in securing the area, and resided in the moshav for a few years. The 4 members participating in Kfar Yona on behalf of Borochov were

474

Moshe Gutvertz, Yakov Friedler and his wife Zipporah, and Itamar Hopen. They trained at the estates of Mataei HaSharon. Friedler set down roots in the village and today serves as vice–head of council.

[Page 368]

The Borochov organization erected the first tents in Kfar Yona

In 1936, they included 3 Turobin emigrants.

The members during plowing for the Mata'ei Hasharon company in Kfar Yona

The members laying down pipes for orchards for Mata'ei Hasharon in Kfar Yona

476

[Page 369]

During that time of flourishing, the Yishuv was dealt a tremendous blow. In 1936, bloody Arab riots erupted. The Arab rioters attacked Jewish settlements, set fire to their fields, and wanted to disrupt the transportation routes between agricultural settlements. After the 1936 riots calmed, British authorities took some steps that were intended to aid the Jews. Among other steps, the Yishuv institutions were permitted to enlist 2,700 Jews as "Notrim" (locals assisting police) and the number of Jewish police officers, which prior to the riots reached only 200, was [more than] doubled. The Turobin emigrants participated in the main activities, including as Notrim (or as they were nicknamed, "ghaffirs[8]") in Kfar Yona.

At the time of the 1936 riots, young men were summoned by the national institutions to serve as Notrim and in the police [force.] Our friend Yehoshua Ben–Ari enlisted that year in the Palestine Mandatory Police and a year later was summoned to serve. Ben–Ari has served in the police for the following thirty years. He slowly, honestly, and alertly ascended through tasks and roles. Thanks to his honesty and loyalty, he reached the role of judicial consultant for the Israeli Police and the Police Ministry.

The activities of Turobin emigrants are reflected in the photos before us. We see the Borochov organization forming the first tents in Kfar Yona, among them three members from Turobin; here they are participating in plowing for Mata'ei HaSharon Co. in Kfar Yona; a fourth photo shows the members as ghaffirs in the Kfar Yona area, and a fifth photo shows the Turobin folks as ghaffirs in Kfar Yona at the time before the days of Wall and Border. Today, it is difficult to describe those days because the most accurate portrayal will seem like a legend or miraculous. Like their friends, the Turobin folks enjoyed their new life in Israel, a life of building and creating, and they were fearless.

The Members participate in the Ghaffirs Security Forces in the Kfar Yona area

[Page 370]

Unfortunately, Mandatory authorities were intimidated by the Arab rioters and wanted to console them by shutting the gates of the country to Jewish immigration and banning land purchase by Jews. However, the decrees and the riots did not deter the Yishuv, which in those days was strong enough to defend itself. Decrees and riots were countered by fortifying existing positions and creating new ones. To bar the Arabs and Mandatory authorities from disrupting the activities of settling, new settlements were founded secretly and hastily. Planks for huts, wooden frames for brick walls, and parts to assemble a guard towner were formed in existing settlements near the designated area. In early morning, a large convoy of freight trucks packed with workers, materials, and tools for construction headed to the site. Everything was built with such speed that the position was ready by the evening. A spotlight was lit at the top of the guard tower, which [was used to] scout the area to discover

478

approaching Arab rioters. Guard tower light notified all nearby settlements of the creation of the new position. That method of settlements was known as "Wall and Tower." Most new settlements in 1937–39 were formed using that method. Many such settlements were founded near borders or the most remote and dangerous areas. Hanita on the Lebanese border before the "Wall and Tower" period was one of them. Turobin emigrants participated in the establishment of Hanita.

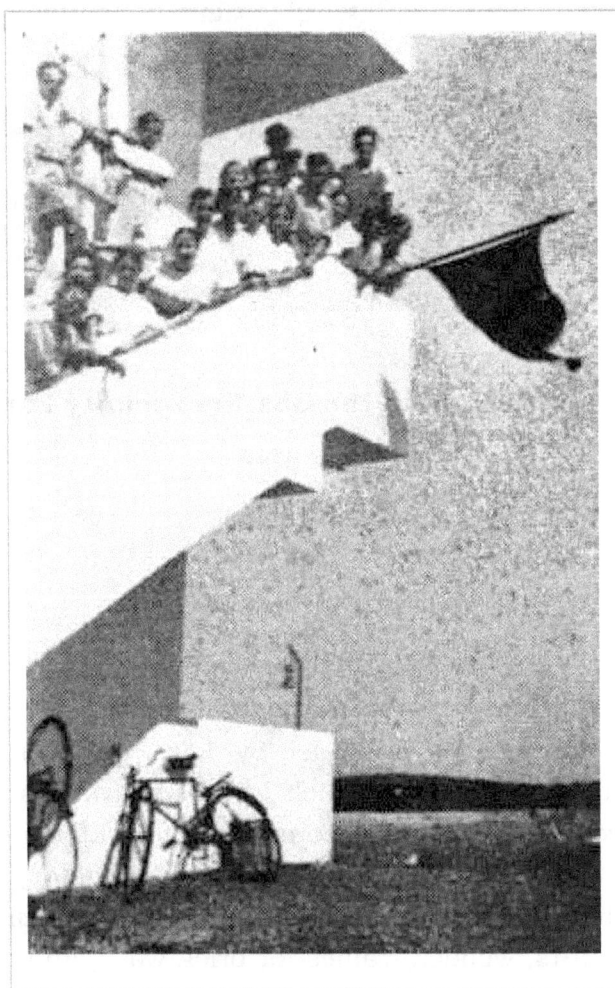

A security building constructed by the Jewish Agency in 1936–37

[Page 371]

The Borochov Organization which, as mentioned, included emigrants from Turobin, joined the ascent to Hanita on the Lebanese border in the Western Upper Galilee. Hanita was formed on March 31, 1938 on Keren Kayemet grounds (4200 dönüm) aided by funds from Keren Hayesod[9]. It was formed as a "Wall and Tower" settlement, the first Jewish position in that mountainous and dangerous territory. The first ascent to Hanita was comprised of young folks whose role was to conquer the spot and fortify it, and it included a unit of workers tasked with paving roads. The members initially resided in crowded shacks surrounded by a protective fence. They erected a fence and built brick homes and a water tower. Hanita is mentioned in the Talmud as a town which served as a spot for lodging on the road from Western Galilee to the ocean and included an Upper Hanita and a Lower Hanita.

The founding of Hanita was a very brave act which left an impression in Israel and abroad. At the height of the bloody riots, a group of young people ascended to a spot remote from any Jewish settlement with no road leading to it. The area was wild and danger lurked behind every rock and bush. For a long while it was a spot of clashes between terrorist squads and military units. Syrian gangs stormed nearby through the northern border of the country. The first to reach Hanita lived in an old house built by Arabs. Tents were raised and surrounded by a security wall – two wooden columns filled with gravel. A watchtower was erected in the yard by the side of the house. On the first night, the people of Hanita were attacked and very bravely beat back their attackers. Their victory cost them the lives of two young people. In its first year, 10 people fell, mostly from explosions of landmines in the area or surprise attacks on the road. The establishment of Hanita in those days was a fair testimony of the power in the ranks of the workers in the country. Hanita was a clear, strong, and brave response to all those attempting to thwart the activity of Jews in Israel.

Only some time later, on November 4, 1939, the protectors of Hanita were replaced by a group of young folks. The Shimron group included many residents of Israel and some from abroad who relocated to Hanita for permanent settlement. In the first days of the Borovhov Organization in Hanita, there was a battle with Arab rioters and Yechezkel Munchik, an emigrant from Bedzin, was killed. Moshe Givertz of Turobin spent ten months in Hanita in harsh conditions until he was replaced; then he returned to Kfar

Yona. He guarded "the Fisher Farm" in Kfar Yona and the area until 1940. He was tasked with signaling and telephone duties. An orchard was planted in Hanita in memory of the casualties during the first year of its existence.

An extension of Turobin folks took a place in the Alonim group. Yisrael Auberois [Oberweiss?] was there from 1939, followed by Yechezkel Bomstein, the Weiss family and others. The Alonim Group also went through twists and turns. At its start, they parked among the oak trees in Bet She'arim. On June 20, 1939, they relocated to designated Keren Kayemet grounds (2000 dönüm) funded by Keren Hayesod, designated for 70 families, a subsidiary of Hakibutz HaMe'uchad. The location suffered much during the riots. On Adar 22, 5699, three of its young members were killed in a mine explosion. A tower was erected for security and another 600 meters from its grounds. Various species of oak grow in the area. Five emigrants from Turobin reside in Kibbutz Alonim.

[Page 372]

For dozens of years, the Turobin community in Israel has been blessed by brotherly unity and devoted friendship. The community enjoys the full loyalty of ordinary working people, sufferers and silent types. Members requested no reward except one: to be worthy of the holy mission of supporting the Young–Ancient state in its journey. They had no satisfaction except for being founding members of Israel and a bolt in the strong arm of the forming Yishuv. These words are devoted to telling a small part of the story of spirit and the bravery of work and persistence in various points in Israel. In memory of friends, young and old, who devoted their lives to sanctify the name of the revival and redemption movement to see the fruition of their soul's desire – the rising of the State of Israel.

Endnotes:

1. Hahalutz – a Jewish youth movement that trained young people for agricultural settlement in Israel. It became an umbrella organization for the pioneering Zionist youth movements.

2. Olim – refers generally to immigrants but is linked specifically to the Hebrew concept of Aliyah, a term used to refer to the immigration of Jewish people to Israel: those who make aliyah are referred to as olim.

3. Yishuv – the group of Jewish residents in the land of Israel prior to the establishment of the State of Israel.

4. Kfar Yona – a city in the Sharon subdistrict in the Central District of Israel.

5. Dönüm – a unit of land area enclosing 1000 square metres. Land area in Israel, the West Bank and Gaza Strip has been measured in dunams since the era of the British Mandate of Palestine.

6. Shochetim – men who have been specially trained and licensed to slaughter animals and birds in accordance with the laws of shechita.

7. Moshavim – (plural of moshav) a type of Israeli town or settlement, in particular a type of cooperative agricultural community of individual farms pioneered by the Labour Zionists during the second wave of aliyah.

8. Ghaffirs – Jewish settlement police.

9. Keren Hayesod – United Jewish Appeal.

With Emigrants from Turobin and the Surrounding Area

Translated by Meir Bulman

As the goes saying, "All beginnings are hard." The organizing of Turobin emigrants in Israel was difficult in the beginning, too. There were Turobin emigrants in Israel before the Holocaust who did a lot to liberate the county through conquering the land and agricultural settlement. However, they did not think to self–organize in the face of global events which Judaism encountered. After the War of Destruction, the remnants [remaining people] from the town began arriving in Israel and the members of the community were tasked with reaching a hand out to their brothers and sisters in order to bring the distant closer and encourage them to reconstruct and resurrect.

The opening words of the piyyut[1] "Ele Ezkera" [I shall remember them] stood out for those who departed Turobin for Israel. Is it possible to not memorialize the martyrs of their town on occasion, as had been done by residents of other towns? It is unknown who were the initiators of the first memorial gathering for Turobin. In 1950, the first such ceremony took place in Bet Hahalutzot hall in Tel Aviv. There are no details about the number of participants, eulogizers, and speakers. Probably a person was yet to be found to record the details of the gathering for protocol. Gatherings in the years to

482

come were yet to planned. One cannot begin with the second or third memorial and skip over the first "anonymous" gathering. Therefore, we found it appropriate to mention some details from the first gathering but due to lack of information about it are proceeding on to the next gatherings according to the protocols.

Leon Goldfarb, Avraham Aurbs [?], Yosef Kopf, and Zalman Frumer initiated and invited all Turobin emigrants to a memorial for the martyrs of Turobin on August 12, 1952. She'erit Hapleta[2] heeded the call and about 80 emigrants from Turobin and the area gathered in Bet Hahlutzot in Tel Aviv. The gathering commenced at 8:00 p.m. by Mr. L. Goldfarb who briefly described the Holocaust and the immense tragedy in which the dear souls perished. Goldfarb called on those gathered to volunteer and build a monument to the Turobin martyrs within the Keren Kayemet[3] project, "Forest of the Martyrs." The project was in the development stage and planned to serve as an enormous monument in memory of all six million martyrs who perished. The forest would be formed with the help of She'erit Hapleta in Israel and abroad.

He was followed by Mr. Yisrael Aubrois (Amir) of Kibbutz Alonim. He eulogized the late Aryeh Rosenfeld who perished in the tragic disaster in Kfar Truman in Elul, 5712 in a coincidental collision with a mine. Aryeh passed away at a young age after he survived the Nazi hell and reached safety. Mr. Amir eulogized him with kind words.

[Page 373]

After they spoke, the cantor, Mr. Peled, recited *El Malei Rachamim*[4] and Psalms. The lights were then shut off, the hall grew silent and the sound of crying and mourning was heard throughout the ceremony.

After the memorial prayer, a report was given on the actions of the committee and the financial state. The attendees were invited to elect a new council which would more actively and energetically turn the monument in the Forest of the Martyrs into a reality. After the report, the members elected and announced Leon Goldfarb as chairman and Avraham Aubrois, Moshe Gutvertz, Yosef Kopf, Eliezer Milkhman, Dov Suntag, Yisrael Tzimerman, Moshe Rosner, and Itamar Hopen as committee members. Yehoshua Ben–Ari was elected as an honorary member. The elected committee immediately sprang into action and 258,615 Israeli pounds were raised.

All attendees gave their addresses which were recorded in a ledger and it was decided to continue to gather the remaining addresses of Turobin emigrants in Israel.

The gathering was attended by Dr. Zvi Heller, chairman of the Israelis of Polish Origin Organization who encouraged the attendees to organize immediately. He explained the need for and the historical value which should be attributed to the Forest of the Martyrs and explained the details of the plan. He promised the help of the Israelis of Polish Origin Organization to the organization which would form and the practical value of such an organization.

The committee members called on the attendees to not make do with the annual ceremony but create options for social and cultural gatherings during the rest of the year to prove that despite everything, "Am Yisrael Chai" (the national of Israel lives) and the spirit of the Turobin martyrs still exists and will continue to exist.

The meeting ended in high spirits and a familial feeling at around midnight. Every member discussed with a counterpart the personal experience from his holy community and the area. The new committee decided to convene in the following days to plan the activities of the organization.

The founding meeting was the cornerstone to the organizational activity and gatherings, meetings, and conferences, and every native of Turobin would know who he can approach with proposals and advice and that there is a public [?] body tasked with improving the relationship between members and scheduling meetings and visits for various reasons. Various matters were discussed and decisions were made at the committee meeting. We will record here only the most important:

a. It was decided to plant a territory of 1000 trees on behalf of the Turobin martyrs, and in accordance with the fundraising for Keren Kayemet.

b. It was unanimously decided to register the organization with the authorities as "Organization of Turobin and the Area Emigrants" whose purposes will be social, cultural, and devoting its activities to uniting all those originating in Turobin so it can serve as an eternal memorial for the martyrs of Turobin and the area. To lend help and advice to those in need and those who will arrive, to create funds to erecting a monument in the "Forest of Martyrs" and other fitting purposes, and eventually to found a charity which will serve persistent social needs.

[Page 374]

   c. It was decided to hasten the registration with the authorities and to contact the organized and unorganized Turobin emigrants abroad and inform them of the founding of the organization and its purposes to bring them closer to the idea of The Forest of Martyrs which will undoubtedly appeal to them and their participation in this effort will be enabled.

   d. It was decided to immediately open a bank account upon registration of the organization for the ongoing expenses of the organization and withdrawal of funds will be permitted only with the signature of two designated members.

   e. It was decided to form a designated ledger to list all those originating in Turobin and the area with their names and addresses to serve as an everlasting memorial and serve the organization.

   f. It was decided to immediately begin recording income and expenses in an organized manner. Of course, the committee is not allowed to guarantee any loan.

   g. To gather details on the Turobin martyrs and the living; eventually it will be necessary to gather details and historical materials on the life in the town and its dilemmas until the day of its destruction.

   h. To order a stamp "Organization of Turobin and the area Olim[5] in Israel" [from?] the organization committee in Tel Aviv.

Keren Kayemet administration invited members to participate in the planting ceremony of the Forest of Martyrs which began on April 12, 1953 near Kislon [?] at the entrance to Jerusalem. The committee decided that at least three members would participate and a notice would be sent to organization members and whoever wants will attend.

Regarding the decisions to gather materials which will serve as the basis for a Yizkor book – activity to fulfill this was weak and thus it barely began. As a result, it was decided to restart gathering photos from all Turobin emigrants as a foundation for an archive and a general album which would represent the town's past. It was also decided to gather materials on people, figures, and families for the Yizkor book.

At the committee meeting on July 11, 1953, letters from Turobin emigrants in America, Argentina and Uruguay were recited after some replied to the calls from the organization. It was decided to send replies to all in the hopes they would maintain contact with Israel and assist with upcoming actions. The Turobin people in America requested a list of all Turobin natives in Israel and the committee affirmed [providing this]. A large amount [of money] was received from Uruguay as participation in the planting of the Forest of the Martyrs.

On December 12, 1953, the third annual memorial ceremony took place at Beit Hahalutzot in Tel Aviv and about 90% of Turobin natives in Israel arrived from kibbutzim, moshavim, Jerusalem, Haifa, and Tel Aviv and the area. It was evident the number of participants was rising each time. The gathering was divided into two parts: the first was designated as a ceremony with eulogies and mourning, Psalms, and El Male Rahmaim. A portion was designated in memory of the young men who fell in the War of Independence, Ephraim Kopf, and Ariel Goldfarb. After reading of a passage from the works of I. L. Peretz, the first part ended. After that, the rest of the event was devoted to practical matters of the Turobin community in Israel. According to the treasurer, all funds were paid to Keren Kayemet for the planting of the 1000 trees in the Forest of Martyrs. Remaining activity was to focus on the next act of establishing a charitable fund, and afterward perhaps a Yizkor book could be approached. Most of the debaters [speakers] mentioned the difficulty of jumping the gun and, in their opinion, only one activity at once should take place. Yisrael Aubrois feared that the publication of the book would be difficult to a lack in intellectual power and proposed an album instead of a book. Dov Suntag said that the members in America are interested in a book and will fund its publication. Ben-Ari held that both are possible; only good will and an honest serious approach are necessary. Based on that, members were called upon again to submit photos and a concentration of details necessary for publication. The decision by participants was given to the newly elected committee.

486

[Page 375]

On the evening of the memorial on October 20, 1957 at the ZOA[6] House in Tel Aviv, recent emigrants from Turobin on the recent aliyot arrived. With much sorrow, they honored the memory of those from Turobin who passed that year: Yosef Dagan (Corndrexler), his Son Yaakov Dagan, and David Milkhman. A proposal was heard to include the offspring in the memorials, fearing that no one will remain to remind those gathered of the memory of the holy town. Mr. Goldfarb invited the participants to write down the names of their families and acquaintances from the town to archive the lists at Yad Vashem and at the sacred tent [?] which would be erected at the area for Turobin martyrs in the Forest of the Martyrs.

Memorial Day at the Forest of the Martyrs, 1965

[Page 376]

Following that evening, another committee meeting took place where the following matters were brought to order: a) whether fundraising among the members should continue among those participating in the memorial ceremonies, b) if the ceremonies should continue in their present format or be changed, and c) what should be done to advance the publication of the Yizkor book. After debates, it was decided to: temporarily stop fundraising; combine a modest friendly gathering with the ceremony and exchange memories; and distribute duties in collecting material and writing for the book, including designating topics and their writers. Yaakov Avituv (Gutwiling) accepted writing about Hasidic figures, Tarbut[7], "Hathiya" and descriptive considerations. Dov Suntag accepted writing about figures and characters, Zionist parties, Mizrachi[8], banks, disputes, and atmosphere. Yosef Kopf agreed to write about Beitar[9], trade, and figures. L. Goldfarb agreed to write about history and partisans. Iyta Pas accepted writing about the Holocaust in Turobin between 1939–1942. Peretz Fink accepted writing about the Bund[10]. Itamar Hopen and Yisrael Aubrois agreed to write about Hahalutz[11] and figures [in town]. Mordechai Yoskovitz–Hopen agreed to write about the Bet Midrash[12], figures, and characters.

At the memorial gathering on October 13,1958 at Beit Hahalutzot in Tel Aviv, eulogies and a ceremony was held for the martyrs and Turobin emigrants who passed away in Israel. Iyta Tzveken [?] then recounted the day of horror of the last liquidation of the Jews of Turobin before the exile to Izbica[13], then on September 16,1942 [when they were led] to Belzec like lambs to the slaughter and parted with their sanctified souls in an awful massacre. May their souls be bound in the bond of life. Yosef Kopf reminisced on unique figures in the town and noted the importance of memorializing them in writing and invited those who have something to detail to come to him or Goldfarb and they would record them in writing. Goldfarb was upset that the Forest of Martyrs was not being visited on Yom HaShoah. He described the beauty of the site and the beautiful view and he invited the attendees to come and participate next year. He also proposed placing a stone in Martef HaShoah[14] in Jerusalem, the site visited from people from all corners of the world. The attendees agree unanimously on that effort.

At the memorial gathering on November 1, 1959 at ZOA House in Tel Aviv, Mr. Zvi Kopf excitedly objected to the reduction in the number of participants

488

and asked, "How could forgetfulness take over such a holy endeavor?" He brought many of the attendees to tears with his passionate words. He concluded with a request to try to expand participation and include the children as well. Iyta Pas demanded that, like other unions have done, a stone should be placed in Mt. Zion in Jerusalem and to conduct the upcoming ceremonies there. Various decisions were made then: a) to hold the upcoming ceremonies in Tel Aviv as it is more convenient for the Turobin folks; b) to invite all immigrants from Turobin to the unveiling of the monument in Jerusalem; and c) to combine the memorial day and the unveiling in one day in Jerusalem. The final decision was changed in a way that the ceremony took place as usual in Tel Aviv and the unveiling served as another chance to gather in Jerusalem.

[Page 377]

Yizkor Ceremony by Turobin Natives at Martef Hashoa, Mt. Zion, Jerusalem

[Page 378]

At the annual memorial ceremony conducted on October 16, 1960 at ZOA House in Tel Aviv, the chairman greeted the guests from abroad: Mr. Berel Papir [?] the grandson of a Turobin emigrant residing in New York, U.S.A. and Mr. Fogel, a relative of a Turobin native residing in Brazil who arrived by chance in the area and met the natives of Turobin, the birth town of their families. After Zvi Kopf recited Kaddish for the martyrs, Yakov Avituv read a piece he had written about Turobin for the Yizkor book; he proposed the book should be written in Hebrew and Yiddish. Mordechai Hopen offered his help with writing essays about life in town. Yakov Friedler proposed planting a public garden in Kfar Yona on behalf of Turobin emigrants. The Kfar Yona council devoted a partially forested 5–dunom plot for that purpose. His relative from the United States agreed to fundraise several thousand dollars from Turobin emigrants in New York. Some also wanted to purchase land in Kfar Yona to found a house named for emigrants of Turobin. Mr. Papir [?] from NY declared that what he does on behalf of immigrants of Krasnik in Israel, he would also do the same for Turobin and he repeated the words of Yakov Frielder. Yerachmiel Freiberg objected to founding a garden in Kfar Yona to commemorate Turobin and was in favor of purchasing land and forming a house anywhere in Israel. Goldfarb proposed founding a cultural house in a town that needs it, other than in the three large cities. The respectable Barak Papir from Bronx, USA and Baruch Fogel from Brazil voted as honorary members.

A week later, the committee council members convened at the Goldfarb home. On the agenda was the proposal of the guest from the United States, Mr. Berel Papir who, at the last memorial evening, proposed establishing a memorial project for the Turobin martyrs at Kfar Yona, establishing a link with Turobin folks abroad. After deliberations, various decisions were made, including to a) purchase a plot in Kfar Yona to establish cultural center to memorialize the Turobin martyrs and b) establish ties with Turobin natives abroad and attract them to join activities to establish various public efforts to commemorate the Turobin martyrs.

At the annual memorial ceremony at ZOA House on October 9, 1961, Turobin–ites from all over the country convened and the hall was full. The Chairman, Y. Ben–Ari, marked the tragedy that befell the organization as three dear souls had passed away: Tamar Goldfarb, Motel Baumfeld, and Chava Bazshess [?]. He discussed the Eichmann trial and the lessons to be learned from it. After electing a new committee, various decisions were made including: a) approaching the survivors of the Holocaust in Turobin and elsewhere in writing or produce other material for the Yizkor book; b) to establish a monument at Mount Zion in Jerusalem; c) to hold an organized visit to the Forest of Martyrs on memorial day; and d) to convene again at a festive celebration in Tel Aviv. According to the chairman's announcement, the plaque was placed through the Organization of Israelis of Polish Origin. Regarding composing a book, it was decided to choose an editorial board whose role would be to form a timetable, gather materials, and promote the effort of publication. It was also decided the chairman would approach the town council of Turobin in Poland and request material about the town and Jewish settlement within it. In the meantime, the material would be held by Itamar Hopen. It was also decided to host a ball on Purim and invite the members.

[Page 379]

The committee conference on July 11, 1962 was attended by a guest from America, Leah Waldman who conveyed regards from Turobin immigrants in the United States. Leah said in America a sum was raised by Turobin emigrants for the organization in Israel. However, $3,500 was in a bank under the names of four former town residents who disbanded the Turobin landsmanshaft[15] and did not want to release the funds in their possession. After a debate, Mr. I. Hopen's proposal was accepted to personally address the four members in the U.S. [and ask them] to transfer the funds in their possession and go through all other means before approaching a lawyer with the demands. It was decided to send a photo of the monument to the U.S. and ensure its distribution. It was also decided to hold the annual memorial ceremony at the Chamber of the Holocaust in Jerusalem and set the pick–up time from Tel Aviv for 1:00 pm.

Meanwhile, another change occurred in the location of the memorial. The memorial was held in the small hall of ZOA House in Tel Aviv with 70 people attending. Two decisions were made: (1) the committee was unilaterally reelected for another year and (2) those gathered encouraged the committee to do anything in its power to publish the Yizkor book for the Turobin martyrs.

From the various items on the agenda, some of which remained on paper and some of which were [eventually] achieved, the need for a book to commemorate [for the community] the Jewish town of Turobin and its colorful life became more apparent to the members, Members had a feeling that there were still no writer, journalists or other literary types. Still, there were some who felt they possessed the necessary expressive ability to describe what took place in their town. Thus, the Yizkor book took center stage at the meetings and all debates surrounded it.

Here are deliberations from the committee meeting at the Hopen home on November 10, 1964. Aaron Bomfeld proposed to approach twenty members to write at least 3 pages each and compose a list of members from whom a writer will write what was dictated. According to Y. Ben–Ari, there is a need to form a central committee which will gather the material. The main issue is gathering the material and photos, and a need to employ a professional who can understand the existing material and add new material. According to A. Goldfarb, the content of the book should be divided by topics: the Zionist movements in the town, Hasidism, and the Beit Midrash. It was decided to choose an editorial committee of three members: Goldfarb, Ben–Ari, and I. Hopen. The board meeting took place on a more regular basis based on pressure from members to focus more on book composition. Indeed, the board members contributed their time and energy, and decisions made were more in line with practical matters.

Here are the decisions of the board from May 11, 1964. Approach Turobin emigrants abroad for donations and photographs. The committee must convene in November to organize the material already gathered. After those actions, the board will convene two months later at the beginning of January. Yosef Kopf proposed to hold a Hanukah ball to mark the 15–year anniversary of the organization. His proposal was not accepted and instead it was proposed to ascend to the Forest of Martyrs on a designated date.

The meeting of the administrative committee on December 23, 1964 at the home of Yehoshua Ben–Ari was devoted to the guest Hinde (Hellen) Wolfson regarding the publication of the book memorializing the Turobin martyrs and entering a dedication in the book in memory of her sister, Zissel.

[Page 380]

At the committee meeting at the home of Yaakov Friedler in Kfar Yona on April 20, 1965. Participation included a guest from Argentina, Nehemya Tapel [?] and his wife. Bomfeld announced that in regard to the publication, there were two fixed matters: funds and written material for the book. Tapel promised that after he returned home to Argentina, he would begin gathering material for the book and will also participate in fundraising for publication. Nehemya also discussed the life of Turobin emigrants in Argentina and revealed some of the mystery of the town memories [among those] living far away. The meeting was adjourned with an expression of trust in Mr. Tapel in the hopes he would do his best to promote matters of concern. Itamar Hopen

492

made a status report on gathering material for the book and emphasized that the missing material was (a) the period of the Holocaust and (b) the time of Turobin emigrants in Israel.

At the board meeting on March 10, 1965, Golda Kenigsman (Cornderxler) and her husband Max participated as guests. Y. Ben Ari reported on the brotherhood of the surviving Turobin community in Israel and the efforts and understanding they expressed about publishing the book. Ben–Ari encouraged Mr. Kenigsman to alert Turobin–ites everywhere about producing material and funds for publication.

Seventy members participated in the memorial gathering on October 24, 1965. Significant progress in publishing a Yizkor book was observed. The treasurer reported several thousand Israeli pounds had been raised for publication, not enough to cover all expenses. However, if the committee would receive a bank loan for several thousand pounds more, it could confidently be said the book could be sent for print within weeks. Some recordings [audio recordings] of members' writings prepared for the memorial book were played. The meeting was adjourned with satisfaction that the "dry bones" had begun taking form and that publishing had become practical and only a matter of time. Itamar Hopen was tasked with preparing the book for editing and publishing; Ben–Ari, Goldfarb, Bomfeld and Itamar agreed to contact an editor who would accept the project and hold a meeting with him as soon as possible.

The gravity of deliberations regarding publication was also noticed at the following meeting. At the meeting on May 5, 1966, Itamar Hopen gave a comprehensive report on the issues concerning editing and printing the book, e.g. numbers of sheets (a reference was made to 20 sheets which are 320 pages); the type of paper (wood–free); the cover; and the editing budget. The number of plates, photographs, and prices were eventually discussed. It was decided to hold the annual ceremony on October 10, 1966 at ZOA House.

The 1966 ceremony was held on the agreed upon date and all progressed smoothly as it was already tradition. Many attended and there was a cantor and service of *El Malei Rachamim*. The Turobin immigrants in Israel commemorated the martyrs of their town every year and made various efforts of commemoration until they reached the immense goal of publishing a Yizkor book, which became a central point in the life of the Turobin–ites in Israel and caught the attention of Turobin–ites abroad.

Since that memorial ceremony, there were significant changes in the operation of the Organization of Turobin Emigrants. Before, the meetings were monotonous and the issue of the book was a matter of the future.

[Page 381]

The meetings were orderly and fixed, and exceedingly boring. But now, matters took a dramatic turn. The activity of publishing consumed the meetings and took center stage. Finally, after exhausting negotiations, a contract was signed with a publisher according to agreed–upon terms with an experienced editor. The editor discovered that the community had existed for centuries and its history and the events experienced in it were worthy of recording. The editor discovered names of notable rabbis and leaders who filled important roles in the life of Polish Jewry. After a while, all material was prepared and divided into different sections, and the activity of organizing and printing began. Ongoing organizing of material and sections spanned months. Organization included proof reading – a 1st, 2nd, 3rd, and sometimes 4th time. At the end of the month of Av, there were already 9 printing sheets which were printed and awaited binding along with the sheets to come. The editor-maintained objectivity in the book, without bias in favor of a movement or party. A designated section was added for Yiddish, for the sake of readers abroad, in addition to the added Yiddish essays in the Holocaust and Destruction section. There are over 50 printing plates in the book. Members recognized they were guiding a glorious effort to commemorate the martyrs of their town, and the Yizkor book that would appear might awaken the leaders of the neighboring town.

The rumor of a Yizkor book already on the printing press reached Turobin members who awaited its conclusion. In the meantime, technical difficulties regarding the print were progressively dismissed. The book began to shine, and the members of the board began to feel they directed a difficult task toward progress and that they would soon be able to see the final product. They were almost sure they could come to the upcoming memorial gathering (after Shabbat Teshuva) and being selling the book which would serve as a collective memory worthy of emigrants of Turobin in Israel and abroad.

In that giddy spirt, the next board meeting took place on July 8, 1967, after no meetings were held since the last memorial ceremony. The first order of business was greeting a guest, Mr. Yitzchak Lichter from the United States. Ben–Ari requested the guest to carry the news to Turobin–ites residing in America that they were on the verge of concluding the effort of printing the book. Bomfeld expressed his regret of the need to discuss financial needs when greeting guests from abroad and the misfortune when guests come and go without activity. Hopen proposed to Mr. Lichter to accept a position as representative of the board and sell the book. He proposed giving the guest power of attorney [?] to sell the book and the board would ship him a few dozen copies. Yitzchak Lichter expressed his happiness in meeting members of his town of Turobin and expressed his satisfaction of Israel which he was visiting for the first time. He accepted the responsibility of gathering funds and distributing the books to members of the town.

General Notes and Footnotes:

These notes and footnotes have been added by this Yizkor Book's translation co–coordinator, not by the original author. They are intended to help clarify certain words, names and phrases.

1. Piyyut – a Jewish liturgical poem, usually designated to be sung, chanted, or recited during religious services.

2. Sh'erit ha–Pletah – a biblical term used by Jewish refugees who survived the Holocaust to refer to themselves and the communities they formed in postwar Europe following the liberation in the spring of 1945.

3. Keren Kayemet – Jewish National Fund.

4. El Malei Rachamim – a Jewish prayer for the soul of a person who has died, usually recited at the graveside during the burial service and at memorial services during the year.

5. Olim – refers generally to immigrants but is linked specifically to the Hebrew concept of Aliyah, a term used to refer to the immigration of Jewish people to Israel. Those who make aliyah are referred to as olim.

6. ZOA – Zionist Organization of America.

7. Tarbut – The movement was a network of secular, Hebrew–language schools in parts of the former Jewish Pale of Settlement, specifically in Poland, Romania and Lithuania.

8. Mizrachi – Mizrahi Jews, Mizrahim, also referred to as Edot HaMizrach or Oriental Jews, are descendants of local Jewish communities in the Middle East from biblical times into the modern era.

9. Beitar – a Revisionist Zionist youth movement founded in 1923 in Riga, Latvia, by Vladimir Jabotinsky.

10. Bund – The General Jewish Labour Bund in Lithuania, Poland and Russia, generally called The Bund or the Jewish Labour Bund, was a secular Jewish socialist party in the Russian Empire, active between 1897 and 1920.

11. Hahalutz – a Jewish youth movement that trained young people for agricultural settlement in the Land of Israel. It became an umbrella organization of the pioneering Zionist youth movements.

12. Bet Midrash – a place used for communal Jewish prayer.

13. Izbica – a village in the Krasnystaw County of the Lublin Voivodeship in eastern Poland.

14. Martef HaShoah – the Chamber of the Holocaust located on Mt. Zion, Jerusalem.

15. Landsmanshaft – a mutual aid society, benefit society, or hometown society of Jewish immigrants from the same European town or region.

[Page 382]

Heroes of the War of Independence

Translated by Meir Bulman

> Beloved men of spade and labor
>
> Who planted and plowed on the roads
>
> Their hidden memory is sanctified here
>
> From this hour forever and ever.
>
> May it be treasured at every place and time
>
> In homeland furrows and deep in the hearts of brothers.

– S. Shalom

The nation of Israel shall remember its sons and daughters, soldiers of the Israel Defense Forces, who bravely and loyally sacrificed themselves in the war for the resurrection of Israel. Israel shall remember and be blessed by its descendants and mourn the light of youth, the chosen bravery, and the sanctity of will and the devotion by those lost in the heavy battle. May the heroes of the War of Victory and Independence be treasured in the hearts of Israel for generations to come.

[Page 383]

He was the son of Eliezer and Tamar. He was born in Turobin and arrived in Israel at age three with his parents. He was raised in a Pioneering–Zionist environment. After he completed elementary school, he was trained in the Montefiore Technical School in Tel Aviv in the field of electricity. He was known as kindhearted and willing to help. While still in school, he worked and helped his parents at home with his salary, although he was very busy and intensely studied books for additional knowledge.

At 15, he joined the Youth Brigades [Gadna], thrilled with a sense of faith and mission in the lines of the Haganah which he joined. Immediately following the United Nations resolution in November 1947, he joined Hish [?] where he trained as a sniper and participated in many actions. He projected confidence to his surroundings. He was destined for officer training courses but it was difficult for him to leave military action. He responded to his family's urging to stay safe with fitting answers about the burden of duty and honor, and he pointed to his father who was also in Mishamr Haganah[1]. He participated in battles in Yazur, Salama, and the Triangle. He excelled as a daring gunman.

Uriel Goldfarb, Born 13/5/30 Died 21/12/48

On a patrol mission near Beit Guvrin, while covering successfully for his unit as they retreated to a safer position, he rescued those retreating but fell [died] himself.

Ephraim Kopf
Born 22 Tamuz, 5688 (10/7/28) Died 24 Kislev, 5708 (7/12/47)

He was the son of Zvi and Rachel and was born in Turobin. In 1936, he made aliyah with his parents. He graduated from Tahkemoni Elementary School in Tel Aviv. Due to his parents' dire financial straits, he went to work at a young age at a factory. He was a member of the youth movement, Beitar. He was athletic and played football for his movement. He then joined the Irgun[2] and participated in their actions.

After the War of Independence began, he left work and enlisted in fulltime service. As he stood guard at his position on the borders of Tel Aviv, he fell after being struck by an enemy bullet. He was buried in the military cemetery in Nahlat Yitzchak.

General Notes and Footnotes:

These notes and footnotes have been added by this Yizkor Book's translation co–coordinator, not by the original author. They are intended to help clarify certain words, names and phrases.

1. The battle of Mishmar HaEmek was a ten–day battle fought from in April 1948 between the Arab Liberation Army and the Haganah.

2. Irgun – a Zionist paramilitary organization that operated in Mandate Palestine between 1931 and 1948.

———

[Page 384]

Arye (Leibel) Rosenfeld

by Itamar Hopen

Translated by Meir Bulman

Leibel was the son of Yaakov and Leah (née Astich) and grandson of Yaness and Chaya Hindels. Leibel was born in approximately 1922. He was unlucky, probably beginning the day he was born, since at a very young age his mother fell ill and suffered partial paralysis for the rest of her life (today we call that disease Parkinson's). After the death of his mother, his father married for a second time to a woman from Lodz, where Leibel and his father relocated.

500

The Trisk shtibel[1] was in his grandfather's home. Of course, Leibel felt at home in the prayer house. All the Hasidim knew Leibel and he became beloved by all. Many Hasidim would tease Leibel by pinching his ear or by saying a certain sentence which he was ashamed of because it had something to do with his mischief at home. But I have never seen Leibel angry (I prayed at the Trisk synagogue for some time). Quite the opposite: the more he was teased, the more his smile grew. Many times, those who met Leibel thought he could not see well, but as it turned out they were mistaken as Leibel was very perceptive. His knowledge and worldview, as can be assumed, came to him from a single strong source – the Beit Midrash, where Leibel first absorbed Torah, where he, as a man, was formed, processed, and eventually, out in the big world, was perfected.

When WWII erupted, Leibel was already a strong man and was well versed in the political environment typical in those days. Leibel was one of many who knew their destination. As the Red Army retreated from the Wisla to the Bug River, Leibel did not hesitate much and joined those who relocated to the territory occupied by the Red Army.

[Page 385]

During WWII, Leibel met much hardship – wandering, hunger, and cold. The reality of war showed its cruelty to Leibel in a sudden way to which he was unaccustomed. Despite everything Leibel had been through, Leibel knew to preserve in his heart the only spark of hope, the yearning for redemption.

After the World War ended, after the Holocaust, as survivors gathered in camps, Leibel joined Hashmoer Hatzair[2]. After he arrived on aliyah, he settled in Kibbutz Sha'ar HaGolan. There he lived, worked, felt well, and was a member of Palmach[3]. In the time of the Founding War, Leibel served in the Harel unit[4].

Leibel joined the Beit Nabla settlement group. The group established a workers' village, Beit Nehemya. The village is located on the side of the Ben Shemen– Migdal Zedek road. Leibel married in Beit Nehemya, where he started a farm and had a daughter. When he met friends, he told them. "I established a home and a family, and I am happy."

In 1953 – 54, as the Fedayeen[5] gangs wreaked havoc, in addition to his work in developing his farm, he also served in the army reserves and participated in securing the village. In those days, the gangs would damage the water supply. In response, the settlers placed landmines near locations where the supply ran.

After a day of reserves service and an exhausting day of farm work, Leibel went out on a dark night to examine the waterline and the landmine he had planted. He was so tired that he forgot where he had planted the landmine and he fell victim. Leibel fell at the front of the War of Independence.

He came to us from afar after many trials and tribulations along the road. He came to us to sacrifice his blood on the altar of liberating the homeland. Many of the town residents did not see him and those who did barely recognized him.

Aryeh Rosenfield became a Hebrew man and soldier, with a good pioneering soul. He went to a remote village. All those who knew him appreciated him very much.

Like a cedar tree, he remained a lone survivor after a storm. His memory shall never leave us. He will forever remain in our hearts, Amen!

General Notes and Footnotes:

These notes and footnotes have been added by this Yizkor Book's translation co-coordinator, not by the original author. They are intended to help clarify certain words, names and phrases.

1. Shtibel – a place used for communal Jewish prayer. In contrast to a formal synagogue, a shtiebel is far smaller and approached more casually.

2. Hashmoer Hatzair – a Socialist–Zionist, secular Jewish youth movement founded in 1913 in Galicia, Austria–Hungary, and was also the name of the group's political party in the Yishuv in the pre–1948 British Mandate of Palestine.

3. Palmach – the elite fighting force of the Haganah, the underground army of the Yishuv during the period of the British Mandate for Palestine.

4. Harel Brigade is a reserve brigade of the Israel Defense Forces, today part of the Northern Command. It played a critical role in the 1948 Palestine war.

5. Fedayeen – a term used to refer to various military groups willing to sacrifice themselves.

The Turobin *Landsmannschaft* in Israel

Translated by Pamela Russ

Turobin is a small town in the Lublin circle, lying between Szczebrzeszyn, Krasnistow, and the Jewish settlement in Turobin, and counted 2,500 Jewish souls before World War Two. Only about 100 of these souls survived, of which the majority can be found in Israel. The rest are spread across the entire world – in North and South America, Canada, Australia.

In the year 1951, with the arrival in Israel of the first survivors of the war, some Turobin friends gathered in the home of comrade Yosef Kopp. Among these Leon Goldberg, Zalman Frumer, Yakov Friedler, and so on. And a committee was chosen with the goal to legalize [form] a union in Israel and to create a connection with all the Turobiner who were found outside of the country. The committee also set out for itself the following objectives that the Irgun stands for:

[Page 386]

1. To designate one day a year to commemorate the Turobiner martyrs;

2. To collect the necessary funds in order to:

    a. Establish a non-profit fund in order to assist with loans the survivors who came over, and also those, who, we hope, will want to come;

    b. To create monuments that will perpetuate the holy memory of the martyrs, and that should at the same time serve as a reminder not to forget the martyrs, and in contrast, the murderers.

At the end of 1951, the Irgun's first mourning gathering was held in the hall of the *Beit Hakhalutzot* [Pioneer House] in Tel Aviv. After the memorial speeches and reports of daily issues a committee of the following friends was elected: Leon Goldfarb – chairman; Yehoshua ben Ari – secretary; Yosef Kopp – treasurer; as well as friends: Avrohom Urbas and Moishe Gutwerc – of Tel Aviv; Milkhman and Montag – from Haifa; and A. Baumfeld – from Petach Tikva.

The Irgun now has over 85 families that are spread across the entire country. At the head of the Irgun is Mr. Leon Goldfarb, a dentist, who himself is a Lubliner, but he practiced in Turobin, married there and established a family, was active in Zionist activities, particularly among the youth. In the year 1933, he made *Aliyah* to Israel where he lost his oldest son in the War of Independence. Mr. L. Goldfarb is active as the head of the Turobiner *Landsmannschaft*, with which he is closely tied.

Near him, Yehoshua ben Ari (Zilberklang) works and is active, who devotes – in spite of his high position as consulting judge of the security – free time for the Irgun to help realize the goals that we had set. Also very active, is Yosef Kopp as treasurer and Avrohom Urbas as the good organizer.

Sixty percent of the members of the Irgun work as laborers in all kinds of vocations. Ten percent are officials, another ten percent are merchants. The rest are on the kibbutzim, and in agriculture in general.

The memorial day of the martyrs is set for after *Shabbath Bereishis* [first Shabbath after the holiday of Sukkot] – this is a tragic date, when the final evacuation of Turobin was carried out. In the memorial gatherings that have taken place in the last years in the hall of the *Beit Zioni Amerika* (in Tel Aviv), about 80% of the Turobiner in Israel participate, as well as from the Turobiner surroundings. After the commemoration ceremony at the gathering, a report is given about the activities of the committee over the last year, and a new committee is elected for the coming year.

[Page 387]

The activities of the Irgun in the early years consisted of raising monies for and providing loans to the needy friends. Until 1956, with the financial help of the Turobiner living outside the country, the plan of planting a thousand trees in the name of the martyrs in the *Yaar Hakedoshim* [Forest of the Martyrs] on the mountains of Jerusalem was achieved.

At the last memorial gathering, all those present expressed their wish for compiling a book that should act as the eternal light for the destroyed community. The book "Turobin" will simultaneously reflect Jewish life in the town with all its nuances of life until the devastation, as well as the brutal, tragic events themselves, going until the moment when the town was totally erased and destroyed by the Nazi murderers – as those from our town who were miraculously saved, who witnessed, or who survived – had seen themselves. In this same book there will be described the incidents of heroic resistance and heroic deaths which were not lacking in our town.

With the initiative of our American guest Berl Papjer and with the support of the Brazil guest Mr. Vogel, it was also decided at the last meeting to build a culture house for the youth in a new border settlement, with the name of Turobin, or as our dear friend Y. Ben-Ari translated, Turo-Bin – *Torah Bina* [Torah and Understanding]. In order to enact this plan, it was decided to establish a specific fund in which all *landsleit* [compatriots] in Israel would take part, and at the same time appeal to all *landsleit* everywhere else, so that with collective energies the funds of this vital undertaking would be covered.

Also, the Irgun plans to set up in *Martef Hashoah* [Chamber of the Holocaust] on *Har Tzion* a marble tombstone in the name of the Jewish community of Turobin.

———

Former Turobin residents in Israel

List of names and addresses

Transliterated by Judy Petersen

Please note that the page numbers on the right side are the page numbers of the original Yizkor Book, not this translation.

Surname	Given name	Place	Remarks	Page
ABITUV	Yakov	Nahariya, Israel	(GOTTWILLING)	387
ORBAS	Avraham	Tel Aviv, Israel		387
IDELSTEIN	Channah	Kfar Saba, Israel		387
AMIR	Yisrael	Kibbutz Alonim, Israel	and Yona	387
AF	Meir	Petach Tikva, Israel		387
AF	Efrat Moshe	Petach Tikva, Israel		387
AKKERMAN	Tzipora	Pardes Katz, Israel		387
BOMFELD	Avraham	Petach Tikva, Israel	living at Aharon's	387
BOMFELD	Aharon	Petach Tikva, Israel		388
BOMFELD	David	Ramat Gan, Israel		388
BOMFELD	Rivka	Petach Tikva, Israel	(PROSZHEN)	388
BOMSTEIN	Yechezkel	Kibbutz Alonim, Israel		388
BILERMAN	Moshe	Ramat Gan, Israel		388
BLUTMAN	Chanoch	Ramat Yitzchak, Ramat		388

		Gan, Israel		
BAR-ARI	Yehoshua	Tel Aviv, Israel		388
BEN YISRAEL	Nechama	Kibbutz Ayin Charod Ichud, Israel		388
BERGER	Bronya	Bat Yam, Israel		388
GOLDFARB	Aryeh (Leon)	Givataim, Israel		388
GUTBERTZ	Moshe	Tel Aviv, Israel		388
GORLIK	Miriam	Petach Tikva, Israel	(KORNDRECHSLER)	388
GIVERTZ	Berish	Tel Aviv, Israel		388
GIAR	Aharon	Netanya, Israel		388
GRINBERG		Haifa, Israel	(ZILBERKLANG)	388
DAGANI	Shlomo	Givataim, Israel		388
DIMANT	Yosef	Kfar Ganot, Doar Beit Dagon, Israel	(LICHTER)	388
HOFEN	Mordechai	Netanya, Israel	(YOSKOVITCH)	388
HOFEN	Yehoshua	Petach Tikva, Israel		388
HOFEN	Itamar	Givataim, Israel		388
HARARI	Emanuel	Moshav Balfuria, Israel	(ZUBERMAN-FERSHTENDIK)	388
VEISTUCH	Reuven	Haifa, Israel		388

VEISS	Sarah	Kibbutz Alonim, Israel		388
VEISS	Meir	Kibbutz Alonim, Israel		388
VISHNIVSKI	Gitel	Hadar Yosef, Israel		388
VALDMAN	Leah	Holon, Israel		388
VAKS	Natan	Ramat Yitzchak, Ramat Gan, Israel		388
ZONTEK	Dov	Haifa, Israel		388
ZISMILCH	Shlomo	Givataim, Israel		388
ZEIDEL	Avraham	Kfar Ata, Israel		388
ZEIDEL	Yisrael	Haifa, Israel		388
TOPLER	Gila	Haifa, Israel		388
TAYER	Moshe	Tel Aviv, Israel		388
TENNENTZWEIG	Miriam	Petach Tikva, Israel	(TZITRENBAUM)	388
TREGER	Moshe	Ramat Gan, Israel		388
KAHANA	Chava	Haifa, Israel	(MILCHMAN)	388
KANARTI	Aryeh	Moshav Neveh-Yerek, Israel		388
LEVIN	Miriam	Tel Aviv, Israel		388
LIBERBOM	Yechiel	Kibbutz Ein Hacarmel, D.N. Haifa, Israel		389

LICHTER	Sarah	Givataim, Israel	(YANOVER)	389
LANDER	Yehuda	Kvutzat Kineret, Doar Kineret, Israel		389
LANDER	Avraham	Holon, Israel		389
LANDER	Yitzchak (It'che)	Bnei Brak, Israel		389
MILCHMAN	Eliezer	Haifa, Israel		389
MITZNER	Yakov	Atlit the Moshava, Israel		389
SKORKA	Channah	Haifa, Israel	(VEIS)	389
FABRIKANT	Yisrael	Tel Aviv, Israel		389
FEDER	Aryeh	Ramat Gan, Israel		389
FOGEL	Yerachmiel	Hadera, Israel		389
POLLAK	Eli	Haifa, Israel		389
FUKS	Avraham	Haifa, Israel		389
FINK	Peretz	Kfar Saba, Israel		389
PAS	Ita	Jerusalem, Israel	(TZWEKEN)	389
FROMER	Zalman	Tel Aviv, Israel		389
FREIBERG	Yekutiel	Tel Aviv, Israel		389
FREIBERG	Yerachmiel	Tel Aviv, Israel		389
FREIBERG	Avraham	Moshav Gan Sorek Doar Rishon Letzion, Israel		389

FRIEDLER	Yakov	Kfar Yona, Israel		389
FRIEDLER	Yechiel	Kfar Sirkin next to Petach Tikva, Israel		389
FRIEDLER	Yosef	Givataim, Israel		389
FRIEDLER	Moshe	Pardes Katz, Israel		389
FOGEL	Yakov	Ramat Yitzchak, Ramat Gan, Israel	and Chava	389
PLISHER	Yosef	Kibbutz Givat Hashlosha, Israel		389
TZUKERMAN	Esther	Kibbutz Kineret, Israel	(LANDER)	389
TZIMERMAN	Yisrael	Haifa, Israel		389
TZIMERMAN	Moshe	Ramat Yitzchak, Ramat Gan, Israel		389
TZIMERMAN	Eliezer	Ramle, Israel		389
KORN	Yechezkel	Yaffo, Israel		389
KOPF	Tzvi	Tel Aviv, Israel		389
KOPF	Yosef	Givataim, Israel		389
KOPF	Yitzchak	Yad Eliahu, Tel Aviv, Israel		389
KISLOVITCH	Hadassah (Yaffa)	Givataim, Israel		389

KORNDREKSLER	Frida	Ramat Yitzchak, Ramat Gan, Israel	and Miriam	389
ROZNER	Nechemya	Haifa, Israel		389
ROZNER	Moshe	Haifa, Israel		389
SHENOVSKY	Yaffa (Scheindel)	Holon, Israel		389

[Page 390]

Former Turobin residents in Other Countries

List of names and addresses

Transliterated by Judy Petersen

Surname	Given name	Place	Remarks	Page
GOODMAN	Harry	Brooklyn, NY, USA		390
GLATMAN	M.	Bronx, NY, USA		390
HYFLER	Hyman	Bronx, NY, USA		390
LIBERBAUM	Morris	Brooklyn, NY, USA		390
LICHTMAN	Hyman	New York City, NY, USA		390
WAKSZUL	Rachela	Brooklyn, NY, USA		390
PANKOWSKI	Sara	Gary, Indiana, USA		390
SHAFER	J.	Brooklyn, NY, USA		390
LACHTER	I.	Bayside, NY, USA		390

GUTWILIK	M.	Winnipeg, Manitoba, Canada		390
ZIMERMAN	I.	Toronto, Ontario, Canada		390
FUKS	Yak	New York, USA		390
WAKS	Moris	Canada		390
LEDER	Hylel	Canada		390
GUTMACHER	Miguel	Buenos Aires, Argentina		390
GOLDBARD	N.	Buenos Aires, Argentina		390
LEVIT	R. G.	Buenos Aires, Argentina		390
KLIENER	Yaime	Buenos Aires, Argentina		390
KÖNIGSMAN	Mauricio	Buenos Aires, Argentina		390
SHNAIDERBERG	Simon	Buenos Aires, Argentina		390
CUKIERMAN	Maurisco	Montevideo, Uruguay	Melbourne	390
CUKIERMAN	Seia	Montevideo, Uruguay		391
KOPF	Samuel	Montevideo, Uruguay		391
TAFEL	Nachman	Argentina		391
TAFEL	Nachemia	Argentina		391
TAFEL	Mendel	Argentina		391
AICHENBLAT	Maurisco	Argentina		391

FALENDER	Maria	Warsaw, Poland		391
DELAGE		Paris, France	Mr. and Mrs.	391
KLOCHENDLER	L.	Paris, France		391
HUARD	G.	Berloz, Belgium	(AKERMAN) Australia	391
BLUTMAN	A.	Melbourne, Victoria, Australia		391
GROPMAN	Yosel	Melbourne, Victoria, Australia		391

[Page 392]

9. An Eternal Candle – Necrology

Translated by Pamela Russ

Families Yafa, Veber [Weber], and Fuks

From right to left

1. Dovid, Khaya, Aryeh, and sister Dvoire Veber

2. Eidel, Nekhe, Moishe, Yisroel, Mashe, and two grandchildren

3. Khane, mother Rifka, Velvel Fuks

4. Malke and Zelig

The three families, Yafa, Veber, Fuks, of blessed memory, are made up of Rifka Yafa and her sister Masha Veber – their son–on–law Fuks, and their grandchildren.

The two grandchildren of Rifka Yafa were killed by the Nazi murderers in France. Leyb and his sister Dvoire, Rifka Yafa and the children – were evacuated with the entire community to Izhbica, and from there to Sobibor. Velvel Fuks was murdered by the Gestapo in the middle of the street in Turobin.

The family Yafa was a multi–branched family, renowned in the town – as modest, honest, and good people. The majority of the families sustained themselves through manual labor, so that the basis of their existence flowed together with other fine qualities such as honesty, and righteousness. These dear and fine people were murdered by Hitler's people. May the names of these fine people be perpetuated.

[Page 393]

The two grandchildren, Dovid and Yakov, survived and live in Argentina today.

In eternal memory – my father Moishe Leikhter, my brother Avrohom, my brother Oizer, my sister Khame–Mikhel, my uncle and his wife and their children, and the entire family – who are represented in the photo that was taken on May 5, 1941.

Family Leikhter

All of you, my dear parents, brothers and sisters, stand before my eyes, and if I stand and think about the tragic manner in which you all died, I shudder, and I lose my speech. But I can utter only one judgement:

The murderous, bestial hands – that cut off innocent young lives, should be cursed!

My dear, holy souls! When I look at your picture, I feel guilty in front of you, because I did not place a tombstone for you. But one God in Heaven knows that I am clean of sin.

516

[Page 394]

The murderers spilled your blood and spread out your bodies in desecration – in a brutal way. And I am the rescued spark.

The one thing that I could have done for you, I did: I placed a tombstone for the community of Turobin on Har Tzion, and the Yizkor book. With these two tombstones, you will be remembered forever, amen!

Yitzkhok Leikter, New York

The first line, from right to left: **Yehudis, Rifka, Soroh**
The second line: **Tzvi ben Tuvia Kofenboim**
The third line from right to left: **Moishe Leybish**

517

For a shining memory, my father, brothers and sisters. I will remember you forever, both in sadness and in joy, how good you were to me and to all the people who were around you. Your refined faces come to me often in my mind, and when I remember, then I ask why they spilled your blood so needlessly? But there is no one to give an answer.

[Page 395]

You innocent, dear souls, I want to give you one comfort – I will always remember you for the good. The eternal light – the Yizkor Book of the Turobin community – will be the living testimony and your eternal tombstone.

Gila Urbas (Kofenboim), Tel Aviv

Shimshon ben Beirekh Geier, of blessed memory

I will never forget my dear father Shimshon ben Beirekh Geier, my dear mother Lieba nee Beker, may their memories be blessed, who died tragically through the Hitlerist murderers, may their names be erased.

I will remember you forever, and you will always be engraved in my memory.

Your daughter, **Laya Waldman (Geier)**

Reb Avrohom Zweken, may his blood be avenged

He was born in Izhbice, came from a fine *chassidic* family, he was a *chassidic* young man, married a girl from Turobin, Reb Zindel Rentner's daughter. He hated going around idly. He was also filled with a love for life, with a healthy sense of humor, and always added a good joke to any situation, and was thus loved by the community, and many craved his closeness.

[Page 396]

He was a Trisker *chassid,* prayed in a Trisker *shtiebel* [informal, small synagogue], and would go to Reb Nakhum'tche Trisker in Warsaw, and would relate stories respectfully of the old Trisker *Maggid.* He was tied to Trisk with his whole heart. He was a member of the city council for one year.

He also was very involved in social [community] issues. He was a member of the *Agudas Israel* and loyally served its interests for the town's community. He devoted himself to the community's needs, he particularly enjoyed a friendship with the simple Jews, used their expressions, and many considered him one of "theirs." He was the secretary and director of the Cooperative Bank and managed all of its matters. His assistant in the bank was Reb Yisroel Janover, a person with excellent traits. At the same time, he managed the *Gemilas Chesed* [non–profit] fund, together with Yisroel Janover and Berl Zontag, and distributed loans without interest. The capital from the *Gemilas Chesed* fund was taken from membership monies from their friends, with the support of Joint [American Jewish Joint Distribution Committee], and they made all kinds of combinations in order to increase the capital of the fund in order to be able to meet the needs of the friends for loans. In particular, the fund felt the salvation that it provided to the friends against the anti–Semitic politics of the Polish officials.

———

Family Freiberg

From right to left: **Male, Perel, Aharon the father, his wife, his youngest son, and Avrohom**

[Page 397]

Reb Avrohom had three talented daughters. Sadly, the entire family was murdered by the Nazis and local Poles, and only the one daughter Yita survived, who started a family again in Jerusalem. She felt it necessary to write about her tragedy during Hitler's war, [material] which is published in the Turobin Yizkor Book.

———

Family Kofenboim

From the top: **Shloime Kofenboim;**
Second line, **Golde and Shaindel Kofenboim; all children of
Khaim ben Tuviah Kofenboim,
Golde survived and lives in France**

[Page 398]

Introduction

Hopen Itamar – Editorial Committee

Transcribed by Genia Hollander

This book is the collective creation of a number of emigrants from the Turobin community now living in Israel. Many of them are not professional writers, therefore, imprecisions, ambiguities and repetitions will be met within this book.

Herein is the history of an ancient small town in the Lublin area – a town of great students of the Torah, Rabbis and Jewish philosophers who lit up Turobin and other communities with their moral learning. And always, this community was represented at the "Four State league".

In addition to history, this book contains reminiscences, folklore and presentation of personalities; a list of martyrs, pictures and an important chapter on the Holocaust – all of which is intended to inspire the reader to thought.

For almost three years, one of the editorial committee devoted himself to collecting and sorting the material, editing and preparing it for the first printing as well as updating the martyr list. Undoubtedly, we have not succeeded in collecting all the material because of the lack of cooperation of some of the community members and the limited time within which the committee was obliged to publish the book. Under these circumstances, it was impossible to give a complete picture of the life of the town. It is important to note that all our applications and requests to the State of Poland went unanswered.

In spite of all these difficulties as well as fiscal and other problems (which need not be detailed here), we have succeeded in reflecting an important part of the community life.

This book will serve as a leading light to our present generation and those to come. Let them know who our parents were and what atrocities Hitler had brought about. May his name be blotted out.

Our special thanks are extended to all those who have helped in bringing about the publication of this book.

INDEX

530

S

T

540

542

www.ingramcontent.com/pod-product-compliance
Lightning Source LLC
Chambersburg PA
CBHW082008150426
42814CB00005BA/256